Being in Love

Finding true love is a journey of transformation obstructed by numerous psychological obstacles. *Being in Love* expands the traditional field of psychoanalytic couple therapy, and explores therapeutic methods of working through the obstacles leading to true love.

Becoming who we are is an inherently relational journey: we uncover our truest nature and become most authentically real through the difficult and fearful, yet transformative intersubjective crucibles of our intimate relationships. In this book, Judith Pickering draws comparisons between Bion's concept of becoming in O, and being in love. She searches for pathways that lead away from relational confusion towards the discovery of genuine relationships, and works towards finding better ways of relating to one another. This is achieved by encouraging couples to enjoy the actual presence, humanity, otherness and particularity of each other rather than expecting a partner to conform to our own expectations, projections, desires and presuppositions.

Pickering draws on clinical material, contemporary psychoanalysis, cultural themes from the worlds of mythology and literature, and a wealth of therapeutic techniques in this fresh approach to couple therapy. *Being in Love* will therefore interest students and practitioners of psychoanalysis, psychology, and couple therapy, as well as all of those seeking to be more authentic in their relationships.

Judith Pickering is a psychoanalytic couple therapist, Jungian analyst and psychoanalytic psychotherapist in private practice in Sydney. She is a senior supervisor and lecturer for the Australia and New Zealand Association of Psychotherapy. She is a member of the Australian and New Zealand Association of Jungian Analysts and the International Association for Analytical Psychology.

Being in Love

Therapeutic pathways through psychological obstacles to love

Judith Pickering

Routledge
Taylor & Francis Group

LONDON AND NEW YORK

First published 2008 by Routledge
27 Church Road, Hove, East Sussex BN3 2FA

Simultaneously published in the USA and Canada
by Routledge
270 Madison Avenue, New York, NY 10016

Routledge is an imprint of the Taylor & Francis Group, an Informa business

Typeset in Times by Garfield Morgan, Swansea, West Glamorgan
Printed and bound in Great Britain by TJ International Ltd, Padstow, Cornwall
Paperback cover design by Sandra Heath

British Library Cataloguing in Publication Data
A catalogue record for this book is available from the British Library

Library of Congress Cataloging-in-Publication Data
Pickering, Judith, 1959-
  Being in love : therapeutic pathways through psychological obstacles to
love / Judith Pickering.
        p. ; cm.
  Includes bibliographical references and index.
  ISBN 978-0-415-37160-5 (hardback) – ISBN 978-0-415-37161-2 (pbk.)
1. Marital psychotherapy. 2. Love–Psychological aspects. I. Title.
  [DNLM: 1. Couples Therapy. 2. Interpersonal Relations. 3. Love.
WM430.5.M3 P595b 2008]
  RC488.5.P52 2008
  616.89'1562–dc22
                                                                2007045125

ISBN: 978-0-415-37160-5 (hbk)
ISBN: 978-0-415-37161-2 (pbk)

The whole world is a market-place for Love,
For naught that is, from Love remains remote.
The Eternal Wisdom made all things in Love:
On Love they all depend, to Love all turn.
The earth, the heavens, the sun, the moon, the stars
The centre of their orbit find in Love.
By Love are all bewildered, stupefied,
Intoxicated by the Wine of Love.
From each, a mystic silence Love demands,
What do all seek so earnestly? 'Tis Love.
Love is the subject of their inmost thoughts,
In Love no longer 'Thou' and 'I' exist,
For self has passed away in the Beloved.
Now I will draw aside the veil from Love,
And in the temple of mine inmost soul
Behold the Friend, Incomparable Love.
He who would know the secret of both worlds
Will find the secret of them both, is Love.
        (Attâr, *Jawhar al-Dhât, Kulliyât*, as cited in Perry, 1971, p. 633)

Eternal gratitude to all who inspire the quest for wisdom and love,
teachers in many guises, 'May all find love's beatitude'.

Contents

What is love?   ix
JAMES S. GROTSTEIN
Acknowledgements   xiii

PART I   1
Being in love

Prelude – shooting the albatross   3

Introduction: a question of true love?   5

1   Love's many facets   18

2   The marriage of alterity and altruism   38

3   Subject relations   53

4   Falling in love: an exogamous initiation   65

PART II   81
The path of love: an obstacle course

5   Love's therapeutics   83

6   Love's uncanny choices   96

7   Veils of projection   104

8   Relational configurations   120

9   Interlocking scenes: a malignant dowry   131

10   A hall of mirrors   151

11   The narcissism of Echo   165

12   Thresholds of intimacy: Bluebeard's Castle   182

13   Don't look back: Orpheus and Eurydice   191

PART III   209
Transformations in love

14   Exogamy: a marriage of all loves   211

15   The iconoclasm of Joy   227

16   *Laetitia*, liveliness and love   238

17   *Alétheia*: becoming in love   247

     Bibliography   251
     Index   264

What is love?

James S. Grotstein

'What is this thing called love?'

After reading and then pondering over Judith Pickering's lyrical, evocative and highly informative book on the psychology of love, I was moved to think of (Bion would have said, 'dreamed') the following ideas in my admiring and respectful response.

Love is one of the most singularly baffling yet most natural emotional states the human being has to contend with (is afflicted with?). It is said that love is a 'moving violation'. It is a violation of our illusion of our independence. There is reason to believe that in the final analysis it is the most fundamental, the ground zero, of our emotions and that all the symptoms our patients bring to us are inescapably tied to love as a defence against the emotional perils, torment, frustration, and humiliation that ineluctably become love's aftermath when thwarted. Bion often propounded that man is born a dependent creature and that he always was in need of a mate as long as he lived. We now have evidence from empirical science that this is true. Infant development researchers such as Colwyn Trevarthen, Daniel Stern, and others now say that there is evidence that the infant is born with what *I* would interpret as an *intersubjective instinct.* John Bowlby and his illustrious followers similarly affirm that the infant is born ready to *attach* to his primary caregiving object, who in turn is biologically as well as psychologically primed to *bond* with him or her. Stein Bräten, the Norwegian anthropologist, states that empirical scientific evidence supports the notion that humans are born with the inherent pre-conception of a partner in mind – that is, the infant is born with an empty place pre-ordained for another. Bion went so far as to state that infancy and childhood constitute *rehearsal* stages for adulthood, the thing-in-itself (Real, 'O'), for man to find his *permanent* partner.

Shakespeare, in *A Midsummer Night's Dream*, used the device of a magical potion which, when poured into one's eyes, caused one to fall instantly in love with the first person they saw when they opened their eyes. Thus, he was keenly aware of the 'chemistry' of love. Freud, along parallel lines, suggested that eros was so strong a force that it in effect tricked its victims into loving so that mating could take place – as if mating were a veritable Darwinian plan to preserve the species and had to accomplish its relentless teleological aims through a deception we call 'love', which would amount to the imposition of a *folie à deux* on two unsuspecting individuals who are suddenly caught in destiny's trap. It is conceivable that love is originally and fundamentally noumenal or archetypal in so far as it seems to be older than its willing, or even unwilling, victims. It constitutes a 'memoir of the future'. It summons or recruits its victims so as to become incarnated in them for its own deceptive reasons.

Love is where it finds *you* while all the while you may think you are looking for *it*, but it is capricious and may quietly depart as unexpectedly as it arrived. There is an uncanny dialectic that seems to occur between the loved one as a real *human being* and the one who reveals a hint of mystery about themselves. Passionate love uniquely becomes a testimony to a 'double transference', not just to transference/countertransference. Love is a mutually unequal partnership. Each lover loves his or her partner more than him- or herself.

In other words, a normal and adaptive idealization occurs in which each lover 'donates' his or her own self-worth to the other. The shadow side of this beloved donation of heightened worth is the commensurately heightened obligations the generous lover expects of his or her loved one in return. Conversely, the lover ever reminds us of our incompleteness and the perilous state of our inescapable dependency on them. Envy lies in ambush to attack our bond with our loved one over this fateful reminder.

The infant must come to accept the ontological fact of dependency, neediness, and incompleteness in relation to his or her mother, father and siblings (family) and must learn to accept the humility of dependency and incompleteness as a fact of nature. Along with this recognition infants must learn to appreciate what they receive from their nurturing. They then introject, not the object, but the legacy of their experience with the object, the experience designating the appreciation. It may take us a lifetime to learn that we are unable to possess or really 'introject' a loved one. All we can hope for is continuingly meaningful *experiences* with the object, really the ineffable, unpossessable other. As we then incorporate the legacy of the object that has been appreciated, the appreciated object experience 'appreciates' within us, filling us with gratitude, the feeling of being profoundly loved and cared for. The infant grows, develops and matures, fed on the milk of loving kindness, the foundation for a sense of being real, alive, vital.

Something more must be said about the infant-development perspective on love, however. Whether we use the developmental protocols of Abraham and Freud, Klein, Fairbairn, Erikson, Mahler, Kernberg, or Stern, we cannot escape the realization that the development and maturation of the infant into adulthood is ineluctably marked by rites of passage, ontological points of no return. Each step assesses the sturdiness and reliability of each of the previous steps to ascertain their capacity to have become a permanent foundation for each succeeding step. The choice of the loved one will depend in large measure on his or her capacity to fill each and all of these gaps complementarily and to become the scapegoat exorcist for the feelings about these gaps by default. The 'trick' of successful love is the ability of each mate to remain a separate individual *vis-à-vis* the other, while at the same time being able to remain immersed in an utterly indivisible duality. Lovers, like analysts, must be able to look past the negativity of the other to sense the emotional distress that invariably sponsors it. But there is more. When I referred to the stages of infant development and their retrospective accumulative significance, I spoke like a psychoanalytically-informed anthropologist, i.e. experience-distant. Now I should like to speak in a manner that is experience-near: each stage of development, including birth, weaning from the breast, toilet-training, etc., represents a progression in the lack of access to mother's body and intimate attention. How the infant → toddler → child accepts or refuses to accept the fact of this veritable ostracism and exile is crucial. (S)he must accept the loss, be able to mourn the loss and maintain the value of the lost object, and then be able to yearn for the beloved stranger of tomorrow ('memoir of the future').

What *is* love? In the first instance love designates the existence of someone on whom one becomes imprinted, to whom one becomes attached – bonded (not a bind) – one who justifies one's acceptance of the stark fact of one's incompleteness. No longer can one function as an autonomous androgyne. This other person seems to make a profound and pronounced difference. Love is where you find it – or more properly, love is where it finds *you*. When we fall in love, the one we fall in love with may remind us of our mother, father or siblings but also of ourselves – as a hand-to-glove complement. Another dimension of the mysterious choice of the loved object maybe traced back to our own ego ideals: the self we were supposed to be and couldn't be – the one we need to complete us. Thus the mysterious choice of the loved one may transcend the imagos of our rearing objects and correspond to an inner but barely imagined self, one which may correspond to our ego ideal *and* to our anima or animus.

Yet Judith suggests exogamous love takes us away from all such regressive bases for our choices. Exogamy and alterity invite us to transcend all such oedipal, narcissistic and self-referential bases for our choices and begin to love the other as Other, not extension of self or stand-in for mother/father. The love object must behave as if they are real and human but they must make allowances for our inadequacies by being mysterious and soaked in the nature of awe, redolent with promises of wonders yet to come. One of the greatest mysteries of love is the unconscious process of *selecting* the beloved.

Although Freud is to be credited for the 'erotic revolution' and placed sex on the high table of psychological worth and cultural respectability, his preoccupation with according scientific respectability to psychoanalysis resulted in his enfranchising biological instinctual drives as first cause for human motivation. He failed to populate the system unconscious with subjects.

It is my belief that the unconscious is populated with preternatural denizens, maybe 'daimons' (I prefer the ancient Greek spelling), 'presences', 'beings', 'homunculi', or other worldly creatures like them, who, as subjects, have will and intentionality. I wonder who is the 'love daimon' who puts provocative chemical potions in our eyes and into our minds. Perhaps a pseudonym for this daimon would be 'Dionysus'.

This is the end of my personal oneiric fugue in response to Judith Pickering's book. Now I shall address her work directly. Her work is rich, extensive, profound, and I am tempted to say that she has left no stone that I know of unturned in regard to the experience of love. I should like to comment on just two of the many rich, redolent, and evocative concepts she has brought to bear to encompass the theme of love: 'exogamy' and 'alétheia'.

Exogamy is not only the prescribed solution to the threat of oedipal incest. It speaks to the racial necessity to dilute the genes by the infusion of the genes of a stranger from a strange land. The 'stranger' is a way of talking about 'mystery', the expectation of the ineffability of the future one who already has been appointed to keep his or her rendezvous and can be spotted by the godhead by a mysterious divination that remains unbeknown to us.

Alétheia, re-introduced to us by Heidegger, means 'unconcealment', which in turn represents the ontological quintessence and epitome of pure intimacy. It connotes a more sophisticated version of our first literal experience of mutual unconcealment when we were privileged to experience being at mother's breast. In love we re-experience it not only literally but utmostly metaphorically: we then feel safe to be naked in all our being – with our mate. Exogamy or otherness is the obligatory prerequisite of love. Alétheia is love's obligatory and constant witness.

Judith Pickering's book is a sweeping, awe-inspiring, fulfilling and erudite revisioning of the most important subject we ever experience and confront.

Acknowledgements

> My heart has become capable of every form: it is a pasture for gazelles
> and a convent for Christian monks.
> And a temple for idols, and the pilgrim's Ka'ba, and the tables of the
> Tora and the book of the Koran.
> I follow the religion of Love, whichever way his camels take.
> Ibn 'Arabi
>
> (Perry, 1971, pp. 791–792)

If, as Bion suggested, thoughts exist without a thinker, needing a container
only to incarnate them, then who is their author? The thinker can claim
authorship for all misconceptions and mistranslations, but not the truth he
or she attempts to realize and convey. This book has arisen out of meetings
of hearts and minds, circling around a core that eludes expression. It has
been a labour of love, crafted from cathartic yet also gradual, incremental
experiences of transformations in O.

Authentic love is never second hand, indirect, or vicarious. Like a hand-
woven carpet, it is about myriad small threads of connection we patiently
weave together. Writing about love is no substitute for the actuality of
encounters with real others, which tend to be unpredictable, messy, disturbing and thus refreshing. Confronting the lived realities of love leads us
to face up to ourselves. We chip away at the crusty barnacles of all the false
accretions that cover our true nature.

Authorial indebtedness goes to so many who have given deep consideration and imparted their insight concerning the ideas behind this book. Others
have given painstaking, detailed help and practical or moral support bringing
this book into being. Doing justice to such contributions beggars description,
particularly as so many must remain nameless. In the following acknowledgements certain individuals, groupings or organizations also represent
many who I have not named. Please, nevertheless, receive my deep gratitude.

Neil Brown, Giles Clark, James Grotstein, and David Russell, have all
been vital intellectual *compañeros*. Daryl Gunter (who deserves a medal
for his perseverance correcting numerous versions of this book), Doug

Bannerman, Anne Morris Bannerman, Richard Cornes, Alison Clugston Cornes, Vesna Hatezic, Patricia Hoyle, Brian Macauley, Anne Noonan, Peter Oldmeadow, Craig San Roque, Andrew Samuels, Walter Sutcliffe and Helen Zilko represent many who have given generously of their time, expertise, intellectual and friendly encouragement at different junctures in this long writer's journey.

Careful, thoughtful supervision underpins the clinical material: my particular thanks to Peter Fullerton and Russell Meares who have bestowed inspiration and poetic imagination. I thank members of peer review groups: Philip Wright, Cécile Barral, Brendan McPhillips, Gail McKenzie, Christina Murray, Antony Gleeson, Annette McInerney, Michael Honnery, John Kelly, and Bruce Lachter.

Colleagues in several analytic communities have provided stimulating fraternal facilitating environments: such as in ANZSJA, the IAAP, ANZAP, the NSW Institute of Family Psychotherapy and editorial colleagues at The Journal of Analytical Psychology, particularly Pramila Bennett, Warren Colman, Michael Horne, Jean Knox, and Marcus West.

Andrew Leon, ANZAP librarian, tracked down numerous articles week after week. Computer experts Rory and Ben at the Academy Store, Bondi saved my computer from viral perdition.

My thanks to Kate Hawes, Editor, Jane Harris and Tara Stebnicky, Editorial Assistants, Kathryn Russel, Senior Production Editor, and all the many other staff at Routledge, for bringing this project into fruition.

I thank all my patients, for sharing your lives and inmost hearts, pains, struggles, hopes, aspirations and growth.

Ann Pickering, Elise Stutchbury, Pamela Oldmeadow, Felicity Bowak, Barry Jarrott, Ralph Pickering, Glenda Cloughley, Leslie Devereaux, Susan Aitkin, Alison Clark, Nida Chenagtsang, Catherine McGrath and Anne Amigo, your loving help has been immeasurable through periods of catastrophic change.

Eternal thanks for imbuing me with first hand knowledge of infinite loving kindness and wisdom: Michael Shirres, OP, Geshe Acharya Thubten Loden, Chögyal Namkhai Norbu, Sogyal Rinpoche, all representatives of vast fields of merit.

Miriam and Naomi, in your birth you revealed the face of love, and in every moment of your lives go on revealing the shocking immediacy of love in the here-and-now. To my mother for intelligent loving kindness, and to my father for showing that love is stronger than death: thank you.

Nemo, thank you ever and anon.

Permissions

My thanks to the following for permission to quote extracts from their works: Andrea Denholm, Hannie Rayson, Andrew Knight and Granada

Productions for permission to quote from 'Love in the Time of Coleridge', an episode of *SeaChange*; Faber and Faber for permission to quote from C. S. Lewis' *A grief observed* and CS Lewis Company: *A grief observed* by C.S. Lewis copyright © C. S. Lewis Pte. Ltd. 1961, Extracts reprinted by permission.

Chatto & Windus for permission to quote from Gillian Rose's *Love's work* by Gillian Rose, published by Chatto & Windus. reprinted by permission of The Random House Group Ltd; Bloomsbury Publishing for permission to quote Anne Michaels' *Fugitive pieces*; Cornell University Press for permission to quote Luce Irigaray's *This sex which is not one*; Hodder and Stoughton for permission to quote from Brian Sibley's *Shadowlands*; Random House for permission to quote Anita Brookner's *Look at me*; Universal Edition for permission to quote from the original libretto for Béla Bartók's *Duke Bluebeard's Castle* (*A kékszakállú herceg vára*) by Béla Balázs, English translation by Christopher Hassall © Copyright Universal Edition (London) Ltd – reproduced by permission – All Rights Reserved; to Martin Armiger, for permission to quote from his article in the *Sydney Morning Herald,* 'Waiting for life and death'.

My thanks to the *Journal of Analytical Psychology*, for permission to reprint material from 'Who's afraid of the Wolfe couple: the interlocking traumatic scene', which formed the basis of Chapter 9. Thanks also to *The Australasian Journal of Psychotherapy* where I also discussed aspects of my concept of the interlocking scene in Volume 24(1).

In Chapter 2 I draw upon material previously published in an article, 'The marriage of alterity and intimacy: a couples perspective' which was published by the Society of Couple Psychoanalytic Psychotherapists in their journal *Psychoanalytic Perspectives on Couple Work: An International Publication*, 2006.

I précis certain of the ideas of this book in a chapter 'Individuation and intimacy: An object relations perspective on love and the development of the self' in *Couple Therapy in Australia: Issues emerging from practice*, Elisabeth Shaw and Jim Crawley, Eds. Melbourne, PsychOz Publications, 2007, pp. 159–180.

Part I

Being in love

Prelude – shooting the albatross

In a television drama called *SeaChange*[1] the drama circles around a palpable but undeclared chemistry between Max, a journalist, and Laura, a local magistrate. Laura is a single mother of two, as well as an escapee from a cut-throat life in the legal fast lanes of the city.

Max and Laura dance around each other, advancing and retreating in a display of faux combat, fending each other off. This circling dance aptly becomes symbolized by the appearance of an albatross: an unexpected, precious creature, which at any moment might take flight and disappear, or be simply ignored, or even shot at. This becomes symbolic of a moment of destiny, requiring decisive, rightful action. To turn away from such a rare moment of grace would be to risk losing all.

Laura's previous love choices had ended unfavourably, so, in spite of her attraction to Max, she decides to opt for prudence, to play it safe and marry a kind, conventional, well-off lawyer instead. The threat of Laura's imminent trip down the aisle into the wrong man's arms finally jolts Max into decisive action. Accustomed to his own disasters in love, he realizes that it is high time to desist from sabotaging yet another possibility of happiness in love. Instead of flying away to an international posting, he valiantly grabs Laura, whisking her away for a boat trip. It's not going to be plain sailing – the motor won't start. Laura ineptly fumbles with the anchor, which plops unattached into the sea. Adrift and floating with the tide, Max relates a personal story concerning how as a child he used to go fishing with his Dad. One morning he saw an albatross circling around.

'I shot it, just on impulse. And there was this moment of real exhilaration; it was a good shot you know, one shot dead. My old man came up to me and he wanted me to go pick it up, hold the body to see what I'd done

---

1 *SeaChange* was a popular Australian television series. The episode in question, 'Love in the time of Coleridge', was written by Hannie Rayson and Andrea Denholm, directed by Ian Watson. 'Max' was played by William McInnes, 'Laura' by Sigrid Thornton. It was first screened in 2000.

and I wouldn't Laura cause I couldn't, but I wish I had because I think it would have meant a difference.'

'A difference to what?' Laura asks a little dubiously.

'To you and me. There was something good circling between us wasn't there? And with my crossbow I shot the albatross.'

Max realized too late, like Coleridge's 'silly bloody mariner', that the albatross was his saviour. From that time onwards, Max circles around in the doldrums, feeling that he can never get his love life right. 'We can't get it right, can we? Is it just me?' He tells Laura how he had been shooting albatrosses all his life. 'I was just hoping that this time the wound wasn't fatal.'

'You can't do this to me Max, not now. I'm so far down the river', she protests.

'Yes', he wryly observes, 'on someone else's boat.'

Introduction: a question of true love?

The quest for true love continues to beckon, however often philosophers, theologians and psychologists may warn us that it is perilous and illusory, and no matter how much we attempt to dismiss it, or rise above it. In our opening story we have an age-old recipe of an elusive attraction between two central characters. Hidden in such stock romantic formulae are often vital truths struggling to be uncovered. True love may be thwarted by fantasies and projections. Close relationships may threaten to tear us apart, but they can also be radically transformative, liberating us from the doldrums of defensive torpidity into new realms of discovery of who we might be and become under all the deceits and disguises.

Our loved ones carry the weight of manifold misconstructions that we layer over them. The work of love involves removing all that obscures the truth of who we are. Revelation of the real person behind our projections is appointment, not disappointment. Real relationships with real others, in all their unexpectedness and complexity, are better by far, even when awful, than any fantasy or illusion we may have entertained. Loved ones don't conform to our expectations, they stop us in our tracks and make us reconsider ourselves. They shock us out of our complacency.

The expression 'quest for true love' contains volumes of meaning. There is a conjunction of truth and love. To be true, love needs to be infused with truth, and truth with love, otherwise love can be blind passion and truth dispassionate. Buddhists speak of the inseparability of compassion and wisdom, of love and the ultimate nature of reality. Mystics speak of God being love, that Being and Love are coterminous.

The word 'love' is derived from Germanic forms of the Sanskrit root *lubh*, meaning desire. True love is desire, but desire for the well-being of the other, as well as oneself.[1] Truth I associate both to 'Ruth' as meaning 'the

---

1 In espousing altruistic love I am not advocating self-effacement. Even the commandment 'love thy neighbour as thyself' implies love is inclusive of both neighbour and self. Self-denigration leads inevitably to denigration of others.

Beloved'[2] and also to 'ruth' as compassion and care. When we talk about someone being ruthless we mean that they are without the capacity to apprehend and value the truth of the other. There can be no truth without 'ruth', that is, altruistic care.

True love requires a marriage of altruism and alterity. Both altruism and alterity derive etymologically from the Latin 'alter', meaning 'other'. Altruism means to go out of one's way to care for others as others, not just as an extension of self, for their sake, not just one's own. Alterity means otherness, difference and the ability to conceive of such otherness. As I develop the concept of alterity in the area of couple therapy, it will refer to more than simply appreciation of difference.[3] Alterity is tempered by empathy, an imaginal act of placing ourselves in 'another's shoes', feeling with them in their joys, sorrows, hopes and aspirations, while profoundly mindful of their ineffable Otherness.

A metaphor for truth underlying this book is epitomized by the Greek word *alétheia,* the 'un-concealed'. Dissolving obscuration, illusion and delusion we seek to uncover and behold the beloved face-to-face at last. Through trying to remove all that is distorted we also uncover and reveal our own true nature. Revelation of ultimate truth occurs in communion with others, through and in love, not alone.

A second meaning for truth is that illustrated by the metaphor of an arrow hitting the mark. The word for sin was originally taken from a term from archery meaning an arrow that falls short of the mark.[4] Eros is often depicted as an archer with a bow and arrow. It is often the ways in which we are just off the mark that cause the most persistent relational difficulties. 'You just don't get it, do you?' our partners and our children complain. We miss the mark by exaggerating each other's faults, being one-sided, off-centre. The attainment of true love requires patient practice to get our aim more correct, to discern the truth and finally penetrate through to the heart of the matter.

The final aim of love's arrow is to pierce through to the core of truth, the bull's eye of ultimate truth where love and wisdom are conjoined. When I speak of ultimate reality I draw on many sources. Within the psycho-analytic tradition Wilfred Bion[5] (1965) articulated a conception of 'O' as

---

2 Ruth in Hebrew means 'pleasant' but also the 'Beloved'.
3 The Jewish philosopher Emmanuel Levinas (1906–1996) has been a major inspiration for my understanding of alterity.
4 In Greek it was *harmartia,* in Hebrew it is *cheit*. It was originally a term from archery meaning missing the bull's eye. In Judaism it refers to everyday situations when one tries to get it right but misses the mark or misses an opportunity, or when one is trying to get it right but doesn't quite make it.
5 Wilfred Bion sought to find language to point towards the indescribable nature of ultimate experience. I draw on Bion's concept of O because it gestures towards ultimate questions in

referring to absolute truth, a numinous domain of reality which is beyond all concepts, and which passes beyond all understanding. O, like a thing-in-itself, cannot be known. It can only be become. It refers to the core truth of a situation, of an object, of each other. O can only be realized through processes of transformation in O.

> I shall use the sign 'O' to denote that which is ultimate reality, absolute truth, the godhead, the infinite, the thing-in-itself.
>
> (Bion, 1970, p. 26)

In this book transformations in O are becoming in love. Individuation, finding one's true self, the search for enlightenment, for the meaning of life, is often described in terms of individual development, as a solitary journey. I am putting forward the idea that finding fulfilment of our deepest potentialities takes place within the fabric of loving relationships, albeit of special and rare kinds.

Relational and intersubjective theories of self challenge the traditional metaphysical division between internal and external reality, self and other, arguing that core psychic processes are inseparable from a relational matrix. It is not enough to say we are inherently relational. If that is the case then the search for meaning and finding ourselves is also a relational activity. We are made and remade in the intersubjective crucibles of our intimate relationships. Love is the energetic force, the *pneuma*, the breath inspiring that quest. It is a *via amoris*.

I call the search for true love an exogamous quest. Exogamy in this book means many inter-related things concerning an authentic relationship with an Other who is related to as a subject in their own right, in all their glorious alterity and pure presence. It is a marriage made in heaven, in that it is a search for something true, right, good and beautiful, a felicity beyond all conception, all imagination, all projection. We are rekindled in the passionate flames of love, in 'the mysterious alchemy of mutual interpenetration with the subjectivity of the other' (Grotstein, 2000, p. 153).

non-denominational and apophatic terms. He describes the mystic as 'being able to see things as they really are – through the filters of disguise' (Bion, personal communication, cited in Grotstein, 2000, p. xxix). This touches on the pre-Kantian Greek for metaphor of truth as *alétheia*, unconcealment, which underlies this book.

As analysts we sit with patients from many different cultural and religious backgrounds, with a range of conscious and unconscious motivations for entering therapy. How each may conceptualize, let alone describe, ultimate questions is utterly unique to them. It is imperative to do all we can to aid each person who comes seeking a sense of authenticity to slowly reach truth as it uniquely manifests to them, through history, culture, gender, religious persuasion (if not anti-religious persuasion or agnosticism).

Exogamy entails identifying and surrendering old, familiar yet psychologically destructive modes of relating based on erroneous views, systems of defence, unresolved oedipal and narcissistic matters and mutual projections, which I call *endogamous* modes.

I will be using the word 'quest' to mean a teleological endeavour, an ethical[6] venturing forwards towards realization of ultimate questions. Uncovering and working through old perverse relational patterns, we cross the threshold into a real-making and consubstantiating marriage with another. We also create a new sense of home or place in the world.

The word 'quest' is related to path; the premise is that there is a way to truly realize transformations in O in love. The path of love means taking in our stride the tides and fluctuations of passion, squarely facing inevitable life-crises, processes of ageing, change, emotional upheavals and set-backs.

Linked to this is the willingness and ability to work for such a goal. The path of love is emotionally wrought: 'All things most excellent are as difficult as they are rare' (Spinoza, 1994, p. 265). The goal keeps disappearing, then reappearing in new guises; the path of love sometimes meanders off in unexpected directions, taking us into areas we did not even know existed.

From an absolute perspective we are who we are, yet this true nature is concealed and occluded. It is dynamic, not static, inter-dependent, not isolated, and thus we are in a continual process of realizing and becoming that which we truly are. In the luminosity of authentic love there is a sense of flourishing and emerging into the fullness of our enlightened being: 'that which stands forth by entering into the light' (Steiner, 1978, p. 51).[7]

'Here I am!' The reality of the real person, however long we have known them, is often a shock of pure presence, a being here now, not as we imagined or expected or fantasized. Being, in the original Greek sense of *ousia* or *parousia*, is a presence, a here-ness, thus-ness, or a 'standing presence' (Steiner, 1978, p. 50).

In the epiphany of love, we honour the sanctity of each other's being. It is not idolatry so much as breaking through the veils of obscuration, valuing each other in our truest potential, our unfathomable opacity and irreplaceable particularity. It is 'real-making' in the sense that to be is to be perceived, *esse est percepi*, as the philosopher Berkeley said. A sense of unreality can occur if we are misapprehended or if we are apprehended, but harshly, without compassion. Feeling understood and loved in all our

---

6 By ethics I mean living in accordance with the Real: living more fully, well, and truly. This has a spiritual and philosophical as well as a psychotherapeutic context. It embraces the ethics of alterity. To live more truly is seen here as an intrinsically relational activity.
7 Greek *phainesthai*, which was taken up by Heidegger, also means 'that which declares itself' (Steiner, 1978, p. 51). I am reminded of Yahweh's 'I am who I am', 'what it is to be' (*to ti ên einai*).

complexity by someone who gives the time and commitment it takes to seek to know and care is fundamental to fostering a sense of meaning, aliveness and human flourishing. The promise an analyst makes an analysand is to be there for the long-haul, through the labyrinthine passages of darkness and despair, to plumb the depths of caverns where angels fear to tread. The cure is affected not by insight or empathy alone, but by both.

Enhancing aliveness and vitality as against emotionally deadening states of atrophy is a major therapeutic goal, according to psychoanalysts such as Winnicott, who speaks of going on being and a sense of personal aliveness: 'To be alive is all' (Winnicott, 1963/1984a, p. 192).[8] The Greek word *eudaimonia* has this sense of flourishing and well-being, of living our inspired nature and achieving true happiness,[9] for to live well and in accordance with truth brings the greatest contentment, serenity, grace and happiness.

Intersubjectivity and interdependence

A fundamental problem that has occupied Western philosophy is the relation of self and others. The origin of this problem is the conceptual premise of an isolated self, who is autonomous, separate and unchanging. The questions are cast from an erroneous starting point: how does that self then relate to other selves? Are others similar or different? How can I know another self?

If our starting premise is a concept of an independent, autonomous self, then it makes relations with others inherently problematic. The philosophical problem becomes a psychological, spiritual and interpersonal one. Alienation and interpersonal pathologies derive from such a narrowly egocentric view. If we begin with relationship, the problem simply evaporates of its own accord. It was never there to begin with. A baby born into the world of loving relations, who feels cared for and minded, does not have to question his or her existence, nor that of others. It is a given.

When the hard, cold kernel of egotistic falsity is dissolved in the warm radiance of love we recognize our interdependence with all beings and all creation. We are not alone.

---

8 See also Ogden, 1997, and Grotstein, 2000.

9 *Eu* means well or true; *daimon* means divinity, soul or spirit. It means living in a way that would be well-favoured by a divinity. It is related to *eu zên* or 'living well'. It is often translated as flourishing, human flourishing or happiness. Buddhism also alludes to the sense of genuine joy when one is aligned with truth and an enlightened attitude. Once free of egoic acquisitiveness and grasping one may feel suffused with rapture and joy (*sukkha*). Further states of enlightened consciousness are described as 'abidings in ease here-now', or 'happy living in this existence', or 'peaceful living' (Majjhima Nikaya, as cited in Chatalian, 1974, p. 361). All these point to the sense of ethical inter-relational well-being I wish to convey, and that it is truly more full of joy than our neurotic modalities.

Birds

Onepach

'The self is a flock of birds', a colleague once declared.[10] The stream of consciousness, the basis for our sense of continuity of self, may also be likened to a bird, 'full of flights and perchings', as the psychologist-philosopher William James put it (James, 1890/1981, p. 236). An 'individual' is a crowd of characters, each with a crowded past![11] A 'couple' is likewise not just two individuals, nor even a dyad, but a trinity containing the two individuals, the 'couplehood', the space in between and the relationship that surrounds and contains them. Or as Augustine argued, there are three things, the one who loves, that which is loved and Love (Augustine, 1961).

A still quiet third

A vital symbol in our opening story is that of the albatross. The growth of a genuine relationship often features a sense of some third presence which circles around the two partners but is controlled by neither. If one listens to its prompting, it intimates the way forward. Yet it is all too easy to control the agenda, act precipitously, and otherwise inadvertently spoil the delicate harmony and beauty of such moments. We turn away, reverting to old, defensive modes, allowing internal destructive elements to attack moments of potential growth. We scare off the albatross. Alarmed, the bird flies off beyond the clouds. Or we even shoot it down completely. The Mariner suffers endless torment for a single, unpremeditated and vicarious act of cruelty. He is redeemed only by a spontaneous gesture of love.[12]

Laura and Max disavow their attraction. Laura, once bitten, and thrice shy, decides to opt for a less risky love choice. In response to the last-minute invitation to the more venturesome dance, she feels it is too late: 'You can't do this to me, Max, not now, I'm so far down the river.' 'Yes', Max wryly observes, 'on someone else's boat.' The proverbial boat Laura is on represents an endogamous boat – a love choice predicated on a defensive rationale, a safe, conservative choice based on fear, precluding courage.

10 Giles Clark, personal communication, 1997.
11 We bring to each new relational situation a host of internal imaginal figures and internalizations of family, friends and other former love relations. These create webs of obscuration that render the new relationship a haunted house. We need to identify and exorcize all such ghostly presences for exogamous love to flourish.
12 Coleridge's *Rhyme of the ancient mariner* of 1798/1999 is pregnant with symbolism concerning redemption by love 'for man and bird and beast' (Holmes, 1998, p. 173). Coleridge saw the killing of the albatross as evil, unnecessarily and wilfully killing something natural and precious. Coleridge's notion of *hospitalitas*, of making the stranger welcome and at home, relates to one of the Greek forms of love, which also relates to zenogamy.

Out of timidity we often turn away from moments of destiny. The Greeks called such moments *kairos*, meaning 'right or opportune moment', an appointed time when we are called to stand forth, rise to the occasion of ourselves, when decisive but right action is called for. It can refer to grace-filled openings between states of being, moments of destiny requiring an existential decision. Rising to the occasion of ourselves is a tall order. We tend to continually shrink away, not dramatically, but in a kind of onto-logically timid way. We beat around the bush of our true destiny, we procrastinate. Not today, we'll do it tomorrow. We do not seize the day, the moment, now. Here again is the metaphor of the bull's eye, to go for it, for life, for love, for wisdom, asking of ourselves, 'how might I best meet this moment, what life asks of me, right now?' When we meet each other, do we treat the encounter as if this is it?

When we unconsciously sabotage possibilities of an experience of grace, of *kairos*, there often follows a period of feeling becalmed, in the doldrums. There is a loss of energy and direction, a shameful melancholia when we realize we have spoiled things, turned away from a moment of possible beatitude, a rendezvous with O.

Even when Max takes Laura on the boat in an attempt to 'go for it' – for life, love and passion – it is not smooth sailing. In couples therapy one is continually confronted with a major impediment to intimacy, which takes the form of an old, stuck, pattern that each partner brings to the marriage. This pattern takes the form of a scripted scene loaded with difficult and traumatic memories, expectations, projections, fears and fantasies. By some strange synchronicity it dovetails perfectly into a corresponding scene brought to the situation by the other partner. Couples superimpose their *tangles* respective scripts to create an entangled drama, which hijacks the relation-ship. I call such scenes 'interlocking scenes'.

The sea that the Mariner traverses could also be seen as the 'rising world of waters dark and deep' which has been 'won from the void and formless infinite' (Milton, as cited in Bion, 1965, p. 151). Underneath and around us at all times is the vastness of O.

The iconoclasm of love

All reality is iconoclastic. The earthly beloved, even in this life, inces-santly triumphs over your mere idea of her. And you want her to; you want her with all her resistances, all her faults, all her unexpectedness. That is, in her foursquare and independent reality. And this, not any image or memory, is what we are to love . . .

(Lewis, 1961, p. 52)

We often assume that life and people will let us down, they will inevitably fall short of our idealizations. Yet the beloved often falls tall, rather than

short, of our limited imaginations. In shattering our illusions and triumph-
ing over our projections, a real relationship with a real Other can be more
life-enhancing and exciting than our fantasies. The real person and the real
relationship are only disappointing because we have failed to keep our
appointment with the other's reality.[13]

Each encounter with one's beloved is a revelation of reality in this
moment, something never experienced before, hence requiring a great deal
of existential courage, as well as the capacity to bear a lack of certainty, to
be open to the call of each moment without turning away.

Every distortion merely conceals the truth, but cannot ultimately obliterate it. Defences have an uncanny knack of revealing the very thing they are
designed to camouflage, of manufacturing the very thing they are meant to
avoid. We delimit the infinitude of being by constructing conceptual strait-
jackets with which to render experiences predictable, predetermined, con-
forming exactly with our expectation. We impute false images and stale
memories upon each other as substitutes for the shock of their actual
presence. We disregard any discrepant evidence to the contrary, expressing
indignation even when another doesn't conform to our negative expectations!

Beyond hopes and fears, when we discover the depths of profundity
beneath our constructions, we may find ourselves wakened to a sense of
delight and even beatitude. This emerges from the endeavour to transcend
the strictures of a self-centred outlook, to cross the psychic threshold into
true intimacy based on an appreciation of the other's ineffable alterity, and
so enter, together, the 'unknown remembered gate' (Eliot, 1935/1959)
towards becoming in O in love.

Love's paradoxes: the elusively subtle language of love

At the heart of this book lies an enlivening paradox. How can alterity and
alétheia ever be reconciled? If the other is Other how can I ever behold the
beloved face-to-face? The arrow of truth flies between the cracks between
knowing we don't know each other and yet being curious about the real
person under all the false imputations. Instead of constructing dualities of
opposites as self-contained, isolated categories of being, a capacity for
paradox concerns the ability to hold the tension between different aspects,
which, although seemingly disparate, properly belong together. There is a
dialectical relation between aspects that are defined or conditioned by their
relationship to each other, by their interdependence. It is in the gaps
between concepts, thoughts and words that we glimmer elusive presentiments of truth.

---

13 A point made by Grotstein (personal communication, 1997).

Inklings of intuitive insight disappear when we attempt to over-define and reify. Insight is often a case of very subtle re-alignments in our understanding. It might be seeing a situation in a more symbolic, less literal or concrete way. We slip off the mark by creating false dichotomies or conflating two aspects of truth which although interdependent are not one. Non-duality is not the same as monism. To say we are relational rather than isolates is not to say we are fused and inseparable. The search for truth as an attempt to uncover another's reality under our projections does not deny their inscrutable alterity. The Buddhist concept of non-self (anātman) does not mean that we have no self and that all is nothing, but it refers to the absence of a permanent, autonomous, persisting, unchanging ego. The Buddhist concept of śūnyatā likewise does not mean simply emptiness in a nihilistic sense but empty of false selfhood. Bion's no-thing (1963, 1965) is not nothingness but an apprehension of the latent plenitude of the void of O. Non-attachment does not mean a schizoid detachment or disengagement from loving relations. It means freedom from a possessive self-centred clinging to an object of desire.

Our relations with each other are all interdependent. So are the terms we use in the attempt to express this. We need to discover a language of subtle distinctions that more finely discern the different and varied forms of love, and so may better catch their respective truths and more accurately gesture towards the ultimate. Can we say love exists as a thing in itself, without lovers loving, or without the daily contingencies of interpersonal experience? Love exists in the particular circumstances of loving which entail lovers relating as both beloved and lover, where the subjectivity of each is created anew in each encounter, ever seeking to be known and ever eluding definition. Love, alterity, exogamy and intersubjectivity can only accurately be understood in terms of interdependent relationships with each other. Alterity becomes meaningless and a form of philosophical dualism if we overemphasize radical Otherness such that no engagement or connection to another is possible. Exogamy incorporates the notion of becoming more fully ourselves in a love which is understood as intersubjective, and which recognizes and respects the paradox of communion and alterity, epistemophilia and opacity.

Love's therapeutics

Sigmund Freud viewed the aim of psychoanalysis as enhancing the capacity to love and to work. I recast this aim as the work of love. Love requires psychological work. Finding our true vocation and fulfilling work enhances our love lives. Psychoanalysis and Jungian analysis have sometimes overlooked the relational ground of our being in favour of more individual aspirations towards self-becoming and individuation. In my analytic practice, with both individuals and couples, heterosexual, homosexual, in and out of love, single, celibate, *de facto* or married, the search for truth in love remain the crux of the matter.

This book presents a therapeutic of love, which grows out of other seminal concepts underpinning the book, namely exogamy, alterity and intersubjectivity. The broad theme of this book is the quest for true love; the psychological obstacles to finding and creating fulfilling and exogamous love relations; and the search for therapeutic ways to understand and transform the many pathologies and impediments to loving. The path out of the suffering of relational alienation unfolds into a possibility of discovering how to find and make enlivening and authentic relationships in which we gradually remove all that perverts our true potential.

The book is clinical in orientation, but I do not wish to hide behind the couch. The search for emotional truth and becoming in love concerns us all: couple therapists, psychoanalysts, psychotherapists, couples and individuals. Although much of what I write is based on the paradigm of a couple, the arguments are not limited to long-term couple relationships but are applicable to many forms of loving engagement with others.

As an analyst I resonate with the idea of philosophy as a practical, spiritual and psychological project to overcome obstacles to uncovering truth, to living and loving well and fully. Epicurus declared that 'there is no use in philosophy, unless it casts out the suffering (*pathos*) of the soul' (as cited in Nussbaum, 1994, p. 13). The philosopher Martha Nussbaum finds 'riveting' the idea of 'a practical and compassionate philosophy – a philosophy that exists for the sake of human beings, in order to address their deepest needs, confront their most urgent perplexities, and bring them from misery to some greater measure of flourishing' (Nussbaum, 1994, p. 3). So do I.

Myths and stories depicting exogamous themes

Therapy concerns personal and interpersonal myths and stories[14] that are sacred to our patients. As Jung said, 'the patient who comes to us has a story that is not told, and which as a rule no one knows of . . . It is the patient's secret, the rock against which he is shattered' (Jung, 1967, p. 138).[15]

In each epoch we reshape such creation stories, our cosmogonies, impressing upon their form elements of both the *zeitgeist* and our own

---

14 Bion saw both collective and personal myths as 'scientific deductive systems' (Bion, 1992).
15 In the interests of protecting such sacred and hermetic stories, all clinical vignettes used in this book are fictional. Although the issues described may be ones commonly grappled with in our personal lives and analytic practice, none depicts any actual couple or person who has consulted me as a therapist.

personal predicaments. In our private lives we myth-make. We may also play out aspects of the big myths. In our opening story Max traces his current romantic tendency to always 'stuff-up' his love life to a moment in time when he failed to act in accordance with the laws of nature and of hospitality by shooting the albatross. Max creates his own creation myth as a way of explaining his central relational dilemma and fall from love's grace. In so doing he draws on another story, that of the Ancient Mariner, which in turn was Coleridge's recreation of a mythic theme of the wandering Jew. The extended metaphor has since entered our common vocabulary and imagination such that it takes on a life of its own.

Myths, literature, works of art, music, film and cultural discourses may be discussed avidly by people in relationship, interpenetrating the intersubjective space. We incorporate elements of tales of love within our own life-stories, amplifying and seeking a wider resonance for our personal concerns.

Signposts into love's uncharted territory: ground, path, fruition

The book forms a triangular structure concerning the ground, path and fruition of becoming in love. Part I, Being in love, creates a metapsychological and philosophical underpinning for the more clinically applied focus of Part II. Love, alterity, intersubjectivity and exogamy form an interdependent quarternity. I explore these four inter-related aspects of becoming in love in the first four chapters of Part I, emphasizing the interdependent relationships between them.

Part II, The path of love, develops a therapeutic of love, drawing on fictionalized clinical material amplified by relevant themes in certain myths, legends and literature, to illustrate a range of psychological obstacles we encounter in the path towards exogamous love.

In Chapter 5 I begin by outlining basic principles of a therapeutic of exogamous love, such as the creation of an atmosphere of safety and containment such that couples can develop a capacity to reflect upon and uncover what is going on at an unconscious level. I compare the marital and analytic third, transference and countertransference in couple work and the marital transference.

Three chapters explore the phenomenology of unconscious obscuration and endogamous patterns overlaying our relational space. The uncanny nature of unconscious factors influencing our love choices is the focus of Chapter 6. Erroneous ideational attitudes, distorted perceptual states, defensive positions and mutual projective processes take a confused array of manifestations, which I outline in Chapter 7. Relational configurations based on attachment styles deriving from early experiences of relationship form the subject matter of Chapter 8.

Fulfilling intimate relationships require a constant emotional and psychological struggle to disentangle the strangleholds which are created by the interpenetration of unresolved traumatic and phantastic complexes stemming from previous disappointing relational experiences. These complexes may manifest as an encrypted pattern of engagement that each partner brings, like a malignant dowry, to the marriage. The dowry box, once opened, releases its nefarious contents to create extremely complex and entangled dramas. Such interlocking traumatic scenes are the focus of Chapter 9.

Love may be obstructed by more endemic structural disturbances and personality disorders such as narcissism. Narcissistic elements formulate themselves in a range of narcissistic intralocking configurations in couple relations, explored in Chapter 10. I draw on Anita Brookner's novel *Look at me* to explore the narcissism of Echo in Chapter 11.

Bela Bartók's opera *Bluebeard's castle* depicts the failure to cross certain thresholds in the exogamous journey, the topic of Chapter 12. Here is the theme of those areas where we demand that our lovers do not enter. Do they represent psychotic pockets in a Bluebeard in each of us, which we enter at the threat of a destructive internal annihilation of a hidden aspect of ourselves? Or do they reveal what must remain hidden?

We may be on the brink of psychological breakthrough and vital change, but at that very moment we may shrink away and look back regressively to the comforts of familiar but non-productive patterns we are used to. This is a perverse attraction to a deathly avoidance of new possibilities and directions in our relational lives. In Chapter 13 we meet Orpheus and Eurydice, and a fictional couple, David and Sybilla, whose intersubjective encounter is driven by the deep morbidity of Orphic and Bluebeardian themes. This is an example of how myths and stories may capture our imagination and so move our interactions because they are potent paradigms of our particular intra- and inter-psychic patterns of relating. In clinical practice we find aspects of certain myths being lived out in the inner world of patients, in their dreams, in their relationships with others and in the intersubjective space of the analysis.

Part III, Transformations in love, returns to the themes of Part I, integrating the major themes of the book with the clinical and literary material of the middle section. I discuss key components related to becoming in 'O' in love: for example, the theme of truth as *alétheia*, the work of love as a process of uncovering all the false accretions we impute upon each other, interpersonal epistemophilia, Bion's K links, what Keats called 'negative capability' (Keats, 1952), *laetitia* or enjoyment and transformations into an enlightened form of love. The marriage of C. S. Lewis and Joy Gresham demonstrates a relationship intertwined with themes of alterity, exogamy, the iconoclasm of love and mortality. I draw on Anne Michaels's (1996) novel *Fugitive pieces* to depict the role of remembrance and pathos in transmuting past trauma into a redeeming love in the present.

This book may well be seen as a philosophically therapeutic and loving engagement between ourselves as authors and readers. Out of this meeting of hearts and minds we may both be taken into areas of experience where neither of us have previously been. We will create new themes and theses, opening ever more fully into the plenitude of our being.[16]

'Wisdom or oblivion—take your choice' (Bion, 1991, p. 576).

---

16 I am indebted here to Ogden's (1994) brilliant opening to his *Subjects of analysis*.

Chapter 1

Love's many facets

Love permeates the stories of our lives, whether we seek to 'write it off' altogether or authorize its inspiration. Being intensely engaged in relationship with another person is one of the greatest joys of being human. It also brings us up against ourselves, our insecurities and our failings. We bicker and fight, we get it wrong. We fall in love inappropriately and unequally. The agonies and disappointments of love can feel impossible to bear. Yet when love throws down the gauntlet (again) do we resist picking it up?

Poets and lovers express and live it, but despite being studied across the ages and cultures of humankind, love as a force can never be conclusively explained. We continue to seek to understand what remains a mystery. 'The language of love is impossible, inadequate, immediately allusive . . . a flight of metaphors', writes Kristeva (1983/1987, p. 1).

The Ancient Greeks gave us six words for love, each of which has given rise to a plethora of different interpretations in the Western tradition. In short *eros* refers both to Eros, the god of love, and to erotic desire, most commonly sensual, but Plato also defined it as desire for the beautiful qualities of the object. *Philia* represents love as friendship, love of ideas, as in the word philosophy meaning love (*philia*) of wisdom (*sophia*). *Agapē* means love of a spouse or family member as well as to welcome in friendship and to cherish. *Storge* means affection such as that of parents for offspring. *Xenia* is the Greek word for love of the stranger and is linked to love as hospitality. *Nomos* means law, by extension, submission to divine law.[1]

These six words by no means cover the lexicon of love, nor other qualities that condition love, such as sympathy,[2] generosity, loyalty, trust

---

1 Irving Singer (1966) developed the concept of *nomos* as the form of Judaeo-Christian religious love in which we surrender ourselves to God's will.

2 Terms such as pity, sympathy, empathy and compassion have their own provenances within different epochs and disciplines; the same word can be used in slightly divergent. Sympathy, from the Greek *syn* meaning 'together' and *pathos* or passion and suffering, refers to a

and fidelity. As well as the Hindu *bhakti*, being enflamed with love as devotion for the divine, Buddhism delineates four boundless attitudes, which translate as: unconditional love, compassion, sympathetic joy and equanimity.

The Greeks also gave an account of a lively debate about different interpretations of one of these words, *eros*. Vestiges of three ideas generated at Plato's *Symposium* continue to influence our thinking about love. These are: love as pursuit of personal wholeness, love as based on lack, and love as a ladder towards higher ideals. In so far as these lend themselves to readings of love that are ultimately self-referential, they compromise the alterity, unique personhood and multi-dimensional nature of an ever-changing beloved other as Other.

'I love you.' That one word 'love' can encompass so many shades of meaning may be confusing, but it also speaks to the nature of love's riches. We have a palette of emotional colours which may be implied in different measure by one word, 'love': awe, passion, desire, lust, excitement, compassion, friendliness, affiliation, care, concern, tenderness, affection and beneficence. We can express so much metaphysically, ontologically and emotionally with three simple words. It is paying homage of one to another. It is Buber's 'I–thou', with love as the bridge, a principle of connection, but which still retains a space between.

True love contains many aspects. We may feel enflamed with love's power, desirous of the well-being and happiness of our lover, compassionate for the beloved's suffering and wish for their greatest good. It falls short, when we overemphasize one quality at the expense of another.

Eros alights upon us unbidden, overpowering us like a sudden gust of wind that sweeps us off our feet. Just as quickly we wonder where it went. Does it mean we don't love each other any more, or is it merely symptomatic of a natural ebb and flow in the tides of passion? Human beings are not good at understanding ambivalence, which is really polyvalence: how we can feel overwhelming infatuation followed by irritation, boredom, jealousy, possessiveness, all for the one person, in varying degrees at varying times. From the perspective of O, they are but passing weather fronts, accident not essence. We shouldn't take them so seriously!

It is not the passionately emotional nature of love that causes ethical problems but its motivation. If it is self-referential to the exclusion of the

---

capacity to share feelings, passions, interests of another. It includes both awareness of another's condition and concern for them (Wispé, 1987). In its German origins *einfühlung* or empathy is stronger than sympathy. As I use the term 'empathy' it will be more in the sense of the German 'feeling into' and 'with', and implies concern for another's sorrows, and rejoicing in another's happiness and well-being. It is closer to the sense of 'fellow-feeling' attendant upon recognizing our fundamental loving and altruistic connectivity with our fellows and all creation.

other as Other, a human being to be loved for his or her own sake, then it leads to a range of erroneous emotional evaluations based on what is good for me. It is the blind exclusivity of an egocentric direction of desire that needs to be surrendered, not the emotion itself, which can be harnessed in all its passionate intensity to love's true aim. We can be enflamed with ecstatic fires which burn up the last vestiges of the hardness of ego.

The quest for Mr and Ms Right

'If only I could find the right person', we say. Who are we searching for when we say 'I'm looking for Mr or Ms Right?' Generally we think of someone who is 'right' for us. When love doesn't work, we often say it was because 'she wasn't right for me'. The idea of Mr Right is often related to the concept that there is one and only one special person somewhere out there, our missing other half. This theory was promulgated by Aristophanes in his theory of the severed whole, at a very famous dinner party, the *Symposium* of Plato.

Love is but 'the name for the desire and pursuit of wholeness'. So declared Aristophanes. If we have the 'good fortune to encounter' our 'own actual other half, affection and kinship and love combined inspire . . . an emotion which is quite overwhelming, and such a pair practically refuse ever to be separated even for a moment'. We seek to be welded together as one person, so that 'instead of two' we should be one, melted into our beloved (Plato, 1951, pp. 63–64). The notion of love as union, that love is perfect when the two become one, has beleaguered Western thought since Plato. Yet as Levinas reminds us, 'two have a better time than one'. Our relations with others are *'better* as difference than as unity . . . The very value of love is the impossibility of reducing the other to myself, of coinciding into sameness' (Levinas, in Levinas and Kearney, 1986, p. 22).

This myth continues to influence ideas about finding one's soul-mate, the notion that there is only one person somewhere out there who is a perfect fit, and that having found the 'one and only', I am at last whole and complete again. Relational breakdown is attributed to misfit – inadvertently hooking up with the wrong mate. Love becomes a quest to heal our disseveration.

If the impetus behind a restless striving to find the right partner is to find a matching half, someone to complete us, it is not actually about a relationship with another person *qua* person. We but seek to reunite two separate halves of a single whole. We indeed need to become less lop-sided and half-hearted to be able to love well, but a partner is not there to fill up all the gaps in our personality. Right relationship is about two whole-hearted human beings, coming together to create a new confederation of wholes not holes.

It is curious that the idea behind Aristophanes' explication of love has been taken so seriously throughout Western history. The idea of original spheres wheeling around doing cartwheels (Plato, 1951, p. 51) surely points up the ridiculous spectacle of two lost souls hooking up with a perfectly matching half.

Aristophanes' love-song can become a monody, if not a monotone, sung by monads tone-deaf to a different tune! True love inspires us to enjoy the richer harmonies of our diatonic if not polyphonic intersubjective natures.

A closer analysis of Aristophanes' statement that love is but 'the name for the desire and pursuit of wholeness' may resound a different tune. The search for the right person may contain a teleological grain of truth, a developmental impetus.

Telos means end, and here teleological refers to the idea that our 'problems' may be there to help us. Problems beg questions, questions evoke solutions, which do not always readily appear. They require patient, at times painstaking, incremental work and psychological insight to uncover what is going on. As Jung argued, instead of reducing all psychological problems to past experiences, crises may be prognostic of the soul's search to become what is there in potential from the beginning. Our various relational predicaments may stem in part from past traumatic, uncompleted or unresolved matters, yet they are also opportune if not opportunistic, for without them we would never be called forth to work things through and thus flower into the fullness of who we might be. This book views the passionate power of love as ultimately having a teleological purpose towards increase and becoming most fully authentic.

Searching for the right relationship may, at heart, stem from a dim intimation that we are interdependent relational beings, not psychological monads.[3] We feel restless because underneath our protestations to the contrary we long to exit the lonely isolation of a defensive solipsism, but not just by simply hooking up with a self-extension.

Right is related to rite, to ritual (*rta* in Sanskrit), and thus rites of passage. Love's initiation rites involve death of an old self, in the form of individual subjectivity, and resurrection into a new mode of being as a couple. Right also has the sense of not bent, distorted or crooked, but upright. Levinas speaks of uprightness (*droiture*) in the sense of consciousness being like an

 love entails loss of old form of self

---

3 The term 'monad' originally comes from the Greek, meaning unity. As a metaphysical concept developed by Leibniz, monads are infinite, eternal, self-reflecting, simple substances. Monads are windowless because they can't see out, and you can't see in (Stewart, 2006, p. 243), they have no beginning and no end. Applied as a psychological metaphor, a monadic stance would refer to treating oneself and/or others as a monadic self-sufficient system, depending on nothing or no one else outside to be what one is. Monadic people avoid interaction, for it would lead to alteration of self and other, which would threaten self-sufficiency.

arrow: 'the urgency of a destination leading to the Other and not an eternal return to self' (Levinas, 1968/1990, p. 48).

Eros, chaos and ecstasy

Love is integrally related to notions of self and other and the desire to bridge the gulf between us. A crucial teleological component of *eros*[4] is that it dismantles the watertight construct of oneself as an independent and impermeable identity. It dissolves our core concept of who we were. *Eros* disturbs our ordered equilibrium and creates pandemonium in our lives.

Eros, according to Hesiod's *Theogony*, was one of three entities there at the beginning of all time, along with *Khaos* (yawning void or chasm) and *Gaia* (earth). *Eros* later becomes conflated with chaos and hence confusion.

Eros as one of the passions was often understood as something to be tamed, sublimated or transformed into 'higher' forms of love. Although most moral philosophers have favoured rationality over passion, the subversive force of *eros* may liberate us from another danger: vegetating into a defensively predictable existence. Eros' action is to:

> melt, break down, bite into, burn, devour, wear away, whirl around, sting, pierce, wound, poison, suffocate, drag off or grind the lover to a powder . . . Very few see him coming. He lights on you from somewhere outside yourself and, as soon as he does, you are taken over, changed radically. You cannot resist the change or control it or come to grips with it.
>
> (Carson, 1986, p. 148)

The arrows of Eros create a piercing that engenders a yearning to overcome the yawning gulf between self and other. Desire makes us restless, opening up a gaping hole that propels us outwards to the world of others. Eros and chaos, the abyss of separateness and the quest to bridge it, go hand in hand.

A salient feature of the state of being in love is the ecstasy of being in a realm of expansiveness in which the duality of self and other is transcended yet not collapsed. Ecstasy means to 'stand beside', as in to be carried beyond one's ego. There is a paradoxical sense of heightened authenticity and realization of our deepest nature – which now becomes also partly defined by our conjoined subjectivity – while respecting the integrity of our beloved whom we can commune with, but cannot have or fully know, let alone be.

4 To differentiate Eros as the Greek god of love from *eros* as a type of love I shall capitalize the word Eros when referring to Eros as a god, and use italics when referring to *eros* as a type of love or principle of connection.

Eros is a ravishing beyond every project, beyond every dynamism, radical indiscretion, profanation and not disclosure of what *already exists* as radiance and signification . . . Love does not simply lead, by a more detoured or more direct way, toward the Thou.

(Levinas, 1961/1969, p. 264)

Kernberg explains how the emotional states associated with the passions of sexual love express 'the crossing of boundaries' bridging 'intrapsychic structures' separated by internal conflicts and past object relations, opening out into new 'personally created' relations (Kernberg, 1995, p. 41).

Such a state of self-surrender is to be distinguished from both terrifying experiences of self-obliteration and regressive fusional states in which differentiation of self and not-self is dissolved, as found in certain psychotic or merger states. A capacity to be alone is necessary to be two. There is an expansion into awareness of our common shared experience of the most fundamental elements of our existence, life, mortality and impermanence:

The separateness results in loneliness and longing and fear for the frailty of all relations; transcendence in the couple's union brings about the sense of oneness with the world, of permanence and new creation. Loneliness, one might say, is a prerequisite for transcendence.

(Kernberg, 1995, p. 44)

We confront and move beyond repetitions of infantile complexes into a new exogamous and consubstantial identity, consisting of two whole people and ~~trinity~~ a new relational third, a relational trinity, a relational space.

Liberated from a confined viewpoint of the solitary ego, we feel an exulted state of being at one not only with our beloved, but also with the whole of creation, with the Divine Lover. This is a theme reiterated throughout the mystical writings of many religions.

Fusion love and non-duality

There is a subtle differentiation between an authentic quest for non-duality and desires motivated by symbiotic or merger fantasies. Symbiotic union refers to a postulated state of fusion with mother, where there is no differentiation between the 'I' and the 'not I'.

The desire for fusion with the beloved can be a pathological defence ~~danger of~~ against difference and aloneness. If we completely merged with our beloved, ~~complete~~ we would not only dissolve our own subjectivity but also obliterate theirs. ~~merger~~ Certain pathological modes of insecure attachment lead to identifying with ~~w/ other~~ the other so adhesively that all separateness and difference is disavowed. A violent assault on the alterity of the other is waged by a cannibalizing attempt to incorporate and thus become the other. Alternatively, self-surrender can degenerate into a form of self-abnegation while idealizing the other, wallowing in a masochistic degradation of self.

A medieval poem by Ulrich of Lichtenstein rather humorously encapsulates the paradox of the aspiration to overcome duality and unite with the beloved, and its impossibility, if not even its undesirability:

> Lady, let our spirits mingle,
> I in you and you in me;
> Let the two of us in single
> Being both together be,
> Each to other let's be true!
> 'Sir, that I will never do.
> I am mine, let yours be you.'
> (Ulrich of Lichtenstein, as cited in Bowra, 1961, p. 30)

Eros and friendliness

A true lover is also our friend and *compañeros*, someone we deeply cherish and take delight in, someone with whom we share everyday difficulties. We have as much longing for the ideals of friendship as we do for romantic love. Romance palls if it is not sustained by other loving qualities such as *philia*, concern, consideration and companionship, as a patient, Mariam, discovered:

Once, when I was a music student on an exchange in Vienna I fell in love with a famous conductor. When I first met him I was over-awed by his brilliant musical flair. He had a wry seductive smile and was dripping with erotic charm. We talked until dawn, wandering the cobblestone streets behind the opera house. He was ardent and intellectually inspiring. But he didn't know how to do friendship. Our romantic whirl was intensely exciting but the days between one heady evening and another started to seem empty and without purpose. I felt homesick and remembered my flat-mate Sam back in Sydney. Sam had popped the marriage question out of the blue just before I left. I just hadn't considered him in that light and I felt like running a million miles, which I sort of did going to Vienna! I suddenly really missed the times in which Sam and I used to go for walks, sharing the humdrum difficulties of everyday life. Fortunately a few warning signals enabled me to see the writing on the wall before it got too serious with 'Herr Maestro'. We were having a romantic dinner and I received a call from Australia about a friend who'd been taken to hospital. I spoke on the phone for five minutes keeping my lover waiting. He stormed off in fury. Then I was wretchedly sick one afternoon and he screamed at me like I'd done it on purpose. I thought, 'what Sam would be doing right now would be making a cup of tea. And Sam would just listen when I was down.'

Different facets of love can get split between different people in our lives. The conductor was pure *cupiditas* and *eros*, Sam pure *philia*. Mariam's experience of the one without the other was, in both cases, not at all satisfactory. Yet she came to reconsider the hidden erotic qualities of Sam on her return home.

'In friendship loving is more important than being loved.' It consists 'more in giving than in receiving affection' wrote Aristotle (2004, p. 213). Love as *philia* desires the good of the other not for one's own sake but for theirs. *Philia* is altruistic and sympathetic. A friend loves what is best for us, and thus might also be our fiercest critic, but we will take their criticism as being constructive, even if we wince in self-recognition.

The Greek concept of *philanthropia* means the 'natural tendency to love' others, a 'way of being which incites to charity and benevolence towards them' (Pseudo-Plato, 412e). Epicurus described 'a very wide form of friendship, as if open to the universal and 'dancing around the world' (Epicurus, 1993, p. 82).

Philia may be enriched by qualities of *eros*. When I talk to a dear friend, I might sense that he is a little in love with me, or I with him. If circumstances were otherwise, we might allow the erotic aspect to deepen. If either is already 'spoken for' or if the rules of our engagement pertain to those of friends, colleagues or mentors, *eros* can still inspire our relationship without inappropriate or otherwise unethical enactment.

We can be in error by being too scared to love. Seeking to eradicate *eros* might amount to a form of denial, which itself could be unethical or at least small-minded. As the philosopher Gillian Rose discovered:

> To spend the whole night with someone is *agapē*: it is ethical. For you must move with him and with yourself from the arms of the one twin to the abyss of the other. This shared journey, unsure yet close, honesty embracing dishonesty, changes the relationship . . . To navigate this together is to achieve the mundane: to be present to each other, both at the point of difficult ecstasy and at the point of abyssal infinity, brings you into the shared cares of the finite world.
>
> (Rose, 1997, p. 65)

Agapē and caritas

Rarely found in classical Greek literature, *agapē* translated the Hebrew word *ahava*, which refers to both divine and human love as well as love toward inanimate objects such as food, wisdom, agriculture and the good.

Agapē (or *caritas* in Latin) became a central term in Christianity to denote a transcendental, divine, unconditional love between oneself and God as well as love for all humanity. God is love and that love is absolute, immutable, all-encompassing, yet it is also deeply personal and engaged. Love as *agapē* is generous, patient, kind, loyal, self-giving, full of joy, hope, peace and truth. *Agapē* is unselfish, does not seek to control, and is not possessive, envious or covetous.[5]

Cupidity, on the other hand, is a ravenous craving for the possession of the other based on a self-centred attitude. As Augustine saw it, the 'perversity of self-involvement is the foundation of cupidity' whereas the 'decentering of the self' is the basis of charity (Moyn, 2005, p. 80). Again we have the theme that the critical factor is whether our desire is self- or other-centred. Love as *caritas* enables us to transcend the lonely isolation of self-centredness. 'As man advances in *caritas* . . . he casts off all that belonged to him as a specific individual.' Love 'destroys the individualization and isolation of man' (Arendt, 1996, pp. 78–79).

Reciprocity and altruism

Many theories of love seek to demonstrate that all love is ultimately self-serving. We only serve others so that they might serve us. We only extend loving, generous gestures so we can receive from the other what we need and want (nurture, idealization, mirroring, sustenance). This was the view of Hobbes, Spinoza, Proust, Freud and Sartre, but not of the Jewish philosopher Emmanuel Levinas (1906–1996).[6] Levinas sees the principle of seeking to serve another without thought of reciprocation as the most fundamental starting point for ethical relations. Putting myself in the place of another is an act of substitution:

> To acknowledge the imperative force of another is to put oneself in his place, not in order to appropriate one's own objectivity, but in order to answer to his need, to supply for his want with one's own substance. It is, materially, to give sustenance to another, 'to give the other the bread from one's own mouth.'
>
> (Lingis, 1981, p. xxviii)

---

5 The very famous passage from 1 Corinthians 13 still rings true, if we could re-open our ears and hear it in a freshly resounded way.

6 Levinas has been criticized for descriptions of love in which he assumes the male 'I' point of view. This may obliterate the 'idea of woman as subject desiring *along with* man as subject' (Irigaray, 1991, p. 115). The position I aspire to is one where the lover is the beloved and the beloved is the lover, the relations are symmetrical, interchangeable and non-gender-specific. Nor should we assume a female or male point of view, or a sexual orientation.

If we place ourselves at the centre of our world, then from such a self-referential perspective we categorize everything in terms of how it affects us. The world of others is only there to satisfy and justify our needs. This is a philosophical, an ethical and a psychological error that is at the heart of many pathologies of love.

Spinoza viewed hatred as an overwhelming affect caused by erotic love (*libido*) due to the self-centred nature of this desire. I love my beloved only if she or he loves me in return; I hate her if she does not reciprocate that love (Smith, 2003, p. 162). Conflict, jealousy, avarice and sexual obsession follow in the trail of self-centred libido. Erotic passion may give rise to frustration, anger and hate as inevitable corollaries of egocentric desire.

Likewise in Buddhism if desire is egocentric it creates a 'tormenting irrationality of possessiveness, acquisitiveness and selfishness' based on self-aggrandizement and self-centredness (Guenther, 1976, p. 42).

When Buddhists say that suffering is created by craving, it is craving that we need to renounce, not the object of our desire *per se*. If we can love one another non-possessively, cognizant of each other's liberty, alterity and separate destiny, then love becomes pure enjoyment, beatitude and gratitude for this moment, now. True love is an experience of 'infinite richness' in which the subject admires and enjoys others as something intrinsically precious and worthy in their own right and for their own sake (Guenther, 1976, p. 41).

To serve another without thought of return is an out-flowing movement away from the self into the world. Paradoxically this enriches us by expanding our horizons. As soon as we expect our charity and generous gestures to be reciprocated we reverse the direction of our attention away from the infinite, back into the limitations of the egotistical mind. Altruistic generosity paradoxically frees us from the prison of limitation whilst also bestowing ethical value to limits – the limits of knowing, the limits arising out of our difference.

Altruism means willingly and lovingly going out of one's way for another. And that is just what altruism does: we get out of our own way. Altruistic love imbued with recognition of alterity frees us from solipsism. 'In altruism, solipsism, the view that the self is all that exists or can be known . . . is transcended: Self no longer perceives self as the only centre of worth' (Post *et al.*, 2001, p. 3).

Love of the other as oneself

The philosopher Roger Scruton claims that love comes into being as 'soon as reciprocity becomes community: that is, just so soon as all distinction between my interests and your interests is overcome' (Scruton, 1986, p. 230). Here we have the real meaning of the commandment, 'love thy neighbour as thyself'. The existentialist Jewish thinker Franz Rosenzweig[7] (1886–1929) argues: 'man is to love his neighbour like himself. Like himself. Your neighbour is "like thee"' (Rosenzweig, as cited in Moyn, 2005, p. 154). In loving one's neighbour one's self is 'confirmed in its place', each one loving the other and being loved in a relation of mutuality and symmetry. Or as Levinas put it:

> 'If to love is to love the love the Beloved bears me, to love is also to love oneself in love, and thus to return to oneself.'
>
> (1961/1969, p. 266)

Storge and the 'erotics of the socks'

Those whose focus is the excitement of *grande passion* often find it hard to sustain and enjoy the myriad small threads of relational connection that are part of lived daily life – how a couple might take their walks together, how they set the table, how they make decisions, day after day, hour after hour – let alone how they mediate disagreements and resolve misunderstandings. There is much to be enjoyed in the ordinary and the daily, in domestic chores and routines, what I call the 'erotics of the socks'. There is also value in acknowledging how messy, neurotic, imperfect and downright silly we sometimes are, as well as the constant stuff-ups we make in our love lives. Through all of this comes a sense of *joie de vivre* and an appreciation of the sanctity of each unique struggling and muddling human being, and a search for a better way to live our lives.

When we can put up with the way our beloved gets us wrong, wakes up grumpy, feels sick, wants to make love when we want to go to sleep; when in other words we descend into our corporeal existence, enter the present and no longer strive to cut ourselves off from where we in fact always were – temporal, limited and embodied beings – then we have achieved an erotics of the socks. It is an attitude of taking delight in what is, not grasping after what might be.

D. H. Lawrence reminds us that erotic sensuality and domesticity are not opposed. It is a quality of aliveness, of transmitting life, of *eros* as a principle of out-flowing connection, rather than in-turned. It is the sanctification of all we do with life-energy that is truly erotic.

> As we live, we are transmitters of life,
> And when we fail to transmit life, life fails to flow through us.
> That is part of the mystery of sex, it is a flow onwards.

---

7 Rosenzweig was a Jewish theologian and forerunner for Levinas's thinking about alterity and love.

Sexless people transmit nothing
And if, as we work, we can transmit life into our work,
life, still more life, rushes into us to compensate, to be ready and we
ripple with life
through the days
Even if it is a woman making an apple dumpling, or a man a stool,
if life goes into the pudding, good is the pudding
good is the stool,
content is the woman, with fresh life rippling into her,
content is the man.
Give, and it shall be given unto you
is still the truth about life.
But giving life is not so easy.
It doesn't mean handing it out to some mean fool, or letting the living
dead eat you up.
It means kindling the life-quality where it was not,   *custodian*
even if it's only in the whiteness of a washed pocket-handkerchief.

(Lawrence, 'We are transmitters')

Some difficulties in love stem from an internal conflict between *eros* and *storge*. The theme of how to reconcile domestic and erotic forms of love is related to unconscious conflicts between endogamous and exogamous libido. We mistake our domestic home-life as consisting solely of familial forms of love such as affection, nurturing or *storge*, and 'outsource' erotic passion onto the face of the stranger.

Freud and Jung both struggled with a conflict between domestic and erotic forms of love in their personal relationships. They both seemed to overlook evidence that their respective partners had the capacity to embody both sharp intellect and power to ignite and keep alive the flames of passion. 'Not a bad solution to the marriage problem' for Freud was to divide two types of love between two types of women: one, his wife Martha, the keeper of the hearth, the other, his sister-in-law Minna, the erotically intellectual companion.

Xenia

Alterity imbues our most familiar intimate relations with a quality of *xenia*, for the strangeness of the real beloved. We should treat our closest lovers, friends, and family members with *xenia*, hospitality for the stranger. Such faith in the ineffable enigma of those most close to us enhances ethical relations, enhances the capacity for breaking through assumptions, memories and expectations. Each time we meet again is epiphany, as if for the first time, yet I also greet you as if you are my dearest trusted friend I have known all my life.

*paradox –
meet as
& for
the first time a
dear friend*

The idea that the beggar who comes knocking on our door might be an unknown guest, God, Zeus or a Bodhisattva appears in many traditions and cultures. The challenge is to do justice to the other as being venerable, 'as I meet him for the first time in his strangeness face to face. I see this countenance before me nude and bare. He is present in the flesh' (Wild, 1969, p. 13).

I think of the kindness and hospitality given to me on so many occasions by strangers who then became dearly beloved friends, mentors and teachers. I remember going overseas on a study tour many years ago when I was training to be an analyst. I had the gall to write to a very famous psychoanalyst asking for a meeting. It was truly a meeting, a rendezvous in O. I arrived at his house where a feast had been laid out in my honour; he had put aside most of his day to meeting with me. We talked avidly about my writing, about Fairbairn and Bion, about Orpheus and Persephone. He treated me as if I were the most important honoured guest, yet he had never met me and I was a nobody. It was pure, unselfish, altruistic hospitality for a stranger. The understandings generated in the conversation were life-changing for me, as was the hospitality in and of itself. He gave generously of his wisdom, his clinical experience as well as his hearth and home. This meeting epitomized the quality of *xenia*, of hospitality as articulated by Levinas: 'Recollection in a home open to the Other [is] hospitality' (1961/1969, p. 172).

'*Viens*, all that I have, all that I am, is at your disposal!' It is the spirit of 'hospitality that does not expect reciprocity and withholds nothing from the guest' (Wyschogrod, 2003, p. 36). For Levinas the demand of the Other issues 'from an unknown God who loves the stranger' (Levinas, as cited in Wyschogrod, 2000, p. xi). The ethical choice is to welcome the stranger, to share their world by speaking to them, using a form of language where there is room for a diversity of dialogue, a readiness to listen without prejudice, an openness, where 'I am never sure just what he will say, and there is always room for reinterpretation and spontaneity on both sides' (Wild, 1969, p. 14).

Love, fear and hate

In the consulting room one is often witness to the many ways people seal off the possibility of engaging with others, with love and with life. The compromises made to avoid the pain of love are covered over in layers of rationalizations and justifications. Staying where we are avoids many fearful prospects: the loss of the neurotic gains of the status quo, the unfamiliar territory of becoming in love, in which each encounter shocks us by its indeterminacy. A real beloved doesn't conform to our expectations. Sometimes a melancholic stasis feels neurotically safer. Often this is the repeated tension of the distance–closeness/closeness–distance of the schizoid personality.

Bion argued that the opposite of love was not hate, but a kind of apathy, *indifference* what he called 'minus love' (–L). The strong passion and desire of love stirs up hate: we may hate our dependence upon the other, our lack of control *model/ obstacle?* over them, our vulnerability, the pain and frustration that love brings.

There is a tension between our longing for connection and fear of our former identity being obliterated. This, in turn, can provoke an arsenal of defences. One defence is to attempt to subsume the other within oneself, denying their separateness. They become an extension of self, or are identified as an inner figure such as an *anima* or muse or mother figure. Freud *celebrity* speaks of a preliminary psychosexual 'phase of incorporating or devouring *chef*— a type of love consistent with abolishing the object's separate existence' (Freud, 1915/1984a, p. 136). The defensive urge to incorporate bits of the other within oneself in a cannibalistic manner forms a major impediment to exogamy. Exogamous love involves a form of dissolution of previous modes of identity, but not via devouring and pillaging.

Sabina Spielrein,[8] whose ideas influenced both Freud and Jung, questioned why passionate love harbours such negative emotions as disgust, anxiety, hate and aggression. Destruction was always part of sexual passion, *loss,* she concluded, because love involves the threat of the dissolution of ego *destruction* (Spielrein, 1994).

Eternity in mutability

> He who binds to himself a joy
> Does the winged life destroy
> But he who kisses the joy as it flies
> Lives in eternity's sunrise.
>   (Blake, 1789–93/2004, p. 153)

Love is in motion, never a fixed, predictable entity cast in stone like Pygmalion's statue. Like the beauty of later afternoon autumn light playing on the water, we might enjoy the 'fleeting, indefatigable alteration of mien, the ever youthful radiance that plays on the' face of the beloved (Rosenzweig, 1921, as cited in Moyn, 2005, p. 147).

A sublime moment when we feel touched by Blake's 'eternity's sunrise' is still experienced in a moment in time. Gratitude protects joyful experiences *gratitude* from being tainted or spoiled by disappointment that they are transient. We may then greet each phase of loving without trying to artificially prolong or

---

8 Much of Freud's theory of *thanatos* and the opposition between life and death instincts was anticipated by Spielrein, as well as deriving from a lineage including Schopenhauer, Wagner, Nietzsche and Thomas Mann.

manipulate it. Rejoicing in what we have, not regretting its impermanence, is an antidote to melancholic reactions to mutability.

Eternity resides in the mutable; it is not '*contrayr*' to *mutabilitie*, as Spenser had it (Spenser, as cited in Miller, 1951, p. 200). We are told that 'passion fades'. Plato maps a course of love in which yearning begets passion, which, in the moment of its satisfaction, wanes. Yet we mistake natural movement and change, the tidal fluctuations of love, as decline. Once we can overcome our fear of change, ageing and impermanence, enjoy this moment just as it is, then love has an uncanny tendency to grow exponentially. It is more often our capacity to contain and embody the full heat of love that is in question.

A particular and beautiful moment occurs unbidden, yet we prevent ourselves enjoying the next moment by wistful nostalgia for what has past. We take an afternoon walk together along a glorious stretch of wild coastline, where, unexpectedly, the conversation opens out into areas of ourselves we had never confided to anyone before. We don't want it to end. Next week we try to replicate the experience and find we are just going over the same ground. You seem preoccupied and when I begin where we left off last week you seem irritated: 'oh yes, you said all that last week'. Yet new manifestations of love arise in the very moment of consummation. It is the very attempt to acquisitively replicate an enjoyable experience exactly in the same way that leads to disappointment. If we can enjoy today's walk for what it is – grey weather, you a bit grumpy – then today is just as much a moment to be cherished in its own way as last week's perfect weather.

As Epicurus said, 'gratitude . . . neither suffers over what no longer is nor regrets what has been' (Epicurus, as cited by Compte-Sponville, 2001, p. 137). When we appreciate and celebrate each moment of life as if it is the most precious gift life can give us, then we are filled with life's graces, not depleted by their passing.

Many relational pathologies stem from the ways in which people will not let themselves deeply love another because to love is to experience risk, change and loss. So much of our suffering comes from wanting things to be so predictable that we would rather create our own misery than be at the mercy of the unpredictable moods and occurrences which loving entails. Understanding change and impermanence, that we are forever in flux, capable of transforming in O, breaking through old neurotic patterns, enables us to give each other the benefit of the doubt.

Love, particular or universal and ladders of love

From Plato, through the Scholastic theologians, Renaissance Neo-Platonists and the Romantics, erotic love has been seen as an intense attachment to and longing for a particular person. This may be displaced, sublimated or transformed into love for other objects (Art, Beauty, God), but it begins with personal attachment. Erotic love encompasses sexual desire, which may be enacted or it too may be refined, redefined and redirected to a non-sexual, non-bodily aim.

Attachment to a particular person has been judged as erroneous, and thus to be avoided, relinquished, or superseded by a 'higher' form of love. This conflict is related to the sense of opposition between spirit and flesh, the immaterial and the bodily, the realm of pure ideas and material reality.

Socrates argued that we love someone because of the noble qualities they possess. Recognition of this fact ideally enables the lover to ascend a ladder of love, from love of the person, to love of their good qualities, to love of beauty, goodness in general, to the beauty of knowledge and through the branches of knowledge to a final vision of the Form of Beauty itself. This gives complete and unifying knowledge of truth concerning the whole universe (Hamilton, 1951, pp. 23–24).

Ladders of love can dehumanize the human beloved who becomes merely the symbolic representation of a set of noble attributes, or is used as a rung on a ladder towards God or the Good. This denies the actuality of the beloved, their particularity and foursquare reality, and can be used very effectively as a schizoid defence.[9] Having ascended past the rung of attachment to a mortal, the real person becomes redundant and expendable. Few like being treated like a rung on a ladder, even for such a worthy cause!

Universalizing love, turning the love of a particular person into an ideal or abstract principle, can be an avoidance of the pain of the loss of a particular unique, irreplaceable person whom we love. The love between Dante Alighieri and Beatrice is not a 'distant, contemplative appreciation' but a love of what is qualitatively unique and irreplaceable which recognizes that both are distinct, individual, with only one life to live' (Nussbaum, 2001b, p. 560).

Being deeply loved and valued as a specific, unique, irreplaceable person ennobles and transfigures the beloved. This is not a simplistic affirmation of unconditional love regardless of a person's actions. It is seeing the divine spark and potential in every person, whilst still retaining a sense of ethical appraisal.

Irigaray expresses the pleasure of love-making in an 'act in which neither can be substituted for the other' or is interchangeable, for 'he is he and I am I'.

And because we are not interchangeable, pleasure is no longer proximity nor duality, neither loss nor regression, nor more or less infantile

---

9 This is a point also argued by Scheler. Love involves loving the person herself, not for her qualities. Furthermore, we can only know the individual personality of another through the act of loving (Scheler, 1954).

perversity, nor failure of communion or of communication . . . a unique and definitive creation . . . ineffaceable, unrepeatable.

(Irigaray, 1991, p. 111)

Love as lack and yearning for completion

Eros, according to Socrates,[10] is a relational force filling the gap between human and divine, enabling the universe to form an 'interconnected whole' (Plato, 1999, p. 39). But in itself, love is nothing but 'lack and tension, desire and movement which never ceases nor finds fulfilment, since it is always in the middle, incapable of dissolving into nothingness or wholeness' (Cavarero, 1990/1995, p. 98).

Love as a yearning that cannot be fulfilled was called *sehnsucht* by the Romantics. Should such desire be sated, its satisfaction would kill love, since one has what one seeks and love is the search for what one has not. This echoes the first and second Noble Truths of Buddhism as dissatisfaction (*duḥkha*). The cause of suffering is acquisitive, possessive desire (*kāma*) and thirst (*tṛṣṇā*). Both acquisitive desire and thirst are based on egotism, which is the kernel of ignorance. This is the critical point: it is not love-as-desire that causes suffering, but love based on selfish desire. Given the self is of itself empty, then it is on a 'hiding to nowhere'.

Desire based on lack if it becomes egotistic leads to feeling 'torn apart and overflowing with absence, replete with the void of its object and of itself, as though it were that very void' (Compte-Sponville, 1996/2001, p. 235). Perhaps it is the void that needs to be squarely faced. There is a deep irony here, at the base of which is redemption from the terror attendant upon dissolution of ego. We are dissolving something that never existed to be dissolved, and if that is the case, what is to be feared?

A sense of lack leading to a restless search for 'The One' is described by many people. Myths across the ages attribute this yearning to return to a former state of perfection that once existed but was then lost, through birth, sin, error, or having an original symbiotic union with mother broken. Aristophanes' theory of the rounded whole and Freud's theory that we seek to regain an original state of oceanic bliss are two variations on this theme. Can something that is lost ever be regained? What if we never had it in the first place? If it existed in the past and then was lost, how can we ever return to and regain what is past and lost?

Drawing on Aristophanes, Freud also argues that love is driven by the search for restoration of an earlier state of affairs. Since all later objects of attachment are imperfect substitutes for our original object of love, our

---

10 Socrates does not credit himself with this theory; it is given as an account of love he heard from a certain woman of Mantinea called Diotima, a priestess and foreigner.

sense of incompletion will continue to haunt us. This condemns us to always look back. The real human adult partner becomes but a stand-in for someone else and is never appreciated in his or her own right. All later love is but an impossible attempt at repetition and all relationships become by default covered over by endogamous transferences.

Other philosophers and psychologists have drawn on the notion of lack in subjectivity. For example Lacan argues that desire is the awareness of a fundamental lack, a hole at one's core which one seeks to fill. Desire is longing for a sense of completeness that can never be achieved. We seek out sexual and emotional relationships to fill this lack, but the need is insatiable. Hysteria, addictions based on primary emotional lacks and borderline frustrations are all strong drives for starving or hungry love.

Lacan on desire

The sense of lack and something missing has a teleological element, propelling the self, which was self-centred in orientation, away from itself outwards towards the world of others. Even desire that is unconsciously self-seeking is drawn forth to seek outside itself for what it lacks. *Eros* is a relational force of connection. Liberated from the desire to have love on demand, on our terms, authentic love becomes a celebration of what is. It is not due to lack and nor is it an abstraction.

Liebestod: who dies in love?

At the threshold of death, a dear friend, David, realized that 'the nature of mind is love'. This was a startlingly unexpected realization, because prior to his long illness his life had been one of spiritual pursuit, predicated on individualistic aspirations for enlightenment. Personal relationships, which he did not eschew, were nevertheless seen as diversions from the path. Through being surrounded by love through the last months of his life, came the realization that love was not a distraction but both the path and goal.

There is an interconnection of symbols of death and rebirth in passionate love, related to the ways in which such love dissolves the unity and autonomy of the self. Hans Castorp in Thomas Mann's *Magic mountain* (1924/1928) declares to Madam Chauchat that the body, love and death are but one thing, pointing to the creative and destructive aspects of love in which self-transcendence and self-annihilation are rarely distinct. We also confront a different form of death: death of a fixed hard core of egotism which we cling to so strongly that we fear its loss as if it means to die to ourselves. The 'transcendence from self to a passionate union with the other person and the values for which both stand also is a challenge to death, to the transitory nature of individual existence' (Kernberg, 1995, p. 41).

shared values

Love and death are inextricably linked not only because to love is to fully confront mortality: ours and our beloved's. We know that both of us will ultimately die. We do not know the time or circumstances, or who will die first. To love is to lose, yet it is a greater loss not to love at all. Even if we die peacefully, in our lover's arms, or surrounded by our loved ones, death is a journey that takes us on different paths. C. S. Lewis recognized in his relationship with his wife Joy as she was dying, that his pain in being with someone who was dying and her pain in being with him in his pain were not the same: 'I had my miseries, not hers; she had hers, not mine . . . We were setting out on different roads. This cold truth, this terrible traffic-regulation . . . just the beginning of the separation which is death itself' (Lewis, 1961, pp. 114–115).

Yet there is no value in attempting to escape the terrible wrenching of loss through death by avoiding love in the first place. This is to kill life twice, since we pre-emptively kill the life of love and the love of the living.

The more fulfilling the relationship was, the less, on one level, one mourns. This is a psychological insight Freud (1917/1984d) articulated, when he argued that melancholia, rather than mourning, occurs where there is unresolved ambivalence towards the beloved. When we truly love, then not only does the beloved live on in us, we keep discovering new aspects of their life and character we never knew before, appreciating them in ever new ways, not *because* they are dead, but because the process of remembering, reconsideration and new discovery continues. Such was Aurelia's experience of being with her lover Daniel when he found he had a terminal illness. I end this chapter with a short story concerning Aurelia and Daniel.

A gentle rain is falling. The fresh scent of wattle imbued with the moistness of dew wafts into the room where I sit, as I have sat, for the last three weeks, by Daniel's bedside. A faint hint, is it just imagination, of a smile flickers across his face at the cacophony of post-rain lorikeets squarbling: 'the dawn brigade', he used to call them.

I suspect, I know, that the blossoming of wattle in September will henceforward remind me of his passing away. And passing away was what it seemed to be, a process so gradual as to be almost imperceptible. What was so striking was not depletion, but the degree of vitality that his frail, emaciated body still emanated. The warmth beneath my fingers as I gently massage his shoulders, the insistent pulse of his heart, the gurgling flow of blood, the rhythmic rise and fall of his chest. His eyes are closed but flicker when I whisper in his ear. He can no longer eat or speak, but holding his hand, he squeezes it back.

When Daniel first found out he really was dying, he asked me to sing at his funeral. He said, 'I want to be transported to the afterlife, like a feather on the breath of God.'[11]

11 An allusion to Hildegard of Bingen's writings.

Now I am flooded with music enfolded with memories of our life together. Like opening a window that had long been closed, I feel awakened to new perspectives of our time together. From where I sit now, the myriad mis-understandings and resentments evaporate into emptiness, to be replaced with a simple sense of gratitude, for his big-heartedness, compassion, wry sense of humour, if not for his messiness. I so often used to laugh at him, 'Daniel. You are so gloriously idiosyncratically yourself!' We are told that life has to be lived in the shadow of dying and parting. That to love means bearing more, more joy, pain, life, a capacity for more all round. And never before have I realized this more than now.

And now we entered a land beyond words, where words no longer mattered, just holding his hand, stroking his face, feeling the warmth of his skin. Days pass into night, I slip into sleep filled with dreams of his waking, alive and well only to wake to his depleted body beside me.

In the darkness of predawn on the ninth day, his eyelids flicker, revealing blue beneath. He whispers, 'I love you'.

And then his breath slowed, and stopped.

A funeral. Gut-wrenching cries of lament well up from the depths of my bowels, resounding throughout the space, transforming my terrible angry grief unexpectedly into a hymn of glorious praise for life. I want to be a feather on the breath of God because only that way would I be able to express my sorrow and my joy, the utterly transcendent gratitude I have for Daniel. Because we are but feathers, and only through singing can I ascend to where he is going, yet I know I remain. Oh how can this ever be expressed. I suddenly feel transported into his bones, into the fire that will any minute take my beloved's body away, as if my voice could lift our spirits to the next life together. I know I will be with him as we have always been, sometimes far away, yet still a couple, sometimes as close as bodies ever get. How can death destroy what we had? Strangely, it expands it. We can never share in the same way, but I sense he is still aware of me as I am always thinking with him. We go on existing in our thoughts and memories, held in mind, like a baby in mind of God. That he existed will always go on enriching me, filling me with gratitude just simply because he is who he is. That doesn't cease. And I feel strangely closer than ever before.

Chapter 2

The marriage of alterity and altruism

Strangers on a plane

When Aurelia first met Daniel it was not love at first sight. He irritated her, serving as a coat-hanger upon which to hang all her prejudices about handsome, middle-class, American men. Which may have been providential, since had she noticed the slightest whiff of attraction, her armoury of defensive and self-sabotaging manoeuvres would have destroyed any possibility of meaningful engagement.

She was on a plane going to Paris where she was to give a lecture on organizational change and gender politics. She had long given up hoping to find 'The One'. Stock phrases, repeated *ad nauseum* to her students, echoed in her head like empty refrains: 'don't look back', 'no regrets', and 'never settle for second best!'

'Third time lucky?' No! Enough was enough! The next best thing was beating a hasty retreat into a comfortable if insular life as an academic.

As she settled herself into the crowded economy section, a man in his forties, dressed in blue shirt and beige drip-dry trousers, sat down next to her in the aisle seat. Out of the corner of her eye she noticed him sitting huddled and absent-mindedly jabbing at his teeth with a toothpick, listlessly glancing at the newspaper on his lap. Jab, jab, jab, he went, then sucked the moisture from the wood. She thought, 'odd obsession, this chewing spears of wood, wonder what that says about him?'

Half an hour later she realized her thoughts had strayed from trying to finish her lecture into making a string of fanciful assessments of his personality: obviously a conservative, probably an accountant without a psychological bone in his body. Married with two children in Washington. Goes to the gym in the morning, expects a cooked supper on his return from work. Control freak with pent-up displaced oral aggressive tendencies as indicated by the toothpick addiction.

He sat down as the food trolley came past. The hostess offered her a copy of *Le Monde*. She asked if there might be a copy of the *Guardian*. He said, 'I can't help you with the *Guardian* but I do have this rather obscure English paper.' She thought, 'he's nicer than I thought, that was a kind gesture'. For a fleeting second she felt an emotion she thought she had long since worked out of her system: attraction. She deftly whacked it back into her unconscious with the stiff reminder, 'any man that age who sits next to me on a plane is bound to be unavailable, unsuitable and dysfunctional. With a blue-on-beige get-up like that, no doubt a fundamentalist Christian chauvinist reactionary to boot.'

'Why are you going to Paris?' she tried to ask nonchalantly.

'To change planes. I'm going to Mozambique.'

'Oh, how exotic, magical, romantic Mozambique, where the couples dance cheek to cheek . . .'

'Well, not much chance for romance where I hang out.'

'Oh. You live there? What do you do?'

'I work for *Médecins Sans Frontières*.'

Aurelia, embarrassed at her gaffe, looked down at the paper. It was *Peace Review* and featured an article about the role of women in peace building. Shocked at her conjectures being plumb wrong, curiosity began to replace irritation and prickly defensiveness.

Conversation opened up, and didn't finish until they reached Paris, dialogue that encompassed every subject under the sun. They each discovered all manner of areas of commonality, yet just as importantly enriching differences between them, the excitement of seeing how their different perspectives opened new vistas on what they each were committed to in their working lives.

'How did you get to work for *Médecins Sans Frontières*?'

'I was on a tour of Africa five years ago. I had been living a very affluent life as a cosmetic surgeon in Montreal. I was visiting a local hospital. A woman was giving birth but she was dying. She had stepped on a landmine. Thirsty and starving she had crossed the field to get to an old well. Behind the well a mangosteen tree dripped fruit, almost lasciviously delicious. I looked into her eyes, the agony on her face, the helplessness. I made a mental promise to her to do all I could. I knew I couldn't save her but I could try to do something to honour her life. The image of this face of a mother, of a child, was like a command, inspiring me over the last five years. Five years later, working in emergency, so few resources, so many tangled politics in the admin, I've had it. I'm haunted by nightmares of children I cannot save.'

'Do you have children of your own?'

'I'd like my own kids but I've given up on relationships.'

'Oh? What makes you think that?'

'Too hard with my life-style. What a joke, there is no style about it.'

By the time the plane landed Aurelia realized she was not only totally wrong in her first impressions, but also totally smitten. This was IT.

The plane landed and they disembarked. The sign giving passengers directions at the airport loomed above them. To the left, 'exit', to the right, 'transit passengers'. She thought, 'this is a moment of destiny, I will never live with myself if I don't follow it'. She said to herself, 'don't look back' as, instead of heading towards Paris, she headed for the transit lounge. A moment later, she realized she was alone. She turned around to see him grinning sheepishly on the other side of the security screen, in the baggage collection area. They laughed at the realization that both had had the same thought.

The marriage of alterity and altruism

difference [handwritten]

> The highest love does not identify itself with its object but instead loves what it knows as different . . . The gap and the feeling of a gap first exacts from love its full force and gives it wings that can beat most strongly.
>
> (Rosenzweig, as cited in Moyn, 2005, p. 113)

Fulfilling intimate relationships require a capacity to discover a non-dualistic yet non-fused relation in which each partner relates to the other as subject to subject and enjoys the shifting rhythms between communion and solitude, togetherness and separateness, familiarity and strangeness, curiosity and opacity.

Intimate relationships require a capacity for feeling with and also appreciating the indeterminate unknowable mystery of each other, for being together and being apart, even being together when we are apart and being apart when we are together.

Alterity [handwritten]

Alterity is the handmaiden of love. Alterity, from the Latin *alteritas*, refers to the 'state of being other, different, otherness' (Brown, 1993, p. 60). It also refers to an individual's conception of another person as an Other.

Alterity as a term has its own provenance in the history of ideas. I use the term alterity as a sublational term rather than 'Otherness' to signal a shift of perspective aimed at avoiding the alienation attendant upon overemphasis on radical Otherness, where ultimately no relation is possible. Similarly alterity also runs the risk of privileging the 'I' point of view, the Other being defined as the 'not-me'. There is the problem of viewing the other as but the object of my epistemological enquiry (the epistemic other), where all I am concerned about is whether and how I know them. The question is ethical rather than epistemological: how to serve the other and be subject to their reality beyond conceptual imputations.

> The 'unknown' is not the negative limit of a knowledge. This non-knowledge is the element of friendship or hospitality for the transcendence of the stranger, the infinite distance of the other.
>
> (Derrida, 1997/1999, p. 8)

I will be playing on the derivatives of alterity: alter not only as otherness, or other-in-self (alter ego, the stranger within), but to alter as in to move, to alternate, as in move between, alteration, as in change, alternative, to provide or find alternatives (from stuck defensive positions) if not also, as so often occurs in couple work, altercations!

Alterity also relates to finding an alternative standpoint, the ability to view things from another perspective, which itself helps resolve something stuck, split or in a conflicted state of opposition.

Both empathy and alterity are concepts that address, from different sides, the problem of otherness and difference (including the philosophical problem of other minds, cultural, sexual and interpersonal difference). Empathy aims to transcend and overcome the alienation created by difference and otherness; alterity has as its aim the recognition of and respect for diversity, the not-same and difference.

Levinas reverses the meaning of subjectivity when he argues that it is only via becoming interchangeable with another that 'I' become substantial, subject to the world. Standing below (to 'sub-stand'), one is subject to the other. From this perspective, our own subjectivity comes into being through an altruistic veneration of another's ineffable being. 'The Other precisely reveals himself in his alterity not in a shock negating the I, but as the primordial phenomenon of gentleness' (Levinas, 1961/1969, p. 50). 'To encounter another is to discover that I am under a basic obligation: the human other's infinity reveals itself as a command; the fact of the Other's "epiphany" reveals that I am his or her servant' (Peperzak, 1996, p. xi).

Alterity goes beyond recognition of otherness, or toleration of difference. It is almost a cliché when we say 'we must learn to tolerate difference' whether interpersonally or on an intercultural level. We can also romanticize difference, attempting to replenish the monotony of our lives with the fascinating allure of the exotic 'other'. An overemphasis on radical alterity can lead to a dualistic attitude, which brings in its wake a sense of alienation and separation in which no relation is possible.

Likewise empathy not conditioned by alterity can err if it leads to mistaken presumptions and identifications, such as assuming that another is just like me, or that we know exactly how another feels. The capacity to recognize another's alterity and opacity are co-requisites for truly ethical intimate relations to occur.

Empathy involves imagining feeling one's way into another's experience, which includes his or her emotions, sensations, memories, thoughts and point of view. True empathy requires alterity in that it is the endeavour to imagine what it might be like to be someone else when we are not someone else and never can be. We imaginably enter their world in their uniqueness: a different body, gender, values, tastes, personality, beliefs, history, culture and family background.

Such empathy is *heteropathic*, based on appreciation of difference. We are simultaneously cognizant of another's enigmatic mystery which forever slips away. It is at the border where we know we are up against the limits of understanding, yet we do not give up seeking to understand, that true understanding dawns. In the gaps where we know we do not know we reach into intimations of infinity.

Alterity conjoined with love has the sense of veneration for the numinous, transcendent, ineffable nature of the other whom I love in the pith and marrow of your being. I have gratitude for each moment your presence graces my life without seeking to control the agenda or prolong the encounter. I make no assumptions or presumptions but give thanks for the briefest of encounters, for you are simply you. Yet I am also passionately committed, engaged and give my utmost ethical fidelity to our relationship.

Alterity, as well as requiring an ethical valuing of the foursquare reality of another, is related to having a theory of mind, the ability to imagine an internal world of fantasy, feeling and mentality in our beloved. It is the opposite of 'mind-blindness' (Baron-Cohen, 1995), which amounts to a failure of altruistic imagination.

Historical contributions

Alterity cannot be considered without its relation to both questions of epistemology and the problem of other minds. The problem of self and other, intersubjectivity, empathy and alterity was theorized by certain German Absolute Idealists and Romantics who showed that self-consciousness and consciousness of the world emerge out of the relationship of the subject to other subjects. Furthermore, this subjectivity can only exist through the realization of the reality of others and their self-consciousness. In other words, our own subjectivity depends on acknowledgement of the other's alterity and subjectivity. We are inter-subjectively constituted.

Herder, a proto-Romantic philosopher, made major contributions to our understanding of empathy. He argued that it requires imagination to feel one's way into another via *einfühlung*, 'feeling-with' or 'feeling into' what is different. Difference is the critical word here, for empathy is not based on identification: *einfühlung* as an inter-personal activity becomes an imaginative act that aims to cross the divide between different self-consciousnesses. If an individual has a self, by extension others must also have a self, and therefore we can imagine our ways into it via interest, curiosity, fear, compassion and love. Herder applied the term cross-culturally rather than interpersonally.

Yet the closer one strives to reach a link through empathy, the more one finds oneself up against the wall of the limits and impossibilities of such empathy: the other (and the lover) remains Other. This became embedded in the notion of Romantic irony[1] and gives rise to the feeling of *sehnsucht*, the intense passion of unfulfilled yearning to be one with the beloved, or re-united with a lost fantasy of childhood.

For Romantics such as Holderlin, Goethe, Novalis and Coleridge, love was exalted as a vehicle by which one sought to understand another's mind through empathy and to overcome interpersonal differences. Yet several of the later Romantics based feelings of empathy on identification (*idiopathic*) rather than on the ability to imagine alterity. The Romantic tradition had a concomitant implication of xenophobia and intolerance of difference.

The very existence of another implicitly places their alterity in me, in that their face-to-face presence immediately confronts me with alterity, theirs and mine, whether I choose to ignore or welcome this fact. As Kristeva writes:

> To discover our disturbing otherness, for that indeed is what bursts in to confront that 'demon', that threat, that apprehension generated by the projective apparition of the other at the heart of what we persist in maintaining as a proper, solid 'us'. By recognizing our uncanny strangeness we shall neither suffer from it nor enjoy it from the outside. The foreigner is within me, hence we are all foreigners.
>
> (Kristeva, 1988/1991, p. 192)

As the post-Kleinian psychoanalyst Thomas Ogden puts it, confrontation with alterity, the otherness of another 'I-ness', radically confronts our sense of static self-identity and does not 'allow us to remain who we were'. We 'cannot rest until we have somehow come to terms with its assault on who we had been prior to being interrupted by it' (Ogden, 1994, p. 14). Up against the limits of knowing we at least shake the fixity of our con-structions and this creates an opening out to the world of others, a receptive attitude to their being. Love is a blinding which 'consents to a night in which I will never know you' (Irigaray, 1994/2000, p. 9).

There is a correlation between interpersonal and intra-psychic forms of alterity – the 'stranger within', our uncanny strangeness, alter ego, or shadow. As Laplanche states, 'internal alien-ness maintained, held in place by external alien-ness; external alien-ness, in turn, held in place by the enigmatic relation of the other to his own internal alien' (1999, p. 80).

The other may become the repository for what we find alien and dis-turbing in ourselves. Our perception of their strangeness can be a projection of what is strange and unacceptable within us. This is like a double layer of obscuration: not only are we incapable of acknowledging their opacity and

---

1 *Ironie* was developed in particular by Schlegel and Coleridge, a concept which specifically refers to the impossibility of knowing the Other.

alterity, but their alterity is covered with a layer of projections of our own uncanny strangeness. They may then identify with the casting of them as alien, becoming truly alienated.

Opacity and negative capability

Levinas sought to remedy what he saw as an overemphasis on ontology throughout Western philosophy which denied alterity and sought to assimilate otherness and difference into 'the Same' (*le Même*) denying all that is beyond Being, transcendent, infinite, alterior, the otherness of the other (*l'Autre*).

The ontological relation, for Levinas, is one based on an erroneous assumption that a relation with another is comprehensible. The human other (*autrui*) defies understanding and cannot be reduced to any construct, expectation, memory, fantasy or other conception of them that I have.

The essential quality of ethical relations with others lies in acknowledging and valuing the ineffable alterity of another as ultimately being beyond conception. Such an attitude is an antidote to projective misperceptions and enhances authentic ethical relations. Seeking to understand another deeply in all their particularity, and feeling that others care enough to want to understand us, is vital in our love relations. Yet the assumption that we know or understand another person inhibits the questioning activity of seeking to understand. It stops the quest for understanding in its tracks. Drawing on Levinas's redefinition of subjectivity as meaning to be subject to another, 'understanding' could be said to be an attitude where we 'stand under' another's dark shrouded alterity.

Levinas is advocating something very similar to what the poet Keats called negative capability. Keats meant by this expression a capacity to dwell in a mode of being full of 'uncertainties, mysteries, doubts, without any irritable reaching after facts and reasons' (Keats, as cited in Bion, 1970, p. 125). Bion advises analysts to actively attempt to develop such an attitude in the consulting room.

Negative capability is one of the greatest servants of *alétheia* in love. Notwithstanding its difficulty and rarity, developing this capacity in our love relations enhances our ability to at least recognize that how we have constructed our loved ones is largely a figment of our imagination. It can be put to the service of peeling away the veils of erroneous ascriptions and false imputations we each layer over each other.

Bion counsels analysts to attempt to actively eschew 'memory, desire, or understanding' in order to move towards an evolution in O or ultimate reality, into that which is 'formless, infinite, ineffable and non-existent' (Bion, 1970, p. 129). This is a discipline based on an act of faith (F) in ultimate reality (O) as being unknowable. Such faith enhances precision in acknowledging opacity: it enables one to be more attuned to and perceptive of subtle nuances of experience concomitant with the appreciation of what remains forever out of reach. It is like starting afresh each time we meet.

Bion's expression 'without memory' doesn't mean we don't try to remember our close ones. Remembrance is a vital aspect of intimacy and feeling we are held in the mind of a loving other. It is critical for the *memory* development of a sense of continuity in a patient whose sense of ongoing being has been ruptured. But if selving is a stream of consciousness, then who we were yesterday is not quite the same as who we are today. Being without memory is about reminding ourselves of this, to approach our next encounter with both patient and partner as if for the first time.

A major impediment to intimacy and to psychological flourishing is the expectation that others will behave predictably according to our memory-laden expectations and prejudices. The words 'always' and 'never' presage such 'memory': 'He *always* has to have the last word.' 'She just *never* listens!' 'He's *always* late.' I call this a 'second order' defence. Partners might work hard on working through their respective individual complexes and counterproductive patterns that have in the past tended to instigate predictable, repetitive altercations. A similar situation arises which would 'usually' provoke a fight, but one partner valiantly tries to resist rising to the bait of false expectation, tries to respond in a less predetermined manner, to be more open and receptive to the reality of this occasion. But the partner who is loaded with expectation based on memory does not realize this and the same old fight ensues.

They may both treat the other as if they are behaving just as expected, even if they both aren't, again the net result being another predictable reiteration of the old row.

> Debbie feels insecure and fearful of being betrayed because a previous partner two-timed her. Mark has a complex about being trustworthy. Rather than being able to reassure Debbie that he loves her, he feels falsely accused and responds by storming off, which evokes her fear of rejection and abandonment. Whenever Mark can't be contacted in the evening after work she fears he is having an affair. Debbie rings Mark and he doesn't answer his mobile because he is having a shower. This time she reassures herself that it will be OK rather than flipping from insecurity to pre-emptive strikes of accusation. Mark sees the missed call, assumes she will be in one of her states, fears her anger, is resentful at the thought of another false accusation, so goes off to the pub with his work mates, where a girl starts to flirt with him. Debbie tracks him down to the pub, witnesses the flirtation, and assumes the worst. She screams at him, 'you fuck wit! Our relationship is over!'

Being 'without desire' does not mean neutrality, indifference or apathy, just as the Buddhist concept of non-attachment does not refer to schizoid disengagement. It means continually examining our hidden motivations for any positive actions. We hear ourselves saying to one another, 'but I did it for your benefit', when really it was for our own. As analysts it means eschewing any unconscious neurotic ulterior motives that might interfere with the therapy.

Without understanding does not mean epistemological laziness, but using every fibre of our being to try to understand, respectfully, while remembering that another being is beyond comprehension:

> The essentially hidden throws itself toward the light, without becoming signification. This unreality at the threshold of the real does not offer itself as a possible to be grasped . . . 'Being not yet' is not this or that . . . It refers to the modesty it has profaned without overcoming. The secret appears without appearing.
>
> (Levinas, 1961/1969, pp. 256–257)

Fear of intimacy is related to fear of the unfamiliar, for each encounter entails entering an unpredictable situation and we cannot quite know what to expect. We seek ways to render each meeting safe by arming ourselves with blanket statements based on judgements of how it was yesterday, making pre-emptive strikes, preferring the predictability of a negative response to the possibility of a gesture of unrehearsed intimacy. We render the opacity of the other into a set of attributes that we jealously guard like prized possessions!

Fear of intimacy [margin annotation]

The power of negative expectation

One defence against being disappointed in our expectations of others is the creation of a negative fantasy. 'Fantasy has the power to create that which it imagines' (Symington, 1985, p. 351). We fear being let down by our partner. We create an elaborate fantasy of being let down 'just as I expected'. We superimpose this negative fantasy upon the actual situation and refuse to let in any discrepant information to the contrary, even if it is positive. Even when a resultant misunderstanding is shown to be based on false fantasies of negative expectation, many find it hard to let go the sense of grievance:

> Diane and Matt described a repeating row concerning how Matt felt Diane didn't do enough to make him feel welcome when he stayed over at her place. His birthday was more than a case in point. He constructed an elaborate fantasy of what he wanted, a romantic home-baked dinner with roast lamb which Diane 'bloody well ought to know by now is my favourite meal'. He arrived an hour late, with the image of the candle-lit dinner

competing with another thought, 'Oh she'll have forgotten she invited me for dinner for my birthday and will be busy on the phone to one of her clients.' The door was open, so he came in, calling out to her. She didn't answer. He presumed it was because she was on the phone, 'just like she always is'.

'She just ignored me, treated me as if I didn't exist!' he complained indignantly. 'But I had been hiding behind the door waiting to surprise you!' she protested, 'where I'd been for nearly an hour, so I went to check your favourite roast wasn't burned. Then instead of greeting me warmly, you screamed at me, "Hello! It's Mr Invisible!" Well, you sure aren't inaudible! You know I get intimidated if men yell at me like my father did when he came home from work.'

'But sweetheart, I had stood there for five minutes and said hello quietly four times before I lost it. You know I can't stand being ignored.'

Even when they each attempted to clarify the situation, it seemed that their attribution of negative intent had more appeal than the fact that both had, consciously, been looking forward to seeing each other again. Diane said she had done everything to make it a memorable occasion. She had prepared a beautiful dinner, and was on tenterhooks making sure it didn't get spoiled. Which it was, by an initial negative expectation followed by a respective triggering of difficult childhood memories in both.

Both were also projecting a parental figure on the other, Diane her father who was verbally abusive and Matt his preoccupied mother who ignored him. The hopeful expectation of a romantic evening was overlaid with an expectation of disappointment, which created the very disappointment it was meant to defend against. Further, the negative fantasies were also contaminated with childhood experiences from which they expected the other to protect them.

The developmental capacity for alterity: being held in mind

The capacity for alterity is not a given, it is a developmental achievement. For a child to develop a capacity for alterity, the child's first caregivers must display the capacity for alterity. It depends on the child's caregivers being both perceptive and at the same time respectful of a child's hidden, private, separate world. A child needs to know his or her parents have the perspicacity to behold them as they are, rather than how they would like them to be, cognizant of their separate and autonomous sentient mind, their own pursuits, interests, different personality and different destiny. A child is born into the world 'trailing clouds of glory' (Wordsworth, 1961, p. 628) and our task is to nurture that child into the fullness of their being in the knowledge that a child's task is to be different, to venture onto another path, to leave us. We bring forth in love, yet such bringing forth is properly a letting go, done for the sake of that brought forth which takes on a life and destiny of its own.

Winnicott suggested that a child needs to be held in the mind of 'Mother'. For Augustine we are held in the mind of God. Being 'minded' has both physical and mental connotations. It means being physically, intellectually and emotionally cared for and about and being held in mind, yet not subsumed. When we love and care deeply about someone we hold them in our loving mind all the time.

The infant first apprehends mother as a subjectively conceived object, that is, as a figment of the child's imagination. The breast appears when desired as if by magic. Gradually the child discovers the breast is attached to a human being: 'Drat! Worse still, she has a mind of her own and is not totally at my beck and call!'

I remember watching a little girl by the beachside summoning the waves: 'Come wave, come! Go, wave go!' The waves obligingly paid obeisance, coming in and going out, as if on demand. I chuckled thinking, 'good thing she got the timing right'.

In the earliest stage of a baby's life, the parent's ability to attune responses to the baby's needs for mirroring and closeness is, ideally, so nearly perfect that the baby believes that the parent is an extension of his or her own mind. This hallucination is in fact the philosophical stance of an Idealist.

Idealist

Gradually, over time, the baby can tolerate mother or father missing the mark a little, creating slight cracks in the seamlessness of its subjective universe. The baby is more able to tolerate the paradox of being neither one entity nor entirely separate. The child finds, in the spaces between self and not-self, a realm of creative imagination.

The baby, says Winnicott, has aggressive fantasies that involve destruction of the image of mother. It is in mother's capacity to survive the baby's attempts to destroy her that the baby realizes she has an existence beyond his mind: 'The subject says, "Hello object. I destroyed you. I love you. You have value for me because of your survival of my destruction of you. While I am loving you I am all the time destroying you in unconscious fantasy"' (Winnicott, 1971, p. 105).

The baby then feels concern about his destructive emotions, a desire for reparation and ruth. Prior to this, relations are based on ruthless love, there is no consideration for the other as Other. Yet this stage is vital, for without it the baby develops a false self, a compliance with the mother's reality.

Care p. 6

Gradually a child can rejoice and empathize with a parent's joys and sorrows, their separate experience and alterity, without it threatening to overwhelm or oppose the child's own experience. 'The object *being at first a subjective phenomenon becomes an object objectively perceived*' (Winnicott, 1963/1984a, p. 180).

When the other is recognized as a whole person in his or her own right, projections may be owned as emanating from oneself; thus the child can begin to distinguish self and other, external reality from fantasy. There is growth of a capacity for concern for the other, for true sympathy and interest in his or her independent foursquare reality and alterity.

However, the omnipotence of the previous idealist position tends to be disavowed rather than truly worked through, transposed into the 'drama of internal objects, shifting from the domain of the intersubjective into the domain of the intrapsychic' (Benjamin, 1995, p. 40). Internalization of objects can be the legacy of an encounter in which mother did not survive the subject's attempt to destroy her.

Fairbairn: solipsism as a schizoid defence against disappointment

Fairbairn argues that we only internalize and orient ourselves within an intrapsychic universe when the external world of relations fails us (see Grotstein and Rinsley, 1994, p. 5). Internalization results from failure on the part of mother to make her appointment with her child's true reality and givenness. Introjection, writes Fairbairn, is 'the first defence adopted by the original ego to a disappointment', when the 'all good' object has critically failed to keep it's 'appointment', leading to a state of dis-appointment. This state is itself internalized, leading to a permeating sense of discontentment. Objects which are 'in some measure unsatisfying' become 'ambivalent' and thereby split into 'good' and 'bad' categories after introjection (Fairbairn, 1954/1994, p. 16).

Fairbairn believed 'that the infant is born innocent and is entitled to be treated as a person in his own right' (Grotstein, 1994, p. 113). Being so treated leads to being able to treat others as persons in their own right. When caregivers fail 'to sustain a sufficiently satisfying interpersonal mutuality' we create an internal world of perverted internalized objects (p. 114).

Distorted internalizations of original objects then become projected upon the face of the beloved, and shape our interpersonal relations. There may be the absence of a theory of mind, an inability to conceive of others as having feelings, intentions and desires (Fonagy and Target, 1996; Hobson, 1985). The schizoid personality is a form of solipsistic and autistic withdrawal from the world of relations; the form of narcissism of schizoids is isolated, detached, withdrawn and overly introspective.

[margin note: Theory of mind]

Mahler: monadic enclosure to dyadic intersubjectivity

Margaret Mahler describes how the baby is at first encased within a 'closed monadic system, self-sufficient in its hallucinatory wish fulfilment' (Mahler et al., 1975, p. 41). This is followed by a symbiotic phase, in which mother and baby form a 'dual unity within one common boundary' (p. 44). Separation and individuation herald a process of psychological 'hatching' followed by a 'love affair with the world'. *Rapprochement*, where the child feels separate but has crises of dependence, is followed by 'object constancy', leading to a sense of autonomy, self–other differentiation and emotional balance.

Levinas and the phenomenology of eros and alterity

Eros, in Levinas's philosophy, should be an exaltation of alterity, not fusion or dissolution of difference such as in merger states of identification. 'The pathos of voluptuousness lies in the fact of being two. The other as other is not here an object that becomes ours or becomes us: to the contrary, it withdraws into its mystery' (Levinas, 1947, as cited in Moyn, 2005, p. 183).

Love represents the paradox of crossing boundaries whilst remaining distinct. We think we overcome alienation by merger, but the implicit denial of difference and autonomy destroys relationship, for there can only be relationship when recognizing the fact of being two, without which relationship is not possible, a relationship with that which forever slips away. Levinas 'situates the phenomenon of love at a border, at the furthest edge of immanence between the immanent and the transcendent' (Wyschogrod, 2000, p. 127). As articulated by Benjamin:

> Only the externality of the other that survives destruction allows a representation of the other as simultaneously outside control and non threatening . . . The loss of externality plunges the self into unbearable loneliness, or escape into merger with like-self beings, creating an identity that demands the destructive denial of the different.
>
> (Benjamin, 1998, p. 96)

Face-to-face

Levinas said that ethics begins in apprehending the face of the Other. The face-to-face encounter is iconic of the primordial reality of a relational context in which ethical responsibility based on doing justice to the otherness of the other person is a metaphysical imperative.

Levinas's description of the face-to-face ethical standpoint is one of standing before the Other as one would approach the holiest of holies. Yet we can both take this attitude of humility and reverence for and with each other simultaneously, giving and receiving, loving and being loved. Lovers behold each other face-to-face. We behold and are beheld by each other simultaneously. This is not an asymmetrical position involving one gazing upon the other who is the object of perception.[2] The gaze of love is predi- ✓ cated upon symmetry, reciprocity and equality.

Authentic love is symmetrical although there is oscillation between symmetry and asymmetry within a relationship of equals. There are relational situations that have a natural asymmetry, such as mother and baby. Even here the baby's gaze at mother is necessary for the baby to see itself in the mother's eye and developmentally later to see through her eyes to her personhood behind.

The face confronts us both with being here, present and embodied, at this very moment. Yet what is behind the face? Thoughts and emotions and memories can never be wholly seen. The face both reveals and conceals, is visible yet cloaks the invisible.

For Levinas the face is 'signification without context'. The 'nudity of a face is a bareness without any cultural ornament, an absolution' (Levinas, 1964/1996b, p. 53). In the 'rectitude of the face' the Other is not a character, an identity, a persona. It cannot become 'a content' which our thoughts could 'embrace', but is 'uncontainable', leading us 'beyond' (Levinas, 1982/ 1985, p. 86). The vulnerability of a face, exposed and unguarded, is a command to do no harm: 'Thou shalt not kill' (Levinas, 1982/1985, p. 89).

The iconoclasm and ecstasy of love

Recognition of alterity may be fiercely resisted, but it can also provide life-enhancing alternatives to the narrow confines of a narcissistic outlook and the webs of obscuration created by projective perceptions. The word 'outlook' is apposite, since being locked inside our self we 'look out' at the world and our beloved rather than the more expansive, spacious vistas of a vision of '*unio mystica*' where one feels 'an all-embracing harmony with one's environment' and 'is able to love in peace' (Balint, 1968, p. 65). We long to transcend the narrow confines of an individual subjectivity

Exogamous love is about the revelation of the actual person behind the erotic object. This

> revelation is almost always painful because the beloved presents himself or herself simultaneously as a body which can be penetrated and a consciousness which is impenetrable. Love is the revelation of the other person's freedom. The contradictory nature of love is that desire aspires

---

2 As it is in 'the look' ('*le regard*') which is a form of gaze which is objectifying, based on a power differential of the one who gazes upon another who is thereby diminished (if not annihilated, as Picasso feared), as conceived by Sartre, Foucault and Lacan.

to be fulfilled by the destruction of the desired object and love discovers
that this object is indestructible and cannot be substituted.

(Kernberg, 1995, p. 44)

When we move beyond hopes, desires and fears, when we discover our
beloved's enigmatic alterity, we may find ourselves wakened to a sense of
revelation and delight. This emerges from an endeavour to transcend the
solitary ego and its self-centred categories, to cross the psychic threshold
into a marriage of intimacy and alterity: not fused and not separate, but
interdependent and intersubjective. In fear, anguish or ecstasy, when 'we
have some presentiment of the Other – it seizes us, staggers and ravishes us,
carrying us away from ourselves' (Blanchot, 1969/1993, p. 51).

Chapter 3

Subject relations

How one becomes what one is.
(Nietzsche)[1]

'Know thyself', Socrates instructs us. 'Learn the depth, extent, bias and full fort of thy mind; contract full intimacy with the Stranger within thee', wrote Edward Young in 1759 (Young, as cited in Grotstein, 2000, p. xvi). But who is this self that we might seek to know?

> How can a human being know himself? He is a dark and shrouded thing; and if a hare has seven skins, a human being could strip off seven times seventy and would still be unable to say, 'now this is really you, this is no longer a rind'.
>
> (Nietzsche, as cited in Kaufmann, 1992, pp. 7–8)

Relational moves in psychoanalysis

This book puts forward a view of self as intersubjective interdependent, relational, dynamic, multi-levelled and multiple. A relational view of self has been increasingly emphasized within psychoanalysis, as it has been in philosophy.

Object relations has been involved in the task of transforming a one-person psychology into a two-person psychology, with a shift from seeing objects as targets for discharge of biological drives to viewing human life as relational in nature. Fairbairn spoke of 'close relationships as the ground of the self' (1952a, p. 109), and Bion said that 'an emotional experience cannot be conceived of in isolation from a relationship' (Bion, 1962/1983, p. 42). Both infant research and infant observation studies have also supported

---

1 Subtitle to *Ecce homo*, as cited in Kaufmann, 1966, p. 657.

and enhanced the inherently relational aspects of the infant self.[2] Following Winnicott, there is no such thing as a baby or self without an other. Jung also stressed the relational, interdependent aspects of self: something lost sight of in much classical Jungian psychology:

> We only become ourselves with people and for people . . . the self is like a crowd, therefore being oneself, one is also many . . . one can only individuate with or against something or somebody. Being an individual is always a link in a chain; it is not an absolutely detached situation, it itself only, with no connection outside.
>
> (Jung, 1988, p. 102)

[margin handwritten note: Jung on individual]

Jung saw a person's life-task as involving the gradual bringing of a conglomerate soul into an integrated unity of wholeness, which he called 'individuation'. 'Individuation means becoming a single, homogeneous being, and, in so far as "individuality" embraces our innermost, last, and incomparable uniqueness, it also implies becoming one's own self. We could therefore translate individuation as "coming to selfhood" or "self-realisation"' (Jung, 1935/1966a, p. 173).

[margin handwritten note: Rather than wholeness, I would say for connection]

Rather than a search for individual wholeness, I see individuation as about un-dividedness, non-divisiveness and interdependence. Levinas turns the meaning of individuation on its head when he says, 'the Other individuates me in my responsibility for him' (Levinas, as cited in Derrida, 1977/1999, p. 7).

According to Fairbairn the task of psychoanalysis is to liberate the person from a closed intrapsychic system into an open interpersonal one. We only orient ourselves within an intrapsychic universe when the external world of relations has failed us. Controversially, Fairbairn argued that we only internalize disappointing, negative experiences, not positive, satisfactory ones. It is 'only in so far as the infant's relationship with his mother falls short' that 'he can have any conceivable motive for introjecting the maternal object' (Fairbairn, 1954/1994, p. 16).

Selving

> Time is a river that sweeps me along, but I am the river; it is a tiger that mangles me, but I am the tiger; it is a fire that consumes me, but I am the fire.
>
> (Borges, 1999, p. 332)

---

2 Stern (1985), for example, proposes a threefold division of self-experiences into a 'social self', a 'private self' and a 'disavowed self' (p. 229). This raises the question of the extent to which there is, as Winnicott asserted, a secret, private, inviolable core which is the seat of the 'true self' and the ways in which social relations require conformity and hence distortion, leading to the 'false self'.

Taking Gerald Manley Hopkins's concept of self as a verb (Hopkins, 1985, p. 51), we can think of 'selving' rather than self, emphasizing the search for authenticity[3] as a dynamic and inter-relational process of becoming. William James coined the term 'stream of consciousness' and sees this flux of images, ideas and memories as the 'self'. The activity of 'selving' is not a 'series of attributes or representations'. 'The shift and flux of inner life, its changing images, feelings, ideas, memories, imaginings to and forth, is at the core' (Meares, 2005b, p. 125).

The question is how to reconcile identity and continuity of self with the flux of consciousness as process. The same metaphor of a stream is used in Buddhism to explain the paradox of how the self seems to be eternal and enduring when it is dynamic and impermanent. When we look at a particular river it appears to be the same river, although what we look at is never the same water; the water we saw a moment ago has flowed onwards. In our mind we impute onto the myriad moving droplets of water a construct of sameness, identity, continuity, cohesion, permanence and autonomy. We give this a name. This 'name-making' imputation of identity, permanence and cohesion upon the self is 'unknowing' (*avidya*), the root cause of all suffering and delusion.[4] James avoids this error by emphasizing self-as-consciousness-as-process, as a function, not an entity in itself. Or in a famous Buddhist passage of the Milinda Panha:

> Just as the king's chariot is not the wheels nor the chassis nor the axle nor the shaft nor the yoke, neither is man matter nor form nor impressions nor ideas nor instincts nor consciousness. He is not the combination of those parts, nor does he exist outside them.
>
> (cited in Borges, 1999, p. 318)

Solipsistic isolation

The legacy of a first-person standpoint, characteristic of post-scholastic Western thought, can lead to feeling psychologically constricted within the windowless walls of monadic alienation. The idea of human autonomy, autochthony and individualism, stemming from overemphasis on 'I am' and 'I think', leads philosophically from Cartesian dualism to Kantian idealism, and psychologically to a solipsistic loneliness. Such philosophical

---

3 I link the word 'authenticity' to the natural aura of authority and integrity which we manifest when we have done the hard work to remove all that falsifies us and become our truest ethical selves.

4 This is a point emphasized in the entire tradition of Buddhist teachings. Authorial attribution would begin with acknowledging my indebtedness to a range of sources, teachers such as the Tibetan scholar and teacher Geshe Thubten Loden, Namkai Norbu Rinpoche and Sogyal Rinpoche.

emphasis on autonomous self

problems are also experiential and lie at the heart of pathologies of love. They are not abstract but highly disturbing experiences, which we may suffer acutely and chronically in everyday personal life.

A patient describes how he exists in an empty echo chamber, all he hears is his own voice coming back at himself. For the most part that is the only voice he wants to hear, only sometimes it echoes hollowly. The Jungian analyst Robert Hobson describes the terror of existential loneliness thus:

> 'I have no being' carries with it the implication 'No-one is there'. I have no sense of contact with another person who can confirm that 'I am me', capable of having an identity separate from the world of people and things 'out there'. Even my body is alien. There is a threat of *non-being* – a loss of the capacity to speak the word 'I' . . . In non-being there is some mysterious uncanny sense of the unknown, of an annihilation in which 'I' cease to be.
>
> (Hobson, 1974, p. 76)

Such are the terrifying states of inner emptiness leading to disorders of self, and the cure, as all therapists know, is via penetrating yet beneficent insight, imbued with altruistic love, over time. Such existential alienation is moved by love, by healing conversations and empathic relational commitments such as provided in both long-term psychotherapy and fulfilling love relations, which involve care, thought, and commitment to bestow love, value and understanding.

Cartesian epistemology and ontology are doubly dualistic, not only splitting mind from body but also cognition from linguistic structures and from other social constructions of knowing. This can lend itself to a non-relational, intrapsychic perspective. Rational reflection (reason) is seen as the source and object of objective knowledge, thereby excluding embodied, sensuous, imaginal and affective experience and intersubjectivity as sources of understanding.[5]

The Absolute of Absolute Idealism, Schopenhauer's inference of the reality of the thing-in-itself through embodied experience of the Will, and Nietzsche's will-to-power were all motivated by a need to overcome dualist concepts of mind–body and self–other relations which were the legacy of Cartesian ontology, rationalism and scientific positivism, and also by the need to explode the idea of the solitary and disembodied self.

Continental philosophy after Heidegger, particularly beginning with Merleau-Ponty, Buber and Levinas, sought to overturn the monolithic tyranny of the isolated subject. Merleau-Ponty held that 'to love is

---

5 Self psychology, founded by Heinz Kohut, and the conversational model, founded by Robert Hobson and Russell Meares, specifically seek to address and heal such inner states of emptiness and the sense of no-self.

inevitably to enter into an undivided situation with another. From the moment one is joined with someone else . . . One is not what he would be without that love; the perspectives remain separate – and yet they overlap' (Merleau-Ponty, as cited in Frie, 1997, p. 92).

Phenomenology also seeks to transcend the separation of idea (theory) from experience. Phenomenal life is seen to be embodied, interdependent and inter-relational. For Heidegger, 'encounter is the existential which grounds human relatedness' (Kern, 1992, p. 43).

Buber's I–thou

my into

'In the beginning is relation' (Buber, 1923/1987, p. 32). Where Heidegger sought to overcome the problem of how we relate to others by asserting that we are with others already, Buber's (1878–1965) focus was the 'with', as in the bridge, the 'between', the elements of the 'interhuman' (Buber, 1947/2002, as cited in Kern, 1992, p. 43).

Buber differentiates two primary attitudes to encounter: the *I–Thou* and the *I–It*. *I–Thou* is a relation of receptivity, mutuality, presence, in which there is veneration for the beingness of the one I encounter. *I–It* is a subject–object relation where one treats the other as a thing, an object. Buber also introduces the terms 'dialogue' and 'monologue' to characterize the respective types of interaction of *I–Thou* and *I–It*. In dialogue we 'experience the other side', which is 'imagining the real' and is an act of 'inclusion'. This enables us to meet and understand the other as he or she is in their particularity. In monologue I make myself absolute, the other relative. Buber differentiates contexts where the experiencing of the other side is not and should not be mutual: such as teacher–pupil, parent–child, doctor–patient (and, by extension, analyst–analysand) (Buber, 1947/2002, p. 119).

In love relations there is a tension between relating to the other as 'thou', a reciprocal encounter between equals, and 'I–It' relations when the other is treated as an object, as an 'it'. 'Love is a reciprocal encounter between responsible equals, in a direct relation. Such an encounter is difficult to achieve and maintain, because in every genuine encounter the Thou is doomed to collapse into the It of "thinghood"' (Kern, 1992, p. 43).

A root cause of relational pathology is a self-centred orientation towards the world, 'relating everything to ourselves, dominating and possessing things which surround us'. It leads to a form of psychological 'slavery, a condition in which we are in turn dominated, captured by our obsessions' (Taylor, 1989, pp. 138–139). So long as the ego remains shut up within itself, it has not 'awakened to reality', a reality which is relational. It is a 'prisoner of its own feelings, of its covetous desires'. A 'dull anxiety' permeates its existence (Marcel, 1945, as cited in Moyn, 2005, p. 223).

possession of other

* covetous desire

Yet such relational alienation may simply be dissolved if we begin with an intersubjective and inter-relational conception of self, the idea that

mineticism

relationships with others and relational energies are there from the begin- ning and part of what it means to be human. Through being with another in a loving relation of mutuality we can redeem each other from the lonely isolation of solipsism.

Alterity and opacity

We continue to exist in a world of things and others apart from ourselves, yet our perception is typically self-centred. We treat others as either exten- sions of the self or alien objects to be manipulated for one's advantage, got rid of, or ignored (Wild, 1969, p. 13). But the person who comes before me face-to-face is not a mere object to be subsumed under one of my categories. We diminish and distort the identity of the other by our presumption that we actually know the nature and motivation of their interactions with us (p. 13). Yet if we relate to one another as in a state of not knowing (without memory, desire or understanding in Bion's sense), the other's reality can be a glorious revelation. A real person is better even when difficult than an intrapsychic projection:

> Ah! Miss Dunbar! I'm glad to find you actually exist – I'd thought perhaps you were only the personification of my conscience.
> (Lewis, as cited in Wilson, 1990, p. 254)

Objects may derive their value for us based on the meaning we accord them, but Subject and Other transcend, exceed and elude our conceptual imputations. To treat the other I encounter as an extension of myself, or bring him or her into a category (mother figure, anima figure, muse) and use him or her for my own purposes (even as a mirror), means reducing him or her to what he is not, a figment of my imagination.

treating other as object

The (dis)embodied spirit and the embodied self

Psychoanalysis is the inheritor of the Western tradition of mind–body dualism, a tradition that has, since Plato, through Christian Scholasticism, Descartes, the Idealists and beyond, tended to render the body and the physical domains as secondary or transitional, something to be tran- scended. Spirit, the mind or psyche is both primary and ultimate.

When we begin to think of love relations and intersubjectivity, we may feel our bodies isolate us, yet they are more porous, permeable and fluid than the illusion of solidity and permanence would have us believe. Bodies as well as separating us are the means of our conjoining and interpene- tration. To be embodied is to be incarnated, to struggle with the limits of our being: sickness, ageing, mortality. It is only through the body, through the senses, through a body which is dependent upon the world around it and which is part of the world, that we get to know and love our body and others, our mind and others. Further, our corporality makes us present to each other and in the world.

I put forward three propositions:

- The self (which, as discussed above, is relational, dynamic, non-unified, multiple, interdependent) is a body–mind self.
- The body is a physical expression of mind.
- The mind is the idea of the body.

The last two propositions need to be considered simultaneously: the mind is an expression of body and the body is an expression of mind. Philosophically there are two issues, identity and causal relations. Cause and effect is the stuff of our psychoanalytic interpretations of psychosomatic states, i.e. our emotions having effects on our bodies, our ideas of bodies compounding that and our emotional responses to our ideas of our physical states, acutely shown in states such as anorexia. To speak of identity is to change perspective to one in which causal principles are not relevant. We cannot have a self without a body. From this perspective the two are one continuum.

The psychoanalytic tradition makes a unique contribution to mind–body relations by seeking to interpret mind–body relations in a particular (psychological) way. It has taken a position that emphasizes the import of the body and bodies as units and relations of meaning. This follows the tradition where the somatic (*soma*) is distinguished from the physical (*physis*). Although I do not want to deny the relevance of psychosomatic cause and effect (such a connection is implicit in everything I am saying), I also want to emphasize the presence of a primary psyche–soma unity that is beyond duality and linear cause and effect. This has been referred to variously as the psychoid (Jung), primal pre-schizoid stuff (Rhode, 1994), the realm of beta elements (Bion, 1962/1983), the primal psycho-somatic unity and the mind–body self (Winnicott, 1949/1992b).[6]

> Since psyche and matter are contained in one and the same world, and moreover are in continuous contact with one another and ultimately rest on irrepresentable, transcendental factors, it is not only possible but fairly probable even that psyche and matter are two different aspects of one and the same thing.
>
> (Jung, 1954/1969, p. 215)

---

6 Federn (1953) asserted that the mind is primary, and that body develops out of mind, in the sense that body-ego develops out of mind-ego.

By the idea of self being a body-mind-self, one might say that both body and mind can be understood as different expressions of one 'substance'. Philosophically this is known as 'double-identity theory',[7] the idea that the mind and body are two aspects of a common substance, or substance monism. I describe my own position as non-dualist. Jung intimates an implicit 'double-identity theory' when he says: 'The common background of micro-physics and depth-psychology is as much physical as psychical and therefore neither, but rather a third thing, a neutral nature which can at most be grasped in hints since in essence it is transcendental' (Jung, 1955/ 1977, p. 538).

Winnicott locates the self in one's body: the body being the root of development, it is out of the body that the psychosomatic partnership evolves. The self is a body-self and psyche means 'the *imaginative elaboration of somatic parts, feelings and functions*, that is, of physical aliveness' (Winnicott, 1949/1992b, p. 244).

And the two become one flesh

'I want to eat you', 'drink to me only with your eyes' – such stock-romantic phrases reveal the ways in which we seek imaginatively to incorporate the visual, visceral, kinaesthetic 'image' of the beloved's body into us.

In love relations there is a psycho-somatic interpenetration in which our experience of our physical coupling and the other's body as well as self is incorporated into our emotional-body-mind. Our psyches discover and embody shared unconscious emotional matter. In love we are transubstantiated.

Language and the self: an embodied view of speech

We use language to cross the spaces between us, voices which are embodied, borne on the wind of breath, vocal chords creating sympathetic resonance, creating a duet in which each voice mimes and amplifies the other, transcending divisions between self and other: 'To find tone, rhythm, meaning. To cultivate the breath until the words can rise up in me and pass the threshold of myself' (Irigaray, 1994/2000, p. 14).

Dialogue is about the creation of a third thing, a creative synthesis which includes yet transcends the original positions of the two interlocutors. And as much as to speak, it is to listen:

---

7 Clark (2006) has developed a Spinozan double-aspect, 'bodymind' theory as an analytic position known as *Anschauunsweisse* or 'active attitudinal approach', which makes interpretive use of psychosomatic transferential/countertransferential communication particularly in borderline conditions.

To listen to the other's love. To contemplate this gift of restrained vibration. Instead of scattering joy about, to transform it into praise, into hymns, into felicity: an alchemy of energy, a return to myself . . . the breath is conserved so that we may speak in a new way: speak love not only with gestures of the body but also with gestures of the word.

(Irigaray, 1994/2000, pp. 14–15)

The gendered subject

Since Freud, psychoanalysis has tended to view gender as fundamental to the construction of the subject, but less and less has it focused on anatomical sexual differences as determining gender identity. Feminist theorists distinguish between our biological sex and our cultural gender. Sex refers to anatomy and the biological substrate; gender is seen to refer to the social construction of what male and female mean in a given socio-historical context.

Feminist thinkers such as Judith Butler, Genevieve Lloyd, Luce Irigaray and Julia Kristeva have, in various ways, radically undermined the traditional essentialist position that posits a distinction between what is viewed as 'masculine' and 'feminine' as being anatomically determined qualities. Gender is now understood as culturally and linguistically created and recreated. Gender identity is fluid, multiple and relative. A woman's subjective sexual identities are seen as requiring their own language based on her own body, her subjective experience of her body and her relations to other bodies. Gender is produced through the shifting play of the powers and pleasures of socialized, embodied, sexed human beings. Genevieve Lloyd, reacting against feminist theories of the 1970s which assumed that sexual differences do not signify subjective gender differences *per se*, has reintroduced hypothetical thinking about the anatomical (as well as social) influences on gender identity, even so far as to say that female and male minds are constructed differently (Lloyd, 1994, pp. 160–168).

The feminine position is less fixated on maintaining boundaries between self and other, but embraces an identity which can be multiple, ambiguous, fluid and open-ended. It is in-between, ambiguous and composite.

Intersubjectivity and subject-to-subject relations

Intersubjective perspectives seek to hold in a rich tension not only the multiple complexities of ways we relate to one another as functions, objects, projections of inner figures and object relations, but also the 'joy and urgency of discovering the external, independent reality of another person' (Benjamin, 1988, p. 44).

One of the main thrusts of recent thinking on intersubjectivity within psychoanalysis is that of the ways in which the encounter creates, destroys and recreates the subjectivity of both participants. There is a dialectical intersubjectivity inherent in this relation. The subjective self emerges 'anew through continuous iterations of change through its interaction with the subjectivity' of the other. 'Each participant inexorably modifies, determines and defines the ever-changing subjectivity of the other' (Grotstein, 2000, p. 153). Ogden points out that the goal of analysis is to 'upset (unsettle, decenter, disturb, perturb) the . . . given of the patient's conscious beliefs and narratives by which he creates illusions of permanence, certainty and fixity of the experience of self and of the people who occupy his internal and external worlds' (1997, p. 12).

change thru interaction

The paradox of self and other remains:

> Thus I and you, she and he, speak to each other and each one forms a subjectivity denying access to the self and to the other prior to all speech. Between us are the world and the word and the universe and the word. One is, in part, common to us while the other remains unique to each of us. You remain a mystery to me through your body and through your word, and our alliance will always be a mystery.
>
> (Irigaray, 1994/2000, p. 12)

As Irigaray concludes, 'we need to love much to be capable of such a dialectic' (p. 12). This paradox is similar to the Christian theological paradox of the Trinity: the co-inherence of the three-in-one that can never be resolved by conflating the three into a monistic ultimate unity nor by positing three distinct godheads. We hover forever between our separateness and interdependence; our bodies and our minds, ourselves and the other, being known and unknowable, becoming one flesh and remaining forever separated in the flesh. Such is the co-inherence inherent in the deepest love relations, leading to an outflow of almost mystical gratitude to the lover for the verity of being, simply, who she or he is:

paradox & Trinity

> I want to live in harmony with you and still remain other. I want to draw nearer to you while protecting myself for you. It pleases me to protect for you the freshness of unknown flesh and the discovery which brings awakening.
>
> To foster growth in difference: tender happiness. This grace flickers across my lips, my heart, my thoughts. I love you upon the threshold of this permanent alterity, offered to my attentive senses and spirit. I wish that the flowers themselves could help me in such fidelity.
>
> (Irigaray, 1994/2000, p. 13)

Life is found in the liminal spaces between people. Ideas, feelings, images, theories are articulated by individuals in order to cross the divide between us, then are given birth in the interpersonal space between us. The ability to encompass alterity is, when we overcome our fears, an occasion for celebration, joy (*laetitia*), ecstasy and liberation:

The universe is our refuge, as is the certainty that we are two. Each remote from the other, we are kept alive by means of this insuperable gap. Nothing can ever fill it. But it is from such nothingness that a spring of the to be is derived for us.

(Irigaray, 1994/2000, p. 9)

A still quiet third

In intimate relationships, as well as there being two partners, there is a way in which the relationship seems to create a subjective entity in itself. As Gillian Rose puts it, 'two times two adds up: three times three is the equation' (Rose, 1997, p. 62). Irigaray speaks of something which is between us but which will never be mine or yours (Irigaray, 1994/2000, p. 13).

Couples in a long-term committed relationship create an intersubjective third subject that is the overlap of their two individual subjectivities. The two individuals, in relation with each other, become a conjoined subject, as well as remaining individual. They identify themselves to the world as a couple, as two partners, as well as retaining individual forms of identity.

A relationship has, as it were, a life of its own, seeming to function with its own directionality or purpose. Gillian Rose calls this thirdness, 'love's work': 'the relationship has a third partner: the work. The work equalizes the emotions, and enables the two submerged to surface in series of unpredictable configurations' (Rose, 1997, p. 131).

The sense of the relationship-as-a-third having its own teleology may give an individual the extra push needed to overcome areas of atrophy or developmental stagnation he or she might never otherwise engage with, taking both beyond their limited notions of themselves. As Jung says regarding the analytic relationship, 'for two personalities to meet is like mixing two different chemical substances: if there is any combination at all, both are transformed' (Jung, 1946/1966b, p. 171). This also applies to long-term love relations.

The relationship as a third presence is indefinable and not to be reified.[8] The 'Desirable is intangible and separates itself from the relationship with Desire which it calls for; through this separation or holiness it remains a

---

8 The 'ontological' status of such a third is a matter for philosophical debate. Gilbert (1989) puts forward the notion of a plural subject, as an entity over and above its constituent members, involving the sharing of goals, plans, intentions, actions and beliefs, which arises out of joint commitment. Tuomela (1995) and Searle (1990) see the subjectivity of the couple, the 'we', as metaphorical. Grotstein (personal communication, 2003) argues that neither the 'group' nor the 'couple' has its own subjectivity, but creates a sense of subjectivity via mutual projections. Nozick (1989) argues that in love we 'form a *we*' and 'identify with it as an extended self', throwing in our lot with its fortunes.

third person, the He in the depth of the You' (Levinas, 1961/1969, as cited in Derrida, 1997/1999, pp. 60–61).

Self, objects and subjects have become selves, intersubjectivites and relations to alterity. The relational third is not only between us but also around us – and cannot be pinned down. Thus there are multiple paradoxes, subjectivities and intersubjectivities. Each relational context creates different and dynamic interdependent self-states that vanish when we shine the torch-light of analysis upon them.

summary

What happens when one (elusive, dynamic) subject encounters another in love? The state of identity that existed until that point is undone. Love unbinds the unity of the self, leading to themes of collision, dissolution, disintegration, obliteration, destruction, death, madness, transmutation, communion, con-fusion, conjunction, fusion, union. 'I melt like wax as the heat bites into it' (Pindar, as cited in Carson, 1986, p. 15).

Chapter 4

Falling in love: an exogamous initiation

'A man shall leave his father and his mother, according to the biblical command and shall cleave unto his wife; affection and sensuality are then united' (Freud, 1912/1977c, p. 181). The transition out of the family of origin into a new grouping one creates with another, non-blood relative, is a fundamental principle of all societies. The psychological process of leaving home, with all its attendant psychological ties, is an essential aspect of growing up:

> The liberation of an individual, as he grows up, from the authority of his parents is one of the most necessary though one of the most painful results brought about by the course of his development. It is quite essential that that liberation should occur and it may be presumed that it has been to some extent achieved by everyone who has reached a normal state . . . on the other hand, there is a class of neurotics whose condition is recognizably determined by their having failed in this task.
> (Freud, 1912/1977c, p. 221)

The quest for true love is a process of psychologically leaving our childhood 'home', finding another mate and creating a new entity as a couple. This entails risks, fear of loss, vulnerability and a loosening of previously solid senses of identity, autonomy if not autochthony. Within such an exogamous relationship both partners are continually surprised, undone, recreated and transformed.

Exogamy, anthropologically, means marriage outside one's own group. This is a common practice across different cultures and historical periods, although what constitutes the group or family is variously defined.

Exogamy is reconceived here as a psychological marriage, involving exit from old defensive habits of relating built up from disappointing familial experiences. There is a teleological endeavour towards becoming in O, to find and make a relationship in which both partners are transformed and made more authentic in their loving, enjoying the opacity, alterity and ever-changing and elusively unknowable nature of each other. I call the quest for such a form of marriage 'the exogamous conatus'.

Endogamy means 'marriage within the group'. Here it refers to being 'married' to, or sticking to, old, familiar, defensive patterns of interaction based on conglomerations of mutually infecting projections of internalized figures and object relations. It can mean being caught in the eternal repetition of unresolved oedipal or narcissistic complexes or of traumatic and disappointing scenes of childhood.

The path of love is continually obstructed by the regressive pull of unconscious endogamous patterns that subvert our love choices, superimpose themselves upon the new relationship and thus hijack the adult, exogamous possibilities for becoming in love. Love's work consists in dismantling such templates in order to liberate the couple into authentic exogamous love.

[handwritten margin note: obstacles + love's work]

Exogamy reconceived

My re-coining of the term 'exogamy' is constructed from a particular combination of the following amplifications of its components:

- *Ex*: Beginning with the prefix 'ex', meaning 'out of' and outside, exogamy involves exiting psychological enmeshment in endogamous, oedipal, incestuous or destructive familial matrices in all their recreations. If becoming is a coming into true being, then it is also a process of coming out of what is unreal, delusional and inauthentic, out of emotional, spiritual and intellectual claustra into more alive, authentic and ethical states of being.
- *O*: There is a death of false selfhood, a conception and consummation of a new mode of being. Exogamy is ultimately an incarnated, mystical relation with each other in O incorporating subject-to-subject relations, alterity, *alétheia* and love.
- *Gamy*: Gamous is from the Greek *gamos* or marriage, which in turn derives from the Sanskrit *gm*, to join or unite. Exogamy here refers to a meaningful 'marriage' or communion with another who is not related to as a father, mother, sister, brother figure or figment of our imagination but as a real person outside our internal object-relational world of projections.

Exogamy also concerns initiations into true marriage and thresholds of intimacy. 'Detaching himself from his family becomes a task that faces every young person, and society often helps him in the solution of it by means of puberty and initiation rites' (Freud, 1930/1961, p. 103). There are thresholds between being a child and becoming an adult, the adolescent transition out of an original relational family matrix with all its positions and couplings. We transact thresholds of initiation between internal psychological positions such as the paranoid-schizoid and depressive positions.[1] We move between stale old defensive scripts and new improvised modes of being with each other. We brush against an inchoate sense of the numinous presence of 'O' which exists before all time. Then it mists over, we trek onwards and upwards, with occasional glimpses behind the clouds, reminding us of its majestic presence.

The exogamous quest: a conatus of becoming in love

The term *conatus* is often translated as 'striving' or 'endeavour'. It was a central concept in the philosophy of Spinoza, who saw it as an energetic process to persist in and enhance one's being. I am adapting the term to refer to the sense of a teleological endeavour, a quest towards realization through love. On one level we are already and always who we were meant to be, and on another level we are in a continual process of becoming. From the perspective of ultimate reality there is nothing to achieve for we are already that (as expressed in the Sanskrit *tat tvam asi* – 'that thou art'). Yet each relationship we are in makes us differently. We become a new 'us' (that *we* are). This means entering uncharted territory, continually unfolding into consummation of our conjoined being.

No exit: the endogamous struggle to leave home

Having left home and ventured out into the world, we all too often discover (after a while) that our new partner has an uncanny resemblance to one or other family member, or family situation. We all too readily project internal figures onto our beloved and set about re-creating old patterns of relating. As Gay notes, 'the pull of early incestuous attachments is invisible, unacknowledged, and tenacious' (1986, p. 22).

Even when people consciously choose a partner with opposite qualities to their parents, they often find to their dismay that all they have done is reverse a situation, or that somehow the partner begins to manifest the very quality they were hoping to avoid. As Klein pointed out, 'a woman may apparently have estranged herself from her mother yet still unconsciously seek some of the features of her early relation to her in her relation to her husband or to a man she loves' (Klein, 1937/1988, p. 59).

Repetitive patterns, memories and internalized figures deriving from childhood situations interfere with intimacy, not only by dictating partner

1 The paranoid-schizoid position is a concept formulated by Klein (1946/1992) referring to an early infantile stage in which experiences are split into all-good or all-bad; the world of others is likewise split into 'all-good' and 'all-bad' objects. In the depressive position (Klein, 1935) the child is able to integrate goods and bads together; another person can be seen as ambivalently both difficult/hateful and satisfying/loved.

choice, but by coming between two lovers in ways very hard to recognize, taking over the conversation, directing how one sees the situation and how one responds. The voices have a tell-tale ring of familiarity:

> A couple, 'Jonas' and 'Jessica', relate how one of the glories of getting married was that they both escaped a restrictive, judgemental parental environment where every detail of even how the table was laid was set down like the tablets of the law. The dinner table had represented a scene of imperious etiquette and exactitude.
>
> In the early days of being married they rejoiced in having dinner parties where they dared to do the unthinkable: leave the dishes to the next day!
>
> One such day, Jonas, came home to find the kitchen sink overflowing with unwashed dishes from the night before while his wife Jessica was languishing on the sofa. 'It was raining and the new woodwork I had done at the weekend was all ruined. There she was moping on the couch, whinging she had a headache. I felt so rotten. Suddenly the dishes seemed to represent all our efforts to make our home nice in our own way coming to nothing. Something came over me and I just yelled at Jessica 'Oh Lady muck, well what a muck!' Jessica retorted, 'Oh go marry your mother then, of course she'd have everything as neat as a pin wouldn't she!'
>
> Reflection and discussion revealed that both were in the grip of unpleasant memories of childhood scenes. The first thing Jessica had to do when she got home from school was help with afternoon chores so that dinner would be laid on the table the moment her father came home. Suddenly Jonas incarnated her father's rage should anything ever deviate from his exacting expectations. Jessica lying on the couch tipped Jonas into an identification with his father's reactions to himself as a teenager should he ever be found 'slouching around' and not 'snapping to'.

Suddenly Jonas and Jessica were back very much at home. Leaving home, is not so easy after all!

Family-of-origin attachments and their influence on our adult choices often have layers of contrariety and inverse logic. Gillian Rose discovered that

> behind my early idealization of men and dependence on them, there lurked a rage at having been deserted by my fathers, and at their having allowed my mother to dispose of them. Then I discovered the even more deep-seated corollary in the lack of independence of my carefully chosen current lover.
>
> (Rose, 1997, p. 57)

Oedipal resolutions and transitions from endogamy to exogamy

Freud (1912/1977c) argues that a union of 'two currents', the 'tender and the sensual', is needed to ensure a 'normal attitude in love'. Tenderness, which 'springs from the earliest years of childhood', continues through childhood, the erotic components 'undeflected from their sexual aims'. In puberty, 'a powerful sensual current' emerges which 'no longer fails to recognize its aim'. The young adult is forced to give up oedipal desires and transfers attention 'from these really unsuitable objects' to others outside the family with whom 'a real sexual life can be carried on'. This would be an exogamous transition, except for the fact that the new objects are 'still chosen after the model' of the infantile ones. Adults live out the 'conditions for loving' laid down in the early years. The new replacement objects will soon have attached to them the tenderness 'anchored' in the original 'imago' of mother and father.

For Freud, love involves unconscious fantasies that derive from childhood relations: we are forever projecting mother or father upon our lover without being aware of it. The process by which we construct the other according to our internal models is unconscious. Not only are we unaware of what we are doing but we resist becoming aware.

Relinquishment of endogamous patterns and attachments is a necessary precondition for exogamy:

> At the same time as these plain incestuous phantasies are overcome and repudiated, one of the most significant, but also one of the most painful psychical achievements of the pubertal period is completed: detachment from parental authority, a process that alone makes possible the opposition, which is so important for the progress of civilisation, between the new generation and the old.
>
> (Freud, 1905/1977a, p. 150)

Some couples do not negotiate this transition effectively and endogamous impulses persist into adult object-choices. 'It often happens that a young man falls in love seriously for the first time with a mature woman, or a girl with an elderly man in a position of authority' (Freud, 1905/1977a, p. 152).

Paradoxically it is harder to take our leave gracefully from a bad parent than a good (enough) one.[2] The psychoanalyst Harry Guntrip reflected,

---

2 Winnicott coined the term 'good-enough mother' (Winnicott, 1949/1992b). By this he meant that a mother who ordinarily does her best to listen, understand and respond to her baby's unique communications does a better job of mothering than one so bent on being the perfect mother that she forgets to listen to *this baby* and trips over the ordinary muddles of domestic life.

after twenty years of analysis, how it was 'harder to give up a bad mother than I realized . . . I'm still unconsciously tied to the mother I hate and resent and regard as bad and a failure: depressing. She early roused a deep need and longing for her which she has never met' (Guntrip, as cited in Hughes, 1994, p. 267).

In Guntrip's mind, mother and the world of others became indistinguishable. He gave up on the 'outer world as hopeless' because 'no one will ever understand'. Others were 'inaccessible' because 'they don't understand'. He couldn't 'find a way of opening their eyes to the fact and they haven't got the human intuition to see it'. 'If mother had been a real mother she would have met that need without my needing to know what it was' (p. 268). Whether the 'mother' Harry was talking about, particularly by this stage, corresponded with the mother who was a person in her own right we do not know. The internal mother as experienced through childhood and particularly adolescence often clashes with the 'real' person as she might begin to appear to be in later adulthood.

Psychologically, the tension between exogamy and endogamy involves a tension between familiarity and the unfamiliar. We speak of 'familiars' as referring to those who are of our family, as well as familiarity in the sense of sameness; what is familiar to us as in known, the place of return where we can feel at home. The sense of going beyond ourselves is at the heart of eroticism, yet we constantly attempt to circumvent and render the experience safe, predictable and unchanging. On the other hand we also need to feel a sense of being at home with each other and in the world to venture forth and initiate new undertakings.

Exogamy does not mean doing away with all the vitally sustaining aspects of what is embedded in the word 'home'. Nor does it imply disowning our ancestry, discarding our extended family of origin, or filial or fraternal disloyalty. It is about taking leave of pathologically regressive forms of destructive, familiar psychic territory, anti-relational or life-denying modes of existence.

We also cannot psychologically leave home when there are unpaid debts to our forebears. Intergenerational family matters need to be worked through, old ghosts laid to rest and untold stories remembered.[3] We need to

---

3 Grotstein coins the term 'the background presence, or subject, of primary identification' as referring to a background presence distilled from tradition and continuity of cultural identity which gives a sense of comfort, as if this tradition becomes a benign familial spirit standing 'behind us in our effort to face the world' (Grotstein, 2000, p. 18). He links this to Winnicott's (1963/1984b) environmental mother, to Freud's (1909/1977b) distinction between the 'remote and romantic parent' and 'the parent at hand, who is more like the caretaker in the gatehouse of the estate' (Grotstein, 2000, p. 17). This links to Fordham's notion of the integrates and deintegrates: from a position of security, integration and safety, from the familiar as *temenos* we can face the initial deintegration as we mate with the world.

work through past experience of family and a current situation. A patient ruefully reflects, 'I know Mum is different now, she's really got her act together, and she's trying so hard, but that makes it confusing. I have this image of her in my head of how she was when I was growing up, and that is who I keep having this internal dialogue with.' Mothers also receive more than their fair share of projections. It is at a very advanced stage in the development of alterity that a child can relate to their mother in her four-square separate personhood differentiated from the internalized mother-figure or archetypal role.

Is the anima exogamous or just another intrapsychic changeling?

Jung attempted to counteract the idea that all love relations are only parental substitutes and consequently endogamous with his concept of the 'anima' (1935/1966a) an inner archetypal contrasexual figure. The developmental function of anima-animus projections is to lure us into life, into the world of relationships, out of the oedipal embrace or incestuous and endogamous matrices which provide support and security at the expense of growth and movement out of the family. Anima-animus projections 'attract the person out into the world and into relationships, away from home . . . One of its functions is to make exogamy desirable. Against this are pulls towards de-animation, depersonalization' (Clark, 1987, p. 106).[4] Where mother-love represents fusion, anima relations involve conjunction of two different entities.

Anima and animus projections can still run the danger of rendering the foursquare reality of the real beloved into a two-dimensional image of an internal figure. The actual beloved is not seen as he or she is but is ascribed qualities which, however ideal, do not belong to him or her, but to the one projecting.

Exogamous love is neither a regressive re-finding of an original love object, nor merely the projection of an archetypal image of the perfect beloved. It is about loving a person who is loved in all their specificity and uniqueness outside any image we bring to the relation. Exogamy requires the ability to make and sustain a relationship with another, not as a

Summary

It enables one to 'accept separation and find the confidence to use their epistemophilic capacities' and integrate 'strange and separate objects to make them familiar' (Grotstein, 2000, p. 18).

4 Colman (1996) views anima and animus as themselves influenced by oedipal object-relations. This is because the contrasexual anima/animus are 'initially mediated by the oedipally loved parent and subsequent manifestations bear the imprint not only of the parent themselves but of the entire complex of object relationships in which Oedipal love is embedded' (Colman, 1996, p. 37).

projection of an idealized fantasy image but as someone who is appreciated in their foursquare reality, independent existence and alterity. The exogamous quest is a surrendering of one system of seeming security and safety followed by the crossing of a boundary into a new one, with no guarantees.

The tensions between exogamous initiations into new realms of being and falling back into endogamous modalities parallel Klein's formulation of the inter-relation between the paranoid-schizoid and depressive positions, which she saw as not only developmental stages but also as two psychic positions one re-negotiates throughout life.[5] The endogamous and exogamous positions operate at both psychological and inter-relational levels. Exogamy is never fully achieved, there being a lifelong oscillation between the two modalities.

Xenogamy and xenophobia

On an intercultural level, exogamy also means the ability to make meaningful connection outside one's group: across cultures, religious persuasions, ideologies or psychoanalytic lineages without demanding, however subtly, conversion or assimilation. It is about being able to converse, generously and receptively, without threatening alienation.

A cross-cultural marriage may encompass intellectual, religious, cultural, racial and sexual differences. Linked to the theme of cross-cultural marriages there are issues of *xenophobia*. The face of the foreigner 'bears the mark of a crossed threshold' (Kristeva, 1988/1991, p. 4). 'They' have entered 'our' territory. Politically the issue is how to value cultural difference without seeking either to assimilate or to eradicate it. The stranger confronts us with our own shrouded unfamiliarity and indeterminable alterity.

Sexual difference may also become a site for projection of all that is fearful and unacceptable in one, thus becoming 'an alien double, uncanny and demoniacal' (Kristeva, 1988/1991, p. 183). Fascination may vacillate with fear, as found in the theme of projections upon women as mysterious and alluring, such as Cleopatra or Iseult. 'Iseult is ever a stranger, the very essence of what is strange in woman and of all that is eternally fugitive, vanishing and almost hostile in a fellow-being' (de Rougemont, 1940/1983, p. 284).

Francis Jacques puts forward a model of dialogue involving reciprocity of 'I' and 'Thou', to overcome traditional constructions of male–female relations in which the female is posited as the 'other' (Jacques, as cited in

---

5 As Ruszczynski puts it, the 'working-through' of the 'depressive position is never fully achieved, and at times of stress, disruption, trauma, or loss there can be a regression to the earlier paranoid-schizoid position, with its more primitive defences of splitting, projection, and blame. The ideal state of maturity, therefore, is never actually reached, but the quest for integration and maturation continues throughout life' (Ruszczynski, 1993, p. 203).

Collin, 1994, p. 288). Only when there is a reciprocal *I–Thou* relation can one avoid condemning the female member of such dialogue to 'subordination, hierarchization, or annexation' (p. 288). One needs to relate to her as not 'another me' whom one can know via identification or appropriation, nor an 'other than me' who is so other that in her solitude, pride, transcendence no relation is possible. Instead it is a case of entering dialogue, relation, and being a co-subject, rather than taking a monological position.

Exogamy can also be applied to mating with ideas that upset our intellectually endogamous status quo. If we cannot tolerate difference on an ideological level then the different ideas may be seen as errors to be eradicated. Often different ideas are identified with their human carrier, leading to ideological crusades: no less in psychoanalytic circles than in the wider political domain. Yet if we are receptive to entertaining, like a guest, new ideas or different articulations of old ideas, then we might be enriched and our perceptions expanded by the robust exchange. Dialogue is not syncretism, which may amount to another form of assimilation and denial of difference. The history of psychoanalysis has been formed through vigorous and often heated discussions between idiosyncratic individuals, each making a contribution from their particular experience, each theory giving a different perspective on a whole. Given that each contribution to the debate is often corrective of a former limited perspective, each theory on its own can become one-sided, and its adherents then create endogamous self-referential groupings intolerant of alterity, even fearful of the slightest deviation from the carefully constructed mould.

Oedipus revisited: a myth of endogamy

Oedipus is the myth that Freud viewed as the creation story at the heart of all human relations. There is 'a voice within us, ready to acknowledge the compelling force of fate in *Oedipus* . . . the oracle laid upon us before our birth [is] the very curse which rested upon him' (Freud, 1900/1945, p. 255). Freud's view was that all later attachments hark back to love of the parent of the opposite sex. The erotic triangle is first enacted in childhood and then repeated in adult life, thus becoming a major determinant of adult love relations.

The oedipal situation relates to the origins of a child's incorporation of an internal model of the couple relationship, essential for the success of later love relations. It also shows how notions of subjectivity, objectivity and intersubjectivity develop through early relationships. The child initially experiences himself as a subjective member of a dyadic relationship. The baby's witnessing of the parental relationship enables a third person perspective to develop:

> A third position then comes into existence from which object relation-
> ships can be observed. Given this, we can also envisage being observed.
> This provides us with a capacity for seeing ourselves in interaction with
> others and for entertaining another point of view whilst retaining our
> own, for reflecting on ourselves whilst being ourselves.
>
> (Britton, 1989, p. 87)

This enables one to take up different perspectives, if not metaperspectives, and entertain different points of view. There is the experience of feeling contained within a monadic[6] space, a dyadic and a triadic space, as well as observing other dyadic intimate relationships. The ability to imaginatively shift subjective positions, imagine how it feels to be inside a relationship from the outside as well as imagine how it feels to be on the outside when one is inside, is related to being able to imagine what it might feel like to be another, and hence to empathy as feeling-into another's internal experience.

The position of observer and of a psychic thirdness becomes internalized as a capacity to observe oneself, envisage how others see us. We can imagine ourselves as if from a first, second or third person perspective. This is necessary for a child's development of a theory of mind. Reflexive thinking develops and the ability to reflect on oneself as an object of consciousness.

A child who feels profoundly loved one-to-one retains a sense of being loved even when the focus of the parents is on each other. If parents display a loving face-to-face standpoint with each other, the child, now thrust into the position of the observer, may feel decentred, but not completely aban-doned or annihilated. The child can observe how different perspectives on life and differences between the partners can enrich a relationship. Either parent may then turn to pay the child attention, the other parent now being on the outer. The shifts between ones, twos and threes recur in different configurations.

Partners who have traversed such developmental territory successfully can, in mature relationships, tolerate their partner's attention being focused on their child, or diverted to another activity, or to friends and outside interests. In other words partners can cope with all the ways a twosome enters triangular intersubjective space. Furthermore, the decentred perspec-tive of thirdness developmentally leads to a decentred yet not destabilized intersubjective self, which is crucial for interpersonal capacity. Thus success-ful negotiation of the oedipal situation enables a sense of thirdness, a capacity for self-reflection and a capacity to be alone as well as able to connect deeply with others.

---

6 That one is encased shows up the fallacy of autonomy: the monad depends on the casing, which itself depends upon mother's body, which itself depends upon an environment. There is no such thing as a monad, in fact, just as there is no such thing as a couple as an entity in itself.

In the following clinical fragment Deborah did not ever feel herself encased in a loving one-to-one relationship with either parent. This meant that she felt forever on the outside looking in, shut out but observing the happiness of other couple relations.

> Deborah's parents were so turned in on each other that she felt forever on the outside looking in, never feeling that she had her own relationship in her own right with her mother or father. As an adult it didn't seem to be any different: all her friends were in relationships and she was 'last on their priority list'. She longed to have her own relationship with a suitable partner *SuperHero* but somehow 'I seem to go for men who always turn out to be "spoken for", married, or otherwise unavailable'. She brought a recurring dream of being a waif, looking through the window of houses full of warmth and light, witnessing scenes of family affection and love.

On fathers

Thirdness is often seen as represented by father. In same-sex relationships and parenting styles incorporating more fluid, less gender-typecast roles, similar negotiations still occur between oneness, being a twosome, a threesome or a witness to a twosome. The critical factor is how parents aid the child's ability to manage different shifts in positions and perspectives. A child becomes an outside witness of another dyadic intersubjective relationship. This might be a 'good-enough parental couple of whatever sex'.[7]

There is a need for a symbolic representative of a third presence, imago, law, objectivity and separation, yet it need not be played by father. Tensions between independence and dependence, separation and togetherness, adventure and comfort, continue to influence adult love relations, but should not be equated with mother or father or a given partner *per se*. Father's role as 'liberator' from the 'engulfing' mother means that qualities of independence and dependence can easily be split and polarized between gender-based parental imagos. Father represents separation, the outside world, leaving home and new heroic ventures. Mother is equated with attachment, nurture, the hearth and home. Winnicott describes the father as a remote figure whose function is to disclose the world beyond the home. Children 'get a new world opened up to them when father gradually

---

7 Here I am appropriating Samuels's (2001) expansion of Winnicott's (1949/1992b) term the 'good-enough mother' to situations where solo mothers take up the role of being a good-enough father as well as mother, and fathers who take up the role of being mother.

discloses the nature of the work to which he goes in the morning and from which he returns at night' (Winnicott, 1944, p. 32).[8] Mahler (1971) sees the role of the father as breaking up the symbiosis between mother and child and orienting the child towards the world.[9]

Schwartz sees Oedipus as an Ur-myth for the Victorian family, its patri-archal configuration itself responsible for exacerbating oedipal tensions:

> This family romance is dominated by an absent authoritarian father, who arriving home, asserts the priority of his own needs over his children's by making overt or covert sexual demands on his wife. The wife, resentful of abandonment by her husband and of his authoritarian attitudes, lavishes her attention on her son. And the son, perceiving rivalry for the mother's affections expressed in sexual terms, responds in kind.
>
> (Schwartz, 1999, p. 79)

There is a delicate balance between oedipal desires and oedipal defeat. Necessary oedipal defeat occurs when the father gives his nubile daughter the message, 'I love you and you are very desirable', but at the same time conveys the message that she cannot marry him or have a sexual relationship with him.[10] She is both valued and admired by father, so gains a sense of self-confidence, yet renounced and rejected as a partner. The sense of loss of being at some level rejected by father is also an exogamous gift of liberation. An adolescent boy also needs to be known and valued by father:

> Anthony longed to be accepted by his father in his fullness and complexity as an adolescent boy. Yet his father was remote and unavailable. Anthony felt annihilated, a ghastly sense of existential void within because his father did not understand and bestow value upon him as he was.

The longing for oedipal conquest, the need to prove one's erotic capacities to 'get mother' or 'father' by repetitive sexual conquests may be displaced onto an adult love object. The complex leads one to focus only on the moment of

---

8 This was an indictment on Winnicott's cultural and personal experience of family life.

9 Samuels calls this 'the insertion metaphor' (Samuels, 1993).

10 Samuels suggests that there is an 'optimal erotic relation between father and daughter' (Samuels, 1989, p. 82) in which the father affirms his love and veneration for the daughter's beauty while not enacting or otherwise exploiting sexual currents between them. This he calls 'erotic playback'. Failure to achieve this optimal erotic relation leads to certain narcissistic relational pathologies.

conquest. Once vanquished, the object of conquest is expendable, their own subjectivity feared and hated, just as a child fears being overwhelmed by mother's own personality, needs and vulnerability.

Oedipal issues in narcissism: Freud's egocentric circle of love

Oedipal and narcissistic issues are both features of early development and thus there is a complex relationship between the two.

Freud's version of the ladder-of-love metaphor is a developmental ascent from narcissistic self-absorption, to linking with the instincts, to oedipal object love, then via the liberating role of the father, to exogamous object love. At the beginning of mental life, Freud argues, the ego is narcissistically self-absorbed, cathected with instincts and capable of satisfying them autoerotically. The 'ego loves itself only and is indifferent to the external world' (Freud, 1915/1984a, p. 133). Under the sway of the pleasure principle, objects that bring pleasure are introjected and those that do not are expelled. The 'world is divided into a part which is pleasurable' and hence lovable, which it incorporates into itself, and a split-off part of the self, 'which it projects into the external world and feels as hostile' (p. 134). Love is nothing but an attraction towards that which gives pleasure, hate a reaction to that which is not pleasurable, perceived threat and hostility a projection of one's own displeasure.

Freud's developmental model tends to be more of a circle than a ladder since for Freud, 'the return of the libido from the object to the ego and its transformation into narcissism represents, as it were, the restoration of a happy love, and conversely an actual happy love corresponds to the primal condition in which object-libido and ego-libido cannot be distinguished' (as cited in Rickman, 1957, p. 121). According to Freud, love for another is merely a circuit back to the self: my desire to be loved is accomplished by loving another who then will love me and tend to my needs.

Liberating thirdness

Freud saw the father as the liberator and protector who pulls the child out of the 'limitless narcissism' of infancy, also breaking up the oedipal symbiotic union with mother.

Freud's view of father as agent of exogamous transitions has been critiqued (Benjamin, 1988) due to its idealizing of paternal authority, which is equated with 'civilization' and individuation. Further, new models of child rearing and the prevalence of single-parent families show that a mother can take up different positions and represent different functions, as can a father.

The re-entry of another loving parental figure of either sex into the space occupied by a parent–child dyad shows the movement between fusion and separation, between subjective and objective states, between being a member of a relationship and being an observer. This gives rise to a linked separateness, the ability to tolerate such separateness and separations and the aspects of each partner's life that are independent, such as their work, other creative interests and friendships.

The resolution of the oedipal situation and the depressive position are linked: 'we resolve the oedipal complex by working through the depressive position and the depressive position by working through the Oedipus complex' (Britton, 1992, p. 35). Attributes of the depressive position include the ability to reconcile one's hating and loving feelings for another, the ability to feel included and excluded, part of a couple and respectful of separateness and difference. The capacity for alterity is linked to the capacity to tolerate being on the outside of another, to entertain and move between states of inner and outer, inclusion and exclusion, union and separation. Green (1975, p. 13) elaborates Winnicott's famous statement that there is no such thing as a baby without a mother, into the idea that there is no such thing as a mother–baby dyad without a father. The father (aside from gender ascriptions, as symbolizing a third presence) is present at every meeting of mother and baby.

Concluding comment

Destructive or neglectful oedipal experience creates major obstacles to exogamy, including the capacity to enjoy one's own and one's partner's plural selves. The father or mother may be incestuous, invasive or abusive, or so defeated and depressed they seem to have been killed by the child. We internalize our parent's conflicts, lacks and destructiveness, their couplings and divisions, as a model of the internal couple, an internal family drama which needs to be deconstructed in order to open us out to wider ranges of possible interpersonal behaviours.

Resolving the oedipal conflict entails the realization that the subject cannot become either mother's or father's lover. This sets the person free to find a mate outside the family. Just as the child might observe their parents retreating to their private realm, even though this might be painful, so too the child may go off without his or her parents. The parents' fulfilling love relations free the child from being overwhelmed by either parent's unfulfilled adult desires being displaced onto the child. Oedipal conflicts represent transitional moments in the relations with others: to separate and destroy earlier modes of relating and to attain new ones. Exclusion can thus be positive as well as painful: adolescents exclude themselves by forming a separate identity, and creating a life and new relationships outside the home, thus fulfilling the exogamous *conatus*.

Oedipal relations are developmentally vital in the understanding of union and separateness, subjectivity and objectivity, being a partner and being an observer of a partnership, of the ability to shift perspective, seeing from the inside looking out and from the outside looking in.

her summary

NO model/obstacle here

The path of love: an obstacle course

Chapter 5

Love's therapeutics

'So the two lived happily ever after.' The fairy-tale ending suggests that the coming together of a couple in love grandly brings the drama of love to a close – all is happily settled once and for all. Yet 'happily ever after' is only another beginning. And as any couple therapist knows, it is rarely 'happily ever after'. The following chapters in the tales of love include intense dramas, boring habits, moments of deep contentment, ecstatic love-making followed by doing the washing-up – the full gamut of domestic emotional life.

Erroneous views of each other form the greatest impediment to love, to contentment, to living 'happily ever after'. The heroic task of the real fairy-tale is to overcome the phantasies, internal demons, monsters and witches of our perverse imagination. Becoming who we are may be a relational activity. Yet such transformations in love are obstructed by the ways we unwittingly conscript each other to play allotted roles in falsely stereotypic and unconscious psychological scenarios. These scenes create an entangled web of projections obscuring the real situation and preventing authentic intimacy from flourishing. Such scenes involve an interpenetration of unconscious defensive, projective and traumatic material, the malignant dowries that each person brings to the new relationship.

True love may be possible, but it is as difficult as it is rare. Its path does not always run smoothly, but goes off course with alarming regularity. Its achievement is never once and for all but requires continual renewal, and is dependent upon how well any two lovers can understand, work through and disentangle the webs of mutual projections and false imputations imposed upon each other. The pathologies of love will be the focus of Part II.

The word 'pathos' etymologically means sorrow and suffering. Love's pathologies give rise to the sense of dis-ease[1] and discontentment in our relationships. We do not feel at ease with each other or ourselves. In love we

---

1 The nuances of meanings of pathos as dis-ease are comparable with the Sanskrit word *dukkha*. The closest expression in English is dis-satisfaction, a sense of physical and mental unease. Another translation of *duḥkha* 'extends its meaning from the actual suffering

suffer daily irritations, not getting what we want, getting what we don't want. We miss the bull's eye of true love through misinterpretations, mistimings and mismatches. We suffer the discomforts of being on the receiving end of unwelcome feelings towards us, and the pain of having our feelings and desires not met in the way we want. Discontent might itself be a disease.

As the Buddha, the Stoics, Augustine, Spinoza, Schopenhauer, Freud, Klein and many others have understood, from the perspective of egocentricity we feel craving for that which brings us pleasure, and antipathy for that which brings pain. It is this egoic core that is the real enemy of true love. Destructiveness in relationships can border on the psychopathic, fuelled by unconscious projections, envy, hostility, blaming, shaming, denigrating, demonizing or retaliation.

Object relations, attachment, intersubjective and relational theorists hold in common the notion that we come into the world as relational beings, and that being loved and minded is necessary for our psychological development. Such perspectives, although diverse, view relational configurations, real and fantasized, internalized and actualized, as integral to personality development, the genesis of psychopathology, and the therapeutic potential of psychotherapy for individuals, couples, families and groups. I shall be drawing on all these perspectives in developing a subject-relational perspective for couple work.

How do we transform endogamous modalities and relationally destructive patterns into new exogamous possibilities? Therapy, from the Greek *therapeia*, is based on the root *dher*, to 'carry, support, hold'. This is the same root as *Dharma* in Sanskrit. The therapist cares and carries the weight of another's soul as does a servant (Hillman, 1989, p. 73). The therapeutic space creates a supportive atmosphere, a holding environment, and provides the conditions for reflection of what is going on under the surface. Conditions developed initially in the therapeutic setting gradually become incorporated into the couple's relationship. There is the creation of a sense of the relationship as a *temenos*, a space of sanctuary and safety, where each partner feels contained yet not stifled. Within this therapeutic space we seek to enhance the capacity for psychological reflection and insight into the tangles of interlocking complexes and object relations in the couple relationship. We amplify developmental and teleological components hidden behind defences, and seek to identify and remove the array of misconstructions and false views we have of each other.

The overlapping areas of couple relationships and couple therapy, discussed in the following chapters, might be expressed diagrammatically as follows:

present in physical pain or mental grief *to any unwelcome state of insecurity, no matter how vague*' (Ñānamoli, as cited in Chatalian, 1974, p. 362). This is the sense of pathos I wish to convey.

Couples relationships	Couple therapy
Marriage as *temenos*, container, facilitating environment and secure base	Therapy/therapist as container for container/contained dynamics between the couple, as a safe space, a transitional environment
Marriage as a container for container/contained dynamics between the couple	Therapy/therapist as container for container/contained dynamics between the couple
Marriage as a 'third', with its own teleology	Therapy and therapist as representing thirdness
Tensions between the *conatus* of the marriage and the individuation process of each partner	Tensions between individual transferences and the transference/countertransference of the marriage in therapy
Marriage as a space in which past hurts are played out, and hopefully resolved	Marital therapy as an arena where patterns of relating are identified, and may be replayed, but in a different and mutative dynamic
Object-choice (defensive or developmental) and relational configurations based on interlocking attachment styles, marital fit	Relationship between object-choice and couple as object-maker: how they make the therapist/therapy a particular object

A relationship as a container

There are several senses in which we speak of containment in analysis, all of which can be applied to couple therapy and couple relations. There is the sense of sanctuary or *temenos*, of being held inside something good, a holding environment, or a transitional zone of experience. Marriage can function as 'a refuge, from within which each individual can venture to explore and develop their interests and capacities and into which the participants can retreat when failure, frustration or humiliation is encountered. It is a place where recovery is possible' (Fullerton, 1996, p. 2). This is similar to Bowlby's (1988) concept of the 'secure base'[2] that stems from

2 Mary Ainsworth coined the term.

early attachment experience. Such containment allows a transitional space in Winnicott's sense, where new parts of each person can be developed as well as new images of coupling explored. Esther Bick (1968) talks of a sense of envelopment like a skin around oneself that protects and enfolds.

The sense of security, continuity and trust afforded by a mutually made commitment to journey together in a partnership can allow such a relationship to function as a space in which partners may further their psychological development, re-encounter and rework areas of developmental arrest and come to know and integrate the different parts of themselves more fully.

The relationship itself may be conceptualized as a container for the two partners, a marital space. This has both spatial and temporal dimensions: the sense of being contained within the relationship and the aspect of relationship-as-process. It can also be personified as being a third party, with a life of its own:

> The relationship itself becomes the container: the creative outcome of the couple's union, to which both partners can relate. It is an image the couple are continually in the process of creating, sustaining and maintaining, while at the same time feeling that they exist within it – are contained by it . . . The relationship is like a third party – the symbolic child.
>
> (Colman, 1993, p. 89)

[handwritten marginal note: The relationship as symbolic child]

In committed and fulfilling adult relationships it is not so much about each partner providing a sense of security and containment for the other, but the creation of a psychological atmosphere of safety and refuge, a container, around both partners. Empathy and mind-mindedness, or the ability to see others as subjects in their own right with thoughts and feelings of their own, are also vital components of creating a secure base in close relationships. When couples have a deep sense of connection they hold the relationship and the well-being of its members in mind continually. One might call this 'relationship-mindedness'.

Couples often present because their marriage has failed to function as a safe space. Therapy may be able to provide a temporary alternative container, the sense of a bounded and safe environment with another caring mind in which thinking and reflection are shown to be possibilities again.

This latter situation is very common when the issue is that of containment of unprocessed primitive anxieties which have never been worked through. Bion called such primitive bits, 'beta elements' (Bion, 1962/1983). These are untransformed emotional experiences and sensory impressions of a very raw and inchoate form, which have not been thought through, but are split-off, disavowed and evacuated in fantasy into the other through processes of projective identification.

Container-contained as processor of beta elements

The mindless repetition and compulsive nature of many marital rows are symptomatic of the activation of interlocking systems of mutual projections of beta elements or undigested traumatic material. Each partner has been triggered into their respective unconscious complexes and is swamped by unconscious anxieties, memories of fear, hurt and misunderstanding. Each urgently attempts to lodge unprocessed beta material into the other in order to rid themselves of its incoherent, chaotic and anxiety-ridden nature.

The therapeutic space as a 'borrowed container' (Colman, 1993), as well as the therapist's capacity and willingness to stand such unprocessed material – to ponder it, experience its re-enactments, digest and reflect on it – enables the couple to feel some reassurance that it is not so unspeakably loathsome and dreadful, it can be thought about. This enables the couple to introject a capacity to contain difficult material and gradually metabolize and modify it into alpha elements. The relational space can function as a therapeutic container for thinking.

Here I am drawing on Bion's (1963) model of container-contained as a model of thinking. One application of this model relates to the mother's containing function whereby she, in a state of reverie, takes in the baby's primitive anxieties, ponders, metabolizes and transforms them via her state of mind. Her ability to contain and ponder is something which she models, and which the child later introjects in the development of self-containment.

A mother, in Bion's terms, doesn't just take in, process and digest primitive material, beta elements, and return them, pre-processed and hence digestible. What she communicates is her capacity to contain, reflect upon and mentally digest such chaotic elements, thus modelling for the child what it might be like to do such reflective work for him or herself. The baby witnesses mother being able to stand in the presence of primitive states of dread, terror or fury. If she can bear to think about it, try to make sense of it and find a constructive solution or well-thought response, then perhaps it is not so terribly and dreadfully unbearable. Thus, through her alpha function, the beta elements can be transformed into something thinkable, into food for thought. Alpha function, which Bion deliberately does not define, refers to the ability to contain and then metabolize and thus transform the almost uncontainable: primitive anxieties, dreads, fears of falling to bits, fears of death and destruction. Through alpha function the mother processes material that has been lodged into her via projective identifications and converts them into nascent sensory data, or alpha elements, which are more able to be consciously thought about.

This transformation creates a link between preconceptions and new information from the world of others. This gives rise to further elaborations in the process of thinking, leading to the formulation of intuition, insight and finally coherent theory-making. All this arises gradually and thoughtfully out of a situation which began as utter confusion. It is this capacity, however psychologically hard-won, which enables a couple to dismantle their co-constructed prisons of projections.

Bion describes an alchemical process of transformation of emotional material from highly primitive destructive elements to their constructive counterparts. Absence becomes transformed into presence, waste into nutriment, fears of death into *joie de vivre*, anxiety into confidence, greed into love, meanness into generosity. It is affected through a capacity for receptivity and containment of such material, reverie, and profound loving kindness.

Container or receptacle?

The capacity for containment is not the same as being used as a receptacle for another's split-off and disowned feelings. If a partner projects psychological material into their partner and the recipient mulls this over, then articulates his or her musings about what is going on, then the one projected into is acting as a container.

However, often the projector simply wants to evacuate his or her feelings into a recipient, in an aggressive, invasive manner. The recipient is made to function as a receptacle rather than as a container. The one projecting does not wish for any processing to take place and certainly does not want to have any interpretations made which might mean owning some of the material, which would involve a painful connection to split-off feelings.

It is common for couples to identify one partner as the carrier of pathology – 'my wife is suffering post-natal depression, I'm just coming to support her' – displacing if not projecting into her all his own insecurities concerning being a father and the primitive material it has evoked from his infancy. 'My husband is suffering depression. He wouldn't come to therapy unless I brought him.' Yet a psychological glimmer of hope lies in the fact that such partners did not just shunt the designated sick member off to a psychiatrist or the local psychiatric ward. This glimmer can be amplified by the couple therapist by gently emphasizing that couple therapy is a chance for both partners to hear and be heard, to reflect on how the mutually created chemistry of their interactions affects them both. Later, when more trust has developed, the therapist might invite the partner of a woman suffering post-natal depression to reflect on his own feelings surrounding having a child.

Couples may also experience difficulty when one partner feels him or herself called upon by the other to be a container for the other's projections. As Colman points out, each will find it difficult to contain the other precisely in those areas where they themselves need most containment (Colman, 1993, p. 88).

Container-contained

In *Marriage as a psychological relationship*, Jung (1931/1991) applies a metaphor of container-contained[3] to the individuals within a marriage. He sees a fundamental dichotomy between the partners where one will feel him or herself to be the contained, the other the container. The contained, 'feels themselves to be living within the confines of the marriage' but depends upon being contained within a personality who is so complex they cannot be fully seen and thus will be felt to be undependable. The container will feel, for their part, uncontained, and will 'spy out the window' (Jung, 1931/1991, p. 195):

> The simpler nature will seem like a room that is too small, with too little space. The complicated nature will give the simpler one too many rooms, too much space so that he/she will never know where they belong. Thus the more complex will contain the simpler . . . without being itself contained. Yet the more complicated has a greater need of being contained, and will feel themselves [to be] outside the marriage. The more the contained clings, the more the container feels shut out of the relationship.
>
> (p. 196)

If there is a shift in the sense of 'who is the container' to the actual relationship, such that the relationship is felt to contain both partners, then both can feel contained within the wider orbit of the relationship. In other words, the 'container' becomes the 'total container/contained apparatus' (Bion, 1962/1983). This alleviates the pressure on one partner to act as a container who has to carry the dependency needs of the other who is thereby contained. Both can feel contained in the relationship, which enables greater fluidity of roles between the two partners.

The spatial metaphor of the relationship as container is similar to Britton's concept of 'triangular space', which I discussed in Chapter 4. Triangular space enables reflective capacity to develop, to entertain different points of view. There is the possibility of being 'a participant in a relationship and observed by a third person as well as being an observer of a relationship between two people' (Britton, 1989, pp. 87–89). As Fisher puts it, 'this provides us with a capacity for seeing ourselves in interaction with others and for entertaining another point of view while retaining our own, a capacity for reflecting on ourselves while being ourselves' (Fisher, 1999, p. 10). Such reflective and reflexive capacities enable couples in

---

3 Jung's (1931/1991) concept and Bion's (1963) concept of container-contained appear to have been independently arrived at and are used in distinct ways.

therapy to begin the process of considering and re-considering their own respective pathologies, complexes and projective processes, vital in the search for discovery of what is going on at an unconscious level in their relationship. Without such a capacity, couples get caught in escalations of mutual projections, there seeming to be 'no exit' from the vicious circles of its enmeshment.

Intersubjective thirds and marital transferences

When psychoanalysts of an object-relational, intersubjective or relational orientation started rethinking the concept of the isolated, intrapsychic self, they turned their attention to the patient and analyst as an encounter of two subjectivities who mutually influence and are influenced. From this perspective they began constructing concepts of additional forms of subjectivity which arise in the analytic space. The analytic space itself came to be seen as a third area. Further, the ways in which each subject *qua* subject was created in that analytic setting came to be re-envisioned as like a third presence[4] that is co-created in that space.

Ogden (1994) writes of an intersubjective analytic third subject of analysis that arises out of a complex, multi-layered dialectic involving an interplay between conscious and unconscious, fantasy and reality, within the analytic setting. The 'analyst' and 'analysand' as such only truly come into being in the process of the creation of the 'analytic subject' (Ogden, 1994, p. 5).

Ogden's concepts are highly relevant to couple relationships and couple therapy. A similar intersubjective third operates within a couple relationship. This 'third' is revealed by the communications of the individuals, but controlled by neither. I call this 'the intersubjective marital third'. This third subject is generated in the inter-relational space as an unconscious co-creation of the couple, taking on a life of its own, yet still sustaining and sustained by the analyst and analysand. The relationship itself operates as if it has its own subjectivity and teleology.

When we speak of 'intersubjective thirds' we are speaking in the same sense that we do when conceptualizing those parts of a personality which seems to have a psychic presence and agency, such as internal objects. These 'third forms' are, in the final analysis, not things-in-themselves but conglomerations of (distorted) images of objects intermixed with projective identifications, introjections, and not 'real' 'subjects' in their own right. As

---

4 Jung (1946/1966b) was the first to conceptualize this, in *Psychology of the transference*. Green (1975) theorized this third subject created in the analytic space as being the 'analytic object' which arises in 'the meeting of these two communications in the potential space that lies between analyst and analysand' and that this object consists of two doubles deriving from the part in each that lives and the part that communicates (Green, 1975, p. 12).

Ogden (1989) points out, internal objects do not have apperception. But, like the denizens of our internal worlds, we experience them as if they have their own subjectivity and agency, and they have their nefarious effects by that alone.

In couple therapy, the therapist turns his or her attention to the particular shapes and forms which such mutual transprojections create, like shadows on the wall. A vital part of work in dispelling them through the torch-beam of analytic insight involves examination of their particular configuration, content and aetiology.

A touchstone of object relations couple therapy is that the 'patient' is the relationship itself, not just the two partners who make up that relationship. In couple therapy there are a number of foci: the two partners, the therapist, the therapeutic intersubjective space, the complex networks and dynamics of relations between them, and the relationship itself which creates a fluid, interpenetrating and interactive field.

There is a second order interplay between the marital third, as representing the 'thirdness' of the relationship between the partners, and the analytic third which represents the thirdness between the patient and the analyst. Given that in marital work the 'patient' is the relationship, yet the relationship itself consists of two individuals, we have two forms of inter-subjective third. The therapist, in her reverie, attends to the interplay between and around these various forms of intersubjective third.

Transferences to the therapist, although including individual transferences, represent this thirdness: there is a marital transference. The way that each partner constructs the therapist can give telling information about how the partner feels about their relationship. There is an intricate inter-weaving between these various transferences and countertransferences.

Two family lawyers sit before me. Mark feels very ambivalent about what he experiences as the strictures of marriage. He has numerous affairs and comes home at an unpredictable hour, with the excuse that he was working on a case. He finds it hard getting away from work to make the therapy sessions and expects his wife to hold the fort on her own. I suggest that given it is couple therapy it is difficult with only half a couple. He reads up about psychoanalytic technique and pre-emptively uses the jargon of analysis to trip me up. His wife Susie baits him into legalistic altercations as if marriage were an adversarial process. They both try to turn me into a judge, able to arbitrate and pass judgment as to who was in the right. Susie keeps praising my therapeutic brilliance, yet I detect contempt lurking under the surface. We discover that Susie's psychological reasons for choosing the legal profession were to be one step ahead of a very intrusive, overly perceptive mother. Likewise Mark's secret sex-life was an attempt to find a realm where no intrusive eye could observe. He wanted me to be clever enough to see past his subterfuges but also equally wanted me not to see. He resented coming to therapy as much as he resented coming home to domestic boredom. In the meantime, Susie was also having an affair with a work colleague. The marital space was an arena for combat and verbal sparring, not love-making. The therapeutic space felt like a courtroom, where I was arbiter, mediator, judge and jury, by turns. Yet being able to speak to this was to reflect on the ways in which their marriage was also needing to be liberated from the prison of the courtroom into a less combative form of relating.

The therapeutic task is to listen in a state of reverie with a 'third ear' to the prompting of the third member of this trinity, attuned to the delicate subtlety of moment-to-moment interactions with their penumbra of associations, hidden sub-texts, conscious and unconscious communications. In addition to listening for this 'still quiet voice', the therapist's capacity to perceive and receive the tangled mass of material, tolerating not knowing, while seeking with every fibre of his or her being to understand, is itself part of the containing function couples are seeking. This affords the couple the possibility of realizing that their terrible anxieties, lack of coherence and confusion might perhaps after all be something that has a possibility of clarity. To jump to a hasty conclusion or make a premature and simplistic interpretation curtails this process.

The sense of the therapeutic process and setting, the therapeutic frame, as borrowed container creates a space for reflection.

Bion's grid

The process of engagement with a couple's interlocking projective complexes could be seen through the lattice of Bion's (1963/1977) grid.[5] Alpha function refers here to the therapist's capacity to sit with an incoherent mass of chaotically loaded, primitive emotional material (beta elements)[6] emanating from both partners and creating a toxic mutually projective confusion. This is related to negative capability, the capacity to observe a mass of confusing emotional material without jumping to a hasty conclusion, to tolerate not knowing while seeking to know. This containment is modelled to the couple, who imbibe its atmosphere such that they also calm down enough for an inkling of reflective capacity to develop. Frustration and the capacity to sit with it, rather than act out primitive emotional

5 I am not going into an exposition of the grid, but rather adapting it to the couple situation as a therapeutic tool.
6 Row A of the vertical axis.

states, generate a capacity for thoughtful consideration. This transmutes the material under consideration into alpha elements.[7] Then gradually dream thoughts, dreams, myths,[8] fantasies and narratives emerge out of a cultural unconscious.[9] These gradually lead to preconceptions[10] and first inklings of what is going on.[11] Further seminal discussions between the analytic trio (mating of ideas) lead to conception, concept and thence theory, in fact to organized thinking.[12] In the horizontal axes the ability to gestate such a process, to deepen one's understanding, without jumping to premature action, leads to the ability to construct preliminary hypotheses, notation,[13] attention,[14] inquiry[15] and thence to mindful, considered action[16] and the final revelation (uncovering) of truth.[17] All put together, publication, as in a well-thought articulation of the emotional situation, may result. The process involves: observation, containment, reflection, incorporation, comparison, analysis, mating with other ideas, conception, gestation, and final expression of a well-thought and well-timed interpretation. When we suggest one should 'count to ten' before one responds to a fraught interpersonal situation, this is the kind of 'counting to ten' Bion would have in mind.[18] Bion did not suggest we should ponder all emotional situations with such an intellectually formulated process, nor did he suggest it might

7 Row B.
8 Here Bion includes not only cultural myths such as Oedipus or Narcissus, but personal myth-making, a personal representation, narrative story, of an event. An example would be Max's use of Coleridge's Ancient Mariner.
9 Row C.
10 Preconception is like a thought prior to mating with a particular set of circumstances which make it real. An example would be a Zen koan which contains truth but does not become a realization until the Zen practitioner, via his or her 'negative capability', suddenly glimpses the koan's enigmatic meaning. This mating of thought with experience renders it real and refers to the subjective experience when one has a realization. This is conception.
11 Row D.
12 Such as interpretation, the tool of analysis.
13 Notation refers to making a note of something, in the sense of 'noticing'. Or a gathering together of data, a description of the phenomenon, prior to really getting to the bottom of it.
14 This is a state of mind in which one is attentive to the phenomenon and can 'discriminate between similar presentations of differing significance' and there is receptivity to the 'selected fact' which 'illuminates the meaning of several previously observed facts' (Symington and Symington, 1996, p. 36).
15 Enquiry implies a seeking to deepen one's understanding via yet deeper probing and amplification of the material under focus, an ever more active investigation.
16 In an analytic setting this is where there is an interpretation which so challenges and confronts the patient that it leads to psychic change.
17 Bion notates in column 2 ψ which refers to interpretations made when the enquirer cannot bear the frustration of not knowing or understanding something: such hasty theories about each other which are born of the attempt to avoid uncertainty.
18 Horizontally, vertically and backwards while forwards!

be useful outside the consulting room. Yet such a reflective process seeks to uncover a distant, buried truth, a conjoint selected fact, in the heart of the most pernicious unconscious interlocking defence system in the couple.

The selected fact

Bion utilizes a term coined by the French mathematician Poincaré which refers to one of those moments where, out of the chaos of a mass of disparate elements, there is a dawning of insight which makes sense of it all. Such would be the feeling when a detective, out of all the trails of evidence, false leads, clues, suddenly 'gets it', or when a mathematician suddenly resolves a previously unresolved problem. In analysis it refers to a particular thought or insight which suddenly occurs to the analyst (or patient), an 'emotional experience of a sense of discovery of coherence' (Bion, 1983, p. 73). This crystallizes all the mass of material the patient was manifesting into an understanding such that one feels that what was previously a seeming mass of confusing, fragmented elements suddenly becomes coherent. As Poincaré describes it:

> If a new result is to have any value, it must unite elements long since known, but till then scattered and seemingly foreign to each other, and suddenly introduce order where the appearance of disorder reigned. Then it enables us to see at a glance each of these elements in the place it occupies in the whole. Not only is the new fact valuable on its own account, but it alone gives a value to the old facts it unites.
>
> (Poincaré, 1952, p. 30)

It takes a considerable degree of negative capability on the part of the therapist witnessing a marital row to be able to withstand being in a 'cloud of unknowing', confronted with a sea of confusion, full of vitriol and destructiveness, and not react prematurely out of anxious identification. Often it is the analyst's ability to sit with the material, seeking to know but not jumping to hasty conclusions, which enables a selected fact to occur in the mind of the analysands or couple themselves.

Alétheia and negative capability

Love's therapeutic depends on increasing our capacity to entertain, like a holy guest, presentiments of truth behind the projections and fabrications. It is to take up an 'as if' stance, receptive to a niggling doubt that we probably have failed to properly understand a situation, that our perception is clouded, and to factor this into our interactions and reflections. We can then ponder, be curious and receptive to new insights that may dawn as tentative hypotheses, entertained as such. It is the language of uncertainty coupled with enquiry, wanting to discover the truth as through a glass darkly. We increase our psychic capacity to contain and psychically metabolize what was uncontainable: primitive anxieties, dreads, fears of falling to bits, fears of death and destruction. We begin to intuit faint glimmerings of the real person under all our obscurations.

Chapter 6

Love's uncanny choices

> He was arrested by the sight of a merry maiden peeling an apple and chatting gaily at the family table . . . That very glimpse was a fatal one.
>
> (Jones, 1953–1957, p. 103)

In a scene redolent with Dante's first sighting of Beatrice, a patient, Ella, tells me: 'I was walking along, minding my business, and I bumped right into Joseph. My files scattered everywhere. He bent down to pick them up. Then he looked up at me, our eyes locked in a mutual gaze, and well, the rest is history.'

How is it that people can convey so much in a first glance? The mutual recognition, across the room, that this is the 'one', the eerie degree of fittingness of the choice which unfolds or unravels over time.

Is love ever at first sight? Such attractions, Freud believed, are always second sight, our eyes lighting on someone who is reminiscent of the real love at first sight, our primary caregivers. Yet the uncanny synchronicity involved in our first glimpse of one another often has the quality of second sight in the sense of intuitive premonition. Of what, is a vital question. A patient, Carole, said:

> I walked into this room where they were having a soirée. He was singing 'Jerusalem'. His voice enveloped me, a voice so strong, warm, and confident, it sent shivers up my spine. I knew then he was the one. I'd made a right mess of things before, but this time I knew this was right.

Is there a fatal compulsion or secret law predetermining those initial moments of attraction? Freud's philosophical ancestors and analytic progeny certainly thought so. 'For a man to love a woman she must resemble the women in his ancestry', wrote Karl Neisser in 1897 (Neisser, as cited in Ellenberger, 1970, p. 708). Klein also believed that 'all later love relations' are influenced by the part that both one's father and mother played in one's early 'emotional life' (Klein, 1937/1988, p. 59).

Love, for Freud, is always at its core self-referential. Love is at first autoerotic. Relations involving others are predicated either upon a narcissistic identification with them or dependence on them (Freud, 1914/ 1984c). In a narcissistic choice we fall for others on the basis of their perceived similarity to aspects of our self. In an anaclitic[1] choice we are attracted to those who resemble the one we depended upon.

Neither narcissistic nor anaclitic object-choices are exogamous. Both preclude altruistic appreciation of the love object as a subject in his or her own right. Both are based on unconscious complexes that not only unconsciously dictate who we are attracted to, but continue to superimpose templates of mutual projections upon the face of each other. To the extent that either narcissistic or anaclitic templates hold sway, we are hindered from making exogamous choices. Psychologically exogamous love transcends autoerotic, narcissistic and anaclitic bases.

so is love at 1st sight by definition not exogamous?

Marital fit and unconscious covenants

Another form of search for our other half involves restlessly searching for a partner whose internal world creates a symbiotic fit with ours. There are complementary shared images of coupling and relationship as well as unconsciously agreed 'pacts' or *règles du jeu*. We unconsciously audition, typecast and impute false templates on each other, according to internal images of parental figures or aspects of our selves, giving rise to a marital space which is overlaid with mutual projective identifications.

Grotstein uses the term 'the covenant' to refer to the 'fact that every relationship, whether between two or more individuals or between internal subjective objects, is always characterized by an implied and unconsciously mutually accepted agreement as to the rules of engagement' (Grotstein, 2000, p. 107). This 'agreement' has its conscious aspect and its unconscious agreement.

Shared unconscious phantasies

Partners are often inextricably drawn to each other on the basis of their shared unconscious fantasies, longings, fears, defences and internal images of relationship. An unconscious agreement to accept the projections of each other creates an initial sense of affinity, but this can also trap the couple into the darkness of a co-created and co-maintained intrapsychic phantasy realm.

---

1 Anaclitic means 'leaning upon' in Greek (*anaklitos*).

Shared unconscious phantasy is a term used by object relations couple therapists to describe the ways in which partners are often inextricably drawn to each other on the basis of their shared unconscious longings, fears, defences and internal conflicts. Loving and hostile feelings are often split, projected into those around us and then re-introjected, giving rise to a layering of projections, internalizations and fantasies.

The term derives from Klein's concept of 'unconscious phantasy'. Klein believed that primitive phantasies cohere around the baby's instincts, desires and fears about his or her object-relational universe. Defensive phantasies are designed to protect the baby from the dread of annihilation or overpowering excitement.

Gratification of desire leads to feelings of love. Frustration of a desire leads to antipathy. We love those who give us what we desire and hate those who impede our desires. We project both loving and hostile feelings onto those around us and then re-introject such feelings, giving rise to complex layers of projections, introjections and phantasies.

The baby attempts to preserve the good by keeping it mentally separate from what is experienced as threatening. Splitting of good and bad experience leads to other defences such as denial, omnipotent control, or projection. The content of our phantasies constellates our inner world; projected outwards they create the tangled web of projections surrounding our intimate relations.

Developmental and defensive object-choices

From the different comes the fairest harmony.

(Heraclitus, as cited in Aristotle, 2004, p. 202)

There is an uncanny alchemical process involved in who we are attracted to. Object relations couple therapists describe how unconscious factors dictating partner choice may be in the service of a developmental impetus towards personal growth or driven by defensive factors which lead to psychological stagnation. Developmental object-choices entail seeking a partner who will enable one to engage with an undeveloped side of one's personality. Defensive choices are driven by the attempt to avoid psychological pain, the marriage being used 'defensively to ward off conscious and unconscious anxieties of both partners and to prohibit development' (Mattinson and Sinclair, 1979, p. 52).

Most love choices involve a combination of developmental and defensive components. The developmental aspect relates to the hope that early disappointments and difficulties might be re-worked and thus resolved. The defensive component entails ceaseless circling in recreations of repetition compulsions. Yet a developmental kernel lies at the heart of every repetition compulsion, containing a selected fact awaiting *alétheia*, unconcealment.

An experience reported by many couples is how the very personality features that were so beguiling initially become the most annoying, bitterly contended traits later on:

> Martin, an auditor, described how he liked his life to be ordered into neat and tidy categories. Yet he fell in love with a 'vivacious, bohemian and eccentric jazz singer from New York'. Piroska was drawn to the image Martin conveyed of a quiet certitude and harmonious aesthetic order.
>
> Martin's apartment was pristine, minimalist, elegant, with sweeping views across the harbour. Once Piroska became neatly ensconced in the marital abode, however, Martin became possessively jealous of Piroska's professional and social life. What he had been at first captivated by in her exuberant spontaneity was now denigrated as chaotic, irresponsible and hysterical. Piroska came to find Martin intensely controlling and boring. Martin couldn't stand her mess cluttering up the apartment: 'she leaves a trail of destruction wherever she goes!' he complained to me.
>
> Martin brought her along to couple therapy because he had been discussing with his doctor the possibility that Piroska might be bipolar, but 'Piroska refuses to go get a proper diagnosis'. Piroska retorted that Martin was just a control freak and if he kept this line up she'd pack her bags. Martin caught my eye and said, 'See what I mean? My doctor said if you didn't make her see sense we might have to consider other options.'

This clinical fragment shows how the same personality characteristics that were so attractive at first come to be felt as abhorrent later on. Such traits represent the developmental aspects of our choice, areas of our personality that we need to work on, qualities we need to develop and incorporate within ourselves, yet we also unconsciously defend against their realization. It confronts us with a sense of our inadequacies, or of traumatic pain. The best defence is dislodging it and locating it in the other. The developmental potential of a love choice is turned into a defensive one.

Even in the most entrenched defence, a developmental potential hides waiting to be actualized. It depends on whether we go on seeing our partner as the sole owner of a given quality or whether we are able to acknowledge that this might be an area we need to work on in ourselves.

> Later in therapy Martin reluctantly agreed that given they were coming to couple therapy, he might say a little about his own upbringing. As a child he was timid and 'labile' but his father used to beat him if he looked as if he might cry. Piroska represented someone who embodied a colourful array of emotional expression. Yet he feared such expression to the extent that he was in

danger of casting her as mad. She became the repository for disavowed emotional material belonging to Martin. Piroska had suffered trauma in her intergenerational heritage as a Hungarian whose family left Budapest in 1959. She longed to find harmony and order in her life, yet she also wished to retain her creative verve and passionate personality.[2]

A hidden truth lies at the hub of even the most pernicious repetition compulsion, since the compulsion concerns an attempt to actualize that which has not yet been actualized, overcome that which defeated us, resolve a situation never resolved. The hope behind the repetition is that one might transcend the limitations created by the failures of early relationships. It tends to be written into the mechanics of the compulsion that this is doomed to fail. However, despite feeling helpless dismay when patients re-invent the wheel of their repetition compulsion in yet another iterative variation, it is usually symptomatic that a central primal truth[3] has not yet been properly understood in our work. It is crises as opportunity, if we can reveal and amplify the hidden truth behind the disguises of the compulsion.

A couple may share a defence, for example when both are fearful of the outside world and seek to create a bulwark against change and otherness. They will tend to emphasize similarity of values, attitudes and concordant experiences. Incompatibilities, differences and areas of conflict will be overlooked.

The collusive unconscious power of shared anxieties makes marriages based on a predominantly defensive mutual object-choice difficult to work with. The relational patterns of such couples show an absence of curiosity that might allow re-appraisal about each other and the emotional situation they find themselves in. Partners hold rigidly to false images of each other and their world, unconsciously agreeing to ward off the perceived threat they both share (Fullerton, 2001, pp. 10–11). In the following clinical cameo Jane and Mary shared a defence against alterity.

Jane and Mary came in and sat down on the couch, folding their hands in their laps and tucking their feet under the sofa in unison. They were dressed in pastel twin-sets, woollen skirts, thick woollen stockings and sensible brown shoes. I could almost imagine them sitting watching me as if I were their television set while they knitted in companionable silence. They looked up at me expectantly. When I didn't say anything Mary started to rise, as if to turn

---

2 A case like this is pregnant with deeper implications concerning projective processes and intergenerational matters.

3 Or selected fact in Bion's 1963 usage, where there is a dawning of an insight which pierces through to the heart of a matter, revealing a central truth which suddenly makes sense of what was a hopelessly confused situation.

me on. Then she settled back down. Jane opened her mouth to speak but Mary began. They finished each other's sentences for each other:

Mary: 'We are here,'
Jane: 'because Mary has been suffering'
Mary: 'anxiety attacks'
Jane: 'about burglars. Our family G.P.,'
Mary: 'suggested I see a therapist,'
Jane: 'I've just come along to support her.'

I couldn't quite tell who was coming to see me for whom, nor even who was supposed to be having the anxiety attacks. They continued in the same manner, from which eventually emerged the following story of their lives.

Jane and Mary worked in the same home-based business running a poodle-grooming salon. Their life was one of predicable routines: they rose at the same time every day, ate the same foods, watched the same programmes on TV, read the same newspaper, often one reading over the other's shoulder. They preferred television dramas to books since they could have the same experience at the same time. Their favourite type of programme was detective stories based on a predictable plot.

Jane and Mary met at boarding school as teenagers. They explained how it was, just as Socrates' beloved youth, Alcibiades, had described it: they knew immediately they had found their other half and they formed a twinship alliance against the world. Lately, however, Mary had started having recurring nightmares of a mysterious young man on a pushbike, appearing from nowhere (leftfield, I wondered) and creating mayhem in the poodle salon. When Mary described the dream-youth she blushed, glancing coyly at Jane. I wondered if this mysterious, youthful stranger might symbolize fresh air breezing into their cosy, predictable life, awakening buried erotic extraordinary longings which alternately excited and terrified them both.

Developmental aspects and defensive adherence to the status quo may be played out between the two partners:

Emmy and Jack were very close, sharing values, thoughts and activities with each other and preferring their own company to socializing with other friends or family. Emmy became interested in studying German, an activity Jack had no inclination for. She suggested it might be good for them both to enrol in a different adult-education course because then 'when we get home we might have something new to share with each other'. Jack feared this would make them grow apart. Emmy thought that sharing new ideas might enrich their relationship.

A couple who have experienced previous loss or rejection might make a conscious or unconscious agreement that they will not inflict a similar crisis on each other. However, the need to negotiate the marital space may become confused with threatened loss and drive the couple into defensive positions in relation to each other. Engagement with issues like losing and finding each other, even going out and coming into the home each night, become fraught (Fullerton, 1996).

Developmental ladders of love: a critique

The idea of developmental versus defensive partner choices is still implicitly predicated on a model of individual development, rather than an inter-relational one, in so far as the underlying premise is that such a choice aids the personal growth of the two individual partners concerned. We fall in love with someone who has qualities that have not been sufficiently developed in ourselves. This could form a developmental version of the ladder-of-love trope, except that we are each climbing up the same ladder on opposite sides (not necessarily at the same speed!).

I meet Jo who has qualities I need to develop. I represent qualities he needs to develop. We find ourselves in conflict because this makes us both confront our respective developmental deficits that we would rather not face. We dutifully trot off to couple therapy and work on these respective areas in ourselves. The real lover becomes superfluous and expendable, just as in Plato's theory.

If we are relational and interdependent beings, then the felt tension between the individuation needs of the individual and the requirements of the relationship is a false dichotomy.

Working with endogamous marital choices

When we realize that our unconscious motivation for our partner choice was oedipal, narcissistic, or otherwise endogamously erroneous, this doesn't necessarily mean that we should therefore leave our partner. It is the endogamous template that has to be relinquished, not the actual person, who never was actually our father, mother or aspect of ourselves, nor even a stand-in. In clinical practice partners are often quite startled when they begin to find an entirely different person behind their unconscious projections of parental figures. The father or mother figure suddenly seems much 'younger, fresher – different somehow', as one patient put it.

Maria's designated role was as a 'stay-at-home mother and wife'. She used to get furiously resentful when Nick stayed out 'drinking with the boys' after work. He talked about how he couldn't imagine sex with her, she was so frumpy, such a 'house-frau'. He had elaborate sexual fantasies concerning a dark mysterious woman. Nick gradually was able to see how he was projecting a maternal image onto Maria, which she identified with. He was also guilty of splitting his image of 'woman' into two: mother and anima archetype. His gradual withdrawal of maternal projections onto Maria paralleled her own growing assertions of her personality. She not only emerged from her identity as perfect housewife to find a world of other creative aspects of herself, but she looked completely different: radiant, youthful, impish, fit and idiosyncratically herself.

Chapter 7

Veils of projection

If relational work in couple therapy can be envisioned as a process of *alétheia*, aiming to uncover the real situation and person behind the mass misconstructions, there is a bewildering array of ways that we misapprehend each other. Projections, identifications, mutual projective identifications, extractive introjections, miscommunications, misinterpretations, fixed ideas, illusions, delusions, idealizations, denigrations, constellations of internal object relations and impositions of relational templates all create an inter-personal mire of Maya, of illusion.

Every emotional engagement with another human being creates a particular emotional environment, a chemistry of interaction, which has the potential to create who we feel ourselves to be in that particular given situation. It is enormously difficult to wriggle out from behind another's image of us and not at some level identify with how we are perceived. It is more difficult to see how we are constructing the other on the basis of our fears, relational templates and object relations. Our intersubjective ecologies are co-created, negotiated and transacted in extremely subtle, unconscious ways.

The intersubjective field of any two people in relationship will include their inner figures projected upon each other, influenced by the degree to which each has enough of a particular set of characteristics to act as a hook for such projections. We may induce each other to incarnate our projections. Responses will be a combination of one's own complexes, wounds and relational pathologies and the natural reaction to being cast in a particular role. We will constantly feel ourselves 'being manipulated so as to be playing a part, no matter how difficult to recognize, in somebody else's phantasy' (Bion, 1961, p. 149). We function for each other as the players on a living stage, where an infinite variety of scenes, identities or states of mind are enacted and worked on. Internal conflicts are invariably played out between partners, so that there are conscious and unconscious negotiations constantly being undertaken both individually and jointly.

Mutual projective identifications

In Klein's (1946/1992a, 1955) original concept of projective identification, we fantasize that we can get rid of difficult and negative emotional experiences by evacuating them into the other. Yet the recipient remains, in essence (if not accident), unaltered. In Bion's (1967) later reformulation, the recipient of our projections takes in what is projected as a form of unconscious communication.[1] The recipient of a projection may feel an accompanying coercion to feel, enact or even incarnate this projection. The process of identification involves separate processes: we 'pick up' on how we are constructed, identify with the conscription, then we incarnate it. Or we may still receive the projection as a communication but we can distinguish that it is not about us. We may take it in and ponder what it is telling us about the projector.

Mutual projective identifications are intersubjective psychic transactions between two people in a relationship involving layers of co-constructions. What concerns couple therapists is intuiting the shape of what is co-created, the particular combination and fit, as well as the aetiology and driving forces behind such projections.

Extractive introjections and the couple

Christopher Bollas (1987) coined the term 'extractive introjection' to refer to a situation where one extracts (steals) qualities out of another and introjects (appropriates) them into oneself. This intersubjective act of 'violence takes place where the violator' 'automatically assumes that the violated' person

---

1 Regarding the debate as to the extent to which projective identification is an intrapsychic, defensive phantasy, as it was in Klein's 1946 and 1955 formulation, or whether it is a form of communication, as it is in Bion's 1959 later development, my view is that Klein and Bion were referring to different yet similar processes. Projective identifications can be phantasies based on wanting to rid ourselves of material we wish to disown or displace into another. Whether the other picks up on such a phantasy and identifies with it or not is a separate matter. Bion's sense of projective identification refers to highly disturbing emotional matters we find hard to contain and process within us. We communicate our disturbance to close others, initially a caring mindful parent, who picks up on our distress, is affected by it and willingly ponders upon what it means through vicarious introspection, empathy and reverie. This can allow us to feel that another shares our pain, sits with us, not through sympathetic platitude, but thinking hard with us and modelling a thinking-caring-containing attitude. Grotstein (2005) argues that we can only project upon our image of the other, not into the 'real' other. However, we all know what it feels like to stand behind the screen (image) of someone else's projections, inwardly protesting, 'but you have misinterpreted me, you have got me so wrong!' Certain emotional states are highly contagious, depression, anxiety and anger being cases in point. We speak of an atmosphere being 'charged so thick you could cut it with a knife'. This is usually an indication that mutual projections are ricocheting through the relational space infecting both in mutual projective identifications.

'has no internal experience of the psychic element' that has been 'stolen' from them. This violation has the effect of robbing the other of the given element, such that they will feel the theft, be 'temporarily anaesthetized and unable to "gain back" the stolen part of the self' (Bollas, 1987, p. 158).

Extractive introjection is a form of psychic theft. Symington (1993, pp. 26–27) discusses a patient who 'gobbled up' Symington's reflections, spilling them out a few days later as if the words had been the patient's own. Extractive introjectors can be enormously impressive when they gobble up other people's original insights and regurgitate them as if they were their own, because they haven't had to do the difficult work of cogitation and consideration that gives rise to a well-thought theory. A partner who uses extractive identification as a defence cannibalizes their partner's psychic material, to the point of hollowing out the other's insides, rendering them empty.

Identifications

Identification, in so far as it fails to imagine, acknowledge, let alone appreciate alterity and the reality of another in their own right, profoundly limits love relations. The phenomenologist Max Scheler (1954) shows how 'identifying oneself with another' is a form of psychic 'infection'. One identifies another in all their 'basic attitudes' with one's own self. Such identification is both involuntary and unconscious. Scheler further distinguishes *idiopathic* and *heteropathic* forms of identification. In the *idiopathic*, one absorbs 'another self by one's own', the other is 'dispossessed and deprived of all rights in its conscious existence and character' (Scheler, 1954, p. 18). This shows similarities to Bollas's concept of extractive introjection. In the *heteropathic*, one takes over another's personality by a form of hypnotic possession, such that all one's own attributes are usurped: 'I live, not in "myself" but entirely in and through the other person' (p. 19). In an idiopathic identification the other as Other is destroyed; in a heteropathic identification one's own self is obliterated.

Adhesive identification, a concept developed by Meltzer (1975) and Bick (1986), refers to a primitive defence where someone is so unable to feel a sense of coherent identity he or she sticks like glue to a partner, using identification like a 'second skin'.

Folie à deux

A couple may be caught up in a *folie à deux*, consisting of mutual projective identifications and introjections of a very perniciously primitive nature, where both are urgently constructing each other on the basis of fixed ideas based on stale memories of previous interactions, projections of internal figures and object relations and projective identifications of emotionally undigested primal material. Each partner is then co-conscripted so as to behave accordingly.[2] Any discrepant information to the contrary is disregarded. The unconscious conscription is so nefarious that it feels like there is little room to move.

The marriage of Guy and Doris seemed predicated on them both fulfilling a proscribed role in each other's shared defensive fantasies. There was little ability to tolerate even the slightest hint of anything other than a two-dimensional caricature they had of each other. They came at a time when cracks had more than appeared in the thin veneer of the reflecting screen between them and hints of other depths began to peep through.

From the first session I felt as though I was enclosed in the claustrum of their internal living room with them, my role merely a prompt to remind them of their lines should they, for a moment, forget and say something unexpected and discrepant. Their system was so pernicious I despaired that I had much to offer against the immutability of the co-conscripted hell-realm they seemed to have created. I tried to reassure myself that if the scene was truly watertight, they wouldn't need anyone to remind them of their lines. I wondered if the fear of forgetting revealed the very possibility it was meant to hide and defend against. An alternative perspective, something unusual, unrehearsed, a discrepant thought, alterior word or action which might create a breath of fresh air in the claustral confines of their interlocking defence system.

In the marriage and in therapy sessions Doris kept most of herself to herself and seemed to function as a 'blank screen' for Guy's projections. Any hint of Doris having any separate personality of her own created existential dread, which expressed itself in an explosion of contemptuous abuse, a litany of her faults, a flight from the alterity of the Other.

Guy's mother had also fled from feeling cooped up and suffocated in her role as perfect mother and wife. One morning while her three sons were at school she left, never to return. Guy, the youngest, recalled how as a five-year-old he had sat in front of the television expectantly awaiting her imminent return. But she never did return. Now, every time Doris left the room for any reason, Guy had no confidence she would return.

Guy wanted Doris to sit next to him on the couch in their living room and watch a video together without any interruption, to share and merge with him in the one (his) experience. If Doris left the room to do anything she was to let him know: 'I'm just going to the toilet. I'll be back in a moment.'

---

2 Grotstein (2005) would call such a situation projective transidentification.

However, at other times, if letting him know why she was leaving the room disturbed his video-watching, he would launch into a tirade of abuse.

Doris wanted to be able to sit in companionable silence, not necessarily glued to 'the box' but sewing or doing a crossword, in other words, be in her own world beside his, not share in exactly the same reality as him. Guy felt this as an attack on their intimacy, a wanton display of insensitivity to his vulnerability to feelings of abandonment. If she really loved him, she would understand and be there for him exactly as he needed her to be.

In the therapy, any glimmer of Doris's separate mindedness set off a chain reaction. It was as if he plugged a particular video into the compulsive mechanical system of his defensive system. Off it went: a litany was recited to me of all Doris's failings and terrible deeds committed since the beginning of the relationship. 'She forgot my frigging birthday the first year we were together, she knows how I like my shirts ironed but no, little lady muck thinks she knows better, she just wanders in and out of the room as she pleases, how would she like it if I just waltzed off into the sunset leaving her to rot in her own shit . . .'

It was aggressively repetitive and ritualistic, the same old tape being played over and over again. It allowed no variant reading on Doris's part, nor any capacity for him to let go and forgive when she pointed out that there was nothing she could do to undo what had been done. She was 'so terribly sorry, I try so hard to get it right, I just seem to always stuff it up, but can't we move on from this?' The tyrannous message in the look in his eyes sent her into a paralysis of indecision: it was a projective order to get it wrong.

There were hidden developmental impulses in their object choice. Guy related how his first impression of Doris was that she was an image of perfect womanhood, nurturing, caring, and so very feminine. But, curiously, he commented in passing that she was obviously 'a bit of a free spirit', a non-conformist who seemed to inhabit her own private day-dream world oblivious to the world outside. His mother's expression of seeking freedom from her scripted set role was to flee, not able to find any alternative within the marriage, thus depriving Guy of any freedom to day-dream in a zone of security, held in the safety of his mother's attentive mind. So being a 'free spirit' was like a *double entendre* for Guy.

Doris said she had been looking for a man who would draw her out of herself, who would challenge her to engage emotionally. During the course of therapy Doris became increasingly intolerant of her scripted role. She wanted to inhabit the shared marital home as a person, not a cardboard cut-out. This represented a developmental move to come out from behind the mirror and emotionally engage with a real Other – Guy – rather than a blustering father figure or her first idealistic impression of him as a heroic, masculine and chivalrous figure. Guy developmentally sought Doris's self-containment and free-spiritedness, but also envied and resented her emotional self-containment because it was so outside his own oeuvre. The unconscious developmental potential in his object choice was that he chose someone who would ultimately assert her own subjectivity, differences and resilience.

Some forms of *folie à deux* involve projecting false self-images outwards. We create a realm of self-deception through selection of partners who will reflect back our self-image. Others function not as subjects but reflecting surfaces for our fantasy image. The deal we strike is a reciprocal reflection back of the other's projected self-image. This form of mutual transprojections functions like a Sartrian 'hell is other people' (*l'enfer, c'est les autres*) (Sartre, 1967/1944).

Projective identification can be positive if it is used as a form of communication, rather than evacuation. Feelings which are congruent with the projector are 'induced' in the other, thereby creating a sense of being understood, or 'at one with' the other person (Ogden, 1992, p. 21). Thus projective identification is related to empathy and vicarious introspection, an ability to identify with another's state of mind (Grotstein, 1985, p. 123).

Splitting and projection

When we cannot manage ambivalence – the ways in which we feel a combination of both loving and hateful feelings for our partner – either the positive or negative emotion becomes unconscious via mechanisms of repression, denial and splitting of the ego (Mattinson and Sinclair, 1979). Emotions oscillate, feeling desire towards our partner one day and repugnance or indifference the next. A negative (or positive) emotion towards one's partner may also be displaced onto others.

For example, both partners might defend against negative feelings and only express positive feelings towards each other. They project elements of antipathy they unconsciously feel towards each other onto a common enemy (such as the couple therapist). The couple may only express indifference or disdain towards each other, projecting their yearning for closeness onto others. Feelings of vulnerability and tenderness may be unconscious, while anger and hurt are conscious. Feelings of enmity may be conscious, while the yearning for closeness is unconscious (Mattinson and Sinclair, 1979, p. 54). In couple therapy, such a projective mechanism may get played out in the transference. They might express annoyance towards each other and longing for understanding from the therapist, each expecting the therapist to take their side. Or they may see the therapist as joining their partner in an unholy alliance against them. The couple may retain the split between them, one partner denying any tender feelings but relying on the other to express affection.

Carla and Laura were executive coaches. They told me how they believed in unconditional positive regard and ran workshops in affective listening skills. But something was going awry in their own communications. At their sixth session they were a bit late, and Carla was obviously very annoyed at Laura about this. Laura explained that she'd slowed them down because her heel had fallen off her shoe. Carla retorted that Laura ought to know that being late indicated unconscious hostility and she should have worn something more sensible. Laura replied, 'Oh you're so predictable', giving her a friendly dig in the ribs.

Laura asked Carla what was really going on. Carla shrugged and said 'nothing'. Laura rolled her eyes at me as if to enlist my support. Carla then said she felt shamed by Laura's remark that she was predictable. Laura ought to know that shame was a big issue for her. Laura burst into tears: 'It's like walking on eggshells with her. Is there no room in the relationship for even an affectionate dig?'

This comment had me wondering just how affectionate the dig might want to be!

Suffused anger emanated from Carla who looked accusingly at me. She was conscious of feeling shamed but oblivious to feeling resentful towards Laura and furious at me that I didn't implicitly take her side and understand perfectly her sensitive inner feeling state. This is one of the inherent difficulties in couple work, when a thin-skinned narcissist needs empathic mirroring and attunement of their inner vulnerable self from the therapist. Yet to enter such a dyadic mirroring dynamic with this partner *ipso facto* alienates the other who also needs such attuned responsiveness.

Laura was conscious of feeling she was in the wrong, unconscious of her own indignation at this treatment. Carla burst out, 'Well there goes our holiday to Bali! No way I'd go with you when things are like this!' Laura just sat looking crushed. I felt my attempts to gently and empathically gather up the pieces of their feelings scattered around the room were as inept and clumsy as a pair of clodhoppers. It was time to finish but they sat in stony silence. I said, as gently as I could, 'I will see you in a fortnight after your holiday'. Carla looked daggers at my insensitivity at ending the session when there was no immediate resolution. Laura sniffed and pulled several tissues from the box. She threw them in the waste-paper basket, drew herself up, and when I opened the door for her, she stormed out, slamming the door, catching my shoe.

I received a call the next day from Carla. 'We both feel that therapy with you is not working. We were appalled that you could just end the session just because the hour was up, as if the only thing that mattered was your psychoanalytic frame, not our feelings. We have found someone else closer to our model of unconditional empathy and positive regard. We won't return after your holiday.' At this point I wondered about the 'slip' (I wasn't going on holiday, they were) and reflected that it was a shame that we would not have the chance to explore possible issues of abandonment surrounding their break, even though it was initiated by them. I had the sense that they needed to leave their unconscious antipathy and resentment towards each other in my room, to safeguard their romantic holiday. Yet, in leaving their bundle of difficult emotions with me, they were also depriving themselves of meaningful engagement with vital if painful aspects underlying their respective and conjointly constructed emotional atmosphere.

Paranoid-schizoid operations

Klein's concept of the paranoid-schizoid position characterizes the first few months of life in which the baby cannot yet reconcile the co-existence of feelings of love and hate towards mother. The baby cannot reconcile how the same person is both the provider and withholder of wants and needs. As infants we split our image of our mother into two: a figure who is good and ideal because she gives me what I want, and a figure who is bad and persecutory because she frustrates me.

The mode of operating at this stage is called part-object relating: the baby cannot conceptualize the other as a whole person but relates in parts, to a breast, hands, lips, face, etc. This can manifest in later life as fetishism, where erotic desire is directed at fetishized body parts, which flies in the face of relating to someone in their foursquare humanity. Directing libido towards an eroticized body part rather than the whole person is beautifully illustrated in Thomas Hardy's *A pair of blue eyes*. Stephen splinters his love for Elfride such that she is related to not as a whole person but as a collection of component body bits.

'What did you love me for?' she said . . .
'perhaps for your eyes.'
'What of them?' . . .
'Oh, nothing to be mentioned. They are indifferently good.'
'Come, Stephen, I won't have that. What did you love me for?'
'It might have been your mouth.'
'Well, what about my mouth?'
'I thought it was a passable mouth enough –
'That's not very comforting.'

'With a pretty pout and sweet lips; but actually, nothing more than what everybody has.'
'Don't make up things out of your head as you go on . . . Now – what – did – you – love – me – for?'
'Perhaps, 'twas for your neck and hair; though I am not sure: or for . . . your hands and arms . . . or your tongue . . .'

(Hardy, 1878/1986, p. 51)

A film director develops an obsession about women with gaps between their two front teeth. As a young adolescent he had a crush on a class-mate who had a gap between her teeth but he felt too shy to approach her. He met her again at a school reunion where she smiled a glorious gap-toothed smile in greeting. She obviously liked him. But he didn't quite have the nerve to ask for her phone number. He continued to dream about her gap-toothed smile into his thirties, which culminated in his desire to make a movie in which he explored his fantasy of what might have happened if he met her again. He marries the gap-toothed actress who comes to play the lead role. Their marriage doesn't last. She leaves him because she says she is more than her two front teeth.

Part-object relating fractures the image of a beloved into bits. Even relating to the other as a set of attributes renders them a list of features, not a person, someone who 'fits the bill'. The culture around internet dating and introduction agencies can fall foul of such attitudes to finding a partner. This is humorously caricatured in Woody Allen's (1992) *Husbands and wives:* 'Spencer was searching for a woman interested in golf, inorganic chemistry, outdoor sex and the music of Bach. In short he was looking for himself, only female.'

In adult relations we see a range of primitive defences belonging to paranoid-schizoid tendencies. Splitting, projecting, idealizing, denigrating and projective identification are used to manage anxiety and contradictions between loving and hating. We idealize a new love interest. When, in some way, they disappoint us, we assume we got it all wrong. They are not who we thought they were. Which is true. The idealized lover is as false an imputation as a denigrated one.

Cheri tells me how she is just 'besotted' with Jenny. She is everything she is looking for in a lover, 'kind, affectionate, nurturing, generous, we're so much on the same wave length, we are both vegetarian, she's following a spiritual path and does yoga, she's a masseur and does the most wonderful massages'. But not long after she tells me she's 'gone off Jen'. 'Actually I was wrong about her, she's quite self-obsessed, bit of a navel-gazer really.'

Cheri was disillusioned and angry with Jenny because she was not as available to her as she had expected she would be. She bitterly resented it when Jenny went off to meditate and abandoned her. Jenny replied that the very thing that Cheri had liked about her now seemed to be the problem. If she didn't meditate, she wouldn't be the person she was.

We uncovered a history concerning an unavailable mother, who went off to her study to write lectures as she was an academic. Cheri said that her mother also complained that she was a very insecure and clingy baby, who had colic and didn't settle no matter how much she breast-fed and held her.

Exaggeration is also a feature of paranoid-schizoid thinking. We project upon a person extreme badness or extreme goodness, which leads us to over-react to a situation.

Typecasting (part-object relating)

'I know I can't expect any one person to satisfy all my needs.' Hannah tells me how her husband is kind and 'a good provider' but 'a bit staid and predictable'. Recently she has been having coffee with 'Ben' with whom she shares her love of literature, *film noir* and Eastern spirituality. 'I know that I can't expect my marriage to satisfy all the parts of me. And Ben is utterly disorganized and impractical, he'd be hopeless to live with.' On the surface we may seek a multi-dimensional relationship, but this belies the fact that we cannot cope with an 'embarrassment of riches' of having a partner who can embody a full gamut of qualities. We sometimes render a multi-faceted person mono-dimensional, splitting-off certain of his or her qualities onto a third person, then creating a false opposition between the two people. This may be due to oedipal tensions, leading to triangular situations in love. The unattainable, sublime object of desire is set against the domestic, non-erotic yet comforting and socially acceptable marital partner. Yet a closer analysis might reveal that the hearth-keeper or breadwinner is also capable of being inspiring, creative and passionate.

Jung lived out a similar split between his wife Emma and the various women he related to as muse *inspiratrices*, such as Sabina Spielrein and Toni Wolfe. Emma united within herself qualities of intellect, maternal, down-to-earth, no-nonsense warmth and a penetrating insight as well as erotic passion. Yet Jung seemed to look elsewhere for qualities of love as *eros-sophia*. He derived such inspiration from his *anima* women, leaving Emma as the shadowy background object of maternal identification.

Depressive understandings

The depressive position, which Klein believed began from around 3 months, involves the gradual recognition that the mother who is frustrating and the mother who tenderly cares for the baby's needs are one and the same person. A mother who is able to cope with her child's primitive anxieties and destructive impulses creates a sense of containment, which aids the baby's capacity for such an integration of feelings of ambivalence, of hate and love.

The child begins to feel concern for mother and fears that his or her destructive phantasies have damaged or destroyed the object. He or she hopes to repair and make good the damaged object. The infant wants the object to survive and be mended; thus feelings of guilt and reparation are evoked. Reparation is also connected to the psychological process of making-whole one's comprehension of the other. Through reparation the child becomes more able to appreciate mother as a person in her foursquare reality. This inaugurates a capacity for relations between two whole and complete persons. Empathy, altruism and recognition of alterity are dependent upon attainment of depressive understanding.

As well as being distinct developmental stages the paranoid-schizoid and depressive positions alternate throughout life. Britton (1998) argues for a process in which one moves from the depressive position to a post-depressive position and on to a new paranoid-schizoid position. Each new experience requires a new resolution, finding insight, understanding and solutions anew.

From the perspective of the depressive position, we see that our lover consists of a range of qualities that completely transcend our limited divisions of experience into all-good and all-bad. We feel remorse for having previously been one-sided, self-centred and destructive. We recognize how much we previously erred in falsely dividing the world into simplistic categories predicated on what is good or bad for me, hating and seeing as all-bad those who frustrate our desires, loving and seeing as all-good those who do our bidding. There is a shift from being concerned with one's own survival and happiness to concern for the other. We can see that our love exceeds our definitions, which are inherently egocentric emotional evaluations based on whether he does our bidding or not. Further, there needs to be a capacity for being without 'memory, desire or understanding' in accepting that our lover is not a static, unchanging entity fixed in time, but continually changing, unfolding – the lover who we meet today is always a surprise. We begin to move beyond fixed ideas about our close one's personality.

The depressive position undermines binary oppositional thinking. The other as a subject in her or his own right exceeds any imputation of loved or hated, good or bad, this or that. A range of colours starts to enter our perceptual field in place of the black-and-white stance of the paranoid-schizoid position. We become many-sided in our appraisal of a given relational situation. We know we can feel a range of emotions about another person and that such emotions are temporary states and not absolutes. We suspect we might be seeing it from a limited and loaded emotional perspective and that we might be projecting something of our own onto the other, that this is about us, not them.

Bion took Klein's ideas further to posit a continual oscillation between the paranoid-schizoid position and the depressive position's attainment of a capacity for ambivalence. Bion placed this sublational Ps↔D movement at the centre of his theory of mind, as representing our tendency to oscillate continually through processes of dividing and reconciling.

In the depressive position more sophisticated forms of defence may emerge. Dependence and ambivalence may be denied. A defensive reliance on autonomy may cover over fear of loss. However, ideally the depressive position brings with it affectionate and healing gestures towards the other who is conceived as a real other. With the 'capacity for concern' (Winnicott, 1963/1984b) gratitude enters into love relations, gratitude for the love received and the other's own separate nature. At this stage of love we are able to trust a relational capacity to contain a range of emotions, that conflicts can be managed and worked through, differences and unpredictability accommodated if not welcomed.

Love based on appreciation of alterity is only possible when the whole object comes to be seen as a subject in her own right and there is an 'internalized symbolic *representation* of the object (in the place where the object used to be). Its predecessor, the internal part-object (in the paranoid-schizoid position) reflects self-object fusion' (Grotstein, 2000, p. 50).

Love, hate and ambivalence

> We had this terrible scene. I screamed at him, 'I hate you, I wish I had never met you'. I stormed out, throwing my keys at him. Yet now all I can remember are all the good times, our first date, our holiday overseas. I want him back.

One of the most confusing aspects of intimate relationships is the contradictory feelings they evoke. We are not very good at reconciling the fact that we might feel a range of conflicting sentiments for the same person. Emotions vacillate in unpredictable succession, from desire to irritation to excitement to boredom to resentment to longing. Emotional responses may become stacked one on top of the other, or succeed each other in a chain reaction. We fear abandonment, which gives rise to unconscious pre-emptive aggressive responses to any imagined sign of rejection, which creates fear that our aggression will destroy the good. This leads to increased insecurity and fear of being left alone, which leads to a cloying demand for reassurance – 'do you still love me?' – unaware that we are as prickly and defended as a porcupine.

Sometimes couples want things to be so predictable that they would rather create their own misery than be at the mercy of the unpredictable moods and occurrences which loving entails. This is the basis for defence systems: in seeking to defend against projected hurt we often inadvertently create the very hurt we wish to avoid.

As well as alternating between positive and negative feelings towards our partner, emotions may be hidden in such a way that the underlying original feeling is buried under strata of other emotional reactions, as well as complicated defensive manoeuvres designed to protect against the associated pain of the initial emotion. Such manoeuvres are not conscious, but have the net effect of thwarting the very thing one consciously seeks.

> Margaret couldn't understand why she was single. Self-help books advised various strategies for catching her man, but to date she was singularly unsuccessful. A sure sign that Margaret was attracted to someone was that she would studiously ignore him. She thought she was merely playing 'hard to get' – a strategy she hoped would make her alluringly desirable – but was unaware of the disdainful expression on her face. All the men she was attracted to felt diminished under her withering gaze. She felt attraction, which evoked vulnerability, which evoked fear of being rejected. She pre-empted the expected rejection by getting in first. Via a form of reversal, she identified with the imagined aggressor and became the rejecter. Even this was not enough: it would feel too shameful to admit of any attraction, so overtly she would decide they were 'up themselves' and not her sort anyway.

Another major contribution Klein made to understanding the vicissitudes of love concerns the problem of ambivalence: the difficulty of reconciling how we can both love and hate the same object. Working through feelings of love, hate, guilt and reparation is necessary for the adult to be able to love freely: 'If we are able to resolve our grievances and forgive our parents for the frustration we had to bear, then we can be at peace with ourselves and are able to love others in the true sense of the word' (Klein, 1937/1988, p. 343).

According to Klein, a 'happy love relationship' involves a capacity for self-sacrifice, deep attachment, the ability to share grief as well as pleasure and to share common interests as well as sexual satisfaction. The sexual satisfaction attendant upon such well-being gives reassurance against the guilt from earlier sadistic wishes and this increases gratitude, tenderness and love.

False oppositions

Relationships require an ability to enjoy a fluid inter-relational space in which aspects which might seem incompatible, contradictory or opposed are understood as interdependent co-requisites. Finding fulfilment in love depends on an ability to resolve apparent dichotomies, to see how the apparent difference between identification, intimacy and alterity can become reconceived as a dance between different positions, a sublational third position incorporating apparently incompatible psychic realities.

We often speak of the 'tensions', 'conflicts' and 'struggles' between different needs, such as the need for closeness and the need for distance, or the individuation needs of the individual partner and the needs of the couple. Partners also often ascribe such a principle or need to the other, creating a polarity of opposites where one partner acts as its spokesperson, gender-stereotypes aggravating the opposition: 'She's the nurturing type, I'm the practical one.' 'She's emotional and lives in fairy land, I'm just a nuts-and-bolts kind of guy.' Solitude, intimacy, socializing, reflection, rationality, emotionality, decisiveness, flexibility, practicality and sponta-neity are qualities that are all needed in an integrated rich life. Helping each partner to de-identify with contrary principles with which they have become identified can help resolve such oppositional thinking.

Truth as *alétheia*: working through projections

Given that all projections are falsifications and what Bion would call 'lies', examination of the particularity and content of mutual projective identi-fications is like examining a haunted house for ghosts. Yet that is what couple therapists spend their time doing.[3]

Every human encounter contains a co-created chemistry of interaction that has the potential to reconstruct who we think we each are. Who I am for you is largely a figment of your imagination. I can identify with your construction of me, or, if I think it is off the mark, I can choose to try to stand aside from it. Yet even if I do not identify with it (which is a tall order in itself) I cannot necessarily change how you see me.

Personality characteristics which we attribute to one another are never essence but accident, in Aristotle's terms, accruing force of habit through re-enforcement by expectations that we will continue to behave according to the construction. Instead we need to give each other the benefit of the doubt, be receptive to who we might be today, not how we were seen yesterday. But negative (and negating) memories always rush in, and take up all the available space, leaving little room for pleasant if discrepant surprises. Memories mixed with exaggerated, overblown fixed ideas become like a cast of grotesque gremlins. There is no room to move in such an atmosphere.

---

3 The couple therapist as ghost-buster?

One of the hardest psychological tasks in relationships involving projections is being able to stand aside from misconstructions of our personality. It is difficult because we are 'guilty by association'. Once associated with a particular conscription our attempts to counter or 'disprove' it often only serve to cement the false imputation. All we can do is make an internal differentiation and de-identification between the projection and our knowledge of ourselves: 'I am not who he/she thinks I am, that is not me.'

Celia described how she had spent her marriage playing a role consisting of a set of attributes for the perfect wife and mother-figure for her husband Mike. They had met through an introduction agency and she had met his list of criteria. Yet after many years of marriage she felt stifled by the need to conform. If she deviated from this list in any way it was met with horror. Mike's father had gone off with his nanny when he was seven. He made a promise as a child that 'when I grow up I will get married, buy a lovely house and be married to the one woman until I die and she will never leave me'. Mike needed Celia to do everything together, on schedule. On Saturdays they did the weekly shopping, did household chores and had dinner with his mother. On Sundays they went to church and had Sunday lunch. On Fridays they had 'date night' and went to the local cinema, 'because I know maintaining your relationship is important' he explained to me. Celia had a recurring dream of a painting of a woman's head, beautifully made up, but with immobilized made-up features. A crack in the paintwork ran down the side of the face. She said she felt like that painting, as if she was just a cardboard cut-out. She felt hemmed in on all sides, yet terrified of destroying Mike's fantasy, of not continuing to conform to his expectations. She still loved him and had her own reasons to be fearful of loss and abandonment. She just yearned to have coffee with a friend on Saturday, or go to a movie he wouldn't like, or read a book in companionable silence, or do an adult learning course on Mondays, or not have dinner with his mother every Saturday, or simply just 'do something different!'

Over time it was like watching a chrysalis emerge from its cocoon. She not only found a world of new interests and creative pursuits, but found to her amazement that all the people she feared would abandon her when she stopped playing the role said, 'Oh thank goodness!' Apart from her husband, that is, who at first thought she must be menopausal. Yet after a protracted struggle to keep her as his constant reliable fantasy object, he was surprised to find a new world of possibility opening out to him; even the changes she initiated dragged him 'kicking and screaming' out of his familial systems of safety. It was a case where an act of freedom and authenticity made by one party eventually may have a liberating effect on the other. This was because

Celia made it clear it was not him she wanted to leave, only the strictures of conformity to an image-based marriage. Reassured that the relationship itself was secure, this enabled him to transform a claustrum into a container in which new growth could take place.

If we are able to disentangle ourselves from relational conscriptions it helps not only ourselves. It might also help the projector to withdraw and reincorporate his or her projections. Even when the projector is not able or willing to do so, it still helps decontaminate the recipient from what is often psychologically toxic waste.

The more we can become aware of our particular unconscious complexes and object relations and how they overlay our perceptions of each other and interfere with our love lives, the more we can factor them in to our healthy scepticism about the veracity of our emotional reactions to others. We gradually learn to identify and see through such templates and projections. It might be like seeing through glasses that we know are scratched, dirty, rose-coloured or have distorted lenses, but it has the advantage of loosening the fixity of projective perception. This requires arduous psychological work such as in an analysis, at the end of which we hopefully find ourselves less under the sway of such endogamous forces or have some insight into what might be going on beneath the surface. At the very least we are able to ask ourselves difficult questions concerning the hidden factors governing our choices and perceptions.

Given that all false imputations and projections are false, they do not exist, so on one level there is nothing to remove. When projections and false identifications fall away, a couple might feel bewildered and amazed: 'what on earth was all the *Sturm und Drang* about?' And often the next thing said is, 'so, what on earth do we talk about now?' We might feel so foolish when we realize that we have been so way off the mark that a sense of shame intrudes, leading us to cover things up again, as if we didn't see through the projections at all.

Chapter 8

Relational configurations

A little toddler plays on a beach, blissfully unaware of anything but the sandcastle he is building. He chirps away to himself, happy as a lark, his dark curls fanning his face, arms browned by the long summer and glistening with sweat. His family sits nearby, eating their picnic lunch. He is dimly aware of background sounds of his mother and father talking, babies crying, other children bickering, screams of merriment, dogs barking, rustle of newspaper, surf pounding . . .

A breeze blows up, a cloud darkens the sun. He suddenly notices it has become very, very quiet. He looks around, rudely woken from his day-dreams by the ominous silence.

The beach is deserted. Storm clouds hang ominously over the sea. The only sign of picnicking of the family clan is the crust of a vegemite sandwich, an orange peel, footprints in the sand, or the indentations from sunbathers. They had forgotten him.

This 'creation myth' of a patient, Jack, encapsulated, not an isolated incident, but a history of growing up in a family where his very existence could be forgotten. He became as an adult terrified of being alone and 'hated his own company'. He came to see me for individual therapy because his girlfriend said she wanted to stay with him but couldn't bear how suffocating and possessive he was. It was driving her away.

A sense of physical containment and being minded by another in a reliable, regular, dependable way in therapy was a vital aspect of our work, of his development of the capacity to play in the presence of another, to lose his need for hyper-vigilance and be able to muse and day-dream safely once more.

A child who is 'minded' in both senses of the word – physically looked after as well as thought about and held in mind – develops a deep sense of internal security, able to venture out into the world, safe in the knowledge of return to the comfort of home. Such experiences become internalized as an inner representation of being at home in the world. Bowlby called this sense of being at home in the world, the 'secure base'. 'Attachment behaviour is held to characterize human beings from the cradle to the grave' (Bowlby, 1979, p. 129).

Bowlby argued that the child is relational from the beginning of life and that coupling is at the core of what it means to be human. Early experiences of attachment and separation become transformed into inner representations (Bowlby, 1979), or internal working models, which have predictable implications for attachment-related situations through life. Internal working models, which are repositories for memories and beliefs derived from early relational experiences, are primarily unconscious, but become re-created in later relationships.

Bowlby showed how two defensive reactions to early separation trauma were clinging and self-reliance.[1] These have become known in attachment theory literature as the insecure-ambivalent attachment pattern and the insecure-avoidant attachment pattern. As described by Holmes (1996), 'insecure-ambivalent individuals cling to the object, terrified of separation'. The 'world appears as inherently unreliable; clinging is the best way of maintaining proximity to an object that she expects will let her down'. 'Insecure-avoidant individuals shy away from their objects, fearful or dismissing of closeness' (Holmes, 1996, p. 70).

Reactions to early caregiving experience become 'hard-wired' and formulate into typical patterns of relating to others, known as attachment style. In a couple relationship different combinations of attachment styles give rise to a series of relational configurations. Insecure attachment patterns become formulated into more rigid, polarized configurations, where each partner conscripts the other in an over-determined, inflexible manner. Partners become locked into fixed positions over issues such as closeness and distance. Common combinations are as follows:

- A securely attached person is paired with another secure individual.
- A secure person forms a relationship with an insecurely attached person (either preoccupied or avoidant).
- A preoccupied/ambivalent individual seeks out a dismissing/avoidant partner.
- Two avoidant individuals create a noncommittal relationship based on maintaining a safe distance from each other.
- Two preoccupied/ambivalent individuals create an enmeshed refuge from any hint of separation or difference.

Where the relationship is based on secure attachment patterns, both partners form confident, secure relationships where both times of solitude and

---

1 These are known respectively in attachment literature as preoccupied/ambivalent and dismissing/avoidant. Later another category, the disorganized, was identified (Main and Solomon, 1986).

togetherness are flexibly negotiated, and have a mature, considered appraisal of the role of early experiences in their life. There is a sense of 'give and take', times when one partner may be studying for an exam and the other provides non-demanding support, or one partner is sick and the other looks after them. The critical qualities are flexibility, a fluidity of closeness and spaciousness, a capacity to connect deeply but without such intimacy being experienced as engulfing or anxious.

Closeness and spaciousness

A patient, Alice, complains bitterly about how she feels abandoned by her partner Michelle when Michelle retreats to her study to write. 'Michelle never has any time for me, she just buries herself in the stupid novel she's supposedly writing.' Michelle, a lover of solitude, wonders how on earth she managed to 'hook up' with such a 'space-invader'.

A very common combination of attachment styles is the avoidant with the preoccupied, giving rise to contracted battles over space and closeness. Solitude and intimacy, which are both necessary aspects of a healthy relationship, become polar opposites, each partner becoming the crusader for either intimacy or space. The overly dependant partner complains that the avoidant one has 'trouble with intimacy'. The avoidant partner dismissively retorts, 'but you are so needy'.

There are developmental aspects embedded in such choices, each unconsciously seeking to find a way to renegotiate their attachment style such that the enmeshed partner may learn to become more self-contained and the avoidant more able to connect.

Relational work with an insecure and an avoidant partner may enable both to become more securely attached as well as self-contained, enjoying the shifting rhythms between togetherness and solitude.

However, such a combination often results in a closeness–distance struggle. The person who represents the principle of connection becomes increasingly adhesive while the person who loves solitude becomes positively eremitical. The more adhesive person needs to develop a capacity to be alone yet connected, the lover of solitude more connected and engaged, retaining a sense of connection and being in relation even when alone.

At the unconscious level an attachment style may be reversed. A defensively self-sufficient person clings like a barnacle to their sense of autonomy, independence and space. 'I just have to have my space!' Their partners are drawn towards their autonomy and self-containment because that represents something needed by the dependent partner. Yet, underneath, the avoidant partner is perhaps too proud to admit how much they need another or else frightened of being gobbled up by an adhesive partner. It is convenient to locate such dependency needs in the other. The person who clings to significant others unconsciously pushes them away, due to what will be experienced as an aggressive demand for an engulfing, suffocating closeness.

Still more complexity is involved, since a relational dynamic consisting of clinging–rejecting may have become introjected.[2] A relational situation where a child whose intrinsic need to be held and understood was not met leads to an internalization of the experience of a needy child and an unavailable or rejecting mother. In adult relations, the partner may be conscripted by processes of projective identification into replaying the rejecting, distancing role, exacerbated by a self-protective desire to recoil from someone who threatens to psychologically obliterate separateness. The partners become locked into a vicious cycle of pursuing and distancing.

John seeks ordinary reassurance from his partner Geoff that he still fancies him. This evokes feelings of insecurity in Geoff, which is a combination of both a projective identification and Geoff's own insecurity about being abandoned. Geoff distances himself from the feeling of insecurity, which he disavows and introjects back into John, who then becomes doubly insecure, leading to an escalating closeness–distance dynamic. John goes off with the postman.

Ever more intense and furious clinging pushes the ambivalent partner away still further in a desperate attempt to get psychological space. 'I can't breathe!' cried one such a partner. All the while her partner was whimpering, 'he just shuts me out'. It goes with the territory of an insecure partner that they will attempt to make their lover of space feel guilty for any time spent in solitary activities. One couple described how even going to sleep felt threatening. 'You just rolled over and went to sleep when I was so needing your comfort and eye-to-eye contact.' 'It was four a.m.!' his

---

2 Here I am drawing also on Fairbairn's discovery that an intolerably ambivalent relationship results in a splitting of one's attitude about the person, such that the *rejected* part of that person is transformed into the status of an 'internal object'. Thus, the shadow of object relations falls upon interpersonal relations and inexorably constrains them. Splitting occurs in the earliest instance of dependent neediness, when the infant's love is rejected. This disappointment triggers a severing of the original object into an accepting object and a rejecting one, with a correlating split in the ego which becomes internalized separately (Grotstein, 1994).

'Pathological relationships are characterized by "object-relatedness" in terms of their need to adapt to or comply with a disappointing real-life situation by internalising the very badness of the needed (but rejecting) person. Indeed, the more unsatisfying an object (eg mother, father) has been in actual reality, the more a child is compelled to internalise it' (Grotstein, 1994, p. 5).

Grotstein points out that 'an important consequence of Fairbairn's theory is that all identifications are either defensive or pathological' (p. 5).

partner protested. The lover of solitude may feel an internal conflict about the validity of their need for solitude. Being able to structure enough time for contemplation into one's daily life and being comfortable about the need for this space can alleviate some of this tension.

One of the major legacies of disappointing relational experience from childhood which obstructs adult relations is unmet developmental needs for either closeness or privacy. A sense of being deeply loved, accepted and understood leads to a positive confident approach to life. We greet the world of others in a friendly, receptive manner, which in turn creates a sense of being at home in the world and evokes positive responses from others we meet in the course of our day. A child who does not feel accepted or lovable can unwittingly emanate hostility, which evokes negative reactions from others.

Unmet needs for acceptance and closeness accrue a sense of entitlement and a grim determination to obtain what was not obtained from our parents from our adult partner. The build-up of a sense of injustice and resentment leads to an atmosphere of hostility that only exacerbates the partner's fear of inveiglement. This causes them to withdraw ever further. Conversely, a child who experienced their mother as controlling and interfering will be ambivalent about relationships and fear intrusion.

A sense of furious indignation and injustice that early disappointments have created fault-lines in our psyche infects some partners with an increasingly insistent demand that their partner or 'life' or the therapist deliver the goods of what was not provided in the first place. They become fixated on ever more desperate attempts to recapture something develop-mentally needed, such as primary love (Balint, 1952). This is tricky psycho-logical territory, since part of the indignation is diagnostic and hence prognostic for therapy. Yet the difficulty is that no matter what a partner or therapist does in the present it will never feel quite enough, the hole will feel unfillable.

Rather than trying ever more hungrily and obstinately to fill a sense of hollowness, loss needs to be transformed into renunciation, mourning, acceptance and integration. Equanimity resides in being reconciled to the fact that what we seek we will not find in the places where we seek it. We don't get it in response to a tyrannical demand from our partners that they make up for what was lost. Even if they tried, it would never feel enough to make up for what has already created a sense of lack.

Renouncing the demand that partners make up for what we never had creates a space for an awareness of a different kind of absence, an absence of false self-constructs. This awareness transmutes absence into openness and being present, to each other, to what is. Absence thus becomes presence. What is, is not empty disappointment. It is fuller by far than hankering after what once was, or was fantastically believed to have been, or we missed out on. It is the restless striving that needs to be relinquished.

Enmeshed relationships

Enmeshment in relationships may be used to ward off anxieties about separation and loss. Any hint of individuality or move towards differentiation is attacked or glossed over. Such symbiotic entanglement militates against genuine relationship and is indicative of developmental arrest. It may be due to early experiences of a mother who was intolerant of the infant's early dependent need for a sense of identification and closeness. Unable to facilitate a movement towards a sense of separateness when the infant was ready, the child remains fixated on a yearning for merger. Aristophanes' creation story of the severed wholes depicts such a desire for what Fairbairn (1943) called a 'Siamese twinship' featuring a desperate desire to swallow the object who simultaneously swallows the subject such that all difference is obliterated.

Avoidance of enmeshment

Fear of engulfment in adult relations may occur if a partner experienced psychic invasion as a child. A mother may fear rejection from her child and find any moves on the part of the child towards separation and individuation threatening and hence cling stiflingly to her child. Such partners may fear that their own separateness will be subsumed, swallowed or seduced, that is, their sense of selfhood annihilated in relationship. Yet in conflict with this will be a developmental push to heal splits, integrate, inter-relate and be known. Thus the partner will hover between fear of being subsumed and longing for genuine affection.

> Jenny and Peter kept everything separate. They had separate bedrooms, were financially independent and moved in a different circle of friends. Jenny was very involved in writing a doctoral thesis and hated any form of intrusion upon her space. Peter was very involved in humanitarian work which took him overseas to East Timor for much of his time. A crisis brought them into therapy when Peter had an affair with an East Timorese co-worker. It was as if he were able to express his longing for fusion and intimacy only if it were split-off from the domestic situation. In other words, he split-off an unconscious yearning for closeness that flew in the face of his stated position of being emotionally independent. This was because he identified all domestic situations with his original familial claustrum which he had experienced as engulfing. His development was arrested at the adolescent threshold of leaving home. A foreign woman in an overseas location represented an exogamous initiation of leaving home, the archetypal stranger in a strange land. His marriage represented the childhood home.

The ocnophile and the philobat

A couple may enter therapy because life and relational circumstances threaten the ongoing viability of their respective attachment styles.

> Melissa was very self-reliant. Her catch-cry was 'I need space!' She did, however, anxiously cling to her brittle structures of pseudo-independence. Melissa feared that her partner Paul wanted to wrap her up in a suffocating clinch. A vicious pattern had developed in which the more Paul sought closeness, the more she distanced, ultimately concluding that the only way to get enough space was to separate.
>
> Melissa's parents split up when she was seven. She concluded at an early age that she would have to look after herself and so developed a grim determination never to rely on anyone but herself. This was fuelled by bitter resentment that her parents had failed to provide a secure home environment. She tended to be attracted to men who themselves were clingy, since this made them more reliable, yet she couldn't stand any sign of emotional weakness (it unconsciously reminded her of her own suppressed neediness) and she felt repulsion towards their anxious dependency. Underneath she felt a yearning to be able to feel held and safe. She wanted a man, unlike her father, who was strong, intelligent and caring enough to depend upon, without being abusive or cloyingly invasive.
>
> Paul described having no sense of himself. He sought to attach himself to his objects of attachment like a limpet to a rock. His intense neediness was felt by Melissa to be suffocating.
>
> Paul related how his father said to him when he was six, 'you'll have to look after your mother now, be the little man', as he walked out the door. His mother's strategy to get through life as a single mother was to focus exclusively on the practical domains, just coping, never giving Paul any emotional reassurance. He became very anxious and insecure.
>
> A crisis developed when Melissa became pregnant. She experienced the shock of realizing that she could no longer be so self-reliant. She needed to know she could rely on Paul to support her, financially and emotionally, but Paul's knee-jerk reaction was, 'but we haven't budgeted for this, I'd have to support you and I can't do that from scratch!' Melissa would angrily retort, 'oh why couldn't I have married a real man!'
>
> Paul was suddenly thrown back into the heart of his traumatic complex. He heard, as if through the corridors of time, his father saying, 'be the little man'. He felt overwhelmed, unequipped and very little.
>
> Developmentally the attraction represented the possibility of engaging with the opposite, underdeveloped side. Yet the experience of actually being in a

relationship but not being able to achieve the qualities they each so badly required, was extremely painful and served to exacerbate rather than alleviate the polarity: neither true autonomy nor true intimacy seemed possible.

Therapy enabled a shift such that both were able to project their needs for security and self-containment into the relationship-as-a-third, and this allowed them to develop confidence in the continuity, viability and stability of their relationship. Paul was reassured of his capacity as an adult to be a bread-winner, Melissa that she could let down her guard and rely on his emotional and physical support. Paul could move from a clinging dependence to auton-omy, Melissa from defensive self-reliance to intimacy.

Their relationship reminded me of Balint's two defensive types, the ocnophile and the philobat[3] (Balint, 1959). The ocnophile clings to objects, feeling lost without them. The philobat, or lover of space, over-compensates for feared loss by becoming defensively self-reliant, in order to maintain himself with little help from his objects.

It can be therapeutically helpful if a couple caught in a tug of war between enmeshment and avoidance can shift their sense of dependence from a partner to the relationship itself. The relationship can be conceptualized as an object of attachment, such that the adhesive partner can cling to it rather than the other person. The sense of the relationship as a safe base or container for both means that it can provide a secure yet spacious environ-ment around both partners, a sense of a safe space which is neither con-fining nor like a leaky sieve. Both may feel contained and secure in the ongoing viability of the relationship, which also allows them to reconsider their respective working models.

Closeness–distance regulation

Various combinations of attachment styles may manifest as a conflict between closeness and distance. Tensions between the need for autonomy and longing for intimacy may occur within each partner as well as be played out between them. We may simultaneously feel fear of being aban-doned and fear of being engulfed. Yet to pursue a partner as they withdraw pushes them further away. Closeness–distance struggles can be viewed as a kind of intimacy-regulation, in which there is an optimal level of intimacy for that relationship, yet the pole of autonomy and the pole of intimacy

3 'Ocnophile' is derived from the Greek οχνεω meaning 'to cling, shrink, hesitate, hang back'. 'Philobat' is derived from the word 'acrobat' which literally means 'he who walks on his toes', away from the earth (Balint, 1959, p. 25).

become split. One partner, as it were, looks after intimacy, the other separateness, in a form of emotional division of labour. As Woodhouse put it, 'if only we were more separate, we could stay together' (as cited in Ruszczynski, 1993, p. 97), or as Gillian Rose expresses it:

> *L'amour se révèle en se retirer.* If the Lover retires too far, the light of love is extinguished and the Beloved dies; if the Lover approaches too near the Beloved, she is effaced by the love and ceases to have an independent existence. The Lovers must leave a distance, a boundary, for love: then they approach and retire so that love may suspire. This may be heard as the economics of Eros; but it may also be taken as the infinite passion of faith: *Dieu se révèle en se retirer.*
>
> (Rose, 1997, p. 133)

Rilke and Andreas-Salomé

The relationship of Lou Andreas-Salomé and Rainer Maria Rilke illustrates how attachment experiences of early childhood, internal working models of interpersonal relationships, resultant adult attachment styles and a mixture of defensive and developmental object-choices, all combine to create the unique relational configuration of a particular couple. The attempt to create an exogamous relationship between Rilke and Andreas-Salomé ultimately failed, as each eventually returned to their more defensive and avoidant default positions.

Rilke had a schizoid mixture of fear and yearning for intimacy, forever feeling a sense of being an isolate, separated from others, life, even himself: 'I have no beloved, no home, no place where I can live' (Rilke, as cited in Freedman, 1996, p. 243).

Lou, on the other hand, felt a sense of being at home in the world, the world contained within her. Lou described her childhood family environment as feeling enveloped in an atmosphere of benevolence, love and fidelity, which created in her an internalized 'secure base', confidence, gratitude and a sense of her giftedness that enabled her to flout convention. On the other hand she wanted to preserve her sense of virginal, undisturbed self-containment, which she theorized as feminine narcissism, which in its essence partakes of a 'primordial fusion with the All in which we repose' (Andreas-Salomé, 1914, p. 11). She feared that sexual union with a man would overpower and shatter her sense of autonomy. All her relations with men prior to Rilke, such as with Nietzsche, Paul Rée and with her husband Andreas, were celibate.

For Andreas-Salomé, Rilke represented the first person with whom consummation did not diminish the flames of enraptured union: 'If for years I was your wife, it was because you were something *real* to me for the first time, at once and inseparably man and body . . .' (Andreas-Salomé,

1951, p. 173). Yet Rilke was more boy-son-lover than an equal match to Lou.

Rilke, thirteen years younger, was her first lover. Rilke, due to his effeminacy and youth, did not threaten to obliterate her virginal universe. Lou's self-containment offered Rilke containment of his terrible anguish, a borrowed secure base, but without in any way overwhelming him, having any needs of her own, or intruding upon his private core.

A year before Rilke's birth, his mother lost a baby girl, Sophia. His mother sought to recover her lost daughter through Rilke and named him René Maria, leading to a sense that he was at some level female, this inner feminine becoming a 'false self' personality organization, one he particularly resorted to when feeling under threat.

Rilke suffered the *puer aeternus* sequelae of the boy who comes to feel himself annihilated by his mother's failure to apprehend him, while at the same time her uncomprehending gaze is annihilating intrusive:

> Oh, misery, my mother tears me down.
> Stone upon stone I'd laid, towards a self
> and stood like a small house, with day's expanse around it,
> Now comes my mother, comes and tears me down.
>
> She tears me down by coming and by looking.
> That someone builds she does not see.
> Right through my wall of stones she walks for me.
> Oh, misery, my mother tears me down.
>
> (Rilke, 1981, p. 65)

Lou was a woman complex, perceptive and strong enough to rescue him from the anguish he felt. He saw his work – if not his life – through her eyes: 'my clear fountain. Only through you do I want to see the world' (as cited in Freedman, 1996, p. 66). As well as lover Lou functioned as mother, teacher, guide and therapist: the latter qualities surviving past the four-year period they were lovers (Freedman, 1996, p. 67).

What could be seen as Lou's masculine intellect and Rilke's effeminacy enabled them both to effect psychological change. Rilke was encouraged to develop more masculine strength of character while Lou felt she could surrender to a man without feeling overpowered and dominated. For Lou, Rilke represented the promise of someone with whom she might finally be able to form a relationship of one whole person to another whole. Her yearning was for two already whole hermaphrodites to meet, rather than each being but half of a whole and incomplete. Sexual love became the dominant theme in her writings from that time on. Such writings feature a concern with a realization of the fusion between inner and outer, self and other, self and world, spiritual and physical, which sexual union transacts.

Rilke sought a maternal function from her, and this both attracted and repelled her. She felt suffocated by his dependence and her consequent withdrawal fanned his depression and clinging, making her withdraw even more.

Ultimately they both failed to fully cross the threshold from their defensive positions to become fully wedded and whole. The relationship never effected an exogamous transition and remained within the endo-gamous, maternal oedipal sphere. Until his death, Rilke idolized Lou as a boundlessly generous, good mother who shielded him from terror and made his unspeakable dreads something he could bear, a mother on whose breast he found a home. Lou was transubstantiated into the Angel of the *Duino Elegies*, a being free from the anguish which so haunted Rilke. Lou, for her part, retained a defensive, non-relational self-sufficiency of aloof feminine narcissism.

Chapter 9

Interlocking scenes: a malignant dowry

> A young woman dances alone in her living room, her eyes half-closed, enveloped in enjoyment of her body in space. She is transported by the music into another realm: a desert in Syria where the women dance a voluptuous snake dance. Soon she is whirling and swirling in an ecstatic trance, her feet stamping an improvised accompaniment to the pulsating rhythms, her arms circling like serpents above her head.
>
> 'Hey Liz, want a cup of tea?' Her husband Greg pops his head around the door. 'Good heavens, what are you up to?'
>
> Liz's expression turns from ecstasy to horror, then from horror to a crumpled look like a child about to cry. Then something else comes over her and she stands towering above Greg as she screams: 'Get out, get out! How dare you interrupt me like that!'
>
> Greg shuffles out, retreating to lick his wounds, mumbling under his breath, 'I was just offering you a cup of tea'.

'Liz', a woman in her early twenties, came to see me shortly after getting married. She described how passionately in love she felt prior to the wedding day, but, 'as I walked up the aisle with my Dad, it was like some kind of curse was put over us – Greg suddenly seemed an alien. And since the wedding day I haven't been able to bear him coming near me.'

As we worked together, Liz began to intuit threads of connection between how she felt towards her husband and her father's responses to her becoming a woman. Talking over with me the scene described above, Liz suddenly remembered an incident with her father, when she was in early adolescence:

> I was in my bedroom with my older sister. We were both naked and having such fun noticing each other's growing breasts. We began dancing around with these pieces of fabric pretending they were magic veils and that we were Arabian princesses in some wonderful exotic tale. Suddenly the door burst

open. It was Dad telling us that dinner was ready. The look on his face when he realized we had no clothes on. He yelled: 'what do you think you are doing? Get dressed immediately! That's disgusting!' We just cowered and tried to cover ourselves up. I couldn't look him in the eye ever again.

As Liz remembered this event she started sobbing to her imagined father: 'you had no right, no right to take away from me my pleasure in my body, my sense of becoming a woman'.

Her husband's interruption as she danced alone in her living room shocked her out of an experience of euphoria such that Liz was neither in the deserts of Syria, nor a suburban house in Sydney, but in a time-warp relating to humiliating and confusing experiences of childhood that created a crippling self-consciousness, particularly concerning sexual intimacy, in the present. She did not realize she was in the grip of painful memories, but experienced what was going on as if it were happening right 'here-and-now'.

It was as if her father handed over at the altar not only his daughter but also a malignant dowry consisting of a series of father–daughter interactions concerning her emergence into womanhood. These were encapsulated in a particular moment when he barged in on her. The memory was profoundly shame-inducing and became played out in her adult intimate relations.

Traumatic memory systems

The husband's intrusion upon her private zone of experience triggered what Meares calls a traumatic memory system[1] (Meares, 2000) in which her husband Greg plays not an errant knight but a deflating, shaming father. Meares defines the traumatic system as 'a collection of memories concerning similar traumatic events, which is stored in a memory system beyond the reach of reflective awareness'. This system is 'triggered by contextual cues which resemble, in some way, the original trauma' (Meares, 2000, p. 53). Chief characteristics of the traumatic memory system are that:

- It is organized 'as a complex of cognitions, emotions and tendencies to respond' (corresponding to Janet's subconscious fixed idea (as cited in Meares, 2000, p. 53)) and may make up a kind of subpersonality.

---

1 According to Freud's original (1915/1984b) theory of repression, unacceptable thoughts, intolerable states of mind or experience are repressed into the unconscious, where they are no longer capable of being modified, processed and transformed. The ego is left with merely a thing-representation (*dingvorstellung*) which leaves its malignant effects upon the ego but cannot be modified by the light of other experiences because, according to Freud, the thing-representation cannot be linked with words and language.

- It is beyond the reach of reflective awareness and is unconscious: the person does not realize they are in the grip of a traumatic memory system but transfers the original experience to the present.
- It is triggered by contextual cues, which somehow resemble the original trauma. Such cues may be externally produced, e.g. by a conversation. Such cues may also be internal, such as an internal voice which attacks the subject.
- In addition to storing memories of a single dramatic traumatic event, it may be made up of an accumulation of a series of small traumata, such as being ridiculed or criticized, not seen, understood or valued, the many disappointments of early life.

Memories of childhood are emotionally detached from their original context and transferred to a present situation without one knowing this is occurring. Traumatic experiences tend to create an uncoupling of consciousness such that reflective consciousness is lost. This gives rise to the concretizing nature of traumatic systems where there is no 'as if' quality or symbolic function:

> Unable to integrate traumatic memories, they seem to have lost their capacity to assimilate new experiences as well. It is . . . as if their personality has definitively stopped at a certain point, and cannot enlarge any more by the addition and assimilation of new elements.
>
> (Janet, as cited by Meares, 2000, p. 54)

Traumatic memory systems involve a multiplicity and layered hierarchy of different memory systems, depending on a highly complex range of psychological, developmental and other intrinsic and extrinsic factors, 'earlier and less accessible traumata underpinning those which are nearer to consciousness' (Meares, 2005a, p. 102).[2]

The intralocking traumatic scene: the malignant dowry

Traumatic memory systems tend to be organized in the form of a particular scene. I call this encryption of a traumatic memory system an 'intralocking traumatic scene'. It is intralocking in the sense that it imprisons the individual in a defensively closed, intrapsychic system.[3] It is locking in the sense

2 Van der Kolk and Fisler (1995, in Knox, 2003) point out that the visual, olfactory, affective, auditory and kinaesthetic aspects of traumatic experiences tend to be retrieved in a current situation but are dissociated from their coherent semantic aspects.

3 Over-identification: Over-orientation towards an intrapsychically closed system of internalized objects is a protective mechanism when the external relationship was in some way untrustworthy, disappointing or dissatisfactory (Fairbairn, 1952a). Fordham likewise argues that in the face of experiences which are overwhelming the infant retreats into an

that it becomes like a mechanical hard-wired lock, entrapping the person into a relentless replay of this scene. It is a concentration of encrypted and scripted manoeuvres. There is no room for reflection, uncertainty or for reconsidering the script in the light of new discrepant information. These intralocking defensive systems are like malignant dowries that each partner brings to the new relationship. The dowry box, once opened, releases its nefarious contents into the marital space to create an extremely complex and entangled drama I call the 'intralocking traumatic scene'.

The intralocking traumatic scene is:

- *intra* from intrapsychic – concerning internal worlds.
- intra*locking* because it is like an *idée fixe*[4] – a system imprisoning the individual in the relentless replay of such scenes. There is no room for 'learning from experience' (Bion, 1983) or for changing the script in the light of new information. It is 'locking' in the sense of an imprisonment – one experiences oneself as a passive victim in a system without agency or power.[5]
- *traumatic* referring to unconscious fantasies, deriving from difficult early interactions with caregivers which become set down as a blueprint intervening in subsequent intimate relations.[6]
- *scene*, meaning a concentration of complex, scripted and choreographed directions that are projected and re-enacted again and again.

In couple relationships each partner brings, as part of their psychological dowry, an intralocking scene. This unconscious drama comes to be superimposed upon their relationship and so becomes an interlocking traumatic scene. Part of this unconscious theatre is the way they may 'audition' the partner. The other person, due to compatible 'hooks' in his or her own internal world, identifies with the unconscious communication of projection.

earlier autistic state (Fordham, 1976). Knox, drawing on attachment theory, describes how the emotionally avoidant reaction to early separation trauma leads to 'rigid and outdated schemas of self, object and inter-personal relationships' because they are not revised by 'new information and experience' (Knox, 2003, p. 209).

4 *Idée fixe*, from the French meaning 'obsession', was a term coined by the composer Berlioz to denote a musical idea used obsessively, applying it to the principal theme of his 1830 *Symphonie fantastique*. At around the same time Balzac used it in *Gobseck* to describe an obsessive idea. It came to be used as a clinical term denoting unreasonable obsession.

5 Such a malignant system is 'an internal and automatic replication' of early traumata or other disappointing experiences (Brandchaft, 1994, p. 215).

6 Here we can synthesize the Kleinian concept of unconscious phantasy and neuropsychological concepts of memory systems. Implicit memories containing procedural representations of self-with-other experiences are only made explicit and knowable when enacted. The interactions of interlocking traumatic scenes reveal the instantiated shared unconscious phantasy. Unconscious phantasy exists in the realm of implicit memory.

Each partner is thus conscripted to replay these stories, which are like intransigent, repetitive interchanges, like a hard-wired model.

The conscripted system takes the form of a pre-formulated script in which no discrepant information can enter. It is characterized by its repetitiveness and incapacity for transformation in the light of new experience, an absence of reflective capacity, philosophical treatment or symbolizing function, or of an ability to form links between past experiences and present circumstances.

True intimacy is based on improvisation rather than conscription. We are able to be spontaneously receptive to our partners as they present themselves in this moment. What distinguishes this from the conscripted mode is that it is adaptive, fluid, creative and responsive. A free flow of imagination, curiosity and emotional resonance is afforded by a sense of containment and trust. We are open and receptive rather than feeling threatened by the constant jolts of revelation of our partner's alterity beyond any idea we have of each other.

In our love lives we oscillate between moments of intimacy and retreat, between trust and fear, of being vulnerable and open and being catapulted by a slight, or look, or another contextual cue, back into an interlocking scene. The critical aspect is that when we are catapulted back into a traumatic zone we do not know that this has occurred or why. We are in its grip.

The improvised and conscripted modalities involve different forms of memory systems. The improvised mode is based on autobiographical or episodic memory. Autobiographical memory[7] is the last in the developmental hierarchy of memory to develop, at around four years. As Meares (2000) shows, the form of language of autobiographical memory is based on the stream of consciousness. It is associational, non-linear, dynamic and gives rise to narratives of self, stories which are open to the light of new experience.[8] It is the memory system most fragile and susceptible to disruption from traumatic shocks.

The conscripted mode is based on a more primitive memory system, which, although still verbal, is not open to self-reflexive consciousness.[9] The

---

7 Meares (2000) outlines how Nelson, following Tulving, called this personal memory system the remote episodic. Episodic memory concerns personal memories rather than just knowledge of the world. Nelson made a further distinction between memories for recent events and more remote personal events of significance (Nelson, 1992, and Tulving, 1972, as cited in Meares, 2000, pp. 35–36).

8 Meares (2000) has made a major study of this phenomenon as it appears in therapy. Traumatic events are recorded in a more formative memory system than the episodic memory system, which depends upon language and reflective capacity as well as on a sense of an internal, imaginal life.

9 It is an example of implicit memory in which an individual is influenced by past experience without awareness of the link.

person finds him or herself in the grip of a traumatic memory system which is not recognized as such but is experienced as the reality of the present, it is as if it is happening right here and now.

Audition and conscription: The introduction agency

The following vignette from a couple I shall call Mimi and Steven shows the processes of auditioning, constructing and conscripting in the dynamics of the interlocking scene.

> Mimi rang me to make an appointment for couple psychotherapy, explaining, 'my partner Steven and I have been going out for nine months but seem to have reached a bit of a dead end. I need to know what Steven's intentions are, so I don't waste any more time flogging a dead horse.'
>
> Mimi, an elegantly dressed Chinese woman in her mid-thirties, dragged a rather reluctant suitor into the consulting room. Before we had time to settle in our seats, she announced, in a slightly imperious tone, that if Steven didn't propose by the end of the hour it would confirm her worst fears. This somewhat tall order for our first therapy session had me sitting bolt upright on the edge of my seat, while Steven slumped down into his chair as if wishing the very fabric might swallow him.
>
> Rolling her eyes in response to Steven's downcast look, she responded, 'Thought so! Just what I expected!'
>
> It was all too apparent that my 'agency' would be deemed utterly ineffectual if this proposal didn't get delivered according to her set romantic formula by the end of the hour.
>
> Under the surveillance of her gaze of appraisal, and attempting to wriggle out from the projection of fairy godmother/matchmaker, I suggested perhaps we might give ourselves a bit of breathing space to ponder what might be going on behind the scenes (and it might take a little longer than one session!).
>
> Mimi explained how she had met Steven through an introduction agency. She had a rigid set of selection criteria that previous contenders had failed to meet. 'I was getting to the end of the road when Steven came onto the books.' He had gone to the agency in response to his father urging him it was more than time to find a wife.
>
> Mimi spoke of how her family emigrated to Australia from Singapore when she was little. As an adolescent she longed to escape her parents' restrictive home environment but felt a social outcast at school. She retreated to her bedroom into an enchanted fantasy realm immersing herself in the world of glamour magazines, making believe she was any one of the celebrities who

graced their pages. Wherever she went, in fantasy, her regal visage shone out beckoning all number of potential sword-crossing suitors.

She was rudely woken from such day-dreams when, in place of the awaited knight in shining armour, her bedroom door burst open to reveal an irate mother demanding that she put her head back down into her school books. She longed for her father's accolade, but when he returned from frequent absences overseas, he just sat in his study staring out the window, his mind a thousand miles away. She would dress up, hoping to find favour in his eyes. Yet he just bellowed at her to stop dressing in such a suggestive manner and to get back to her studies.

Steven did not volunteer information about himself or his family's back-ground. But Mimi filled the breach, telling me how his parents were Lithuanian and he was the youngest of three children.

In response to Mimi's prompting, he diffidently described how as a child he suffered from psoriasis which made him feel very self-conscious. His father, not able to tolerate any sign of weakness, demanded he prove himself in areas of physical prowess. 'Get on with it! Be a man!' was a constant refrain.

Mimi's almost literal foot-stamping insistence he 'get on with it' and propose trip-switched him back into how he felt as a child when he was made to jump through hoops and did not feel able to do so. The expression 'shotgun wedding' came to my mind: in fact it conjured up the shadowy image of a shotgun at his head.

Visibly wilting like a proverbial violet, he whimpered *sotto voce*, 'please, I'm not ready, give me time'. Time, with its penumbra of associations with bio-logical and oedipal clocks, was of the essence. A catch-cry for Mimi was that 'time's running out, no one will ever want to marry me anyway'.

Steven sensed her insecurities, but said he felt he was in a 'Catch 22': if he proposed in response to her insistent request, she would just think, 'oh he's just saying that to make me feel better, he doesn't really want to marry me'. He kept muttering, 'if she would only get off my back a bit, I could run the marriage and horse-drawn carriage number past her.' I wondered whether Steven's hesitation related not just to resistance to perceived pressure but to insecurity about his own sense of masculinity and worth.

Reading his uncertainty as rejection, Mimi's face crumpled and she whim-pered like a Cinderella whose prince had finally come to claim his bride, only to wince at her ugly, smelly feet.

The slightest sign of any hesitancy to propose shocked Mimi out of her wide-eyed expectation in such a way that she was no longer either in my consulting room or in a Vogue fairy-tale, but in a time-warp relating to shame-evoking events of childhood. In place of the imaginary lover so enchanted by her beauty that he sweeps her off her feet, Steven wore for Mimi the mask of a deflating, shaming father.

Mimi was locked inside a lonely internal fantasy world. She longed to be rescued from its grip, yet her increasingly desperate attempts to liberate herself by interviewing then dismissing a string of potential suitors only served to cement this encryption. Seizing on Steven as a 'last-ditch stand', her insistent demand that he propose 'now or never' triggered a reciprocal system in his psyche. To attempt to do something so momentous as propose to someone he feared would reject him and when he did not feel ready, tripped him into his own traumatic complex.

Both Mimi and Steven were locked in an altercation which had all the hallmarks of a traumatic complex covering an all-too-soft underbelly. Underneath Mimi's fantasy of being adored as the princess-bride and Steven's fantasy of being a dashing athletic hero, both were more alike than met the eye. What manifested as vacillation on Steven's part and imperiousness on Mimi's masked shameful feelings of inadequacy and fears of abandonment.

What had been triggered was a superimposition of two traumatic scenes.

Neither Steven nor Mimi realized they were in the grip of such traumatic memory systems but experienced what was going on as if it were happening right 'here-and-now'. The link between past and present only emerged much later in the analytic context.

The interlocking scene

Due to the complex factors dictating partner selection (auditioning), shared unconscious phantasies and mutual projective identifications operating between couples, there is often an interlocking in which the individual 'traumatic scenes' of each partner come to be superimposed. In other words, it is an interlocking of two intralocking scenes.

While simultaneously living in one's own traumatic zone one is inadvertently playing a proscribed part in the other's internal drama. Two plays are performed simultaneously. In many cases the imaginal space between the two partners can be seen as a two-sided projection screen, upon which are superimposed two separate phantom plays, both projected on each side of the screen. The superimposition of two individual scenes upon a permeable screen creates a third play, made up of a combination of the two individual scenes. Three plays are being performed simultaneously. There is an entanglement of systems because, first, each person does not know the extent to which he or she is locked up in his or her own scene and thus how he or she is also co-opting and entrapping the other into playing their part in it. Second, one does not recognize that while one might have been catapulted back into the experience of the traumatized child, one may inadvertently act the part of the traumatizing adult in the other person's world. Third, each partner is being unconsciously played out by the combination of the interlocking of two systems which gives rise to this third play. In couple psychotherapy we attend to both the individual intralocking scenes of each partner and also how they intersect to create this 'third play', the interlocking traumatic scene.

When the traumatic complex which is the puppet master behind such a script is impervious to modification from alternative experience, the model scene may border on the psychotic, in that the person caught up in such a scene cannot distinguish the 'play' from reality, the partner from a ghost in their nursery.

A shape-changing cast of characters

Object relations theory proposes that as children our disappointing experience with primary caregivers becomes internalized. Our unconscious will symbolize and introject entire scenes with all their participants. These scenes, people and experiences become introjected, not as whole people or memories, but as parts. Our internal world then is made up of symbolic fragments, parts, or, as in the name of the theory, objects.

In later life, when a contextual cue triggers this memory, we find ourselves compulsively acting out this scene, projecting various parts onto those around us. Furthermore, given that the entire disappointing interrelational dynamic has been internalized, we may identify with any member of that drama, not just our childhood self. Thus we may also act out the part of the mother or father and treat our loved one as our mother treated us, switch from being the one who feels victimized to the victimizer.

For example, the experience of a mother who is preoccupied and does not respond to a son's exuberant displays may be internalized as an interaction between the two figures of vivacious child and uninterested mother. Later, as an adult, this son might find that whenever he enthusiastically launches into a display of intellect he has an anxious expectation that his partner won't be interested. His partner picks up this expectation from facial cues and tones of voice and responds accordingly. On the other hand, the son, having internalized both positions (uninterested mother and deflated son), is just as likely to identify with that rejecting mother – in other words, a form of identification with the aggressor. Thus such a person may also be disdainfully unenthusiastic towards his partner's exhibitionistic displays, because, in that moment, he identifies with the uninterested mother in his own original experience.

A further complexity is the way in which we may identify with any member of an internalized family drama, not just oneself as a child. We incarnate our internal archetypal witch-mother or tyrannical father, we switch from being the one who feels victimized to the victimizer. The perceived reactions of any other family members who were present (or absent) will also be incorporated. Various ideas, fantasies and projections onto the reactions and interactions of others are also internalized. This leads to a mass of self-positions and object relations with which we identify and which we replay, giving rise to an extremely convoluted internal drama.

Thus when two such intricate traumatic scenes are superimposed in a marriage, the possible combinations operating simultaneously lead to an almost impossibly complicated marital drama.

Traumatic memory or unconscious fantasy

Interlocking scenes may involve a varied mix of internalizations of traumatic experiences and relational disappointments, defences, shared unconscious fantasies and phantom presences in the relationship. For clarity, I shall now attempt to unpack this somewhat dense array of concepts.

Trauma means shock. As Symington (1993) points out, trauma may refer to any unpredictable experience the child was unprepared for and thus cannot adjust to, which radically alters the structure of inner and outer relations. In other words, the critical traumatizing condition is that the child was not prepared for this event and hence not able to integrate it. The sense of continuity, stability, going-on-being (Winnicott, 1971) is shattered, development arrested.

There is a sense of shock, indignation and profound disappointment when a child's need for recognition is not met. Such was Mimi's repeated disappointment at her father's failure to meet her and affirm her emergence as a young woman.

Another form of shocking experience derives from psychic invasion and possession by unprocessed (sometimes unprocessable) traumatic material from one's ancestors. Such forces may form themselves into sinister alien inner figures manifesting in dreams and scenes as witches, burglars, intruders, ghosts, uncanny presences and 'chimerical monsters' (Grotstein, 1997a). These are the intergenerational phantom presences in the relationship.

'Psychical trauma, or more precisely the memory of it, operates like a foreign body which must still be regarded as a present and effective agent long after it has penetrated' the person's psychic system (Freud and Breuer, 1895/2004, p. 10). Laplanche describes how parents relay 'extra-verbal' messages to the infant that are doubly enigmatic, because they are unconscious to the parents as well as being incomprehensible to the child. What the child can make sense of he or she can 'translate' and thus incorporate; however, there is often still a residue which constitutes an unconscious perception of foreign bodies (Laplanche, 1999, p. 79).

Such messages are triply enigmatic if relayed to the child at a time prior to the development of autobiographical memory and narratives of self, as well as a 'shared interpretive system' (Laplanche, 1999, p. 79). The young child's psychic skin is very permeable at this stage and he or she has no way of sorting out what derives from another source outside his or her own immediate experience. The child's undeveloped mind is being made to act as a receptacle for what could not be contained by the parents.

Thus traumatic scenes can encapsulate an accumulation of layers of traumata, various unexpected, shocking, disappointing, incomprehensible and unaccepted experiences in the early and intergenerational relational matrix.

Fantasies can be seen as defences designed to protect the baby from the dread of disintegration arising from such psychic impingement. They also create hope for a different and better way of being, the determination that things will be different 'when I grow up' or 'when I get married' or, as Mimi's and Steven's immigrating forebears might have said, 'when we get to the new country'.

The content of our fantasies constellates our inner world. Projected out upon those around us they create the entangled unconscious dramas of our relationships. Unconscious fantasy shapes how we internalize difficult experience; external life-experiences and environment affect our fantasies. How we view and hence interact with the world also shapes how the world reacts to us.[10]

We have seen how partners are often inextricably drawn to each other on the basis of their shared unconscious longings, fears, defences and internal conflicts. Loving and hostile feelings are often split, projected into those around us and then re-introjected, giving rise to a layering of projections, internalizations and fantasies.

The fantasies Mimi and Steven brought to the introduction agency were based on a mixture of adolescent fantasies, childhood oedipal longings and much earlier disappointments and traumata, all bundled into the vain hope that the magical fairy-tale ending would eventuate.

A honeymoon cruise

Through therapy we discovered much about the origins of Mimi and Steven's overlapping traumatic scenes and were able to untangle their adult relationship from its grip. Steven proposed and Mimi gratefully accepted

---

10 The self may be inherently interdependent, intersubjective and relational; however, infant research shows that the original infant subject is also an active ideational agent in the creation of his or her relational worlds, not a *tabula rasa*. Overemphasis on a two-person, relational approach can overlook the role of psychic creationism (Grotstein, 2000). Knox suggests that 'wishes, desires, fears' may distort how we experience events and 'also form part of that experience, and so themselves become incorporated into the memories of those events' (Knox, 2003, p. 219).

his hand in marriage. We all hoped it might be 'and they lived happily ever after', but of course life in the marital therapy room is never as straight-forward as a fairy-tale ending.

Mimi rang a few months after getting married saying they were having difficulties in the form of a repeating pattern of rows: could they come back for some more therapy?

At our first therapeutic reunion Mimi launched right in:

> We went to the Great Barrier Reef for our honeymoon. It was meant to be so perfect, but it was a horror show. I could just hear my mother's mocking voice – No man will put up with you! – ringing in my ears, like she had her revenge. Steven's doctor told him he should swim in the sea to help his psoriasis, so a scuba-diving cruise on the Great Barrier Reef seemed just the thing. Well, we went on this wonderful boat trip but when it came to jumping into the water he got cold feet! I said, 'For goodness sake, we came all this way, just get in.' It's like he sees me as this nag and I'm just trying to help.

We mused on what might be going on. Mimi reflected, 'I guess on one level I can understand his reluctance to get in. I remember when I was a kid my mother was forever on my back to do things that were supposedly good for me. I remember swimming lessons when she'd constantly badger me, "in you go!" and I felt so hassled I'd just sit on the edge saying, "No, it's too crowded" . . .'

At that moment Mimi clapped her hands to her mouth and exclaimed, 'Oh my God, I must have seemed like my mother!'

'So when you saw Steven sitting there, reluctant to dive in, it was like he was you as a child, sitting on the side, and you were your mother cajoling you into doing something "good for you"?'

'How ghastly! I know how sometimes I make him into my bad mother, but how could I ever end up acting like that nag-hag?'

Even more alarming was Mimi's realization that the puppet master behind this script was an internal saboteur ensuring she never escaped her intergenerational familial system, preventing her finding the intimacy she so longed for, but had never before experienced.

In this incident Mimi became the mouthpiece for an internalized 'nag-hag' while Steven became the young Mimi who did not want to jump into the pool – a role he could identify with due to parallel issues in his own history.

Steven also became conscripted into playing the role of her father. He had been sitting on the deck gazing contentedly out to sea when Mimi approached to cajole him into the water. Abruptly woken from his day-dream, he suddenly snapped and furiously retorted, 'Oh go take a running jump yourself, back into your own little world.' She beat a hasty retreat to her cabin to lick the wounds of her hurt pride, just as she had as a girl when her father humiliated and belittled her.

All the while Steven was caught up in his own scene. When Mimi told him to get into the water he heard his father yelling at him to get back onto the sporting field when he had been injured and the other children made him a laughing stock. He snapped suddenly into the role of the aggressor, incarnating his father's voice, unwittingly simultaneously being the mouthpiece for her father's voice.

The distant echoes of other voices, on another boat, also reverberated down the corridors of time, relayed from father to son, but this link in a longer chain of intergenerational transmission only emerged much later.

Two totally different scenes were thus simultaneously enacted with manifold roles for each player. Steven identified with and played out both Mimi and himself as a child. Mimi incarnated both her nagging mother and his domineering father. Steven wore the mask of Mimi's preoccupied father staring into space, then enacted her father's demeaning retorts, concurrently switching from the intimidated boy to his autocratic father . . . and so it went on and back.

Mimi and Steven, on their honeymoon in a boat, were transported backwards, to scenes of childhood and earlier, as Steven's and Mimi's families were also transported on their respective vessels to a new future in Australia.

Phantom presences and the malevolent third

We have seen how in couple psychotherapy there are variable transferential and countertransferential foci, different depths of field. There are the two partners, the complex networks and dynamics of relations between them, and the relationship itself, which creates a fluid, interpenetrating and interactive field, the intersubjective marital third. This is revealed by the communications of the individuals, but controlled by neither. It is within this complex of interactions that the work of couple psychotherapy occurs.

A couple might report in therapy how they had a row during the previous week. As they relate the story, it sparks the system and they get locked into yet another re-enactment of the scene before the eyes of the therapist. The difficulty is that once this system is in full swing there is little possibility for any reflection on what might be going on. They are, as it were, possessed by the complex. However, the containment and safety of the therapeutic space, as well as the therapist's capacity and willingness to stand such unprocessed material – to ponder it, experience its re-enactments, digest and reflect on it – enable the couple to feel some reassurance that all this is not so unspeakably dreadful that it cannot be thought about. This alleviates anxiety so that things can be slowed down rather than escalating.

New little inklings begin to penetrate the psychotic chambers. However, in working with interlocking traumatic scenes an additional sinister force or presence seems to be at work. The moment a breakthrough to a new possibility of understanding and hence intimacy is imminent, it raises its ugly head, re-enforcing the deadlock of the malignant inter-relational system. I call this contrary element 'the malevolent third'.[11]

In dealing with interlocking traumatic scenes, therapists need to remember that they are not just speaking to the patient's conscious parts but to various malevolent phantoms in the relationship that vociferously defend against consciousness and change. I am reminded of Fraiberg *et al.*'s (1975) 'ghosts in the nursery', the vestiges of the parents' unremembered and unredeemed past, transmitted as if by possession to their offspring.

Such phantoms haunt both the adult relationship and the analytic space. In the complex transference–countertransference play it is hard at times to know who is the therapist, who the child, who the malignant witch or bullying tyrant. In the incident above, the moment I made a humble observation about Mimi's mother it was as if a witch-like character incarnated herself in the room and she screeched at me in a spine-chillingly sarcastic voice, 'Oh aren't we the clever one, you with all your oh-so-brilliant observations. Well, you just have no idea do you, what a honeymoon might feel like, you dried up old prune', muttering under her breath, 'same old . . . same old . . .'

Such expressions as 'same old' are indicators that an intralocking scene based on a traumatic memory system has been re-constellated, with its repetitiveness, invariance and arrested time-frame. Within its confines nothing seems to change or get better, nothing shifts or transforms. The activation of an intralocking traumatic scene in the couple has definite telltale signs: 'It's utterly useless, we just go round and round in the same old argument. It never gets better, we're just crap communicators.' Traumatic memory systems, as we have seen, are arrested in time, existing in an eternal past-in-the-present, like a psychotic pocket. Other signs are a ghostly, unreal, dark and highly charged, persecutory atmosphere, a sense that we have been taken over by some menacing emotional force we don't understand, feeling possessed, under the influence of confusing emotional forces

---

11 The malevolent third could be compared to Ogden's (1994) 'subjugating third', transposed into the arena of couple work involving an interlocking scene. Using Grotstein's evocative language, it is formed by 'mutual unconscious transprojective identifications' of both parties into a third area. 'This new invisible entity is felt by its creators to have taken on a life of its own, one that omnipotently' possesses and controls each partner – and, at times, the therapist. The couple are 'therefore unwitting "ventriloquists" for this mythic, preternatural homunculus' (Grotstein, 2000, p. 114).

that are overpowering. The level of affect is way out of proportion to the situation. We know we are over-reacting terribly but not why.

The following incident, which occurred several months later, shows how the marital analytic third as the agent of transformation is in combat with the power of the malevolent third.

The bookshelf: intergenerational matters and the malevolent third

Mimi and Steven wanted to renovate their marital home. They related to me how the previous Saturday the 'game-plan' had been to paint 'just one wall' of the front room, which meant 'simply emptying a bookshelf', before enjoying a rewarding afternoon tea at their favourite café, or so they optimistically thought.

'Such a minor task', said Mimi, 'but what a scene it brought on! We both recognized something was being stirred up without knowing quite what, we'd look at each other and think of you and we'd take a break, so as to tackle the job from another angle . . .'

Here there was some indication of 'borrowed containment' (Colman, 1993) being incorporated into their relationship, as well as the growth of a reflective capacity, as symbolized by the figure of the therapist.

Mimi went on, 'but what was so weird was that as soon as one of us backed off, the other would start up again. It almost felt like some sinister third party was directing us!'

This 'sinister third party' is the malignant third, the nefarious hidden director of the interlocking scene. This is experienced as having its own autonomy, like Jung's traumatic complex, which 'forces itself tyrannically upon the conscious mind. The explosion of affect is a complete invasion of the individual, it pounces upon him like an enemy or a wild animal' (Jung, 1928/1966c, pp. 131–132). Although either party may be its 'ventriloquist', it helps the couple to see the shared nature of what has been co-created and co-maintained if we de-identify the one who is its mouthpiece at a given time. Both parties (if not also the therapist) are the tyrannized victims of this destructive force. Further, the malignant third has the effect of reinstating the destructive relational patterns just at the junctures where change is possible. The very tools of therapeutic change and mutative insights can be turned into weapons to attack each other.

What followed from this was a concatenation of cues triggering Mimi and Steven's respective systems.

For Mimi, the bookcase conjured up a vision of a little girl looking up at a wall of books in a foreign language that she was meant to master. She started piling all the books as fast as she could onto the floor. Steven threw up his hands in horror, 'Wait a minute, don't just dump them like that, you'll damage them, you need to keep them in order!'

Unbeknown to Steven, an intergenerational traumatic memory had been triggered. He saw not only Mimi but a shadowy flashback of an officer throwing books on the ground.

The expression 'keep them in order' triggered Mimi's memories of her mother's insistence on an overly ordered studious existence. She stormed off in a huff and they didn't speak to each other until this next session.

Negative capability and the conjoint selected fact

I mused aloud, 'I wonder what books might have meant for you growing up'.

'Well', said Mimi, 'the first thing my mother ever thrust into my hand as a baby was a book. I dropped it. She picked it up and put it back in my hand over and over again until several years later I could begin to read it.'

Steven said that adventure stories were his way of escaping his father's rages into an imagined place of safety. 'I loved "Biggles" books. But my father would just grab the book out of my hand and hurl it across the room and as the book fell it broke the spine and I felt he had broken my spine.'

Thinking it over in therapy, Mimi suddenly had a very moving insight. She realized that the wall of books may have reminded Steven of all his family had been deprived of. Mimi leant over and gently touched Steven on the arm.

'Oh Steven, your parents came to Australia without a thing to their name. Perhaps the bookcase reminds you of everything you were deprived of?'

'That's it! You've hit the nail on the head', Steven replied, so touched that tears came to his eyes, which he hurriedly wiped away.

Steven's ancestors were Lithuanian. His parents met as teenagers on the boat that brought them to Australia in 1948. They eschewed all that reminded them of their background. The topic was a closed book.

Both the scene on the boat and the fight about the bookcase signified an intergenerational component of which both Steven and Mimi were not at first aware. It was long after beginning couple therapy that Steven began to intuit links with intergenerational elements affecting his life through a trail of clues. Steven had been brought up oblivious to his Jewish heritage and to the horrendous history his parents had escaped and survived. His grandfather, he discovered, had been a *shleger* or strongman in the Jewish police. His father survived due to youthful teenage cunning and agility. Steven's father's emphasis on Steven's being a strong able-bodied sportsman made new sense, as both unconscious identification with his father and an overwhelming paternal protective impulse. To be strong was to survive.

Mimi's insight was an instance of the mutative process when someone makes a link which transforms the trauma into something that can be jointly mourned and held. One might call it a 'selected fact' (Poincaré, 1952) where, in a previously fragmented, whirling chaos of unprocessed beta elements, there is a dawning of insight which brings coherence and meaning to the whole.

I posit a 'conjoint selected fact' in the case of unlocking the gridlock of an interlocking traumatic scene. Mimi and Steven realized that books had an essential symbolic meaning in both their respective histories (two individual selected facts). But what books signified for each was very different. 'Oh my God, so the central fact for you, Mimi, is having a book thrust into your hand, whereas for me, it's having it grabbed out of my hand!' said Steven. Yet it was not only realizing the meaning which books had for each that helped unlock the system, but the fact that both parties could see both meanings simultaneously. The word 'conjoint' refers to the third thing created by the combination of the two individual selected facts. It is related to the intersubjective marital third.

There is often considerable pressure on the therapist to alleviate the terrible dreads and anxieties by relying on premature solutions. As the therapist, or either partner, gains insight into what is going on in an individual system, there is a tendency to seize this as a sure sign that everything is now solved. All too often one partner 'sees exactly' what is going on in the other's unconscious or family 'dysfunctional behaviour', but not their own, and will be quick to pip the therapist at the post. As therapy progresses and reflective capacity increases, they may even have some inkling of what is indeed going on and where it comes from for them. But it is not until such time one has have got to the heart of what is going on in each and in both – the system of each person, their interlocking system, in other words a central conjoint 'selected fact' – that the therapist or either partner is in a position to make a mutative interpretation.

The conjoint selected fact thus refers to those hard-won moments when the therapeutic trio finally understands a central element, a key organizing principle or symbol in each person's system, each person's history, as well as how this dovetails into the marital dynamics and has a double meaning in each person's psyche. There is an extraordinary sense of relief, an 'aha!' experience which dissolves the glue that sticks the system together. Thence one is able to begin to dismantle the structural prison because we have made the necessary links of recognition and understanding.

Here we also see how defensive and developmental aspects of choice go hand in hand in the auditioning of a partner to play a role in one's intralocking scene, and how at the heart of a repetition compulsion lies the kernel of truth waiting to be disclosed. A selected fact lies at the heart of every repetition compulsion. In the couple the repetition compulsions of each are superimposed to form an interpersonal interlocking scene. A conjoint selected fact lies at the heart of every interlocking scene.

Second order interlocking scenes: the role of 'memory'

Even when a couple have gained understanding of their interlocking dynamics they may find the scene reiterates itself in a new form – a second order interlocking scene. In a second order iteration a partner will defensively expect their partner to behave according to script even when this partner is 'bending over backwards' not to. Further, the prejudiced partner may interpret any look, gesture, silence or action on behalf of the judged partner as typical even when it is different. Partners nurse their grievances like treasured possessions, holding onto the grudges they bear, wanting some undefined degree of recompense before allowing things to move on. Psychological change is incremental, subtle and often invisible, given it often relates to how a partner is thinking and feeling which cannot be directly observed or known.

Unto the third or even the fourth generation

In couple therapy there are four layers of history that need to be taken into account: relational dynamics operating in the here-and-now; the history of the couple's relationship, with all its joyful memories as well as the myriad slights, misunderstandings and disagreements; the history of each partner's family of origin; and intergenerational matters.

Interlocking traumatic scenes can function as conduits for the transmission of walled-off chambers of horror deriving from trauma suffered by ancestors, which were previously incomprehensible and unspeakable (Pickering, 2002). The word 'unspeakable', Wajnryb observes, indicates the sense that such matters are so terrible and unthinkable that words can never do justice to the enormity of the experience, as if serving to contain that which is not confinable. Yet to not speak perpetuates the sense of isolation and alienation between survivors and 'the unmarked' (Wajnryb, 2001, p. 107). Steven said, 'There was always a cloud of secrecy and a sense of there being more to it all, which permeated my childhood.' As the hidden, broken fragments of this history gradually became coherent and could be spoken about, it opened a door of understanding between Steven and Mimi. Mimi's own ancestors also had firsthand experience of the horrors of imprisonment, war and dislocation. So often, when we penetrate to the heart of the interlocking scene, an uncanny concordance between the different intralocking scenes of each partner is revealed.

It is often the children of survivors of trauma who are unconsciously driven to enter therapy by the need to uncover and piece together an ancestral and cultural history, before the stories and the keys to comprehending what they carry die with their forebears. Such material will haunt the marital and family dynamics of the next generation until it is uncovered and worked through.

The therapeutic work, then, is to sift through the unredeemed wounds of the past, transmitted into current interactions, distinguishing them from the present relationship. The current partner often protests that no matter how much reassurance they give, how much they try to be there for the other, it can never be enough, because the deeds have been done and can't now be undone by another person. Yet the past exists in present memory and having another stand beside you in an act of *memoria* can ameliorate if not undo the effects of the facticity of irreversible events.

> History is amoral: events occurred. But memory is moral; what we consciously remember is what our conscience remembers. History is the Totenbuch, The Book of the Dead . . . Memory is the Memorbucher, the names of those to be mourned, read aloud in the synagogue.
>
> (Michaels, 1996, p. 138)

Summary of therapeutic interventions

I will now summarize the progression of therapeutic interventions aimed at deconstructing the interlocking traumatic scene:

- Retelling a recent conflict during a therapy session tends to constellate the traumatic complexes, often leading to a re-enactment of the interlocking traumatic scene in the consulting room.
- The role of therapist represents a reflexive capacity that gradually becomes incorporated into the couple's system and ability to seek understanding of what goes on. This adds a new element, the intersubjective analytic third.
- The iterations and reiterations of the system now contain an incorporated reflective element. When these incidents occur, the couple are beginning to be able to ask themselves, 'what is going on here?', but at the same time they are able to suspend judgement or premature understandings.
- In retelling the incident to the therapist in an atmosphere of reflection and non-defensiveness we can begin to unpack the intricacies of what occurred still further until such time as a conjoint selected fact emerges.
- However, moments of revelation are all too often followed by a turning back, a reinstatement of the gridlock of the system, which is often experienced as occurring under the operation of a third destructive force in competition with the analytic third, the malignant third.
- It is only when we have found the central selected fact in each individual case as well as the conjoint selected fact that we can really begin to disentangle the system.
- The couple themselves begin to recognize the triggers, catch the complex in the moment of its constellation, and then can back out.

- This backing out is a moment-by-moment transition. If either one 'loses it', reverts to script or 'back-slides', then the system will get the upper hand again and be reinstated.
- Expressions such as 'here we go again' indicate a conscious recognition of being drawn back into the system, which in turn indicates the incorporation of reflective function.

Conclusion

There is a common united thread running through five psychic factors concerning the interlocking scene: trauma as various shocks and disappointments; fantasy as necessary defences and management of these traumas; malignant dowries as encapsulating these defences; disturbing malevolent thirds; and intergenerational phantom presences which infiltrate the adult relationship.

In a sense one could see the therapist as an anti-director, working against the malevolent third which is the hidden, ghostly, but potent director of the play. The ghastly pyrotechnics of the destructive dynamics exert at times a fascinating and addictive power, and safer because familiar and predictable.

Couples need to develop faith in the incremental nature of change which is about moment-by-moment alive responses. Such fluid states of improvised interactions are enhanced when defensive anxiety is relieved via the 'borrowed' containment of the consulting room and therapist which gives one the sense all can be slowed down and thought about.

True intimacy is improvisatory rather than over-rehearsed. It is about responding rather than reacting to one another as we are, in this moment, here and now, not as any ghostly phantom, and not according to predetermined expectations, entrenched interlocking scripts and stale memories.

Not all shocks are traumatic or dramatic. Some are life-enhancing surprises, such as when we are startled by the revelation of the unmasked beloved.

Chapter 10

A hall of mirrors

He that cannot chuse but love,
And strives against it still,
Never shall my fancy move;
For he loves 'gaynst his will; . . .

Is there then no kinde of men
whom I may freely prove?
I will vent that humour then
In my owne selfe love
          John Donne, 'Selfe Love', 1650–1669

Narcissism has been explored in psychoanalytic literature from a variety of perspectives. My focus is the hall of mirrors as reflecting surfaces obscuring Echo and Narcissus from each other. These two characters are personifications of narcissistic intra-relational (if not anti-relational) systems that are antithetical to exogamous modes of loving based on alterity and empathy. They feature an intralocking chemistry of connection and non-connection. Narcissus displays a desperate need for recognition coupled with fear of emotional entanglement. He wants to be seen but does not want to see. Echo, who is both an echo chamber and a seer, does not feel seen. She yearns to be acknowledged and embraced because she feels invisible and insubstantial. Gazing at the glassy surface of a pool, Narcissus yearns to pluck out and recover his lost love. Mistaking reflection for depth, he never reaches through to find what lies beneath the empty illusion. Fatally stuck in his disappointment, he never discovers that the river itself could surprise him with its lively variety and depth.

Narcissism involves a form of object relating built on projections and denials in which the partner is not related to as an Other but merely as a reflecting surface for projections of an idealized self-image. Narcissism is object-relational rather than subject-relational due to the inability to apprehend the other's alterior reality and personhood. There is a longing for an other, but one who is merely a reflection, an extension of oneself, a servant, a function, a role, without a mind of his or her own.

Behind a narcissist's apparent disdain for the subjectivity of the other there often lurks a fear of the unpredictability and three-dimensionality of the other's alterity. Such intolerance of alterity masks a terror of the reality and independent existence of the other. Real human others don't behave according to plan. They are not like mirror images that do our bidding, but jump out of the mirror and grab hold of us, or disappear out of sight.

Echo forms two reflective functions: echo and mirror, auditory and visual. Echo must repeat back parrot fashion Narcissus' monologue so that Narcissus feels heard; she must mirror his every gesture so he feels real. If she is a perfectly attuned, mirroring selfobject she may remain in Narcissus' orbit, for a while.

> So did he fall in love with his own creation? . . . If love, as some assert, is a purely self-referring business, if the object of love is finally unimportant because what lovers value are their own emotions, then what more appropriate circularity than for a dramatist to fall in love with his own creation? Who needs the interference of the real person, the real *her* beneath the sunlight, the lamplight, the heartlight?
>
> (Barnes, 2004, p. 89)

Yet, as the myth tells us, narcissism always takes place within a relational context. Other people are involved – his mother Liriope, the nymph Echo who adhered to him like a shadow, his suitor Ameinius who killed himself on Narcissus' sword, and a string of other admirers who were strewn like wilted flowers in the path of his cold-blooded rejection. It is the inter-relational aspects of narcissism I am interested in exploring here.

The gaze of a narcissist is fixated upon the injury of not being beheld in the loving lights emanating from the gaze of mother's eyes. To what degree this was because there was an early absence of such beholding, to what extent the narcissist imagined such lack, the net result is a feeling of being a 'reject'. The narcissist then launches himself into being one who rejects: he rejects the vulnerable part of himself that once felt so hurt. This vulnerable inner representation of self becomes projected onto others who show any need or desire. In narcissism we have a relational dynamic of rejecter–rejected. To enter such a dynamic, those on the receiving end of his cold-blooded rejection often have inverted narcissistic hooks in their own psychic make-up. It is thus a narcissistic dyad, an intra-relational system, that we are speaking about.

Narcissus projects an air of superiority while feeling desolately empty and insubstantial inside. Grandiose phantasies compensate for the sense of inner emptiness. In searching for a love object the choice may be based on what one lacks, as if by finding that quality in another one will at last become complete. Another form is seeking a mirror. As Kristeva puts it, the mode of relating for the narcissist is often one in which: 'Its Highness the Ego projects and glorifies itself, or else shatters into pieces and is engulfed, when it admires itself in the mirror of an idealized Other – sublime, incomparable, as worthy (of Me?)' (Kristeva, 1983/1987, p. 6).

Identification, looking for someone just like me (someone just like how I would like to be), is a common dynamic in narcissistic object-choice. The attempt to construct a perfect other half is an avoidance of love, for the other person is no longer 'someone else'. The implicit denial of separation might seem like union but there can be no union where there are not two separate and different persons to be united. A tell-tale sign is the unspoken demand for understanding, without taking the effort to bridge the gulf, to find ways to communicate, the idea that 'if he loved me truly he would know what I want without my having to tell him'. This is a regressive wish deriving from pre-verbal infantile life where mother was to intuit our non-verbally communicated needs.

In intimate relationships we find an oscillating tension between narcissistic and exogamous modes of relating, similar to the ways in which one moves from the paranoid-schizoid to the depressive position, but this is never fully realized and has to be continually re-negotiated. This is a theme amplified by Fisher (1999). Bion (1992) posited a narcissism–socialism tension similar to the Ps↔D.

The pathology of narcissism lies in its denial of intersubjectivity and interdependence. The self-absorption and self-worship displayed by narcissists is viewed by many psychoanalysts as deriving from being fixated on a primary state of self-containment or as a defence structure which arises when the early environment has failed, leading to a lack of healthy self-esteem and sense of being intrinsically lovable. Other characteristics of narcissism are an aloofness, a ruthless exploitation of others, and delusions of omnipotence and grandiosity which compensate for an underlying sense of futility and emptiness. Narcissists are easily injured, this leading to both narcissistic rage at the separate life of others and emotional withdrawal into a non-relational but brittle cocoon.

The narcissist's fear of alterity precludes a 'face-to-face' ethical stance. The autonomy of others, their emotional worlds and demands are experienced as being too frightening and dangerous. At the same time others are needed to fend off loneliness, so one narcissistic solution is to turn the other into an extension of self, a selfobject.

This has its roots in a state in infantile development where a sense of perfect fit and nondifferentiation between mother and child is developmentally appropriate. This includes a need for highly attuned responsiveness and the ability of the mother to intuit the baby's needs without verbal communication. Furthermore, the development of a sense of self depends on being seen and mirrored. As Winnicott described it, 'the mother is looking at the baby and *what she looks like reflects what she sees there*' (Winnicott, 1971, p. 131). When the baby looks at the mother's face he sees not the mother in her own right but himself reflected in her expression, in the gleam in her eye. The capacity for self-reflection grows out of having one's own being and nature reflected back by a loving other, who responds with empathy, acceptance, understanding and appreciation of the child's different authentic self.

Taken into adulthood, due to the failure of this developmental stage to be superseded by a more subject-to-subject one, a need for perfect attunement creates major obstacles to those qualities of genuine loving, such as mutual interest, care, concern and appreciation of each other's multi-dimensionality, necessary for mature, sustained and fulfilling relations.

Psychoanalytic theories of narcissism: paradise lost or cramped quarters?

The philosophical debate as to whether self is initially autonomous or intersubjective is echoed in psychoanalytic history. Psychoanalytic theories of narcissism are divided on their conceptualization as to whether uterine life is intra- or inter-uterine. There are those that view the aboriginal self as inherently self-maintaining and non-relational, and those that posit the original self as relational and aware of its connection with its uterine environment. If the original state is seen as being one of sublime self-containment, then contact with the external world of relations with others at birth is equated with disintegration and threat to this perfect autonomy and unity. If inter-uterine life is seen as already conditioned by contact with the uterine environment in the mother's womb, then there is no such original state of pristine isolation. Theorists of this persuasion argue that the foetus is already aware of feeling impinged upon and cramped, aware of sounds and vibrations. From the beginning the internal and external worlds interpenetrate. Another conception predicated on a concept of original unity is that of symbiotic union with mother. According to these views later love relations represent a desire to reunite with feelings of oceanic bliss, whether the bliss of fusion with mother, or the bliss of self-sufficiency.

Just as both intersubjectivity and alterity theory refute the solipsistic position, object relations and relational theorists reject the idea of primary narcissism, viewing the primary state as relational. Narcissism is a secondary phenomenon caused by failures of early relationships, which may include a failure to provide the child with a (necessary) illusion of a symbiotic union and perfect fit.

Narcissism often covers over grief and loss of a vital connection with another. In 'Mourning and melancholia' (1917/1984d) Freud analyses the psychogenesis of one form of narcissistic sado-masochistic relations, which manifest both internally and inter-relationally. Melancholia, as distinct from true mourning, is based on an inability to tolerate the mixture of painful and negative feelings evoked by loss through death or separation. A chain of emotional reactions occurs. Ambivalent feelings towards the other evoke anger in response to the hurt for dying which is experienced as a form of abandonment. This anger is turned away from the person who died and turned in on our self. We blame ourselves for destroying the other who is retained as an ideal, all-good object. At the same time that we preserve the lost object as an ideal we see ourselves as good because we are preserving the object. What is also being avoided is recognition that we have lost not just an object, but a relationship with its unpredictable mixture of ups and downs, goods and bads. The unconscious image and idea of the lost beloved, who becomes an internalized object, is split into the idealized and the denigrated parts. To preserve the idealized object, the ego takes on, becomes and is felt to be 'all bad', the lost object is 'all good'.

Thus the memory of the loved one (the 'shadow of the object') falls upon the ego in such a way that the ego ideal is identified with the lost object, the ego with one's own difficult feelings. Sadism is projected onto the ego, expressed by a self-reproach for the lost object, as if the mourner willed it to occur. Mourning, as distinct from melancholia, concerns the incorporation of mixed feelings about the other who died, remembering the whole relationship in all its complexity. Such ambivalent mourning explains the melancholia of Orpheus who realizes he is responsible for Eurydice's demise.

Ambivalence in love relationships becomes expressed as self-reproaches, as if the mourner has willed it. Hate comes into operation, deriving sadistic satisfaction from one's suffering: hence one is open to dismemberment and pernicious attack (such as one could interpret the dismemberment of Orpheus by the Maenads).

The erotic connection to the external person undergoes a double vicissitude: one part regresses to narcissistic identification; the other part, under the influence of ambivalence, becomes sadistic. Sadism explains the suicidal impulse of the melancholic: the ego treats itself as an object that can be pleasurably and pseudo-potently destroyed. This is a repetition of (and therefore sense of power over) the lost object relationship. Symington (1993) takes this distinction to flesh out the dialectic between those who forswear and those who choose to remain connected to the 'lifegiver': whether one deals with traumata of narcissistic injuries by surrender to an internal malevolent saboteur, or whether one maintains a sense of faith, and holds onto the gift of life personified as the lifegiver. This lifegiver is connected with a 'primordial object' such as the mother who is able to transmit liveliness and metabolize her child's anxiety. This life-giving mother is contrasted with its opposite: the 'dead mother' whose emptiness is taken in by the child who really expected nourishing love.

Klein, who saw narcissism as an omnipotent denial of dependence, distinguished narcissistic states and narcissistic object relations. Narcissistic states refer to the situation where 'the ego-ideal is projected into another person, this person becomes predominantly loved and admired because he contains the good parts of the self' (Klein, 1946/1992a, p. 13). Narcissistic object relations are connected with a pre-verbal relational modality involving projective identification, whereby disturbing envious and aggressive aspects are projected into the object via projective identification: 'the relation to another person on the basis of projecting bad parts of the self into him is of a narcissistic nature, because in this case as well, the object strongly represents one part of the self' (1946, p. 13).

Balint, Winnicott, Fairbairn, Bowlby and Fordham are among the theorists who emphasized the original self as inherently interdependent and relational. They connect both what the child brings of his own personality into his relational universe, and also the contribution made by the real mother and by early environmental factors.

Balint (1952) replaced Freud's concept of primary narcissism with his concept of 'primary love' or 'primary object-love'. Balint's self is interdependent, intersubjective and inter-relational, the baby coming into the world actively loving the mother and seeking a harmonious relationship with her. The attributes of narcissism such as oral sadism, aggression, envy and mistrust, described by the Kleinians, were, according to Balint, secondary reactions to a primary need for love, harmony and physical contact not being met.

Fordham's model of the self encompasses both unity and interdependence, as well as both passivity and activity. For Fordham the primary self is a primary integrate. This self, or self-process, is, however, intrinsically relational in that it is programmed to go out and meet with the environment and with others. Such meeting (what Bion would call mating) brings a temporary state of de-integration, until such time as it can re-integrate these new elements of experience into its system (Fordham, 1957, p. 127).

Ledermann has taken Fordham's theory of integration–deintegration into the area of narcissism. Arrogance, aloofness, grandiosity and pseudo-independence are defences against the terror of the sense of emptiness and fear of non-existence such emptiness gives rise to. Healthy interdependence is replaced by pseudo-independence. Not feeling loved, a narcissist cannot develop the capacity to love (Ledermann, 1986, p. 24).

Kohut's selfobject and marriage

Kohut (1984) depathologized narcissism, arguing for a place for 'healthy narcissism'[1] throughout life. Kohut believed that needs for mutual, self-esteem-enhancing mirroring and idealization, or what he called selfobject needs, are part of a healthy marriage. Each partner might need to use the

---

1 Symington comments that often what theorists mean by 'positive narcissism' is not narcissism at all but self-esteem or self-confidence (Symington, 1993, p. 8).

other partner at different times as a selfobject in order to regain a sense of cohesion.

However, my point is that if the primary mode of relating to one's partner is as a selfobject, this becomes not only limiting for the partner, whose only function is as 'mirror', not person in their own right, but it constitutes a narcissistic object relationship. One could also consider whether it is the partner or the relationship that is providing selfobject experiences – the other as selfobject or the relationship as selfobject.

Thick- and thin-skinned narcissism

I apply Rosenfeld's theory of thick- and thin-skinned narcissism to inter-locking narcissistic scenes. A particular form of intralocking narcissistic scene occurs when a thick-skinned narcissist hooks up with a thin-skinned one, which is almost as common as the combination of preoccupied persuers with dismissively avoidant individuals. Thick-skinned narcissists, according to Rosenfeld, are those whose narcissistic structure provides a 'thick skin' that renders them insensitive to deeper feelings. They take the world in their stride and criticism seems to bounce off them like water off a duck's back. Thin-skinned patients are hyper-sensitive, easily hurt in everyday life as well as therapy (Rosenfeld, 1987, p. 274). Britton points out that inside every thick-skinned narcissist is a thin-skinned one trying to get out and vice versa.

Rosenfeld emphasizes the denial of the separate identity of the object as a defence against the pain of separation and dependence, as well as the resultant envy such dependence stimulates:

> Dependence on an object implies love for and recognition of the value of the object, which . . . stimulates envy, when the goodness of the object is recognized. The omnipotent narcissistic object relations there-fore, obviate both the aggressive feelings caused by the frustration and any awareness of envy.
>
> (Rosenfeld, 1964, p. 333)

Rosenfeld uses various metaphors to describe the destructive aspect of narcissism which are similar to what I describe as the 'malignant third': 'a Nazi-like structure, a delinquent organisation, a gang . . .'; and his approach is to help the patient become aware of this internal attacking force which prevents the patient from 'thinking and observing what is going on' (Rosenfeld, 1987, p. 90).

In couples relations thin-skinned and thick-skinned narcissists often seek each other out. They see in the other their reversed inner state. At the unconscious level the situation is in fact reversed: the rhinoceros hide protects an extremely tender, soft, sensitive inside, and the sensitive person is often very thick-skinned in regard to their treatment of others. Thin-skinned people often say the most brutally cutting things about their thick-skinned partner without realizing it, since, like most narcissists, they are only really aware of how easily hurt they themselves are, not the effect their reactions have on others. There can be a despotic aspect to such over-sensitivity. As C. S. Lewis said, 'what is commonly called "Sensitiveness" is the most powerful engine of domestic tyranny, sometimes a lifelong tyranny'.

> Did we pretend to be 'hurt' in our sensitive and tender feelings when envy, ungratified vanity, or thwarted self-will was our real trouble? Such tactics often succeed . . . and so we win: by cheating.
>
> (Lewis, as cited in Sibley, 1985, p. 129)

Case vignette: 'Annette and Bruce'

'Annette' initially consulted me about separating from her husband 'Bruce' whom she described as a loud-mouthed oaf who verbally and physically abused her. Annette was very thin-skinned. I had a sense of a baby being born into a world with skin so thin that she found the very swaddling clothes that wrapped her rough and prickly. This suggested a maternal mismatch where mother was felt to rough-handle her as a baby. She described her partner's numerous failings with pursed lips and a sense of great moral indignation.

Bruce presented as someone who took things in his stride, laughed things off, but underneath this jocular veneer I sensed someone shy, insecure and sensitive. When he heard her descriptions of his 'abuse' he was utterly mortified as if he couldn't believe his ears. What for him was merely an affectionate placing of his hand on her back was cause for accusations of sexual abuse. Putting the sugar spoon in the sugar bowl without drying it properly was experienced by her as a soiling of herself, as if she were the sugar.

Annette wanted to be the apple of her father's eye. She hated her mother who was seen as malignantly deliberately misunderstanding. She did everything to be father's favoured son, to win his affection. But when her brother was born, her place beside him was taken from her and she could never get over the fury this evoked.

Unlike Annette, Bruce was the apple of his mother's eye. He could do no wrong in his mother's estimation. He certainly could in Annette's: she seemed driven by a mission to pull him down a peg or three. She was attracted to him because he had the qualities she wanted so much to have herself, but bitterly resented his monopoly of them.

Annette could not tolerate any interpretation directed at the relationship rather than just a perfectly attuned mirroring of her subjective experience.

Any attempt to address the shared issues, however sensitively phrased, was like having an objectifying persecutory interpretation shoved down her throat. It seemed impossible to say anything which did not hurt, however softly murmured. I felt reduced to uttering soft maternal soothing 'ahs'.

Couple therapy for such thin-skinned patients is inherently disjunctive. Frozen at a very dyadic 'one-to-one', rather than triadic, stage of development, they are not capable of tolerating the various relationships of thirdness, the subjective feelings and reality of their partner, or an observation addressing the relationship itself. The therapist may feel torn between the thin-skinned patient's expectation for perfectly attuned empathic response from the therapist and the role as couple therapist whose task is to tend to the relationship-as-patient. If one attunes to the thin-skinned partner then the other partner has, *ipso facto*, been alienated and left out of a maternal dyad, as if to become 'father'. If one tends to the relationship-as-patient, the thin-skinned patient may feel alienated by the objectivity of this intruding third.

Britton sees the states of thin-skin and thick-skin narcissism as the result of two different relationships of 'the subjective self with the third object within the internal oedipus situation' (Britton, 1998, p. 46). In therapy this can manifest in the following ways: if the analyst attunes herself to the subjective feelings of the patient she will be identified as an understanding maternal selfobject. If the analyst offers an interpretation, she will be identified as persecutory and objectifying. The triangulating structure of couple therapy tends to *ipso facto* create this set-up with narcissistic couples. Often the thin-skinned partner will complain, 'my individual therapist understands me, you don't', because the couple therapist is seen as an objectifying third observing the couple rather than as a dyadic empathic selfobject for the individual.

Britton also differentiates three forms of narcissism. Firstly, clinical narcissism entails self-preoccupation and turning away from relations with others. Secondly, narcissism may involve 'an innate tendency within the personality which opposes relationships outside the self' (Britton, 2004, p. 478). Thirdly, narcissism refers to personality disorders. Britton further notes that narcissism may be alternatively seen as a defence against painful relationships or hostility towards object relations.

The narcissistic intralocking traumatic scene

People involved in a narcissistic relationship ostensibly play out a dyadic drama, but it contains two monads, and is not truly intersubjective. They share in common the fact of their being locked inside themselves. There is no room for the other person to enter the system except as a fantasy object. They are each caught in a narcissistic intralocking traumatic scene. What distinguishes it from the interlocking traumatic scene is that the narcissistic system is so non-relational as a modality as to make it *intra-* rather than inter-relational: 'intralocking' meaning the imprisonment of an intrapersonal fixed system of non-relating; 'traumatic scene ' as in a scripted, repetitive story.

If we consider the scene in which Narcissus looks at his reflection in the water, there are three aspects: Narcissus, the reflecting surface and his reflection. The mirror is itself clear. It has properties such as being a reflecting surface in which one can see the reflection of form and colours, but in itself it is not those forms or colours. When applied to narcissistic relations we have two people and a reflective mechanism at work. One presents to the other a reflection of that other: the admirer admires, but the admirer is not usually admired in return. Yet the admired is dependent upon there being an admirer to feel admired. If there is no mirror then there is no image of self. The narcissist is dependent upon having admirers, yet repudiates any such sense of need. The mirror in itself creates a third presence which paradoxically and simultaneously reflects absence, difference, and thirdness. For it brings in a third element, the space between, which forms a divide that must exist in order for us to want to cross it. The space creates a sense of separation and difference, a no-thing that is neither Narcissus nor Echo. Triangular space exists even though it is not acknowledged.

The relationship of the reflector to the reflected is given symbolic form in a parable by Oscar Wilde[2] where he says that the river loved Narcissus because, 'when he leaned over my waters, I saw the reflection of my waters in his eyes' (Wilde, as cited in Ellmann, 1987, p. 337). The river does not love Narcissus for himself but for the way in which the river himself is reflected in Narcissus' gaze. In the original myth there are two counterparts of Narcissus: Echo and his reflection – a vocal and a visual re-presentation of Narcissus' speech and body.

---

2 Wilde and other Victorian homosexuals theorized on the theme of the beautiful youth admired by the older, wiser man who mentors and initiates him into the adult world, taking their cues from Plato's *Symposium*.

Freud, controversially and questionably, equated homosexuality and narcissism. Implicit in this view is a primary state of identification with mother. Freud explained homosexual object-choice as due to repression of a child's love for his mother in which the boy identifies with the mother and takes himself as a model for object-choice. They 'look for a young man who resembles themselves and whom *they* may love as their mother loved *them*' (Freud, 1905/1977a, p. 56, note added in 1910).

I am not equating homosexual love with narcissism. Both homosexual and heterosexual object-choice will have narcissistic elements in so far as they are predicated upon seeking in the other an idealized reflection of oneself.

To take the components of this intralocking traumatic scene, we have Narcissus, a reflecting surface and a reflection. We also have the figure of Echo. Echo and the mirroring function can be seen as one continuum or as two separate aspects. Further, Echo sets up a triangular structure consisting of herself, Narcissus and herself as an intervening reflecting surface for his projections.

Focusing on the reflection motif, these three components can take a number of combinations in a narcissistic set-up:

1 Narcissus–Echo: admirer–admired

- I am the object of your admiration and you are the admirer. When I look at you and see your admiration for me, I see my beautiful form reflected in the surface of your eyes (e.g. the reflection in your eyes is me).
- I am the admirer and you are beautiful. When I look at you I imagine you, your beautiful body, to be my reflecting surface: you are the image I would like to see reflected in a mirror.

These two positions can be superimposed and operate concurrently such that:

- While the beautiful person is basking in the admirer's admiration, the admirer identifies themselves with the beauty of the other. Both feel beautiful via different identificatory processes.

However, the admirer might not identify with the beautiful admired person but only feel themselves to be abject. Their only role is to echo, admire, applaud, while the beautiful person takes the spotlight.

Regarding the first situation, the beautiful person is Narcissus, the expression on the face of the admirer is the reflection. If I am beautiful and you admire me, then when I look at you I see your face lit up with adoration. I am reflected in the gleam in your eye, the admiring expression on your face.

If I feel myself to be unattractive, but have managed to 'score' a beautiful young woman, or man, I might use their physical attractiveness as the image of how I would like to present myself to the world. We see this operating with 'trophy brides'. Their beauty is made mine via possession and identification: they become the mirror reflecting me (e.g. their body is me).

'Adam', a middle-aged married man, spoke of how he was attracted to Adonis-like youths of great physical beauty, fitness and virility. They represented everything he would like to see if he were looking in the mirror, a compensatory substitute for his actual mirror-image. He fell madly in love with Amare who represented his inner *anima*, his lost youth and inner soul. This signified an interlocking traumatic scene, because, as an adolescent, he had longed for his father to reciprocate his quasi-eroticized adulation and yearning for mentoring. His father did not know how to respond, and Adam felt profoundly rejected.

Amare was a beautiful young poet who, torn with inner conflict and confusions about his sexuality due to a very strict Catholic upbringing in Italy, was looking for a man of wisdom, integrity, honour, a mentor figure. Amare did not want to have sex with Adam, but wanted Adam to act as his patron, an older and wiser philosopher-friend. He succumbed to allowing Adam to cuddle him, but felt very uncomfortable about having sex. What he sought was a wise man, not a lover. He put Adam on a pedestal, but was not physically attracted to him.

In ancient Greek culture love often involved an asymmetrical demarcation between the *eromenos* and *erastes*, the lover and beloved. Although these roles could switch, the same person was not seen as simultaneously both lover and beloved. The *eromenos* is the beloved, a 'beautiful creature without pressing needs of his own', supremely aware of his 'own attractiveness but self-absorbed in his relationship', with being desired rather than desiring himself (Nussbaum, 1986, p. 188). In the case of Adam and Amare, Adam fitted perfectly the *erastes*, Amare the *eromenos*. The youth proffers his beauty and sensuality, the older man provides moral, spiritual and philosophical mentoring. There is an implicit 'deal' being transacted: the *eromenos* provides 'favours' but seeks intellectual, spiritual guidance. As Pausanias describes it in the *Symposium*, the *eromenos* is not meant to be physically attracted to the older man, sexual gratification is not the aim of the game for him.

2 The beautiful duo (Narcissus–Narcissus)

- I am beautiful and you are beautiful. Both partners are beautiful and see their beauty reflected in the other.

Both members of a narcissistic duo may repress feelings of abjection and only project a beautiful image: 'we are the beautiful people'. It is the reflected atmosphere of beauty that is sought, not a three-dimensional person behind the image. Both use each other as a reflecting surface for their own imagined beauty. The narcissist still focuses on his or her own reflection in the eye of the beholder.

3 The abject duo (Echo–Echo)

- I identify myself as an abject wallflower and I seek out other non-descript companions. This could be an inverted form of masochistic narcissism, or else the Echo–Echo couple make a career out of being echolalic admiring audiences to narcissists who need to be surrounded by admiring audiences.

4 Beautiful couple with world as Echo (Narcissus–Narcissus – Echo)

A beautiful duo may present themselves to the world as the beautiful and powerful admirable couple, icons of success, glamour and richness. The world as Echo pays homage to them. The world's adulation becomes the reflection and reverberating accolade.

5 The beautiful duo with admirer duo (Narcissus/Narcissus–Echo/Echo)

Two echolalic people might hook up to create a dyad who then become the joint admirers of a beautiful duo.

In all narcissistic duos each narcissistic participant is only interested in being seen. A narcissist only looks at others as a reflection, seeking expressions of adoration in their face, or by identifications with another's beauty. No one sees.

Given that the narcissist's grandiosity is a defence against feeling unattractive and empty, the internal split between the part that imagines itself all glorious and the part that feels abject may be reproduced in love relations. In the third position above, both partners create a pact to defend against the abject part that is either repressed or projected outwards onto another imagined object (the world is one's audience). The abject person may take masochistic pleasure in wallowing in their ugliness, turning loss into a fantasy of pleasure.

Regarding the third (and fifth) situation, we have a person who feels themselves to be an abject, empty mirror, who feels their only role in life is to pay homage to beautiful or powerful people, never to feel admired themselves. This can become a form of sado-masochism, finding a pleasurable power in ugliness. The masochistic part will take pleasure in the fact that the sadistic part enjoys taking pleasure in the masochist's ugliness. There is a pay-off via identification with the pleasure of the other person.

To apply Hegel's master–slave metaphor to the sado-masochistic paradigm, the slave gets secret pleasure from identifying themselves with being the master and with the power their slavery affords in terms of creating pleasure for the master. They realize that on another level the power dynamic is reversed, because the master depends for his mastery on the slave.

The neurotic gains of such a narcissistic system are closely related to the power and pleasure gains of sado-masochistic relations. In the latter both the masochistic and the sadistic sides or positions seek gains through identification with the phantasy of the other.

The mirror of revelation

Dorian, the narcissistic hero of Oscar Wilde's *Picture of Dorian Gray*, was once given a 'curiously-carved mirror' surrounded by white-limbed Cupids (Wilde, 1891/2000, p. 210). The mirror showed his true soul, which had become as two-dimensional and lifeless as a portrait. His attempt to live life brilliantly on the surface led merely to being hideously destroyed by his own murky depths. Wanting desperately to destroy the mirror that had come to mock him, he flung the mirror onto the floor and 'crushed it into silver splinters beneath his heel'.

The splinters under his feet that he so wished to grind into dust reveal the true self, the state of Dorian's soul, the mirror in which Narcissus comes to know himself. Throughout the novel there are moments when the brutal truth stares Dorian starkly in the face, and moments of *kairos* when he could choose to fully acknowledge what he has done and take full responsibility for it, with the desolation concomitant upon such sober moments of depressive understanding. But the abyss which he would have to cross is too terrifying. What tends to occur in a narcissistic system is that the system itself co-opts and appropriates any insight back into itself: this is the mechanism of the narcissistic malignant third at work.

Narcissism as a defensive system represents a life-denying, devouring, anti-relational *thanatos* that is the enemy of *eros* and the inter-relational, interdependent domains. Envious of life, richness and creativity, it hollows out, vaporizes, sucks in and implodes.

Although a narcissistic intralocking system represents a defence against psychic development, the mirror reveals the true face of narcissism. There are elements that, like shards of glass reflecting the sun, have the potential to illuminate the play house, dispelling the shadows on which a narcissistic shadow play depends. Such shards represent the developmental aspect of any relational 'fit'.

Narcissus' reflection also revealed the truth. He came to realize that 'Alas! I am myself the boy I see. I know it: my own reflection does not deceive me.' The truth is there, staring him in the face all along.

Chapter 11

The narcissism of Echo

'I lacked the patience or the confidence to invent a life for myself, and would always be dependent on the lives of others', realizes the narrator in Anita Brookner's *A friend from England* (1987). Anita Brookner's novels depict lives of quiet desperation led by sad, lonely, self-contained wallflowers, observers of life who are always to be found hovering in the shadows of the limelight of their more exhibitionistic counterparts. Such characters are the descendants of the nymph Echo and they find their niche in forming echolalic mirrors to those who live out an undeveloped part of their vivacity. As Scurr points out, 'her fastidious characters suffer intricately, washed up on the moral high ground while the less fastidious sail blithely on in life's stream. At the heart of this disappointed suffering is something mawkish and shamefully passive' (Scurr, 2002, p. 24).

The fascination of those who take the role of observers and researchers of life, who form a mirror to narcissistic people, needs examination: if they were not narcissistic in some disowned, way, why would they be drawn to such exhibitionists? Self-effacers are fascinated with those who show their face.

We have seen how there is an intralocking sado-masochistic loop involved in narcissism in which one is outcast and one casts out. One is Narcissus and the other is Echo. The masochistic fidelity of Echo reaffirms Narcissus' contempt, enforcing her melancholic, self-absorbed, compulsive ruminations.

The echolalic is one who imitates, identifies with those admired and idealized: repeating their words, ideas, gestures, dress and interests. Echolalic children, according to Tustin (1972, p. 48), 'hide themselves behind a facade of parroted words and phrases' in order to hide the heartbreak of too abrupt a disillusionment. 'The artificial voice of the echolalic is a mockery of the real thing.'

In this chapter I focus on the narcissism of Echo: in other words those who for various reasons are drawn to play out an echolalic or mirroring role to narcissistic people.

My point is that although the story is about the inability to relate, there are always two people in the story, Narcissus and Echo. While narcissism takes place in a pseudo-relationship, a real other, whose reality is not perceived as such, is inevitably on the receiving end of such imperceptions and suffers accordingly.

Who is Echo and why is such a person drawn to Narcissus? As characters, Echo and Narcissus are a perfect match. Neither can initiate and sustain true dialogue, neither can love an-other as an Other. Both are fascinated by appearance. Real interaction is fatal, since in real interaction, images and illusions dissolve. In the narcissistic scene Echo does not offer anything new, jarring, disjunctive or different to the stream of consciousness of Narcissus' monologue.

Narcissists take themselves as love objects, hoping by this to avoid disillusionment, the demands and needs of the other and the possibility of separation. To realize they have a need for love but that they are not loved is so awful they cannot survive it. To fully know that their desire is unrequited and impossible to requite and that they themselves have constructed their own self-referential system that prevents this, can lead to utter alienation. While they don't know it (or forget it) they can live on within their fantasy.

Narcissus doesn't know how to engage with an Other to make and go on remaking a relationship. There is the sense it either works or it fails. If it fails it is due to the imperfections and limitations of the other. The narcissist passively awaits for a more perfect one to appear. But after any idealizing projection upon a new love object comes inevitable disappointment and denigration. A real, full-blooded and complex person with passionate desires of her or his own shocks Narcissus' ideals and fantasies like freezing water. Narcissus flees, denying himself the experience of finding that the real person is actually more exciting and challenging than a mere idea, image or fantasy.

Narcissus rejects Echo because she appears to have desires of her own. Yet the irony is that this expression is merely his own desire echoed back at him. The paradox of Echo is that she isn't even what he fears – she too lacks substance, is not three-dimensional. She all-too-perfectly mirrors his narcissistic needs, simply parroting and playing back his words. He cannot bear to hear his own desire reflected back at him: 'Let us come together here', he cries, but when Echo joyfully rushes to embrace him echoing, 'let us come together here', he shakes her off and runs away. 'I would die before you ever lie with me.' Narcissus is right to reject Echo, but he does so for precisely the wrong reasons.

There are categories of people who live their life vicariously: as spectators not partakers in life. This is an occupational hazard for therapists as well as writers. Such self-effacing onlookers form the audience to their exhibitionistic counterparts. Those who feign distaste for showiness and display nevertheless often seem to be attracted to take up a position in the outer circles of the famous (never in the spotlight, of course).

In couple therapy involving narcissism it is often the case that the relationship is predicated upon the model of Narcissus and a mirror. This occurs for example where one partner has been diagnosed with narcissistic personality disorder and the other comes to therapy just to 'support' them. Both collude with the assumption that the diagnosed partner is the selected 'problem' and both assume that all attention should be focused on that person. When I challenge this one-sided focus, the person playing the mirroring, supportive role is just as likely to be threatened by the idea that he or she might come out from behind the mirror as the one playing Narcissus that she reveal her personhood and foursquare subjectivity.

Anita Brookner's *Look at me*

Brookner's (1983) novel *Look at me* begins with a homage to unknowing:

> Once a thing is known it can never be unknown. It can only be forgotten. And, in a way that bends time, so long as it is remembered, it will indicate the future. It is wiser, in every circumstance, to forget, to cultivate the art of forgetting. To remember is to face the enemy. The truth lies in remembering.
>
> (Brookner, 1983, p. 5)

These words form an echoing refrain in *Look at me*. It seems to echo the decree against Narcissus knowing who he was, the prophecy pronounced at his birth. It is also like a Sibylline prophecy concerning the defensive nature of a narcissistic system, the rationale of which is to defend against seeing who one really is, against knowing. 'So long as it is remembered, it will indicate the future.' This expresses the developmental potential that the truth points to.

Frances Hinton is a classic observer of life. The story concerns the tragedy of what happens when she tries to become a participant by attempting to form a relationship with another observer: we could call it the case of Echo meets Echo, when the only scripting possible in the narcissistic intralocking traumatic scene is that the character of Echo is there to reflect and observe, not to herself partake and relate.

Frances closets herself away in the labyrinth of a dark, dusty, musty medical reference library, where, from the safe vantage point of a non-descript status as blue-stocking spinster, she can peer out at the visitors to the library through horn-rimmed spectacles, seeing, but not being seen.

A submerged loneliness pervades her existence; she is locked into a self-referential universe, a system so watertight in its internal logic that any move to break free merely tightens its bonds. The exhibitionists and socialites of the world carry the projections of an undeveloped, split-off part of her:

> Sometimes . . . I wish I were beautiful and lazy and spoiled and not to be trusted . . . Such thoughts sweep me to the edge of panic. For I want more, and I even think I deserve it.
>
> (p. 19)

Writing is her fantasy of making public what is behind those glasses, an imagined way of calling out from behind her façade:

> When I feel swamped in my solitude, and hidden by it, physically obscured by it, rendered invisible, in fact, writing is my way of piping up. Of reminding people that I am here.
>
> (p. 19)

To write is to imagine communicating and being heard, but, unlike the real world, one can order, change and have agency in a fictional world. Her characters act as imaginary objects into which to displace unbearable emotions. No one reads her writings and thus she maintains the purity of the fantasy that someone will actually see her beneath her mask, unimpeded by the messy interpersonal experience of someone actually reading them, having his or her own thoughts and reactions, taking it to another, more intimate, yet fearfully unpredictable level.

Nick Fraser swoops into the library and with a 'ravishing smile' asks Frances to do a series of jobs beyond the call of duty, before sweeping out again, 'leaving a trail of disorder and excitement'. She finds herself vanquished by fascination with his good looks, carefree presumptuousness and utter insensitivity to the needs of others, yet this draws her to him:

> People like Nick attract admirers, adherents, followers. They also attract people like me: observers.
>
> (p. 14)

While the handsome beauty of someone like Nick has accustomed him to continuous gratification, his attention span, she notes, is very limited. This limited attention span is alluring yet safe:

> I find such people . . . quite fascinating . . . I recognize that they might have no intrinsic merit, and yet I will find myself trying to please them, to attract their attention. 'Look at me', I want to say. 'Look at me'.
>
> (p. 15)

Implicit in her attraction to 'such people' is an unconscious wish to be the recipient of such accolade. Her real desire is that they look at her. '"Look at me", I want to say', as she looks at them. Her unlived life, reflected in others who did live fully, continued to draw her, even though it made her feel unseen and unknown.

Narcissists, of course, need someone like Frances to be their mirror: and it was not long before Nick and his 'equally dazzling' wife, Alix, 'adopted' if not co-opted 'Orphan Fanny', as they nicknamed her, into their life, her role being to appreciate, reflect, respond and feel *so grateful* to be drawn into their lively, social orbit. There are oedipal themes of triangular space, the third as observer, combined with the narcissistic couple's reliance on a mirror to shore up their fragile image. As Kernberg describes them, narcissists:

> present an unusual degree of self-reference in their interactions with other people, and a great need to be loved and admired by others, and a curious apparent contradiction between a very inflated concept of themselves and an inordinate need for tribute from others.
>
> (Kernberg, 1975, p. 227)

Frances was a willing participant in her allotted reflective role. She loved the 'feeling of being taken over', 'after that kingdom of the shades in which I had been living for so long'. One is reminded of the glades and forests and caves in which Echo hid her shame of being discarded. She feels dazzled and grateful that Alix would introduce her to the club thus: 'Be nice to her. She's an orphan.' This is an example of the masochistic pleasure of the abject, a theme I link to the master–slave paradigm of Hegel.

The gratitude of Echo is related to her own intrinsic emptiness and hollowed-out inner state:

> I felt as if I had been reprieved from the most dreadful emptiness . . . I had been rescued from my solitude; I had been given another chance; and I had high hopes of a future that would cancel out the past.
>
> (p. 36)

It was as if Alix and Nick's 'golden quality' held up the mirror and amplified her lack of life, whilst she bestowed upon them her own split-off vivacity and undeveloped passion. In the face of such extraordinary physical presence she immediately felt 'unfed by life's more potent forces, condemned to dark rooms . . . an obscure creeping existence . . . which would allow me gently to decline into extinction'. Again, one is reminded of Echo wasting away in the shadows until she was but a disembodied voice.

The extractive processes of narcissists have the effect of hollowing out the insides of others who are seen merely as shadowy objects, for at the heart of the object-relational world of the narcissist is the 'image of a hungry, enraged, empty self' (Kernberg, 1975, p. 233). The 'world of outer object relations [is] robbed of vitality by the narcissist's envy and hatred' (Schwartz-Salant, 1982, p. 30). This is what Bollas (1987) describes as extractive introjection.

That Nick and Alix were turned in on each other created a safe vantage point from which Frances could continue her stance as audience. This was a much safer vantage point than if Nick had suddenly turned his gaze upon her. Yet Alix and Nick also needed their audience:

> They found my company necessary: they exhibited their marriage to me, while sharing it only with each other . . . I was there because some element in that perfect marriage was deficient, because ritual demonstrations were needed to maintain a level of arousal which they were too complacent, perhaps too spoilt, even too lazy, to supply for themselves, out of their own imagination.
>
> (p. 57)

Frances was fascinated by how Nick seemed to prepare 'an atmosphere of affection for himself' as if it were his 'natural climate'. He was born to it, ignorant of the 'sad compromises and makeshifts, the substitutions and the fantasies, that constitute the emotional baggage of the average person'. Such 'diapason of love' seemed to have 'followed him from home' yet there was a 'restlessness', 'urgency', as if 'however spectacular and satisfying his life might be' he always had the 'capacity for more, for other experience, for infinite fulfilment' (p. 38).

Nick and Alix seemed impervious to pain, which starkly contrasted with her own sensitivity and easily bruised, thin skin. Here is another example of the combination of thick- and thin-skinned narcissism. Frances sought in their company relief from the constant reminders of mortality and frailty, from the realization that:

> human beings were vulnerable, that everyone was, more or less, dying . . . I needed to know that not everyone carries a wound and that this wound bled intermittently throughout life . . . I needed to learn, from experts, that pure egoism that had always escaped me.
>
> (p. 43)

One night Frances arrives at the Frasers' house to find another person present, Dr James Anstey. It does not escape her attention that she and this newcomer have a great deal in common. Both are lonely and habitually take the role of observer rather than participant in the emotional dramas of life.

She gradually finds herself doing what she had not expected herself to do, to be drawn into the plot as a full participant, wishing to initiate a relationship of her own. James walks her home on that first night, and she reflects that it was the happiest night of her life: 'beginnings are so beautiful' (p. 83).

She does not write for many evenings after that and the meaning of her defensive system reveals itself to her in one fell swoop, upon finding the joys of actually relating. She realizes that writing is for her but an attempt to reach others and make them love her, an instinctive protest against her subservient status of being but a nonentity:

> when you find you have no voice at the world's tribunals and that no one will speak for you. I would give my entire output of words, past, present and to come, in exchange for easier access to the world, for permission to state, 'I hurt' or, 'I hate' or, 'I want'. Or, indeed, 'Look at me'.
>
> (p. 84)

She saw James in the library every day where they would share a morning cup of coffee, and it wasn't long before he would accompany her on the walk to the Frasers for their evening entertainment. Then he would walk her home to her flat. A new ritual developed, of being walked home, a cup of cocoa and conversation by the fake log electric fire, before James would walk home alone to his mother. They felt shy and reticent alone with each other and were relieved to have such awkwardness alleviated by the dinner-time company of Nick and Alix in whose reflected light they continued to bask.

The whole late autumn was spent as a time of comfort, anticipation and enjoyment. Involved in a real interpersonal relationship Frances found she could dispense with her internal world of fantasy figures. 'There were no images in my head. I did not write. I was happy.' She 'knew it would take me a long time to unlearn my lessons, to let down my defences, to find out how to be carefree and trusting' (p. 96). She took every pleasure that the unresolved situation offered, without ever wanting it to become a full-blown consummated relationship. James was her friend, 'and I held his hand as confidently as a child holds the hand of its parent'. Frances related as a child to a father, not a lover to her beloved.

The narcissistic intralocking system does not include within its set positions the possibility that one might really feel or be loved. Certain modes of relating are allowed; others, such as an Echo getting together with another Echo, are prohibited. Furthermore, narcissists are possessed by hidden but very intense envy of any sign of life on the part of their entourage. Alix is threatened by the growing friendship between James and Frances and demands to know all about it, subsume it back into her system. Frances's protestations of innocence that there is, after all, nothing to tell, fall on disbelieving ears.

Alix pressures James to move in with them, thus sabotaging the intimate nightly routine between Frances and James. Slowly but surely, Alix, Nick and James-as-mirror become a threesome and Frances is left out in the cold. When she tries to assert her right to be included she realizes how much she is at Alix's mercy. 'I felt as if I were about to come up for judgment, at a court which was already prejudiced against me. And I still could not see what I had done that was so wrong' (p. 121). All she wanted was 'contentment and peace for myself and for him and I wanted the approbation of others' (p. 122).

She rebels against the realization that her only way back in would be to renounce her attachment to James. She decides to oust herself from the prescribed scripting and 'throw her lot in with James' at the risk of offending Alix still further. She demands to see James alone that night.

Alix predictably interferes with an invitation to dinner that evening. 'I can't', Frances replies, 'James is taking me out.' But Alix has already taken care of that. 'Yes, he rang to tell me. I thought it would be simpler if you came over here and then we could put you in a taxi and all have an early night' (p. 124).

Frances, frightened, insists on her rights and gets her way with James. But she finds to her dismay that over dinner James does not even look at her; he seems to be addressing a point 'somewhere to the right of [her] head' and she realizes he is being deliberately inconsequential, defending himself against her. 'I make no inroads on his attention although I knew that it was there, warily, waiting for an ambush, and determined to avoid one . . . I could not engage his attention. He would not even meet my eyes. Look at me, I wanted to say. Look at me' (p. 126).

Back at her flat he sits away from her, looks wary, distant. She sums up her courage, takes him to the bedroom, for the first time, and pulls him towards her, reaches up for him, but then he tears angrily away saying, 'not with you'. She goes to him as he stands by the bookshelf, asks him what is wrong, turns him to face her, but he does not answer. 'And then, I think, I knew that I had lost him long before the evening had ever started' (p. 127).

When she becomes Echo to him, calling out to him to love her fully by consummating the relationship, he, although himself an Echo, switches to take on the role of Narcissus who is utterly repulsed by her desire and spurns her. She, like Echo, is left with her words going nowhere. She slowly wastes away, to a shrivelled old age, her anxious thoughts keeping her awake, making her pitifully thin, until only her voice remains, a solitary writer. She now knows herself, and once a thing is known, it can never be unknown, and for a narcissist this is a fate worse than death.

Discussion

The intralocking narcissistic system of this story consists of two Narcissi and two Echoes: Nick/Alix are admired by Frances/James.

This system breaks down when Frances, whose only scripted role is to echo and reflect, tries to become a participant in her own right. When she turns her gaze on James rather than on the beautiful couple and the two begin an incipient relationship, it constellates an Echo–Narcissus relationship between Frances and James, both of whom are frightened of real relationship. Further, it inculcates intense envy and alarm in Alix who cannot tolerate any more than one Narcissus in the equation. As in the ways in which the master depends on the slave for his enjoyment, Alix desperately needs her mirrors, her Echoes to defend against her hollowed-out insides.

James finds Frances's tense and conflicted discomfort about her atrophied areas of healthy exhibitionism as repugnant as a narcissist feels about a woman's full desire. For Frances, the giddy heights of love consist in an innocent, non-sexual relationship, in which she trustingly puts her hand in his, has a cup of cocoa before he leaves again. As an echolalic she has no self and thus cannot be desired, let alone loved. In the master–slave dynamics of this set-up James cannot do otherwise than reject her. Like most thin-skinned narcissists she gives off the unspoken command, 'do not hurt me: do not tell me the truth about myself or I'll be so upset'. Alix and Nick live out her split-off exhibitionism and appetite and desire. Furthermore, James cannot bear to see in her gaze of love for him an awful reflection of himself. He is attracted to those in whose image he would like to pretend to be. He cannot bear an image of his dull, conservative and insecure personality looking up at him from a position of innocent abjection.

Frances has constructed her universe so self-referentially that it cannot be deconstructed and reconstructed in the light of experience. Her relationship with James is merely constructed in her fantasy. When she reveals her actual passion he responds with repugnance, as if a sister, nun or friend was to proposition him. Having projected an image of a non-sexual person, she cannot easily be redefined even when she attempts to break out of this role and seduce him.

To date Frances had not ever identified herself with the beautiful people of the world but she begins to feel vicariously special by being included in the orb of Alix and Nick's social set. As her own sense of attractiveness develops, so does her self-assertiveness. As her relationship with James develops she starts treating herself like someone who deserves love. 'I wanted to be spoilt, at the same time, in the way, I suppose, that fortunate young women are spoiled. Or lucky ones. I wanted to be treated like . . . Like a bride of course' (p. 95).

Remembering that the narcissist's grandiosity is a defence against feeling unlovable and empty, the narcissist defends against the part that feels abject by surrounding himself with those who are worthy objects for receiving the split-off abjection and whose role is to bolster his ego. Frances takes masochistic pleasure in wallowing in her 'wallflower' status, turning loss into a pleasurable fantasy.

The neurotic gains of such a narcissistic system are closely related to the power and pleasure gains of sado-masochistic relations. Both the masochistic and the sadistic sides or positions seek gains through identification with the phantasy of the other. The sado-masochistic dynamic comes out in Alix's sadistic mocking of 'Orphan Fanny' and Frances derives masochistic pleasure from that, just as the slave gets secret pleasure from identifying himself with being the master and with the power his slavery affords in terms of creating pleasure for the master. Alix's sense of inherent threat when Frances begins to assert herself is like that of the master threatened by the intrinsic power of the slave.

Not only is Alix threatened, but when Frances tries to throw that role over and be desirable in her own right to the other abject mirror, James is disgusted.

Narcissists need other narcissists to maintain a narcissistic defence system against full-fathomed relationship. Yet built into the mythic creation story are the elements of its own destruction. The agreement to live life on the surface is merely another thin veneer disguising longing for real relational connection. This is expressed by the inevitability that one or other participant will actually fall in love. Like Echo, when desire for genuine full connection is expressed, several horrible possibilities follow. If the mirror turns around and becomes a real flesh-and-blood, vivacious, passionate, sensuous person in his or her own right, Narcissus is left stranded with his own mirror-thin shallowness. He is appalled by the reflection of his shallow insubstantiality and either faces it or faces away from Echo, as Dorian did Sibyl. When Frances shows her face, James turns away, won't meet her eyes.

> I make no inroads on his attention although I knew that it was there, warily, waiting for an ambush, and determined to avoid one . . . I could not engage his attention. He would not even meet my eyes. Look at me, I wanted to say. Look at me.
>
> (p. 126)

The echolalic for her part has internalized a fear that if yearning is expressed she will inevitably be rejected because there is nothing to love, or she will disappoint. In an internal solipsistic grandiose way, she will feel at some level too good for the other. The defence against humiliation is to feel superior.

Nick and Alix also fear humiliation. In the case of the denizens of the library, a private, hidden, intellectual arrogance is mixed with the fear that their specialist intellectual area is of no consequence to the rest of the world. The defence reveals the very thing it defends against.

Turning from narcissism towards relationship

Narcissistic defences such as grandiosity, pseudo-self-sufficiency, aloofness and self-isolation derive from the pain of alienation and from original traumatic disjunctions. They are difficult to treat since they often form a self-protective *modus operandi* which has been built up over a lifetime, and therapy amounts to the renunciation of an edifice of defences against the pain of vulnerability. Therapeutically the task is to support the 'struggling life-enhancing side against the side that desperately wants to keep within the narcissistic refuge and remain anaesthetized' (Symington, 1993, p. 80).

Within every defensive system are developmental aspects struggling to come to light. These shards of glass are all we have to work with therapeutically. They tend to contain within them the selected fact that both signifies the original trauma and points the way out of the stalemate of the self-reinforcing dynamics of the system.

Therapeutic metaphors of transformation rather than of dismantling such a defensive structure are more apposite, such as ice that can melt, or a screen that can fade away like clouds obscuring the sky. Such changes to narcissistic structures occur when the whole affective system is challenged to its roots by the mirror of an understanding of the whole, or if a slow realization of the roots of this system is steadily assimilated so that the system and its powers evaporate.

A crumbling of the fragile defences of thin-skinned narcissists may reveal underneath a mixture of something ferocious and cruel, but at least this has energy. It may melt down into depression, then further into mourning. A melting of the thick skin occurs, leading into emotional tenderness, which can be enlivening but also can fall into depression. The issue is one of how to challenge the system without provoking the endless repetition of the system which has served the patient for so long.

Given that we are dealing with a system involving two individuals who to some extent must both be treated as suffering narcissistic problems, the therapist needs to attend to the dynamics between the two and the narcissistic system. In the case below the couple formed a Narcissus–Echo dynamic in their marriage.

'Mr Gray' and 'Mrs Gray' came into therapy when it had been revealed that Mr Gray had been leading a double life. This was revealed because Mrs Gray contracted a sexually transmitted disease from Mr Gray. This secret life involved cross-dressing and sex with male prostitutes.

I noticed that the couple presented a perfect match of narcissist and blank reflecting screen. The implicit assumption of the set-up was that Mr Gray was the patient and Mrs Gray there only to help him with his problems. He spoke about all the childhood reasons he might have been led to such behaviour and Mrs Gray merely joined in by adding details he had forgotten. She never volunteered any information about her own background, but echoed and affirmed all he said.

Mr Gray's cross-dressing fantasies began when he was a little boy. He had been a replacement child for a sister who died. His mother's room was surrounded by photos of the little girl and she used to cradle the sister's dolls in her arms as if they were a baby. In a desperate attempt to win his mother's love, he used to dress in his dead sister's clothes. He would stand for hours in front of the mirror, gesturing and watching the reflection gesture back.

As Mrs Gray nodded her head in sympathetic agreement as he related this story, it seemed to reflect the image in the mirror gesturing back to the little boy.

What were Mrs Gray's reasons for wanting to be a screen? I wondered if Mrs Gray was just waiting for me to invite her to speak about her own family background, but when I invited her to share something of this I realized from her startled reaction that Mrs Gray was as uncomfortable about revealing anything of herself as Mr Gray was in listening to it. This led me to speculate about whether Mr and Mrs Gray had created an interlocking traumatic scene consisting of, on Mr Gray's part, a developmental arrest whereby he had been denied the experience of mirroring and affirmation from a mother who did not impose her needs upon him but amplified the gestures of his true self.

I continued to make the observation that it seemed she was uncomfortable revealing anything of her own self by way of holding the mirror up to her participation in the system. And over time Mrs Gray made tentative moves in the direction of revealing some of her own feelings, particularly unexpressed hurt, betrayal and anger at what had happened to her.

I noted that Mr Gray visibly shifted uncomfortably whenever Mrs Gray talked about her own feelings. It was as if he could not bear hearing it. Again, making an observation about this seemed to shift things a little, but it was only when I was able to get to the heart of what all this represented for Mr Gray that he softened and opened up.

On one occasion Mrs Gray, unusually, began the session saying she wanted to relate something that had happened during the week, which affected her. She didn't feel safe about bringing it up at home but said, 'the thing about this room is there is one place, once a week, where I feel I can begin to say things I'd never normally say to anyone'. Mrs Gray was all the while looking at me. I noticed Mr Gray shifting uncomfortably in his seat and looking very uncomfortable. I was struck by two things: I noticed how little Mr Gray could tolerate any expression of Mrs Gray's own personality, needs and feelings. I also noticed that Mrs Gray was oblivious to his discomfort, because she was only looking at me. I wondered if she did so because she might hope to have a sympathetic ear. It was as if unconsciously she was setting up a dyadic, responsive dynamic which was a model for how it ought to be with Mr Gray.

She related how she had been really upset the other night because they had gone to visit a friend whose father had just died, on the other side of town. After visiting the friend Mr Gray suggested that they have a meal together and take advantage of being in a different part of town. Mrs Gray said she thought it was not the night for celebrating, but reluctantly agreed. Mr Gray said there was a Lebanese restaurant he'd always wanted to try and so they went there. There was a belly dancer, which brought up all Mrs Gray had been through in coming to terms with the reality of Mr Gray's double life. But furthermore, her mother had been terribly depressed and unavailable to her family due to grief about a twin sister who had died *in utero*. Her father had numerous affairs as his response. The restaurant brought it all up for her. She wanted to leave but Mr Gray said, 'we're here now, can't you just get over it?'

As she was relating all this to me he burst out: 'You don't understand that this life was something else, it was never meant to affect us, my love for you.'

When Mrs Gray was confronted with the reality of her husband's other life, it was as if he was also confronted with it being real, not merely a compartmentalized fantasy life.

When I linked how he felt with his wife to how he felt as a child, his defensiveness melted and tears came to his eyes. He looked to me for sympathy and this mirrored the times when Mrs Gray sought the kind of response from me she needed from her husband.

I asked Mrs Gray to reflect on what was going on for her in all this and whether some aspects had echoes with her own childhood.

She reflected that her reasons for taking the stance of observer with no needs of her own derived from how her twin sister had died *in utero*. She always had the sense of a missing half, and when she met Mr Gray, he seemed to incarnate that other half. They were unconsciously drawn to each other due to shared traumatic experiences of the loss of a sibling, a twinned part of themselves. She felt she had to be very, very good and not make any trouble for her mother, who, like Mr Gray's mother, entered a deep post-natal depression. Mrs Gray mirrored and echoed her mother, providing her mother with empathic attunement.

Mrs Gray's story reminded me of the version of the myth of Narcissus by Pausanius where Narcissus searched for his lost twin sister in the reflection in the water. Narcissus sought relief in gazing at his reflection, seeking in it her likeness. It was not love of self but melancholic love for a lost sister that gripped him.

Mr Gray tried to incarnate and thus resurrect his lost sister, by cross-dressing since childhood. Mrs Gray tried to become her lost twin and make up for her. At the heart of their narcissism was loss and longing to connect, not a desire to turn away from relationship.

Mr and Mrs Gray reported that a curious phenomenon of the terrible crisis of discovering Mr Gray's cross-dressing was that they actually felt closer to each other than ever before. The shocking revelations meant that for the first time in their lives they began to reveal all of themselves to each other, including the core meaning and source beneath the enactment. Both had been hiding vital parts of themselves from each other, showing only their surface selves. Both had been living behind screens, Mrs Gray presenting a blank screen to her husband and Mr Gray hiding his other life behind a wall.

Mr Gray's other life was an acting out of very crucial aspects of his personality which when understood symbolically and developmentally were aspects with which his wife could feel sorrow and sympathy. They represented an unmet longing for connection, for love, for acceptance from his mother, which he tried to achieve through becoming the little sister who died, by cross-dressing. He found no sense of empathy from the male prostitutes, but he did finally feel a sense of being understood by his wife when he was able to articulate these areas of longing rather than act them out.

Mrs Gray took the courage to come out from behind the mirror entailing her playing a masochistically abused blank screen to a depressed and split mother/husband and philandering father, and so was able to be an effective agent in her marriage and adult life.

Thus the relationship-as-a-third also changed from a locked prison to a more open and mutually supportive intimate space.

This illustrates how discovering the conjoint selected fact, consisting of both the insight pertaining to the aetiology of each partner's narcissistic traumatic scene and the ways the superimposition of both create a third play, is necessary to unlock the system. It also shows that there is a teleological element seeking to come to light and be known, encapsulated within the system.

Concluding remarks

At the heart of narcissism is grief: grief at the loss of a twin sister, or one's soul, for the perfection of basking in the orb of perfect empathy, a face whose utter radiant love is a reflection of one's truest nature.

Loss of such vitality of being leads to a fissure in the cracks of our being. If we are not lovingly beheld in the mind of another we do not feel ourselves to exist. We therefore search forever for such love, for a perfect picture of beauty, for a reflection of our true being, and hold to it without letting go, seeking to absorb it into us, to drink in the reflection until we can satisfy our endless thirst.

Narcissism is a denial of the relational, the true self and the other. There can be no relation where both persons are unconsciously treated as identical; there can be no con-junction without two separate, discrete, but mutually interested persons to come together. A hatred of the relational leads to a presumption that the other has no independent life that is different from one's own. To allow one's admirer their own freedom and autonomy means to allow them to be unpredictable and this capacity depends on having the 'experience of a relationship with one's internal objects in which their freedom is a genuine possibility' (Fisher, 1999, p. 226). In turn, this depends upon the original sources of such internalized object relations having been predictable and reliable enough.

In narcissism there is an implicit expectation and presumption that the other should perfectly understand one without being told. Normal confrontation and disagreement are avoided. Depressive anxiety and paranoid fear preclude ambivalent understanding and integration. The narcissist is one who fails to achieve the depressive position and remains locked into a paranoid-schizoid world.

Liveliness and the possibility of relationship with the contingencies of being in an other-peopled world are cripplingly tense for the narcissist, leading to the intricate defensive manoeuvres associated with narcissism, which aim to defend at all costs against dependence, separation, suffering and depressive understanding. The narcissistic system often fails and collapses in the face of life events, such as broken relationships, which in some cases shock the narcissistic into a moment of recognition of the emptiness, depression and the horrible nature of their devouring greed.

The narcissist is torn between wanting to maintain the self-referential system and also to be freed from it. This conflict between developmental and defensive aspects is reflected in object-choices: the narcissist often unconsciously chooses someone who seems to reflect a non-intrusive, responsive, blank screen but who actually has an edge of difference and depth which is feared yet needed (the shards of glass). This is another example of how even a defensive system tends to contain developmental elements.

In terms of therapy with a narcissistic couple, interventions are somewhat different from those of individual therapy. Couple therapy is inherently disjunctive for a narcissist because dyadic relationship severs the monadic illusion. It is not really possible to create a symbiotic-like attunement and selfobject experience for the individual in the context of couple therapy. Therapy proceeds along the lines of first creating a space in which some of the defences can be melted via carefully timed interpretations, linking the current dynamic back to its sources. This creates a space in which the original trauma can be mourned, and doing so in the presence of empathic companionship heals the lack of empathy which was an essential aspect of the original trauma.

A the particular task of couple therapy involving narcissism involves uncovering the central locking device which clamps tight the narcissistic interlocking traumatic scene, which consists of two histories that have been superimposed. This is predicated upon having a sense of containment and negative capability that enables one to discover the conjoint selected fact.

In the case of Mr and Mrs Gray above, this was the realization that they were *both* hiding the fullness of their many parts and aspects behind a mirror. The revelation of what was behind the mirror did not, as they feared, destroy their marriage, it actually brought them closer. All they destroyed was a narcissistic illusion which, not being real, could not be killed. It could only evaporate in the clear light of day.

As the system unlocks, there is a space for mourning the original trauma of each, in the presence of two caring witnesses: the other partner and the therapist. The therapist, as well as having the function of creating the sense of containment, models her capacity for alpha function, to think in the face of a seemingly impossibly loaded, confused, conflicted situation. The therapist represents both the analytic third and the marital third. She has to be on guard for the inevitable re-emergence of the malignant third which will attack such insights.

Emergence out of narcissism into true exogamous relationship oscillates, like the movement between the paranoid-schizoid and the depressive position. In the territory of therapy the mirror metaphor takes on a different meaning: as revealing and concealing the other and the relationship and oneself within that relationship:

> Reciprocal love, such as I envisage it, is a system of mirrors which reflects for me, under the thousand angles that the unknown can take for me, the faithful image of the one I love, always more surprising in her divining of my own desire and more gilded with life.
>
> (André Breton, as cited in Mitchell, 2002, p. 58)

Hidden in the metaphor of the mirror is the way forward which will liberate us out of narcissistic systems. The mirror, itself empty and clear, reflects only what is set before it, young, old, beautiful, deformed, but these reflections do not in essence modify the mirror. The mirror retains its absolute nature. 'In any object, material or immaterial, resides the unknowable ultimate reality, the "thing-in-itself". Objects have emanations or emergent qualities or evolving characteristics that impinge upon the human personality as phenomena', but these 'differ from ultimate reality' (Bion, 1970, p. 87).

Buddhism would teach that our primordial nature is clear, pure and empty and we can realize that state simply by looking in the mirror of our mind. Such emptiness is close to what Bion describes as O, or, as Milner describes it, zero, void, emptiness, the divine ground of being (Milner, 1987, pp. 258–274). Narcissism is a system built of phantasmagoria, denials of reality, mortality, of who we actually are. Yet that reality is always there behind the phantoms and falsehoods we create.

Chapter 12

Thresholds: Bluebeard's Castle

Threshold: how do two lovers take it,
to be wearing down slightly their own older threshold
of the door, they too, after the many before
and before those to come . . . lightly.
                    (Rilke, Ninth Elegy, 1923/1992, p. 89)

Thresholds of love

When two people meet and begin to form a relationship, there is a time of
transition between previous states of identity as a single person, a member
of a family of origin and of other social groupings, and a new identity as a
member of a couple. It can be a period of what Bion (1970) calls catastrophic change, of loss of a former identity. There may be fears of losing
ourselves in the new relationship, as well as joyful hope and romantic
fantasies. Each partner brings expectations of what life as a couple involves,
these expectations not necessarily being shared by the other.

One or other partner may turn back out of timidity or fear from crossing
love's various thresholds into deeper states of intimacy. There are also
developmental thresholds to cross, such as the adolescent threshold between
the childhood world and adult relationships. Threshold failures also occur
when moving from an oedipal, narcissistic, orphic or solipsistic template to
true marriage.

Two related aspects of exogamous initiation involve exit from enmeshment in the endogamous realm of childhood, and entry into a new adult
state of being as a partner in a marriage, symbolized by stepping over the
threshold of the new marital home. In a truly exogamous relationship both
partners step over the threshold into an intersubjective space that symbolizes a bounded container for both to live within. Leaving their former
life as a single person behind and becoming one flesh, together they go
about creating a new home which expresses the new reconfiguration of their
identity as a couple.

Bluebeard's Castle depicts an asymmetric relational pattern regarding thresholds and Bion's container/contained. Bluebeard's new wife is invited to cross the threshold of his castle. She is given the instruction to respect those private domains that he wants to keep hidden. Yet there is no reciprocal process on Bluebeard's part of getting to know his wife or entering, on invitation, gradually and respectfully, the labyrinths of her psychic chambers. In an equal relationship both are interpenetrated, both encompassed, both also retaining their dark indeterminate opacity. Rather than one partner coming to live in the other's pre-existent residence (psychic or physical), together the couple might build a new home, symbolically and physically, which comes to contain them both, including its secret recesses where either might retreat for solitude.

The legend of Bluebeard, who murdered his wives and kept their severed heads in a secret room in his castle, has horrified and fascinated readers since Charles Perrault wrote *Barbe bleue* in 1697. No fewer than six works exploring the legend were written in the first twenty years of the twentieth century. The story of Bluebeard depicts a failure of initiation and a psychologically murderous attack on psychic change and the possibilities of becoming in love. It also speaks to the terrifying fear of loss of identity in becoming a couple.

Béla Bartók's lonely castle

> I prophesy, I have a foreknowledge, that this spiritual loneliness is to be my destiny. I look about me in search of the ideal companion, and yet I am fully aware that it is a vain quest.
> (Bartók, in a letter to his mother, 1905, as cited in Demény, 1971, p. 53)

Béla Bartók's *Duke Bluebeard's Castle* of 1911, based on the libretto of the symbolist poet Béla Baláz,[1] is a psychological study of male–female relationships, and the elusive quest for a beloved. Bluebeard, in Bartók's treatment, is not a wife-slayer, but a man who is locked into the windowless walls of a monadic alienation. He both longs for but is terrified of finding a soul-mate who can plumb his depths, discover all he is, without destroying him or being destroyed in the process.

The opera's setting is a huge, circular, windowless, Gothic hall. As they hover on the threshold, Bluebeard asks, 'Judith, are you coming?' She knows the rumours – he has been married before, and no one knows what became of his wives. Disregarding these, Judith cries, 'yes, I am coming'. She wants to assume the burden of her beloved's fearful obscurity, his

---

1 Baláz (1884–1949) was a symbolist poet, novelist, cinema critic, dramatist and communist. Baláz was also deeply interested in psychology and Western philosophical currents.

mysterious greatness, to enter and redeem the suffering reflected in his piercing eyes, open his dark recesses to the light of day.

Judith, the stronger of the two, initially occupies the musical foreground, Bluebeard answering her in short motifs. The roles reverse as the drama unfolds. The musical portrait of Judith proceeds in a diminuendo, that of Bluebeard in a crescendo.

The melodic motifs Bartók composed to represent Judith allude to the ending of Bartók's *Portrait of a girl*, Op. 9, dedicated to Márta Ziegler, the wife to whom he dedicated *Bluebeard's castle* as a wedding present, thus strengthening the autobiographical associations between Judith and his own wife Márta.

Bluebeard keeps asking, 'are you afraid'? Judith reassures him nothing will turn her away. Fumbling in the darkness Judith asks why the walls are sweating, but Bluebeard is evasive. Judith is fearless in her love, with her own lips she would dry the weeping walls, with her own body warm the icy marble. All must be revealed and opened up.

Judith hammers on the first door. A cavernous sighing, like the night wind sighing down endless, gloomy labyrinths, makes her shudder, but she says, 'Come we'll open, I'll unlock your doors, very gently, let me have the keys because I love you.'

Reluctantly he consents. The first door opens to reveal a streak of red light, marked by a semitone trill, the blood motif. It is Bluebeard's torture chamber. The gruesome tools of torture are conveyed by metallic shrieking up and down the span of a tritone, the traditional *diabolus in musica*. Yet Judith overlooks the weapons of torture and persuades herself that the red light is the crimson radiance of dawn. She asks to see the next door. 'Judith, careful, 'tis my castle.' Judith promises to go gently, softly, into the night. Ignoring the brutality of warfare in the second room she looks to the stream of light, demanding he give her all the keys at once.

Reluctantly he gives her three more keys, which open the doors to the pleasures of power – a treasure chamber bathed in golden light representing his spiritual richness, a flower garden washed in blue-green light, and the dazzling brightness of the vast panorama of Bluebeard's realms.

She lays jewels, a crown and a cape upon the threshold, but jumps in alarm when she sees they are stained with blood.

The fourth door opens upon a pristine spring day in the castle's secret garden. Her gasps of delight at the beauty of the castle's secret garden turn to horror when she plucks a rose and finds that it is bleeding. 'Who bleeds to water this garden?' Bluebeard only answers, 'Judith, love me, ask no questions'. Now it is Bluebeard who urges her to open the fifth door.

'Now behold my spacious kingdom, Gaze ye down the dwindling vistas. Is it not a noble country?' Judith screams a high C as a monumental organ peal, timpani, brass and orchestra proclaim the power, majesty and vastness of Bluebeard's domain. In her shriek she meets like with like: her high

C is the height of Judith's light, her power, in the epiphanic moment of vision when she perceives the heights and majesty of his creative power.

All is placed at Judith's feet, 'All is thine forever, Judith. Here both dawn and twilight flourish, here sun, moon and star have dwelling, they shall be thy deathless playmates.'

Yet she is rendered almost speechless and stammers unaccompanied. She feels silenced, awestruck by the numinous might of Bluebeard's imagination.

Judith notices that beyond the velvet green pastures, the silver streams and distant mountains, the clouds cast a blood-red shadow. Bluebeard implores her to ask no more questions, to refrain from opening the remaining two doors. He warns her that she had begged for sunlight and now the sun filled the house. Was that not enough?

This is the point of no return. Judith could content herself with what she has seen behind the five doors so far opened. The conflict deepens into the most intense battle of wills between them. Judith's demands that the doors be opened reaching a climax of dissonance. 'Open, open!' She hammers on the last two doors. The castle answers with a sigh.

As she turns the key to the sixth door a deep sobbing sigh accompanies the revelation of a sheet of white, tranquil, sleeping water. 'What is this mysterious water?'

'Tears,' he explains sadly, 'tears, tears.'

She gazes intently into his eyes. 'Come, my Judith, let me kiss you. The last door must stay shut.' Thinking she has guessed his secret she shrilly demands that he open the last door. 'All your former wives have suffered murder, brutal, bloody.' The shrieking blood motif combining all manner of dissonant tonal relationships proclaims her doom.

Bartók's leitmotif for pain, suffering and sadness, a C minor seventh chord with major seven, accompanies the opening of the last door. The sorrow, tears, darkness and violence of Bluebeard have not been transformed by the bright, light, major character of Judith and C major becomes C minor as the last bride becomes but the cryogenized image of beauty.

The seventh door opens on the realm where the brides of Bluebeard live a deified but ghostly half-life in the dark chamber of his memory. Bluebeard falls in homage singing: 'Radiant, royal, matchless beauty, immortal, who gathered all his riches, bled to feed his flowers, enlarged his kingdom, all is theirs.' Judith shrinks in horror, 'Living, breathing. They live here!'

The wives each have their own tonality and here autobiographical references to Bartók's own life are manifest. The motifs for each wife contain 'cross-references' to motifs used in works dedicated to his own former loves.[2]

---

2 This was a musical discovery I made in researching this story (Pickering, 1996).

The first bride he saw at dawn, 'crimson, fragrant early morning'. There is a musical allusion to Bartók's first love, Felicitas Fabian.

The second bride is that of noon, 'silent, flaming, golden-haired noon'. Here Bartók makes a musical allusion to his beloved Stefi Geyer.

The third love he found in the evening time, 'quiet, languid, sombre twilight'. The melody contains an allusion to a motif of the Second Fantasy which was dedicated to another love, Irmy Jurkovics.

'The fourth I found at midnight, starry ebony mantled midnight.' 'No more, no more, I am still here', protests Judith, but it is vain and the all-too heavy mantle, diadem and jewels she had herself selected in the treasure chamber are placed upon her shoulders. 'Thou art lovely, passing lovely, thou art queen of all my women.' They gaze into each other's eyes before she walks along the beam of moonshine, bowed by her robes and crown, to take her place within the hall of memories.

Bluebeard's respite from the prison of his soul is over, his brief attempt to find light, life, joy and love has failed and he recedes back into his dark lonely soundscape. Another attempt to find one able to withstand the terror, the brutality, the pain, the torment, the riches, the beauty, the might, the vastness and power of Bluebeard's psyche, has again failed. The piece ends as it began, in the dark key of F sharp pentatony, in the deep, inexplicable loneliness of one who cannot find redemption, who rather than being changed by the light, ultimately seeks to overpower it and who seeks repeatedly for another feminine soul to dispel the gloom.

Analysis

Bartók's Bluebeard is locked into a solipsistic state of aching loneliness. He yearns to have his interior castle penetrated by the gaze of loving comprehension, to allow a mortal beloved to enter his inner recesses and come to know him in all his richness and complexity, yet he can do so only by making his love object an inner figure, subsumed into his windowless monadic isolation. When a real beloved wants to know all, she must be rendered safe by being made but a memory, an image. Here again we meet another version of the isolated self, encased in its own sublimely monadic independence, a state of autarchy involving a fantasy of total self-sufficiency and freedom from others outside itself except as figments of its own creation.

> The same sound resounded and yet was everywhere heard only in one's own interior; no one felt the human element as the human element in others, each one only immediately in his own self. The self remained without a view beyond its walls; all that was world remained without. If it possessed the world within itself, it did so as personal property, not as world . . . It itself remained the only other one that it saw; every

other one wishing to be seen by it had to be contained in this its field of vision and to forgo being regarded as another. The ethical norms of the world thus lost all their own meaning in this field of vision of the self-willed self; they became the mere content of his self-inspection.

(Rosenzweig, 1921, as cited in Moyn, 2005, pp. 143–145)

Bluebeard's castle can be seen to depict the problematics of exogamous transitions relating to fears of psychic penetration of an all-seeing eye which is experienced as annihilating. In Orpheus we have the theme of looking back and losing all at the brink of re-entry into the conscious world. In Psyche and Amor we have the theme of a prohibition against seeing one's beloved: love needs to be blind, yet through exile and labours Psyche is reunited in a new way with her lover, face-to-face. In Bluebeard there is the theme of a prohibition against knowing too much. Yet who is it who lives in the locked room? The untransformable past wives? Unintegrated, split-off psychotic aspects of ourselves? Does the story represent a failure to mourn, a failure to integrate or transform? Bluebeard doesn't dare look at the actual present or the future; he had a defensive compulsion to check that nothing had changed, that his wives were the same, iconographic images in a hall of memories.

In response to the steadfast devotion and fearless love of his last wife, Judith, the doors of Bluebeard's heart opened one by one, penetrating ever deeper into his inner recesses. The unlocking becomes an integral part of the relationship, of the struggle for full, uncompromising, unconditional love. The two are locked in dialogues of pleading, restraint, submission, disclosure, reaction, reinterpretation. Yet Judith herself clings to illusions and ignores the true, stark nature of all she sees – her love gilds the reality of the torture chamber and she sees instead the red light of sunrise. As much as Bluebeard fears psychic invasion, Judith seeks to obtrude. It is thus another form of pursuer–distance dynamic. Under Judith's insistence Bluebeard reveals more and more of his spiritual treasures, the dazzling greatness of his ideas; he becomes passionate, enamoured, animated and at this point wishes to unite with his beloved in a never ending embrace. Revelation is a dramatic and psychic necessity. That he believed love could freeze at the juncture where only his greatness has been revealed means Bluebeard is locked in a cycle of searching out new mates, requesting they leave the doors unopened, having them disobey this injunction and take their place as living portraits on his walls, fictionalized memories rather than flesh-and-blood women, leaving him alone once more.

The yearning to uncover and reveal all, to do the very thing that is forbidden that leads to greater consciousness, is located in the figure of Judith. Against this is Bluebeard's admonition, 'never question me', pointing to a fear of the penetrating eye of insight, the seeing, making, naming, inveigling eye. Picasso also spoke of the devouring nature of the gaze of the beholder. For Sartre, the very capacity of the other to look at me creates a 'drain hole' in the middle of my being (Sartre, 1943/1958, p. 256). This is because the other can make of me an object in his[3] universe. He can also create a feeling of disintegration of my universe as he reorganizes the world around himself. His 'space is made *with my space*; there is a regrouping in which I take part, but which escapes me . . . Thus suddenly an object has appeared which has stolen the world from me' (p. 255). One senses it is this fear that a partner will reorganize the house around her, psychologically and physically, that terrifies a Bluebeardian personality.

Judith enters Bluebeard's castle and sets about bringing a healing light of day. Bluebeard is eager to have Judith behold his spacious kingdom but also fears this: is she capable of seeing accurately but not intrusively? Does her penetrating gaze objectify? Will she see too much or not be capable of comprehending his depth and complexity?

There is the theme of warning against a devouring prurient and intrusive curiosity which seeks to intrude too far into our partner's private realms. Ujfalussy József states that 'Bluebeard is in reality every man. His soul is a mysterious, dark castle, and if the woman who yearns for brightness and warmth penetrates its secrets, she destroys the love between them, and herself becomes part of the past.'[4] Serge Moreux shares this view. Locked away in 'man's interior world' are secrets as mute as the seven doors of Bluebeard's castle. Here we see the gender identification, with woman as prurient in her inveiglement, man as needing to have his privacy respected:

> Only the shining intoxication of fresh love can dissipate this dark threat; but let the new woman in a man's life be discreet; the hidden places of the masculine self are forbidden to her and above all those where, richly adorned by kindly memory, past loves live. However total a passion may be, it will not survive their exhumation.
>
> (Moreux, 1953, p. 108)

Bartók saw an image of himself mirrored in the glass sheet of the lake of Bluebeard's tears. Bartók's music radiates the entangled passions, the destructive patterns of human behaviour, his lifelong conflict between fear of intrusion and longing for connection. His longing for a soul-mate was as fierce as his rebellion against interference with his inner life. Like Bluebeard he sought all his life for a soul-mate who could revere him in his sparkling greatness but not intrude into his murky shadowlands.

---

3 Sartre refers to the other with the masculine pronoun and uses the first person to refer to the Subject.
4 József, sleeve notes for Béla Bartók's *Bluebeard's castle*, Qualiton, Hungary, LPX 1001.

He was torn apart by inner conflict between yearning for a soul-mate and a desire to rise above all emotional entanglement. It was almost as if he played this out by treating his inner loves as Bluebeard did his wives. He could not effect a full transformation in love but sought instead to effect a schizoid detachment from emotional life:

> Each must strive to rise above all; nothing must touch him; he must be completely independent, completely indifferent . . . It needs a gigantic struggle to rise above all things! How far I am yet from doing so! What is more, the further you advance, the more intensely, it seems, you feel!
> (as cited in Demény, 1971, pp. 49–52)

As a student in Budapest Bartók wrote pieces addressed to Felicitas Fábián and cast himself as Schumann to her Clara. He wrote a scherzo which he later alludes to in the theme for the first of Bluebeard's wives. Bartók sought refuge from the pain of relational longing in solipsism:

> For solace, I would recommend to anyone the attempt to achieve a state of spiritual indifference in which it is possible to view the affairs of the world with complete indifference and with the utmost tranquillity . . .
> (as cited in Demény, 1971, p. 53)

Stefi Geyer, another beloved, was the recipient of long philosophical expositions. He longed to find his views mirrored in another, yet only if they matched his:

> For life is so beautiful! There's so much beauty in nature – the arts – science . . . That is the most beautiful thing you have written to me so far. And why? because it reflects my own view of life . . . There may be some interest . . . in exploring a conception of things which is quite alien to one's own. But to come upon a fellow human being – more, a friend who shares, albeit in a different form, the ideas on which one's whole conception of the world is founded: that is one of the purest joys.
> (as cited in Demény, 1971, p. 75)

Bartók's *Bluebeard's castle* depicts a failure to cross a threshold into a full conjoined intersubjectivity. It describes a wedding, but Bluebeard expects his wives to become subsumed as internal figures into his psychic domain. It never occurs to him that he might leave his interior castle and venture forth to create a new co-created intersubjective realm with his new love. When the wife makes her presence felt in her husband's home, he feels diabolically threatened. There are strictly demarcated 'no-go' zones, displaying more than healthy fear of psychic intrusion. The punishment for trespass is to become a portrait, an internal object, in a hall of memories.

In *Bluebeard's castle* the wife is only an image, a function, not a human being in her own right. Bartók's composition is the poignant, heart-rending song of his own melancholic loneliness and longing.

Yet it could also be argued that the preceding analysis of Bartók's opera represents the story from Judith's point of view, the respondent to this cry. In other words, my interpretation above could itself be interpreted as a counter-transferential response evoked by Bartók's agonized lament. Bartók's music calls forth the response of wanting to be the one who succeeds in saving him, by entering his castle and bringing light, redemption and the salve of warm love.

Chapter 13

Don't look back: Orpheus and Eurydice

Who is Eurydice? The face of ultimate wisdom who withdraws into her mystery, to be sought through heroic descent into the labyrinths of memory, of longing, of underworld subterranean domains? The story of Orpheus and Eurydice epitomizes thresholds of becoming, initiations in the journey into the underworld to find and redeem, to harness all our courage, resources, wisdom in the exogamous quest. We confront, face-to-face, Persephone and Hades, two faces of dark wisdom. Eurydice–Persephone is the epitome of apophatic wisdom, the dark shrouded face of Sophia. To see is to become: one cannot gaze upon the face of wisdom without it being heirophany. In one moment we are ready to make the appointment with the Real or we lose all. Yet that is not enough. Having made that appointment, what next? This is the critical factor. We have to integrate the moment of realization, initiation and ontophany into life as it is lived, keep the inner vision clear, translate it into how we go on living each day. It is how we walk out of experiences of epiphany and live them that is the ultimate heroic test.

Orpheus depicts our tendency to return to old destructive modalities. It depicts the melancholia that results from recognition of failures of moments of destiny. Intrapsychically, this myth depicts aspects of an analytic journey and in particular the tendency to look back and lose all, just on the point of crossing psychic abysses into new areas of growth and transformation. It also describes particular relational configurations that become constellated by those caught in an orphic complex.

The story of Orpheus and Eurydice also symbolizes the attempt to cross the portal from family-of-origin domains, into adult relationships. The threshold is situated at the point of the adolescent's first exogamous relationship: symbolic and actual and the oft-repeated failure to cross such a threshold.

Intersubjective fields of love

Winnicott talks of an intermediate area of experiencing that lies between fantasy and reality, a locus of cultural experience and domain of creativity

(Ogden, 1997). This area of potential space, which Winnicott saw occurring between mother and infant, also occurs in the analytical relationship and may occur between lovers.

We have seen how perceptions we have of one another are a shifting combination of reactions to 'real' persons and the projections of internal complexes or of the *dramatis personae* built up over one's life. We simultaneously enact our own scenarios while playing the parts ascribed in the other's fantasy, with a cast of shape-changing characters. In this chapter I show how a particular interlocking phantasy scene may involve the replay of aspects of certain mythologems which depict common inter-relational themes concerning thresholds of intimacy.

In an intimate human encounter we may find ourselves in a unique imaginal and embodied environment, a dynamic, interactive space, in which there are fluid realms of experience between internal and external reality, conscious and unconscious communications, shared states of mind, bodily sensations, attunements and malattunements, or, as Balint put it, a 'harmonious [disharmonious?] interpenetrating mix up' (Balint, 1959, pp. 62–69).

The imaginal realm between us will not only be peopled with projections of inner figures, but may also be crowded with aspects (images, sounds, dialogues) of films, music, novels, plays, cultural discourses and the meanings we derive from them. When we both have read a certain book, or seen a film, opera or play, discussing its significant scenes and meanings for us may generate multiple associations which further our creation of a future relational history. When we refer to the story it is as if we are referring to something we have both lived through, as if we are an amalgam of the characters as well as ourselves. The images, characters, passions of the story become incorporated into the choreography of our *mundus imaginalis* (Corbin, 1972), thus generating new landscapes for us, new worlds of associations.

In this chapter, a short story, based on a script for a play, takes the place of a clinical vignette. It narrates the unfolding of a relationship between a man I will call David and a woman he encountered, whom I call Sibylla. This genre has been chosen because it more appropriately reveals the intersubjective nature of love: the complexities and confusions of two people in relationship and ways in which it is difficult to disentangle who is experiencing what in the field of mutual projections. Is it all a phantasy or a memory of love related by the narrator? Are David and Sibylla real figures or internal figures speaking their interior dialogue?

David cum Sibylla

'David' and 'Sibylla' found themselves, in their encounters with each other, living out aspects of both the Bluebeard and the Orpheus mythologems.

David was eternally caught between his search for a beloved who was capable of knowing all and fears of intrusion into his secret inner chambers. An orphic complex reformulated itself in his love life repeatedly: falling in love with an idealized *femme inspiratrice*, losing her to the underworld (or unconscious), a heroic quest to redeem that aspect of himself, then a fatal looking back to old defensive modalities. This was inevitably followed by a psychic wailing in the wilderness, torn apart by furious maenadic forces of self-destruction. Sibylla, due to her own identifications with sibylline aspects of the myth, provided a perfect match for such complexes to be played out in her encounter with David.

Our two antagonists were intimately acquainted with various operatic and filmic interpretations of the story of Orpheus, films such as Jane Campion's *The piano*, versions of Bluebeard's Castle such as the Bartók opera and an Australian play *Blue murder*, popular psychology books and Buddhist philosophy. The *mundus imaginalis* between them was richly littered with images, sounds and ideas derived from these sources.

Orpheus and Eurydice: a myth of exogamous failure

The story of Orpheus' descent into the underworld in order to redeem Eurydice is one of the most persistent and potent myths in Western civilization, endlessly retold in drama, opera, poetry, art and, in the twentieth century, film. Each element of the tragedy of Orpheus is dense with multiple layers of meaning which can be read simultaneously on individual, collective, psychological and historical levels. The way it is retold, the choice of which elements of the story are emphasized, tells us much about the psychology of both the individual artists who reinterpret and represent this theme and the collective unconscious of the particular era.

Unlike Oedipus and Narcissus the myth has not been as extensively analysed in psychoanalytic literature, thus I will outline some of these historical depictions below.

Orpheus – poet, composer, musician, shamanistic priest, giver of oracles, magician – through his melodious voice, the power of his rhetoric and the beauty of his lyre-playing pacified birds and beasts, confronted the gods and acted as psychopomp between the worlds of living and dead, past and present. As *Theologos*, he sang of the gods, founded the mysteries and introduced sacred rites and writing.

Orpheus, according to accounts such as those of Virgil's *Georgics* and Ovid's *Metamorphoses*, was born of the union of Apollo, the Sun god, and Calliope, the muse of epic poetry and eloquence. He was given a lyre made by Hermes and thus was empowered by the gods to communicate divine inspiration through his singing and playing. He was able to mesmerize rocks, tame animals, gods and humans and had power over the gates of Hell.

Orpheus met and fell in love with the nymph Eurydice. Eurydice died from a snake bite on the heel, trying to flee the advances of Aristaeus, and was taken down into Hades.

The grief-stricken Orpheus determined to enter Hades and recover her, to overcome death by entering alive where only the dead had gone before him. He thus effects the ultimate initiation between life and death, transversing the underworld, his powers of rhetoric and song charming the ferryman Charon, the dog Cerberus, the three Judges of the Dead and alleviating the tortures of the damned. His eloquence and beautiful singing swayed Persephone, queen of the underworld, who pleaded with her spouse Hades to grant his request. Hades relented – Orpheus could take Eurydice back to earth on one condition: he must not turn back to look at her following him until he entered the world of daylight.

Orpheus begins the ascent from Hades, his eyes on the path ahead, remembering the admonition, repeating under his breath, 'Do not look back'. But doubts as to her faithfulness beset him. Is she behind him, can he truly trust her?

At the last moment he loses faith and turns around to reassure himself that Eurydice is still following. With a cry of reproach dying on her lips, she fades into a wraith and Eurydice is whisked away for ever into the underworld. Nothing would allow a second entrance. The doors of Hades were closed shut, Eurydice gone from him for ever.

Orpheus thenceforward abandoned all connections to the social world of relationships and wandered the wilderness year in year out in inconsolable anguish. He sang ceaselessly of his torment and his rejection of all women, comparing them unfavourably with Eurydice. Maenads, female followers of Dionysus, heard his misogynist outpourings and in indignation tore him apart. His severed head and lyre were thrown into the river Hebrus, floated down to the Aegean Sea and eventually were carried onto the barren shores of the island of Lesbos, all the while still singing its laments. Caught in a fissure of rock (in a cave sacred to Dionysus) it issued oracles until eventually Apollo, finding his own oracles at Delphi, Gryneium and Clarus were deserted, decreed it to be silenced. However, oracles purporting to be from Orpheus gave rise to a growing body of esoteric philosophical literature.

There are different accounts of why Orpheus was dismembered. One was that it was the revenge of the followers of Dionysus because Orpheus served Apollo and neglected Dionysus. Another was that his sacrificial murder was actually a partaking in Dionysus' dismemberment. Some said Zeus killed him for divulging divine secrets, instituting the mysteries of Apollo at Thrace as well as those of Hecate in Aegina and Subterrene Demeter at Sparta. Another was that Orpheus' advocacy of 'the love of tender boys' post-Eurydice enraged the Thracian women both for his rejection of them and for his homosexual enticing away of their husbands and sons.

Orphism is characterized by its dualism: the soul is capable of salvation, but is entombed in a body from which it must be released. Redemption is attained by physical and spiritual purity in this life, via asceticism, celibacy, avoidance of any contact with death and attunement to the divine harmony instituted by the lyre of Orpheus. This is followed by a cycle of reincarnation in which purgation in the underworld is followed by rebirth until release from the earth.

Don't look back

> He stopped . . . he looked back . . . there all his effort was poured away.
> (Virgil, *Georgics* IV 490–492)

At those moments in our lives where we are on the brink of breaking through old stuck patterns, we all too often shrink back, the old being reassuringly familiar, the new being unknown and fearful. There is grave temptation when on the verge of psychological transformation to have second thoughts, falter at the gates. This 'looking back' is a repeated miscarriage of psychic birth and the crux of the tragedy of Orpheus. It is the terrible threshold to what Melanie Klein called the depressive position: the area of Bion's allusion to catastrophic change. The attempt to make this transition tests and uncovers all one's disabilities.

There is a dawning of a realization. In this moment of insight, when the cracks between the worlds are open, one sees the possibility of being able to negotiate the road to the underworld to retrieve a vital lost aspect of oneself and return with it.

Yet just at the moment of re-entry into the light of day, the thought of the comfort of the familiar, the old unreconstructed life, seems more alluring than the existential fear of the unfamiliar. We want a more fully human life, to grow beyond old patterns, to 'experience a greater range (and play) of thoughts, feelings and sensations' that are felt to be our own (Ogden, 1997, p. 11). But, there is a part that violently resists any such change. We are literally demoralized when there has been a failure to transact the threshold from the paranoid-schizoid to the depressive position.

All too often we drop into a half-alive state of apathy, predictability and torpor. We initiate destructive actions that deaden ourselves and those around us even more and undo whatever good is built. We are torn apart by the maenadic forces within us.

The abandonment of Eurydice may also signify the ways in which a woman who is used by a man to function as muse or *femme inspiratrice* so often finds herself abandoned once her function is fulfilled, as Ariadne was by Thesius. Lou Andreas-Salomé, Anaïs Nin, Christiana Morgan, Toni Wolff, Sabina Spielrein all played inspirational or prophetic functions to numinous seeming men, such as Henry Miller, Henry Murray, Sartre, Jung, Freud and Rilke.

The lament of the one left behind is echoed by the lament of he who has lost his beloved for ever. Orpheus' reaction to his own folly is to wallow in self-pity and hatred for all other women. Orpheus loses Eurydice through his own actions. In Jean Cocteau's *Orphée* of 1950 the hero betrays Eurydice by looking at her reflection in the rear-vision mirror of the car.

Dismemberment is indicative of a literal cutting off from the more earthy, disruptive, Dionysian way. Like the music or the poem Orpheus creates, his spirit must soar. The attempt to repress libidinal energies, the rejection of women, orphic ephemeralizing becomes one manifestation of the mind–body, head–heart split that has beset Western culture. This story is intimately about the perils of such splits. Atonement, or 'at-one-ment', requires healing, integration of the divided self, recognition of the interdependence of psyche and soma, of self and others, of love and a spiritual path.

Blue Orfeo: a monodrama

They meet at a Buddhist initiation ceremony, Sibylla running headlong into David in her eagerness to avoid the flight path of a 'Peter Pan kind of man', who had recently given her a hard time. He immediately engages her in deep conversation – in five minutes she has given him a potted history of her life, occupation, marital status and interests. He gives her his phone number.

She had spent the winter in hibernation, a self-imposed retreat. Her work had been so intense she needed her walled garden to contain it. But now she decided to throw a garden party to induce her rebirth into the social world. It took a week's prevarication before courage took the better part of discretion in ringing David, and another week before he returned her call, with an 'on the run' 'deep and meaningful' response, to which he added a list of his more noteworthy credentials – lawyer, journalist, script-writer, theatre politico in some high-flying job . . .

'I'd love to come to your party', said David. 'Do you mind if I bring my ex-wife who's visiting from London?'

'Sure, no worries! spice, ex-spice, mummies, significant and insignificant others and Grandmas are all welcome.'

She dresses carefully in honour of the occasion – bronze flowing Grecian number, gold slippers, amber bracelet, her dark hair loosened from its knot.

He arrives halfway through the afternoon, *sans* ex-wife. Sibylla raises her eyebrow quizzically commenting, 'You left the exes at home, I see.'

'Ex, only one', he corrects her.

He invites himself to a guided tour of her house, pausing before each etching or *objet d'art*, asking her to explain its significance.

'Do you have a shrine?'

'Yes', she answers, a little hesitantly.

'Can I see it? I'm really curious about how people set up their shrines. You don't mind, I'm just nosy.'

It was in her bedroom. He examines her *tanka* of the Buddha of Compassion, 1,000 arms outstretched in the gesture of open-hearted giving.

'How old are you?'

'Why do you ask?'

'Like I said, I'm just a snoop.'

An image of a man pinning the wings of a butterfly comes to mind. She hopes if she says nothing he'll go on, but he stares silently waiting for an answer. She finds herself revealing too much of herself whilst asking herself, 'why do I capitulate?'

He moves on to her study, where it is her wedding photo in a dark corner that catches his attention.

'That woman is so beautiful, like a Renaissance princess. God, look at your book collection!'

Concerned lest she neglect her other guests, she tries to guide him back outside, but like Anna Karenina at the ball with Vronsky, she finds herself enveloped in his spell, unable to tear herself away.

Eventually he finishes his inspection of her home, shepherds her outside, saying apropos of nothing that he did have more than one ex, he'd been married three times.

'It's a bit embarrassing, they nickname me Liz.'

'Liz? what does that stand for?'

'Liz Taylor.'

'Or is it Bluebeard?'

'Speaking of Bluebeard, did you see Beatrice Christian's *Blue murder* at the theatre festival? An Australian version with the castle, Black Rock, in the middle of Sydney Harbour. Great place for New Year's Eve fireworks!'

'I found it unconvincing that this modern, liberated, Evelyn character was so hoodwinked by his metaphysical pondering she couldn't wait to get her clothes off. Even when the writing was on the wall she didn't leave.'

David muses, 'Why does one enter and stay in a relationship you know is going to be disastrous?'

She tries to detach herself again, but after a few minutes talking to the many friends floating through the garden, she sees him standing alone. He puts a hand on her shoulder saying, 'I didn't miss your somewhat pointed reference to Bluebeard before. Do you know Béla Bartók's opera? I gather it was somewhat autobiographical.'

'Yes, apparently Bartók dedicated it to his third wife on the occasion of their wedding. What a wedding present! Kept marrying teenage girls, then felt lonely because he couldn't share his tortured soul and Nietzschian philosophical musings with them. It's funny, Bartók's music evokes in me a sense of compassion for his loneliness and longing. I have so wanted to reach out to him and say I heard, I cared. Only he's dead. Now I'm older and more cynical I question my reaction. I think that's the reaction that a man with that sort of complex evokes – the saviouress. Yet, his music still inspires a sense of wanting to get inside his psyche, to open within the walls of his castle, the multi-faceted rooms of jewels and tears and poetry and indoor gardens . . .'

'Sounds like you're in love with him. Pity he's dead. Interesting how the Bluebeard theme keeps cropping up. Have you seen Jane Campion's film, *The Piano?*'

'Many times over. That film is so loaded with innuendo about male–female patterns of relationship . . . and the will to live winning out over the lure of the silent, ocean grave.'

'You know Campion had Ada drown. It was the preview audience that saved her.'

'Excuse me while I reel from that . . . Her turning back is the most critical point of the film. Campion had her drown then?'

'She drowns. The whole Nelson domestic bliss scene is a tack-on, filmed in Philadelphia. Harvey Keitel called back to strut his stuff again. He is such a hunk for women, can't see why myself.'

'Not entirely. In the beginning of the film where he is trying to get what he desires by power games he's repulsive. But when he surrenders the will to power, when Ada comes of her own accord and finds him desolate upon his bed, vulnerable, honest and sick with longing, then he's incredibly attractive. You see, where there is a will to power there can be no love . . .'

'You sound as bad as Campion.' He seems annoyed.

'Sorry. I do tend to wax a bit lyrical on this subject. I reckon you can tell a lot about a man by asking him what he thought of that film, which aspect he related to, or didn't, as the case may be.'

'The voyeur scene rang bells for me. Been there, done that.'

'Really? I read one review by a man who was offended by the idea of women finding a naked pot-bellied man desirable. But I don't think women get hung up on the physical appearance of men in the way men do about women.'

He changes the subject. 'I love your dress – you look like a Cretan maiden soaking up the sun's rays. I lived in a cave in Crete once, part of my dropping out phase. The cave where the Cyclops was born. I had a house on one of the Greek islands later, but my first wife got it when we divorced . . . Don't ever marry a lawyer!'

'Thanks for the warning!'

David muses, 'Three wives and all three left me.'

'Or did they leave you because, in a sense, you had already left them?'

She wonders what is guiding her tongue to say such things.

'Funny you should say that. The ex-wife who was here this weekend said she left me because I left her emotionally ages before. The thing is I've come to recognize that for me it was about possession. I had to have them. And then when I had possessed them sexually I lost interest, put all my energies elsewhere, work, writing.'

'That's horrible! I suppose at least you're honest.'

'Yes, well this isn't something I tell everyone. To most people I'm just a good Buddhist.'

So, she thinks, am I supposed to feel some kind of special privilege that you're telling me?

'The middle wife was amazing, incredible, beautiful, cultured Jewess. I just had to have her.'

'And when you had her, you lost interest and then she left you.'

'She went to America. I didn't want to go, it didn't suit my timing. Now she's really happily married to a New York businessman.'

'At least it seems your ex-wives get to have a happy ending.'

'Yep, all happily remarried. I lost my children though. But you just leave them behind and on you go in life . . .'

'At your peril!'

'Yes, at my peril', David says a little more quietly.

Sibylla feels a wave of empathy at this glimpse of a bruised man lurking underneath. 'Hold on', she reminds herself, 'don't get too compassionate here, beware your special brand of being sucked in.'

'So I'm not getting married again', David continues, 'I'm determined on that. I enjoy the company of women, but I won't sleep with them any more. It's deadly. My last close shave was when a woman came to visit me in India. But I resisted the temptation to marry her, I've risen above all that now. I suspect I'll end my years as a monk.'

She raises an internal eyebrow at how he makes resisting relationship seem a blood sport.

'What made you think you possessed your women just because you married them?'

'The women I never married remained fascinating. The sense of wondering about what it would have been like.'

Alarm bells clang in the spring air. The parallels with the play *Blue murder* become alarmingly close. Blue's three wives who languish, cryo-genized, bickering among themselves about the lack of attention, uncomprehending that after he went to such lengths to capture, seduce and marry them he lost all interest. This Blue thinks he gets over his power games by being celibate. You don't have to sleep with someone to play seduction games. What has he been doing all afternoon with this mesmerizing act of his. Do I really need to run this tape again? Want to be hurt by a *puer aeternus*/Bluebeard combo again? It was almost as if he were not a real being but just a tormenter, a phantom presence delivering his lines from an old, old tale.

'What do you think is behind this power game of yours?' she asks.

'I guess not having any relationship with my father, I don't even know who he was. He left when I was born and my mother remarried when I was five. I remember the wedding. I've never found out why he left, anything about him. I don't want to hurt my mother by asking. I'm really bright, I mean *really* bright, but I'm really stunted in the emotional department. How about you? Do you think you'll ever get remarried? How do you reconcile love and your spiritual quest?'

'I think marriage can also be a valid path. I'm also suspicious of the ways a spiritual path that renounces relationship can be used as a defence against psychological maturity. A committed relationship and having children can really make you face your stuff. A daily stubbing your toe on reality.'

'I just got bored, what do you do with the boredom?'

'Stick to the boredom and out of the deadness may rise a real relationship not based on conquest, domination or projection. Actually, the real relationship may be far more interesting than any fantasy one concocts out of one's desires. There are more things in heaven and earth, David, than are dreamt of in your philosophy.'

Later, when he has gone, she tugs angrily at the hooks that despite her circumspection had managed to lodge in her heart. In the days that follow she feels a strange sense of poignancy, like someone was calling to her on the wind, someone very young, fragile, neglected. She knows too well her tendency to be drawn into *eros* out of compassion. But this was out of proportion to her own stuff. She felt lumbered with a very sad, wounded, vulnerable part of him. And she didn't want this burden. She felt some sense of duty to speak to him, however futile it might be. She struggled with this for a week till prudence won, at which point she found a message on her answering machine from David asking her to the opening night of *Who's afraid of Virginia Woolf*.

At the theatre she soon sees her role as an appendage, a bit of fluff to ornament his Gucci suit. He seems to know everyone, the place full of politicians and upwardly socially mobile-phoned people, and he is networking like networking is going out of style.

Afterwards he invites her back for A-grade Darjeeling tea at his top-storey apartment.

'Welcome to Bluebeard's castle', he ushers her in.

'Thanks Blue, or is it Liz?'

He puts on a CD. Gluck's Orfeo serenades a reluctant Euridice as they sit contemplating the city lights below.

She found herself strangely impressed by his aesthetic sense and also by his devoutness; the apartment was like a shrine or ashram and exquisitely, yet sparsely, decorated.

'Funny what social animals we are despite being born alone and dying alone', he comments.

'Yes and the incredible energy we spend refining communication skills and ways of knowing another, despite the ultimate futility of such a quest.'

'I like the Abhidharma philosophy because it is so straightforward, clear, logical. None of this emotional stuff.'

'Have you encountered the Cittamatra school? That is about how the world we live in is so much a reflection of our state of mind. We sit here in this room yet inhabit a different psychic world . . .'

'Yes, I bet what you and I are experiencing right now in emotional terms is very different . . .'

'I suspect so.'

He asks her to interpret a dream he had the night after her party.

'I dreamed I lost my canine tooth, it was surreal, I put my hand to my mouth and it just came out in my hand. It looked very worn as if it had been through a lot.'

'Well, apart from it being a classic symbol of castration anxiety . . . only joking of course!'

'Hardly think that applies!'

'I've no idea where this thought comes from so take it or leave it. It feels like letting go of something maybe you don't need any more. Surrender and softness are words that come to mind.'

'I could do with some softness. I feel on the edge of some huge, momentous change in my life . . . perhaps it's meeting you.'

He lends her Robert Drew's *The drowner*.

It is a week when she finds herself submerged in images of watery graves, pools of tears, drowning and being saved, sinking and swimming. The image of a wraith-like, adolescent girl sinking back into a watery grave. She can't seem to shake off this sense she must warn him . . .

She asks him to dinner.

She is preparing a vegetarian feast when he arrives. She feels self-conscious and awkward – some presentiment of the heaviness of the evening's agenda. Gradually she warms to the occasion as they sit down to eat, candle light taking over from the last light of day, soft colours and light playing patterns on the table, a huge bowl of salad, Arvo Pärt's hauntingly beautiful music . . .

He continues relaying the story of his many relationships with women, this evening talking of the ones he didn't marry. An eighteen-year-old he rescued from an alcoholic father. He felt flattered she fell in love with him. So he took her into his home, made love to her, initiated her into the adult world. But while he was out leading a busy political life, she, at university, began an affair with a man her own age. He was hurt, momentarily.

Then, at a public function for a Buddhist teacher he was confronted by the image of a blond, smiling woman at the opposite table. Something in this open, beaming smile he found irresistibly endearing.

'I swear I've never done this before in my life, but I walked right up to her and asked for her phone number. So began a two-year relationship with a woman who I later found out was schizophrenic. I didn't believe it . . .'

An eighteen-year-old girl living out her father stuff with David. A beautiful, schizophrenic woman. Again the apparition of a pool of cool, green water, within it Eurydice, a ten- to twelve-year-old maiden, sweet, soft, fragile, innocent, stretching a pale, small hand out, her deep eyes imploring Sibylla to take her hand in hers and pull her through, not let Orpheus abandon her by looking back.

'David, I'll be honest here . . . I don't quite know how to say this, or even whether it's wise. Disregard this if you like, put it in a box and ponder it when you're eighty . . . But if the shoe fits, wear it.'

He smiles, bemused.

'When you left my party I thought a lot about what you'd been telling me about your life, your marriages, your loves. And I felt connected to a sad, lonely, part of you. It made me cry. I keep being reminded of Eurydice, just at that point where there is still that chance, that hope, that Orpheus can fulfil his heroic mission, bring her to light, not look back . . .'

David looks at her as if on the brink of breakthrough, tears form and gather in the corners of his eyes, he suddenly drops the persona and the bravado and cries:

'I have grown up not knowing who my father is. I have lived an amazing life, travelled the globe, written film scripts and books but nothing of real substance. I have had numerous relationships none of which has come to anything. It's all futile, meaningless. I have lost both my children, been denied any relationship with them. I am nearly fifty and nothing has touched my soul!'

He takes off his glasses and wipes his eyes. She desperately wants to put out her hand to him, show she cares. In that moment of his own compassion for himself she can almost see him emerge from the watery depths, Eurydice in tow.

But before her eyes she witnesses him contemplate the two roads before him, the choice. In a brief, split second the old wins out over the new, he looks back to the old. The apparition of Eurydice fades into a wraith and disappears, a silent reproach dying on her lips.

He goes on to completely deny his pain.

'Oh, but what am I talking about, in the scheme of things that's so unimportant. What is important is my spiritual practice. Last year, when in retreat there'd be days when I wrote and wrote about my experiences and the writing is really good, Sibylla, really good. I felt if I spent my life in retreat it would not be a life wasted. I look around and its so beautiful here –'

He points to the candle-lit table in front of him, including her in the scene as if she is merely part of some vision put before him to tempt him off his path –

'It is so beautiful it is shining, but it is nothing but phantasmagoria.'

She feels really insulted at this point, his disavowal of her, the scene, all she is offering as being but the temptation of the devil.

'Don't dishonour me by misinterpreting my motives.'

She adds to herself, 'I am not trying to personally offer salvation from your celibate path. Thanks, David, but I am a real person, not some tempting vision. And I have no intentions towards you. I'm not that gullible.'

She realizes his response is precisely what Orpheus did. No wonder he ostensibly advocates the path that renounces love, relationship, marriage . . . He has become the misogynist Orpheus wandering in the wilderness, lamenting his lost soul, decrying womankind.

'Do you know what happened to Orpheus?'

'What?'

'For his misogyny, he was torn up by the Maenads, the out of control, frenzied, female forces within him.'

She tells him that she thinks the tooth dream might be positive, a falling away of the need to suck the blood of women, using them, milking them dry, then spitting them out.

'I agree, I can't go on notching up women like scalps on a belt. And some of those women didn't like being scalped . . .'

'What are you trying to avoid?'

'Loneliness.'

She keeps reminding herself not to invest in his winning through, to renounce attachment to motives of salvation, know, cynical though it may seem, not to hope. Dracula's well-worn tooth has fallen, but one remains . . .

She thinks, 'well I have delivered my message, Messagera-like, of his lost, dead, regressed anima and it is his path to choose to negotiate the underworld to win her back, not mine. My job is done . . .'

A few days later Sibylla receives a 'thank you' card:

Dear Sibylla

Thank you so much for a relaxing, entertaining and stimulating dinner the other night. I do apologize, however, for being a less than scintillating guest: I'm afraid when some of the dark moments of my past float up, I tend to become strident.

As for my life, the case is simpler than it seems: for whatever reasons, I am still emotionally less-than-competent and for this reason try to discipline myself to avoid (causing) further hurt. Thanks again! David.

The loud thud of battening hatches echoes between the lines. She feels a maenadic fury at the strength of his defences, that he could be so successful at renouncing all need for relationship (would that her defences were that strong!). She feels insulted that he misinterpreted her motives. She paces her study, composing a suitable reply:

You say you try to discipline yourself to avoid (causing) further hurt. You don't get off the hook that easily, you don't avoid hurting yourself or others by avoiding relationships, you only have to walk down the street and converse with a woman and you inflict your wounds upon her. Further, you continue to play the same seduction/possession games only more subtly and unconsciously in all manner of ways.

Am I to presume by the last part of your message you feel it necessary to warn me off? Is this a 'dear Johnny'? I feel insulted by such insinuations. I repeat: do not dishonour me by misinterpreting my motives.

If you want a sometime companion for theatre, film, dinner, conversation, fine. But I'm not in the game to form a more intimate relationship with someone like you. Anyway the sort of woman you would be attracted to 'ain't me babe (no, no, no, it ain't me babe, it's not me you're looking for', as Bob Dylan might say). I've played the role of Messagera, Persephone and now a Maenad, but I don't 'do' Eurydice. I'm not fragile, neurotic or nubile enough, to be your object-choice. I'm a real McCoy, not a wraith. Like in Waltzing Matilda, you'll never get me alive, said she!

And his ghost may be heard, as you pass by that billabong, bodilessly intoning his Buddhist mantras.

Analysis: the orphic complex

David and Sibylla can be read in a number of ways:

- David and Sibylla and the '*mundus imaginalis*' or intersubjective field between them. David's complexes infect and catch Sibylla in their web. Her responses are a combination of her own hooks from her own complexes and responses to being constructed in a certain way.
- David conversing inwardly with and projecting outward a dramatis personae of inner figures – Eurydice his soft, virginal, innocent figure, Sibylla the prophetess/wise woman, Persephone as psychopomp of the underworld.
- Sibylla as a woman conversing with internally or projecting outward her collection of figures and relational configurations: her need to penetrate into forbidden Bluebeardian zones, her quest to redeem an alienated yet powerful masculine figure, to retrieve from the underworld her own soul, her longing for an orphic man of wisdom who would meet her at her own levels of Sibylline prophetic intelligence, her enchantment with an eternally youthful spirit.

Within an intimate relationship all of these processes operate simultaneously. The intersubjective field consists of a complex matrix of simultaneous processes of projection and introjection: David's projections onto Sibylla with which she identifies, her constructions of him, which he also plays out. Within this multi-layered dialectic both are continually destroyed, recreated and transformed, and in that process creating one another 'as a subject that has not existed to this point' (Ogden, 1994, p. 2).

The figure of David is a personification of a particular form of relational pathology which I call the orphic complex.

David's spirituality was characterized by an Apollonian aesthetic sensibility, a love of literature, music, the world of ideas, vegetarianism, an orphic emphasis on physical purity. David utilized his own reading of Buddhism to construct an ideological rationalization for an elaborate defence structure which attacked, in Kalsched's words, 'all elements of experience and perception' that were 'linked with his "reaching out" into the world of objects that traumatized' him. This led to a persecution of his need for significant others and an attack at the threshold between self and other (Kalsched, 1996, p. 102).

The experience of a gaping 'black hole' within was intellectually defended by David by recourse to a misreading of the symbolism of Buddhist doctrines of *anātman*, non-self, *śūnyata*, the void. Such emptiness (*śūnyata*) as (misunderstood) philosophical belief is one thing, but as 'psychic reality . . . it feels so appallingly awful and lonely that the child/patient must retreat into an inflated alienation, and dares not consciously experience or acknowledge either the loneliness or the panic that such uncontainedness and abandonment induces' (Clark, 1987, p. 73).

David was fascinated by the 'idea' of woman, but a real woman bored him, which is to say she emotionally frightened him. He was infused by a sense of de-animation, depersonalization and apathy, which is a passive form of hate, a narcissistic sadism.

Women whom David encountered were typically provoked by this orphean complex into assuming particular responsive roles, highly similar to what an analyst might experience as a congruent, syntonic countertransference. The woman might feel drawn to play out the role of his weak, young, inexperienced love object, to be his Eurydice. She might feel drawn to act the psychopomp, who will show him the way to recover his lost soul (Persephone). A maenadic rage might be provoked by the implicit misogyny of his eschewing of women for the (higher) spiritual plane. She might want to save him, personally offer salvation like Judith wanting to bring warmth and light into Bluebeard's castle. She will probably find herself alternating between a combination of these roles. Sibylla found herself playing all these roles, one by one, except that of Eurydice. She would tell herself it was because she stood her ground, but she would not in any case have got the part should she audition: David's unconscious casting agency would not have given her the part. Yet she felt a tearing poignant sense of pity for a vulnerable Eurydice-like figure within David who seemed to call out to be rescued.

David had an almost obsessional need to manipulate women by possession, stemming from unresolved issues concerning a domineering yet emotionally distant mother. All his love objects complained of being left for dead once locked into their safe and unchanging position. In such a way he always looked back, as if to say, 'I've still got you, you're still my inexperienced, virginal woman'. He could never look forward to new growth or the shock of the other's radical alterity.

His own answer to his predicament was to 'rise above' entanglement with women, sublimating all vestiges of such urges in spiritual practice. He now led his life like a post-Eurydice Orfeo wandering an emotional wilderness passively wreaking his revenge for his previous disappointments. These were attacks on integrative connections in order to break his desire, thereby never retrieving his lost soul from the shadowlands.

Despite his avowed celibacy, there remained a strong seductive current in his overtures towards women, whom he still hooked into some kind of pseudo-relationship with him. He sought out the company of intelligent, glamorous women who could accompany him to 'first nights' at the theatre, political functions, where one is 'seen'. These 'escorts' were ignored once he felt he had engaged their interest. Thus the compulsion to reach out to, engage the attention of, then withdraw from women continued in a more subtle form.

It was not surprising that the scene in the film *The piano* he most related to was the voyeur scene. David's psychic reality was 'voyeuristic, masturbatory, and second-hand', evading 'real related sexuality . . . assertiveness, non-sentimental affection, love and its emotional demands' (Clark, 1987, p. 70).

Freeing the spirit from the terrifying loneliness of its isolation cell is as much the goal of Buddhism as it was the individuation task confronting David. Non-duality (*sunyata*) points to the travesty of a dualistic orientation that views oneself as an entity independent of and separate from the integrated wholeness of the universe and that fails to comprehend the interdependence of subject and object, oneself and the world.

The barrier to a more interpersonal integration of this view was a fear that his own precarious separateness would be seduced and eaten, that his self would be annihilated by forced psychic intrusion. Thus he hovered forever, half-alive, on the brink between his 'phobic fear of being pulled back into the powerful, suffocating, dark embraces of mother' and his 'longing to come alive and develop' his 'atrophied identity' (Seligman, 1982, p. 1).

David attempted to construct a watertight defence structure against psychic pain. Sibylla's saviour's arms inevitably proved insufficient to dissolve the powerful, habitual obstacles to change. He would have to become real, mortal and needy, and she, for him, would have to be able to become human, complex, with a mind of her own. This was bound to fail. He only wanted to relate to the image of a maiden and imagine himself as a celibate knight. He was locked for ever in looking back, thus missing all possibility of embodied love and vitality, which he so desired, and so feared.

Sibylla came to recognize that she was the recipient of a disowned part of David. She attempted to dislodge it via seeking to understand the subtleties of his intrapsychic dynamics and then to deliver back to him her insight *Messagera*-like on a platter. This failed because David, predictably, refused to swallow her gratuitous offering.

David was ambivalently drawn to her because she was capable of understanding him, yet the idea she might want real connection repelled him. Then he abandoned her for knowing too much, as Bluebeard did Judith. The intersubjective sphere created by both parties was one in which they danced on the line of whether to give or withhold. From his side there were competing impulses to reveal and to hide, to know and not to know. On her side there were impulses to understand and a fear of sucking him dry, trampling uninvited into his secret recesses. Furthermore he both wanted and didn't want her as seer and initiator. She picked up his ambivalent conflicts and was devastated by them. He got a vicarious satisfaction out of the devastation he caused. The story was thus destined to unfold much like its orphic template.

In the mutually constellated psychological field there was an unconscious projective usage of each other. At first Sibylla identified with the role of medium, and played out the role of a pseudo-therapist with a vengeance. Sibylla had her own neuroses that allowed her to be hooked into playing such circumscribed roles. She unconsciously was motivated by the desire to redeem herself through redeeming another who had a similar teleological task to herself. Her own mother's narcissistic possessiveness of her soul had trapped her, and her desire to free him was linked to her desire to escape the claustrum of the maternal matrix. At those levels there was a link, a magnetic attraction between them. They were soul siblings coping with the same threat of being devoured. Sibylla's mother had made unconscious demands of her to not be herself in her otherness but to become a clone, as if singing the lullaby, 'don't be yourself; be my unknown and unfulfilled needs. You are here to become my existence, my identity; you must not and do not exist for yourself' (Clark, 1987, p. 75). Consequently Sibylla had grown up learning the subtle permutations of performing mirroring functions to others in the way she had been required to mirror her mother. This meant that she unthinkingly picked up and enacted the roles others scripted her to play.

Thus, too, she needed a robust heroic Orpheus figure to help her negotiate her own underworld, find her way back to the light of day, to develop and find the real power to take the leap and not look back. But David (like his prototype) was never in the running to effect such transitions. The strength of her adamant declaration, 'I don't "do" Eurydice!', belied the truth it attempted to cover – her own Eurydice had long since been left to languish, buried beneath layers of fierce pride and submerged grief. The apparition of a tender maiden was both a disowned part of David as well as a dislodged lost part of herself. Her admonition to David to redeem his soul was also a call to resurrect her own wounded spirit.

Concluding remark

The focus of Part II has been clinical and applied. We have looked at many possible obstacles to being able to achieve authentic intimacy in couple relationships. While the number of such possible impediments is limitless, I have examined five major areas of difficulty: projective processes in the couple, the gridlock created by the superimposition of traumatic systems deriving from childhood, narcissistic relations; failures to negotiate thresholds of intimacy; orphic and solipsistic defensive systems; and fantasy lovers as defences against authentic loving. To augment the more exclusively clinical material I have also analysed themes of endogamous obstructions to exogamy using examples taken from literature, opera, myth and film. I have discussed therapeutic ways of working with such issues.

All the various obstacles to fulfilling love relations can be seen as various pathologies of the subject-centred self, who imputes his or her internal constructs, narcissism, fantasies, false representations and expectations upon the face of the beloved, camouflaging and preventing the revelation of her or his being. The path of love is a path of transformation out of the conceptual prison of the isolated monad into true intersubjective, inter-dependent realms of becoming in and through love.

The emphasis of Part II has been on the problematics of exogamy. The next section outlines some of the components by which exogamous relations are made possible.

Part III

Transformations in love

Chapter 14

Exogamy: a marriage of all loves

Ultimate love is a harmonizing of all loves: *eros, philia, agapē, storge, xenia, nomos* affection, compassion, altruism, tenderness, care, appreciation, patience, equanimity are all aspects of becoming in love. Such love is not based on lack so much as upon a capacity an ever-growing beneficence and non-possessive enjoyment, in wonderment and gratitude.

The constituents of such a kind of loving can be gathered together as follows:

- an intertwining of *eros, agapē, philia, storge, xenia*;
- appreciation of the other's foursquare independent reality and alterity;
- love as enjoyment, based on increase rather than lack;
- the capacity to encompass the shifting tides of intimacy and solitude;
- love as a continuum of ever-moving, ever-changing, unpredictable becoming;
- subject-to-subject relating rather than subject-to-object (Buber's I–thou as distinct from I–it);
- transcendence of the alienation arising out of the fallacy of separate selves, as a state of non-duality rather than fusion;
- altruistic considerations such as compassion, care, consideration, gratitude, trust and fidelity;
- a sense of being able to surrender rather than trying to control, where such surrender is not subservient or masochistic but receptive and responsive;
- a sense of thirdness, of the relationship having its own teleology;
- curiosity and wanting to know the other, while recognizing that one cannot truly know, the continual rediscovery of each other;
- a sense of humour, or *'heaven in ordinarie'*;
- a coming to terms with loss, ageing and mortality;
- a capacity to tolerate feelings of ambivalence;
- a capacity for forgiveness.

Love's increase

Most romantic accounts of love focus on the experience of falling in love and have, as their necessary corollary, the decrease of love and passion after the first heady moments. When we move beyond narcissistic, fantasy-bound and projection-based constructs, through disillusionment to mature love based on appreciation of others for their foursquare reality, then love grows exponentially. It is no longer delimited by the constructs of our egocentric desires and fantasies. We are continually refreshed and expanded by the unfathomable plenitude of our beloved's multi-dimensional, ever-changing nature. This is not being sentimental, one-sided or defensively idealistic but rather psychologically realistic. Love is about a creative force of increase, based on a capacity to feel more, which means, when we are less defended against loss and sorrow, deeper joy.

> Lovers know well how sensual, voluptuous, and intense it is to make love in joy rather than want, in action rather than passion, in pleasure rather than suffering, in the fulfilment rather than the frustration of our capacity – in other words, to desire the love we are *making* rather than the love we dream of, do not make, and are obsessed by.
>
> (Compte-Sponville, 1996/2001, pp. 250–251)

Intimacy and solitude

A good relationship is predicated on the 'capacity to be alone', in Winnicott's sense, as well as the capacity to be together, a communion in solitude and a solitude in communion. Yet it takes as much existential courage to be together with another authentically as it takes to be alone.

Rilke said that in marriage, 'each must be the guardian of the other's solitude'[1] (Rilke, 1901, as cited in Freedman, 1996, p. 146). John Bayley also felt that solitude was one of the greatest pleasures in his marriage to Iris Murdoch (Bayley, 1998, p. 36). This was not *solitude à deux*, an isolation from the world, but being able to enjoy separate experiences knowing one would share it later. The more Bayley got to know Iris, the less he felt he understood her.

---

1 Rilke, 1901, as cited in Freedman, 1996, p. 146. Rilke fiercely guarded his own solitude. I am a little suspicious of the oft-quoted aphorism of Rilke, who struggled with his conflict between intimacy and need for solitude, resolved only by having an epistolary marriage with Clara, physical distance coupled with intellectual closeness through letter writing. Horace Walpole also famously declared he preferred the epistolary form of marriage, avoiding as it did, 'tiresome first-hand exchanges' (as cited in Kiberd, 2003, p. 5). Certainly, in Walpole's case, it indicates that secondhand experience was far superior to the irritating shock of firsthand reality.

The capacity to enjoy unpredictability and separateness as well as meeting is beautifully illustrated by Clare Winnicott describing her life with her husband Donald:

> Donald was, and always would be, completely unpredictable in our private life . . . This unpredictability had its advantages, in that we could never settle back and take each other for granted in day-to-day living. What we could take for granted was something more basic that I can only describe as our recognition and acceptance of each other's separateness. In fact the strength of our unity lay in this recognition . . . Our separateness left us each free to do our own thing, to think our own thoughts, and possess our own dreams, and in so doing to strengthen the capacity of each of us to experience the joys and sorrows which we shared.
>
> (C. Winnicott, 1989, p. 15)

Idealization

According to many philosophers and psychologists, romantic love involves an elevation of the love object into an idealized figure, whose every quality is exalted and glorified. In so far as the qualities and the person seeming to display them are not the same thing, love is therefore deemed as false or misplaced. In so far as it depletes the lover, who ascribes all their own positive attributes to another, it may be pathological. It can also be pathological if the tendency to idealize originates from what Fairbairn (1943) called the 'moral defence'. This occurs when the 'putative badness' of another person, upon whom one depends, is taken in as being one's own badness in order to keep the external object ideal, a 'laundering' of the image of the idealized person at one's own expense (Grotstein, 1994, p. 115).

Love, for Santayana, 'is an imaginative search for unattainable ideal objects which do not exist and thus cannot be attained' (Singer, 1966, p. 29). Stendhal believed that love is obscured by idealizing projections, imbuing of the beloved with all good qualities, which are one's own. The lover empties himself and invests his energy in the beloved. 'He underrates his own good qualities and overrates the least favours bestowed by his beloved.' 'From the moment he loves, the wisest of men no longer sees any object as it is' (Stendhal, 1822/1957, p. 60). Freud saw such overvaluation of the beloved and denigration of oneself as a form of displaced primary narcissism. Such love is but self-love and hence anti-exogamous.

Idealization can be both defensive and developmental, as illusory as a gleaming display of salt crystals upon a leafless branch, an obstacle to exogamy or a natural aspect of loving.

For Freud, idealization in love involves the lover becoming, 'as it were, intellectually infatuated . . . by the mental achievements and perfections of the sexual object' (Freud, 1905/1977a, p. 62). For Freud, idealization is a process by which the object, 'without any alteration in its nature, is aggrandized and exalted in the subject's mind' (Freud, 1914/1984c, p. 88). Given that for Freud love is always reducible in the final analysis to self-love, idealization is 'a state suggestive of a neurotic compulsion, which is thus traceable to an impoverishment of the ego as regards libido in favour of the love-object' (Freud, 1914/1984c, p. 82).

There can be a developmental aspect involved in idealization whereby the idealized figure acts as a projection screen for our own developing capacities in a given area. By ignoring ordinary human failings and amplifying the praiseworthy aspects of the other we may invest faith in our own capacity for such achievement. This is similar to the Buddhist practice of seeing all those around us as enlightened beings, or the Christian virtue of seeing the good in others. Such a practice enhances our own virtuous potential, generosity and goodwill. Buddhist teachings often speak of how the guru represents our own enlightened nature. Projection of our potential enlightened qualities followed by re-introjection is a spiritual technique. We project our own potentiality for enlightenment onto the figure of the guru, divinity or saint, then at a later stage we re-introject enlightened qualities of wisdom, compassion, generosity, patience, loving kindness, morality and insight as something to be realized within us. Such idealization and identification processes occur in ancient mystical practices. The 'adept, by inducing a state of ecstasy, becomes aware of his true identity in the being, life and destiny of the god or goddess – becomes, in short divine' (Scheler, 1954, p. 20).

Freud (1921/1955) argued that through loving someone with qualities we value ourselves, we might incorporate and enrich ourselves with these very attributes. This reiterates the Platonic idea that idealization involves admiring in the beloved the qualities to which we aspire ourselves.

Applied to love relations, such idealized love can lead to ennoblement of the lover and beloved, an enhancement of values, ideals, virtues, a sense of beauty and harmony with the world. It can also be a defence against coping with disappointment, conflict, ambivalence and feelings of helplessness. The objectifying quality of projection-based idealization can be an obstacle to exogamous relations that are predicated on the capacity to embrace the full gamut of another person's personality, goods and bads, strengths and weaknesses.

Idealization thus has both anti-relational and relationship-enhancing qualities. On the one hand it renders the other an image or a screen upon which to project our ideals, rather than a flesh-and-blood, foursquare and complex person. We defend against the uncontrollable and unpredictable qualities of real lived love by replacing it with images, because images, being abstract and universal, can protect one against the pain of losing 'that' particular, non-replaceable relationship. On the other hand, where idealization is based on a sense of awe, wonder and gratitude for the beloved's existence for his or her own sake, it enhances the virtue of rejoicing in another's merit, which enriches the lover as well as the beloved.

Illusions, disillusionment and revelation

Idealizing and disillusionment are two sides of a false coin. We decide someone we meet is 'A' (admirable, marvellous, talented, heroic). Then a discrepant fact shatters our illusion. So we then decide they are 'not A', failing to see that both 'A' and 'not A' are equally limited ideas we have imputed or projected upon them, closing ourselves to all the other things they might be if we could open our eyes to a greater range of possibility. In our disappointment we fail to appreciate how they happen to be a whole range of other things we never imagined, perhaps, in fact, much more interesting and challenging than our first impressions. Disillusionment is often just as false and limited as the illusions of false idealization. We are disappointed because the person is not a figment of our imagination, even if the real person is much better than our fantasies. The first deviation from our projected template is met with indignation: how dare you deviate from your allotted role in my fantasy, side-step the screen of my projections and reveal your true face?

Exogamy requires negative capability as well as realization of the depressive position: the person who is able to tolerate a greater range of confusion, intricacy, diversity, and therefore ultimately wholeness. Furthermore, it requires more than a realization of ambivalence, for the person we relate to is likely to be not just a mixture of the good things and bad things we impute upon them. The things we like and the things we don't like about someone are both constructs connected to an egocentric stance. The only way to avoid such limitation is to remind ourselves that our beloved's depths will always elude and surprise us. This is what Bion meant by K in the sense of the impetus of curiosity, wanting to know, while being able to tolerate the knowledge that one doesn't know. Marion Milner had such an insight:

> I saw that to see only the ridiculousness of humanity was just as misleading as to see only its dignity, that what one said or thought about a thing must always be a distortion, that the mistake was to believe that any one expression could be the last word, for experience is always bigger than the formula.
>
> (Milner, 1934, p. 157)

Romance has its stages, as so much of the popular literature on this topic reiterates: from initial attraction with its attendant states of infatuation and idealization, to first meetings and first kisses, from the joys of finding love reciprocated to a sense of fusion and a 'honeymoon phase'. Thence 'inevitably' it moves on to disillusionment, from passion to indifference and boredom, if not contempt and hatred. And 'if one sticks with it', so we are told, we will attain a deeper form of loving based on active choice to love rather than being a victim of compulsions, infatuations and emotional vacillation. This trajectory describes the move from a sense of being perfectly attuned and at one, idealization, to disillusionment. It is a hard stage to achieve to realize that one's beloved is both ideal and not ideal, satisfying and disappointing, exciting and boring, and to realize that we can and do fluctuate endlessly between such feelings, which are entirely subjective: the real beloved is always one step ahead of any such projections:

> Richard met Daphne when he was thirty. They were together for twelve years, then emotionally grew apart to the point where they drifted off, without really discussing anything, into other relationships. He described to me how he had a string of passionate affairs with other women, but wondered why he kept thinking and dreaming about Daphne. He couldn't quite 'get rid of her' in his mind. He drew up a profile of the perfect woman and the perfect relationship and trawled the internet RSVP site. He kept realizing that the characteristics were ones that somehow reminded him of Daphne. They were still friends and 'there for each other' when the going was tough. He eventually decided to open up the topic of their relationship with her. He didn't feel he could 'move on' until he had worked out 'what was going on' in his relationship with Daphne. In fact it was going on, just at a different level. Like a stream whose course goes underground, it continued onwards at a subterranean level. He asked and she accepted, not his hand in marriage, but an invitation to enter couple therapy! They worked hard on 'what was going on' in their internal object relations and how it interpenetrated. Much later they re-emerged together in a newly reconfigured relationship which, he observed, was startlingly moving, full of nuances and depths of mutual understanding. 'Even the sex is pretty damn amazing.' He felt surprising gratitude to her and for her, and 'it is miles better than anything we had at the beginning, she's so much more interesting than all the women I dated via the internet. I really can't believe my luck.'

Discovery

When we open out into intimacy rather than neurotically seeking to defend against its mysterious alchemy, there is a sense of being continually surprised by the limitless horizons that ever unfold.

Sometimes we are suddenly startled as we realize that
We have ventured beyond
The bounds of mapped love;
That we have reached places
Previously unimagined,
First sightings of richly blessed lands
Yet to be explored,
New matters to be touched,
Senses to be revealed to us;
Extraordinary new life seems to come to
Meet and welcome us.

(Impala, 2001)

Clouds of unknowing

Plato's iconoclast

'I'm going to tell the truth. Do you think you'll allow that?'

(Plato, as cited in Nussbaum, 2001a, p. 165)

Imagine a dinner party, a banquet, a gathering of (male) intellectuals, a symposium. Several of the literary celebrities of Athenian society have been invited to celebrate the poet Agathon's win at a poetry competition. It is proposed, as an after-dinner activity, that each member composes a paean in praise of *eros*. Yet then a curious thing occurs. A drunk wanders in, a beautiful young general and erotic admirer of the philosopher Socrates, called Alcibiades, overturning all the formal rules of etiquette, disturbing the highbrow air of the *symposium*. Discrepant facts pop up like hiccups everywhere.

Alcibiades is not the slightest bit interested in ascending a ladder of ever more spiritualized love from the human to the divine forms of beauty. Rather he is there to seduce his former boyfriend, Agathon. He is so drunk he has to be helped to a seat. All the while,

he kept trying to take his ribbons off so that he could crown Agathon with them, but all he succeeded in doing was to push them further down his head until they finally slipped over his eyes. What with the ivy and all, he didn't see Socrates, who had made room for him on the couch.

(213a)[2]

---

2 Plato (1989).

Instead of a paean to Eros, Alcibiades substitutes a speech about his love for Socrates, a mortal and physically ugly man.

Alcibiades describes how he has developed a confusing but powerful desire to know Socrates. Having spent his life closed within his impenetrable self-absorption, desired but not desiring, finding himself loving and wanting to know all there was to know about Socrates' inner being is an experience of sudden opening, a desire to know and to be truly perceived. To be seen and spoken to becomes a 'siren music (216a) that rushes into his body in this person's presence', 'something he deeply needs not to avoid' (Nussbaum, 1986, pp. 188–189).

This is a union of erotic and epistemic aspiration: he wanted to 'hear everything' that Socrates knew (217a). As his love opens up, so does his curiosity grow and understanding deepen. The metaphor Alcibiades uses is of a statue of Silenus, which has a crack running down its middle. When it is opened up it reveals divinity, 'the treasure inside' (216e), a beautifully carved scene of trees, animals and humans, 'that is the surprise, and the reason for awe'. Alcibiades is overpowered by Eros as a genuinely two-way relational energy and by the epistemophilic yearning for insight into the depths of Socrates. Love involves the inseparable union of erotic and epistemophilic yearning, the desire to open up what is concealed inside the 'magic box' of the beloved's body-mind, through emotional, sensual, and intellectual exploration.[3]

Alcibiades locates the theme of love in his direct experience with Socrates. It is not a rhetorical point but an expression of desire for a particular, embodied, unique and contingent human being in all his mysterious being. The tale he tells is one of understanding born of direct experience (*pathonta gnōnai*), and, as Nussbaum argues, 'it is precisely its groping, somewhat chaotic character that makes it so movingly convincing as an account – and an expression (even now) of love' (Nussbaum, 1986, p. 188).

The experience of being seen and wanting to see into Socrates liberates Alcibiades from the schizoid ivory tower of sublime self-isolation and invulnerability into the fertile and verdant realm of ivy and wine.

A fundamental human need is to be loved and to be understood. Yet we also remain mysteries to ourselves and to each other. We reserve a sacred hidden part, which we may wish to reveal, tentatively, in small poetic measure, a line here, then silence. In exogamous relations, there is a constant unveiling of the numinous presence of the other in ever new epiphanies, yet ever deepening senses of ineffable mystery.

Our relation with the other (*autrui*) certainly consists in wanting to comprehend him, but this relation overflows comprehension. Not only

---

3 See Nussbaum, 2001a, p. 190.

because knowledge of the other (*autrui*) requires, outside of all curiosity, also sympathy or love, ways of being distinct from impassible contemplation, but because in our relation with the other, he does not affect us in terms of a concept. He is a being (*étant*) and counts as such.

(Levinas, 1951/1996a, p. 6)

Knowledge and being are relational states: being known by another, I come into being that which I am. As Berkeley said, *esse est percepi*, to be is to be perceived. Winnicott said:

When I look I am seen, so I exist.
I can now afford to look and see.
I now look creatively and what I apperceive I also perceive.
In fact I take care not to see what is not there to be seen (unless I am tired).

(Winnicott, 1971, p. 134)

The corollary of this statement is that not to be seen is to feel one does not exist. Babies who do not experience being seen sufficiently and perceptively by a good-enough mother thereafter doubt the existence of the outside world and others, doubt their own mind and so doubt all relationships. The philosophical problem of *esse est percepi*, 'becomes and remains a vital one, a matter of life and death, of feeding or starvation, of love or isolation' (Winnicott, 1988, p. 114). Winnicott explained that there were increasing degrees of this dis-ease, from various narcissistic defences, to borderline, psychotic or psychogenic autistic-like states. Or, as Winnicott (1988) implied, it leads to philosophers and philosophy.

Some mothers see too much, and we also want to remain private and separate. Winnicott also protests the right to remain silent in the face of 'the frightening fantasy of being infinitely exploited' of being 'eaten or swallowed up' (Winnicott, 1963/1984a, p. 179). There is the traumatic experience of 'being found, altered, communicated with' by forced psychic intrusion, which is experienced as 'a violation of the self's core' (p. 187).

Holding the relationship in mind

A quality of relatedness is having a subliminal sense of the existence of our partner even when we are apart. An example is holding our children in mind. A mother usually knows where her child is every moment of the day, what the child will be doing, concerned for their safety and well-being. Likewise as couples we hold our partners in mind, not necessarily at the forefront, nor intrusively or possessively, but as an empathic act of imagination. A caring awareness of each other's existence subtly permeates our consciousness.

When partners show in small ways that even apart they are together in each other's imagination, separation is not experienced as loneliness but an apartness which is part of togetherness. There is a need to feel the other intuitively comprehends us,

> that our secret self should find a home in the eyes of another person, who will look upon this intimate aspect with pleasure . . . The longing for love is the longing that our sense of isolation will be pierced and that another will enter into the private areas of our existence in a tender and appreciative way.
>
> (Armstrong, 2002, p. 53)

Love involves confidence, we confide, we trust. Yet we need to be confident to trust, in ourselves and in the other, to revere and never abuse such sacred secrets.

> Chris and I sit, silent in my consulting room, the room growing gradually darker, awe-struck by the enormity of what he tentatively had confided. He had waited a lifetime for this moment and the secret-sacred nature of the stories seemed so precious it beggared all description. Like messages in a bottle he had kept his secrets in little indecipherable jottings, waiting for a trust-worthy recipient. And now he went out, back home to a woman he had hardly spoken to in years, confident that now he might also have the courage to begin to open up to her, as he had never been able to do. She had waited a long time for this, knowing something was plaguing him, unable to help, reaching out with gestures of compassion.

The epistemophilic impulse

The epistemophilic impulse is a desire to know, discover something and categorize it. Yovel talks of the *conatus intelligendi* meaning the conatus to understand, to 'interpret our existence, to make sense of it, to endow it with *meaning*', that 'human beings *strive to exist in an interpreted, meaning endowed way*'. This means we are, 'existentially, both a question – which breaks down our compact being in the present – and a rudimentary answer, which does not repair it' (Yovel, 1999, pp. 54–55). This includes both an endeavour to understand (an epistemophilic impulse) and also a quest for infinity.

Freud linked sexual curiosity with the epistemophilic impulse. 'Thirst for knowledge seems to be inseparable from sexual curiosity' (Freud, 1909/2001, p. 9).

Epistemophilia can be intrusive and disrespectful of another's inviolable privacy. 'Knowledge' can become inveiglement, a way of categorizing and thus controlling the other. There is the fantasy of omniscience, the danger of assuming our partner is 'fully knowable, assimilable, subject to our internalization. The notion of a transparent understanding of the other implies a transparent self, a self which does not allow the existence of its own negative, its unconscious otherness' (Benjamin, 1998, p. 101). Between intrusiveness and apathy lies the positive value of being respectfully curious:

> To perceive what the other is, while not knowing it. Not to use such knowledge but to make my gaze helpful to him: an aid, a resource. And to accept that he will be the one who discovers innocence lives there, if it is capable of contemplating without violence or capture: to insist on transcendence here and now, with us and between us.
>
> (Irigaray, 1994/2000, p. 14)

Clouds of unknowing and the plenitude of the void

> The Zohar says: 'All visible things will be born again invisible.' The present, like a landscape, is only a small part of a mysterious narrative.
>
> (Michaels, 1996, p. 48)

For Bion, ultimate knowledge of the reality of the other is unknowable: 'It is impossible to know reality for the same reason that makes it impossible to sing potatoes; they may be grown, or pulled, or eaten, but not sung' (Bion, 1965, p. 148).

The object of knowledge is one's own or another's psychic reality. Emotions such as anxiety, fear, love, hate, cannot be apprehended via the sense organs. Their existence can only be deduced through interpretation of their manifestation, which is notoriously open to misinterpretation. Contact with external reality is mediated by models and constructs derived from intuition, abstraction and transformations of O. As Irigaray so poetically writes:

> For you, for us, between shadows and light. Always being in the light wounds. Modesty requires a bit of secrecy, a silence over what is known, a reserve: to respect you and leave obscurity between us.
>
> Who I am for you and who I am for me is not the same, and such a gap cannot be overcome. We are irreducible in us, between us, yet so close. Without this difference, how do we give each other grace, how do we see each other, the one in the other?
>
> (Irigaray, 1994/2000, p. 10)

Bion, asserting the unknowable nature of ultimate truth, places himself in the same Idealist and Transcendentalist tradition as Plato, Berkeley and Kant, modified by Freud and Klein. He says that O is like Kant's unknowable thing-in-itself, except that this O can become known through its transformations in experience.

In our love relations, knowing we don't know helps ameliorate false certitudes. We can do well to remind ourselves that we are always seeing the situation from a particular limited, coloured perspective. In so doing we free ourselves up from the fallacy that any one perspective is all-encompassing. In the gap of uncertainty other discrepant facts may be allowed to shock us out of our complacency. Remembering we are not always right in our interpretations of each other is not automatic. It is a discipline. We will continue to see things erroneously, but at least we have some inner voice reminding us that our view may be distorted, which loosens the fixity of our opinions a little.

Symington (1986) points out that we have a natural tendency to be frightened of one another, and this fear of each other is fear of the unknown. If we are not a little apprehensive each time we meet, something is wrong, for it assumes we know what will emerge, 'and if you know, then what is the point of having the encounter?' (Symington, 1986, p. 52).

We defend against fear of encounters with others by internally arming ourselves with an arsenal of stale memories, ossified constructions, ways of rendering the opacity of the other into a set of attributes.

What Bion calls the K link refers to the emotional experience present when two persons are related to each other, or two parts of a person. It is both intra- and inter-relational. The K link is the link formed by a subject attempting to know an object. It is an active link, with an emotional character expressed by the frustrating feeling implicit in wanting to know while knowing one doesn't know. The epistemophilic impulse or *wissenstrieb* is the expectation of knowing something that is not yet realized. The essential characteristic of the K link is the toleration of not knowing while being receptive to new knowledge. One can defend against the pain of not knowing via a *piece* of knowledge: this is what Bion calls 'memory', and this precludes the establishment of a K link and learning through emotional experience.[4]

What Bion calls minus K (−K) is a tyrannous imposition of a false 'knowledge' fuelled by envy for the other being outside the sphere of one's

---

4 Freud spoke of *Verleugnung*, the 'blindness of the seeing eye' in which 'one knows and does not know a thing at the same time' (Freud, as cited in Britton, 1998, p. 15), which Strachey translated as disavowal. There is a non-psychotic form of disavowal in which one believes and does not believe a thing at the same time. Such is the suspension of belief necessary to engage imaginatively in watching a movie, or play, or reading a novel. Yet in everyday life we may willingly suspend belief in order to avoid the emotional consequences, which leads to a state of psychic unreality. Ambiguity may be used as a defence against ambivalence (Britton, 1998, p. 16). Further, counter-beliefs may be used defensively against other beliefs, such as omnipotent fantasies used as a manic defence in order to deny psychic reality.

epistemological control. Minus K is an evasion of the pain of not knowing and not being able to know (= delimit and control) the other. The emotional aspects of −K are envy, greed, a spoiling, destructive impulse where meaning is denuded of vitality, militating against discovery. According to Bion, this belongs to the psychotic part of the personality.

The desire to be known and the desire to not be known

As Winnicott points out, there is a tension between the desire to be intimately connected with another and the desire to protect privacy: 'At the centre of each person is an incommunicado element, and this is sacred and most worthy of preservation' (1963/1984a, p. 187).

This is particularly the case for those who in the past have been violated by either sexual or psychic intrusion. The analogy one patient used was the difference between someone being invited to visit, knocking respectfully on the front door, and being welcomed in, as distinct from a burglar who forces their way in. Doris Lessing describes how she developed a 'hostess personality' to wall off and thus protect her inner core:

> *You will never get access here . . . this is the ultimate and inviolable privacy.* They call it loneliness, that here is this place unsharable with anyone at all, ever, but it is all we have to fall back on. Me, I, this feeling of me. The observer, never to be touched, tasted, felt, seen, by anyone else.
>
> (Lessing, 1995, p. 20)

There is a conflict between a longing for relationship and a fear of being encroached upon, particularly for children who did not have a chance to play in a private space and thus did not develop a sense of a hallowed inner core. For them aloneness is a confrontation with nothingness, yet the danger of closeness is that they might be subsumed into another's psychic insides.

Realizing one cannot ever really get 'inside' the other, but a coupling of respect for privacy with genuine interest, is a feature of the capacity to enjoy alterity. It gives rise to a sense of richness, nuanced by 'generosity, receptiveness, aesthetic reciprocity; understanding and all possible knowledge'. This is 'the locus of symbol formation, and thus of art, poetry, imagination' (Meltzer, 1992, p. 72).

Intrusive projections, on the other hand, give rise to the phantasy of being inside the other by forced psychic penetration. Sometimes the sense that we know our partner becomes a way of warding off the fear of not knowing: the motive being to establish security and predictability over the unpredictable, knowingness over the unknown.

In couples relationships there may be a combination of one partner who in early life experienced a parent as invasive with another partner who felt shut out. This partner might seek to inveigle their way into their partner's space, entertaining a phantasy of omnipotent intrusion into their partner's insides:

> Julia was labelled by her husband 'a closed book'. Matthew was experienced by Julia as 'intrusive'. This dynamic became symbolized by the door to Julia's study. He couldn't bear it shut, and she couldn't bear him hovering at the door anxious to be let in. The more she defended against intrusion by emotionally withdrawing, the more desperate he became to penetrate into her imaginal world.
>
> In therapy this manifested in the opening of each session. Julia sat silently as if in her own world. Matthew would break the silence with a question aimed at ascertaining Julia's private ruminations. Julia would visibly shift uncomfortably at having her thought process interrupted.
>
> What struck me as curious, witnessing this interaction, was that neither Julia nor Matthew showed any curiosity about what might be going on in Matthew's head. For both the focal point was Julia's insides.
>
> Matthew's overt position of being 'a pursuer' of her thoughts served to distract attention from what might or might not be going on in his inner world, while Julia's pointed silences merely drew attention to her, like a beacon announcing, 'I have a secret, don't you want to know what it is?'
>
> Julia's seeming self-containment concealed a tension between the longing to be found and the fear of intrusion. Julia had experienced her father as impenetrable and her mother as invasive. Julia's adult stance of self-sufficiency was but the final result of giving up the futile attempt to get inside father's world, and protect herself from mother's encroachments on her private world. Thus one aspect of the tension between Julia and Matthew was a playing out of the internal conflict between Julia's parents and herself as a child, where she identified herself as her father and Matthew as her childhood self. Matthew's mother had also rejected his need for identification and closeness, but instead of withdrawing into a defeated blankness masquerading as self-containment as Julia had done, he became relentlessly determined to find a way into his objects of passion.
>
> Matthew was hollowed out and two-dimensional in the sense Meltzer (1975) describes of adhesive identifiers. Thus he enviously wished to scoop out Julia's insides which he saw as full of depth.

Negative capability

In attempting to transform a stuck pattern of inter-relating, one of the major impediments is memory, the expectation that the other will behave according to script. We want to be one step ahead, be prepared for how we fear that they will react. Unfortunately such an expectation acts as a screen which blocks out information to the contrary – that the other was not in fact thinking or behaving according to how we anticipated. Memories are cloaked in blanket statements such as 'he's so unreliable', 'she always has to take over'. The ability to entertain uncertainty enables curiosity, receptivity, open-mindedness to the presentiment of another as they are, beyond our expectations, memories, desires and false imputations.

Bion's advice to discard our memories and expectations prepares us for a becoming in O. This requires an act of faith (F) that enhances precision in unknowability: it enables one to be more attuned to and perceptive of subtle nuances of experience concomitant with the appreciation of what remains forever out of reach. Faith in O 'approaches an attitude of pure receptiveness. It is an alert readiness, an alive waiting.' We are acutely uncomfortable in such a state, since we must tolerate 'fragmentation, whirls of bits and pieces of meaning and meaningless, chaotic blankness, dry periods, and psychic dust storms' (Eigen, 1998, pp. 219–220). Becoming in O in love depends on negative capability:

> What is to be sought is an activity that is both the restoration of god (the Mother) and the evolution of god (the formless, infinite, ineffable, non-existent), which can be found only in the state in which there is no memory, desire, understanding.
>
> (Bion, 1970, p. 129)

Predictions, pre-emptive manoeuvres and preconceptions are defensive strategies serving to reinforce old patterns, hijack new endeavours and insights back into old endogamous systems.

Mr and Mrs Epstein consulted me concerning the effects of Mrs Epstein's manic-depression on the relationship. The problem was the ways in which the family's fear of a manic episode created an emotional strait-jacket such that any sign of even ordinary humour, effusiveness, or simple pleasure in life was met with terror lest this signal another manic episode. This in itself became a vicious cycle, because Mrs Epstein felt so emotionally hemmed in and constricted that she would eventually break out, and take herself off for what she described as retail therapy and her family saw as a sure sign she was on a 'manic bender'. I found myself wondering if some of the so-called 'manic episodes' were not displays of ordinary pleasure in life. For example, Mr Epstein described attendance at a sports event put on by the school. 'She kept yelling at the top of her voice "Go, go, go!" to urge our son on. He was so embarrassed.' She protested, 'well, even the headmaster was yelling'.

As we began to uncover the history of the marriage, it became apparent that fear of a manic episode had become a pernicious systemic perpetuation of a clamping down on any element of *joie de vivre* that had not only childhood origins (in both) but had transgenerational origins.

Mr Epstein grew up in a household where any sign of exuberance was met with a look of abject horror on his mother's face. This was due to his mother's childhood family experience of being in hiding in Nazi Germany where survival depended upon silence. This made more sense of his reaction at the football match: with its unconscious associations to the mass hysteria of Nazi rallies, and the fear that any outburst equalled bursting out of the safety of a hiding place into certain torture and death.

Over time, we tried to suspend the 'false knowledge' that if Mrs Epstein expressed laughter at a comedy, or swore when watching a sporting event, she was heading for another manic episode, and that in fact it might be the reverse. When there could be some sense of safety and containment such that normal expressions of gladness and mirth could be allowed, it was less likely a break-out would occur.

Thus, for this couple, one form of 'memory', in Bion's sense, needed to be eschewed, whilst another uncovered, in order to allow a new reality to peep through; a new understanding and a new evolution.

Alétheia

The nature of illusion, being unreal, cannot destroy truth but only conceal it. Revelation of another's difference and foursquare reality might be defended against, we may fear it being painful and disillusioning, but it can also be gloriously refreshing. The reality behind the veils of projection may, when expectation, fears, defences fall away, be more exciting and enriching than the dim shadows of our fantasies and the thin veneer of the reflecting surface we cover with our fantastic and illusory imputations about the other.

Even delighting in the ordinary, messy, fallible, sometimes down right silliness of our daily love lives is more exciting than the boredom of our neurotic repetition compulsions and fantasy-bound manoeuvres.

Chapter 15

The iconoclasm of Joy

> The most precious gift that marriage gave me, was this constant impact of something very close and intimate yet all the time unmistakably other, resistant – in a word, real.
>
> (Lewis, 1961, p. 18)

The story of the marriage of Joy Davidman to C. S. Lewis illustrates many of the central tenets of the book: appreciation of alterity as the site for a life-enhancing revelation; thresholds of intimacy and the sense of a third presence pulling one forward into areas never traversed; the teleological conatus of becoming in O in love; Bion's concept of catastrophic change and transformations in O; transformations which are physical, intellectual, emotional, and mystical; being 'surprised by Joy' or *laetitia*; love and mortality; the sense of eternity in an ephemeral moment; unity and aliena-tion; and the intertwining of mythological truths and history.

A sense of wonderment, revelation, negative capability and *laetitia* was what drew both Joy Davidman and Lewis towards each other.

Joy Davidman's relationship with C. S. Lewis began with what Kohut would call an idealizing selfobject transference. Out of his writings and letters Joy constructed a fantasized image of the perfect spiritual mentor. When she actually came to meet the real person she was shocked by his alterity: he looked nothing like the image she had of him in her head.

Lewis was equally 'surprised by Joy' – her abrasiveness, self-assertiveness and strong-minded Jewish-American intellectualism were a breath of fresh air in the hallowed cloisters of Oxford to a large, red-faced, fifty-four-year-old, emotionally retarded academic and bachelor.[1]

Born Jewish in 1915, Joy Davidman became, in adult life, an atheist intellectual, writer and active member of the Communist Party. In 1942 she

---

1 Many accounts of C. S. Lewis's life emphasize his bachelorhood, when he had had a major relationship which he could not extricate himself from, with the mother of a friend killed in the First World War, Mrs Moore. This relationship began in 1918 and only ended with her death in 1951.

married a fellow communist, Bill Gresham, with whom she had two sons. Bill was an alcoholic and unfaithful, and had a nervous breakdown soon after they were married. Joy's sense of helplessness led to a religious conversion. She described the sense of surrender to a third presence, a greater power, that had other designs on her than those constructed by her limited, egocentric desire for control: 'All my defences – the walls of arrogance and cocksureness and self-love behind which I had hid from God – went down momentarily – and God came in' (Davidman, 1951, p. 23).

Joy maintained that this conversion was no 'comforting illusion conjured up to reassure'. It was, 'terror and ecstasy, repentance and rebirth' (pp. 23–24). Such an experience could be seen as one of transformation in O, residing in her own aliveness and reality in the presence of ultimate reality. By comparison all else seemed like a shadow play:

> It is infinite, unique; there are no words, there are no comparisons. Can one scoop up the sea in a teacup? . . . I myself was more alive than I had ever been; it was like waking from sleep. So intense a life cannot be endured long by flesh and blood; we must ordinarily take our life watered down, diluted as it were, by time and space and matter.
>
> (Davidman, 1951, p. 23)

Lewis had experienced his own conversion as a demand of 'total surrender, the absolute leap in the dark', a demand not for just 'All or nothing' but simply 'All' (Sibley, 1985, p. 43).

Joy sought to 'consult one of the clearest thinkers of our time for help' in her confusion about her marriage (Davidman, as cited in Wilson, 1990, p. 99). A lack of social inhibition and strident strong-mindedness were apparent from the first. As Warnie, Lewis's brother, described it, she was:

> quite extraordinarily uninhibited. Our first meeting was at lunch in Magdalen, where she turned to me in the presence of three or four men, and asked in the most natural tone in the world, 'Is there anywhere in this monastic establishment where a lady can relieve herself?'
>
> (W. Lewis, 1982, p. 276)

Lewis found this refreshing. He found in Joy a woman with whom he could be himself. She enjoyed walking, drinking beer, telling jokes, swearing, as well as having intellectual arguments, 'with no holds barred'. He delighted in the ways Joy broke through his defences, and admired her sharp dismissals of self-deception or any idealization of her:

> Her mind was quick and muscular as a leopard. Passion, tenderness and pain were all equally unable to disarm it. It scented the first whiff

of cant or slush, then sprang . . . How many bubbles of mine she pricked!

(Lewis, 1961, p. 8)

The exogamous conatus pushed Lewis out of his self-satisfied comfortable life as a bachelor into the catastrophic transformation of a relationship with Joy. They moved from being strangers to acquaintances to friends to loving each other more and more authentically – haltingly, evasively, and out of time with each other.[2]

Lewis was reluctant to move out of his comfortable life at home with Warnie and the daily routine of a largely male academic life. After her divorce from Bill, Lewis agreed to marry Joy, but merely as 'a pure formality designed to give Joy the right to go on living in England'.[3] The civil ceremony on 23 April 1956 over, Lewis took a holiday in Ireland, alone.

Lewis knew that for sixty years he had felt emotion to be 'something uncomfortable and embarrassing and even dangerous', and thus to be avoided. Something was happening in the relationship with Joy to shatter that shell and expose him to the tempestuous world of 'a love which threatened to upset or even to destroy the very fabric of his life' (Wilson, 1990, p. 257).

In October 1956, in excruciating pain after a fall, Joy was rushed to hospital where she was diagnosed as having a terminal cancer, which had eaten through her left femur. 'We live in the shadows', Lewis realized, but it was only under the shadow of losing her that he crossed the threshold from *caritas* and *philia* to *eros* and realized the brute force of the 'disturbing fact' of his love, a love which created a bridge 'by which I might get back from exile, and grow a man' (Lewis, as cited in Sibley, 1985, p. 142).

Lewis and Joy now wanted desperately to be allowed to solemnize the realization of the reality of their becoming 'one flesh' before God, and to 'claim the grace of the sacrament' of marriage before Joy died. The marriage previously enacted for ostensibly pragmatic reasons became a real marriage. As Sibley writes, there was a 'terrible poignancy about the exchange of vows' in the 'stark, sanitized setting of the Wingfield Hospital' on 21 March 1957 (Sibley, 1985, p. 123). Embracing the reality of *liebestod* in its non-defensive aspect was part of the demands of their marriage. In a letter to an American

---

2 Most accounts of their relationship suggest that Joy was deeply in love with Jack at a time when he did not consciously reciprocated such feelings. She was 'quicker off the mark' in pushing them tumbling over thresholds of whose significance Lewis seemed to be oblivious. Wilson points out that Lewis's autobiography shows a tremendous capacity for 'thinking he saw human situations extremely clearly, but actually getting them plumb wrong' (Wilson, 1990, p. 255).

3 It was not regarded by either as possible to marry in the eyes of the church due to Joy's being a divorcee. This was a difficult theological issue for Lewis to reconcile.

friend Lewis wrote, 'I am shortly to be both a bridegroom and a widower . . . There may, in fact, be a deathbed marriage' (as cited in Sibley, 1985, p. 119).

Lewis was confronted first hand by life-and-death issues that previously he had written about: not only the problem of pain, illness, separation, mortality, but also full-blown romantic love. The love lyrics he had so long studied and written about became lived reality:

> Years ago when I wrote about medieval love-poetry and described its strange, half make-believe, 'religion of love', I was blind enough to treat this as an almost purely literary phenomenon. I know better now . . .
> (Lewis, 1960, p. 102)

Gillian Rose also recognized that writing is no substitute for a real, embodied love:

> However satisfying writing is – that mixture of discipline and miracle, which leaves you in control . . . it is a very poor substitute indeed for the joy and the agony of loving. Of there being someone who loves *and* desires you, and he glories in his love and desire, and you glory in his ever-strange being, which comes up against you, and disappears, again and again, surprising you with difficulties and with bounty. To lose this is the greatest loss, a loss for which there is no consolation . . .
> (Gillian Rose, 1995, p. 54)

Lewis and Joy's relational history lived through the horrific discovery that Joy was suffering a terminal illness, being nursed by Lewis through her sickness. Then it transformed into an experience of a seemingly miraculous recovery that allowed their marriage to flourish ever further. Lewis wanted to take on and bear Joy's pain. By some seeming miracle, which he saw as Substitution (the doctrine that one can opt to literally 'bear one another's burdens'), Joy had a remission which allowed them to live out their love, cancerous spots in Joy's bone disappearing, new bone being made.

If the body is the mind's idea of itself and in love relations the two are inextricably intertwined, then despite 'magical thinking' there is still a mysterious capacity for love to exert a healing power when the 'two become one flesh':

> I have stood by the bedside of a woman whose thigh-bone was eaten through with cancer and who had thriving colonies of disease in many other bones as well . . . The doctors predicted a few months of life . . . A year later the patient was walking (uphill, too, through rough woodland) and the man who took the last x-ray photos was saying, 'these bones are as solid as rock'. It's miraculous.
> (Lewis, 1959, as cited in Wilson, 1990, p. 278)

Lewis also knew that there 'is a limit to the "one flesh"' and that the feelings one has for the other might correspond but do not unite:

> You can't really share someone else's weakness, or fear or pain. What you feel may . . . conceivably be as bad as what the other felt, though I should distrust anyone who claimed it was. But it would still be quite different . . . All their love passages have trained them to have, not identical, but complementary, correlative, even opposite, feelings about one another.
>
> (Lewis, 1961, pp. 14–15)

Joy's remission did not engender in either an omnipotent denial of impermanence and eventual death, but a sense of profound gratitude for what time they did have together. Time, space, the body – these were the very things 'that brought us together' (p. 15). Cut one off and the conversation ceases. As Lewis said, 'of course, the sword of Damocles still hangs over us; or should I say, we are forced to be aware of the sword which really hangs over all mortals?' (as cited in Sibley, 1985, p. 127).

Thus in his sixties Lewis found the happiness that had passed him 'by in my twenties'. They 'feasted on love; every mode of it – solemn and merry, romantic and realistic, sometimes as dramatic as a thunderstorm, sometimes as comfortable and unemphatic as putting on your soft slippers. No cranny of heart or body remained unsatisfied' (Lewis, 1961, p. 10). It was a multidimensional love – intellectual, spiritual, emotional, sexual, and, not least, domestic, which I call 'the erotics of the socks'. It was a marriage in which 'jointly the two become fully human' and, by a paradox, the 'carnival of sexuality leads out beyond our sexes' (p. 41).

Then, in 1959, the cancer returned. Yet still more joys in the here-and-now awaited them. Despite being terribly ill, Joy wanted to visit Greece. There were moments of 'inherent excellence' – at Daphni, visiting the temple of Apollo and the Byzantine church with its vast mosaic portrait of Christ – 'the last of the great days of perfect happiness'. They journeyed through 'richly scented pine woods' and 'olive groves shining silver in the sunlight', drank ouzo, retsina, and dined on fresh squid, red mullet, ewe's milk cheese and fresh oranges at the coastal village of Aegosthena. The appointment with the Real was made, and it was no disappointment. 'Greece was wonderful. We badly need a word meaning "the-exact-opposite-of-a-disappointment". *Appointment* won't do!' (Lewis, 1959, as cited in Sibley, 1985, p. 139).

Although they both knew she was dying it didn't detract from the joy of this time. As Lewis expressed in a letter to Father Walter Hooper, 'Joy knew she was dying, I knew she was dying, and *she* knew *I* knew she was dying – but when we heard the shepherds playing their flutes in the hills, it seemed to make no difference' (as cited in Sibley, 1985, p. 138). Their love brought them both fully into the present, while knowing their ability to be here now incorporated their ability to not deny her inevitable death.

Joy came back 'in a *nunc dimittis* frame of mind, having realized, beyond hope, her greatest, lifelong, this-worldly desire' (Wilson, 1990, p. 280).

Five weeks later she underwent a mastectomy, but after only a month, in June 1960, Joy fell into a coma. There was another reprieve, allowing a car ride into the Cotswolds, and more poignantly joyful domestic scenes. 'It is incredible how much happiness, even how much gaiety, we sometimes had together after all hope was gone. How long, how fully, how nourishingly, we talked together the last night' (Lewis, 1961, p. 14).

Part of such love includes allowing the dying to die, to depart in peace without trying to keep them on earth. Joy once reassured him that 'even if we both died at exactly the same moment, as we lie here side by side, it would be just as much a separation as the one you're so afraid of' (Davidman, as cited in Lewis, 1961, p. 15). He asked her, 'if you can – if it is allowed – come to me when I too am on my death bed'. She replied, 'allowed! Heaven would have a job to hold me; and as for Hell, I'd break it into bits.' Lewis knew that 'she knew she was speaking a kind of mythological language, with an element of comedy in it. There was a twinkle as well as a tear in her eye. But there was no myth and no joke about the will, deeper than any feeling, that flashed through her' (Lewis, 1961, p. 59).

The next morning Warnie awoke to hear her screams of agony; she was taken to hospital, where an afternoon and evening passed peacefully. Later in the evening Lewis told her the end was near. She was ready, it was the best news they could have. After receiving final Absolution she told Jack, 'you have made me happy . . . I am at peace with God.' She died at 10.15, smiling – 'but not at me', Lewis recalled (Sibley, 1985, p. 143).

It was, his brother Warnie observed, 'a short episode, of glory and tragedy: for Jack, the total (though heartbreaking) fulfilment of a whole dimension to his nature that had previously been starved and thwarted' (W. Lewis, as cited in Sibley, 1985, p. 145).

> And then one or other dies. And we think of this as love cut short; like a dance stopped in mid career. Thus bereavement is a universal and integral part of our love . . . It is not a truncation of the process but one of its phases; not the interruption of the dance, but the next figure. We are 'taken out of ourselves' by the loved one while she is here. Then comes the tragic figure of the dance in which we must learn to be still taken out of ourselves though the bodily presence is withdrawn, to love the very Her, and not fall back to loving our past, or our memory, or our sorrow, or our relief from sorrow, or our own love.
>
> (Lewis, 1961, p. 41)

In mourning Joy's death Lewis strove to keep alive the tender, vulnerable, newborn self she had nursed into being, but at the same time strove to avoid turning her memory into a hagiography, to 'sink back horribly into being not much more than one of my old bachelor pipe-dreams' when 'the reality is no longer there to check me, to pull me up short, as the real [Joy] did, by being so thoroughly herself and not me' (Lewis, 1961, p. 18). The whole point of their relationship was that she was not an internal figure projected outwards, not an *anima* or *femme inspiratrice* or muse, no ideal image of femininity, not a mother-figure or any such reality substitution, but Joy. The worst insult to the person she actually was would be to internalize her, turn her into an introject or symbol, to sentimentally idealize her, turn her into an abstract principle or apotheosize his beloved into a divinized image. 'As if I wanted to fall in love with my memory of her, an image in my own mind! It would be a form of incest' (Lewis, 1961, p. 19).

Lewis recognized the tyrannical desire for omnipotence inherent in introjection. 'The image has the added disadvantage that it will do whatever you want. It will smile or frown, be tender, gay, ribald, or argumentative just as your mood demands. It is a puppet of which you hold the strings' (Lewis, 1961, p. 20).

Lewis and Joy both lived out the principle that love entails the ability to live more fully, more undiluted. Yet he was only able to do so by allowing himself to be taken up in a process of transformation in true marriage with a 'worthy opponent'. As Austin Farrer wrote of Lewis:

> He took in more, he felt more, he remembered more, he invented more . . . [he displayed] an intense awareness, a vigorous reaction, a taking of the world into his heart . . . His blacks and whites of good and evil and his ecstasies and miseries were the tokens of a capacity for experiences beyond our scope.
>
> (Farrer, as cited in Sibley, 1985, p. 167)

And as Lewis wrote of Joy:

> Her palate for all the joys of sense and intellect and spirit was fresh and unspoiled. Nothing would have been wasted on her. She liked more things and liked them more than anyone I have known. A noble hunger, long unsatisfied, met at last its proper food.
>
> (Lewis, 1961 p. 17)

Love and remembrance: Anne Michaels's fugitive pieces

True intimacy is about the capacity to dwell in a state where we want to know but know we can never know: we share this moment, this time, as deeply as is possible, but we did not live each other's past, and we have access to it only through what we confide. We stitch together the tapestry of our relationship through the telling of our stories of origins, the vital narratives of our personal history. We vicariously share a past that we never shared, thus transcending the immutability of history, our separate lives. We were not there. But we can participate in the stories of that past, and take our beloved through relaying those stories, into that territory. In sharing another's history we change the memory of that history, in so far as our memory of that history now incorporates another memory: that of another bearing witness:[4]

> The shadow past is shaped by everything that never happened. Invisible, it melts the present like rain through karst. A biography of longing. It steers us like magnetism, a spirit torque. This is how one becomes undone by a smell, a word, a place, the photo of a mountain of shoes. By love that closes its mouth before calling a name.
>
> (Michaels, 1996, p. 17)

Exogamy is not about a unilateral severing of ties to the past, breaking free of the family-of-origin by walking out the door and never looking back. Our ancestry is integrated into the tapestry of our lives after we leave home and make a new coupling. It is paradoxically through fulfilling loving obligations to our ancestors that we are freed to create our own life and family with another. What creates obstacles to exogamy is the *failure* to work through that which needs to be known and mourned in our history, the failure to disentangle ourselves from the webs of unconscious complexes. That which is unresolved may become a compulsion to repeat, but the repetition also has its kernel of teleological truth. The compulsion is also about something striving to be avowed, understood and resolved. When one human being stands – as closely as is humanly possible – in the face of another's magnitude and vicariously witnesses and in an imaginal way enters the forests of another's past, this loving *participation mystique* begins to heal the terrors and sadness and disappointment of the past until every cell of memory, once containing terrifying memories of trauma, 'has been replaced, suffused with peace'.

Anne Michaels's (1996) novel *Fugitive pieces* shows the vital role of remembrance in the growth of a loving relationship. When Jacob first meets Michaela, it is reverence for history and her ancestry he first values:

---

4 Here I am talking about a positive aspect of how we can redeem memories through how we re-member them in the presence of a loving other, not forgetting the terrible ways in which totalitarian states seek to re-write history, whitewash the past, or Bion's reminder that such memories are in the first place distorted by desire, by inattention at the time, by judgement. 'Desires distort judgement by selection and suppression of material to be judged' (Bion, 1992, p. 380).

In Michaela's face, the loyalty of generations, perhaps the devotion of a hundred Kievan women for a hundred faithful husbands, countless evenings in close rooms under the sheets, discussing family problems; a thousand intimacies, dreams of foreign lands, first nights of love, nights of love after long years of marriage.

(Michaels, 1996, p. 179)

Jacob, a refugee, is found hiding in a bog by a Greek archaeologist, Athos. Athos rescues him, hides him in his coat, secretly takes him to his home, on a small Greek island, Zakynthos, where he lives until adulthood. Before they leave their beloved isle of Zakynthos, Athos says, 'We must have a ceremony. For your parents, for the Jews of Crete, for all who have no one to recall their names.'

Athos's love, his unfailing fidelity to truth and wisdom, to researching the past and resurrecting the souls of the dead from their prisons of unremembered graves, redeemed Jacob from the bogs of Biskupin so that he could be born again. Athos's kindness, love of the stranger, the patient, calm faith in what makes us human, the warm, heavy hand of reassurance upon Jacob's shoulder, the upbringing on Zakynthos which opened to him the world of knowledge from archaeology to philosophy: these many manifestations of love are what makes it possible, in turn, for Jacob to love. Athos's love for Jacob was initially *xenia*, love for a stranger who came across his path, later transmuting into love as *storge* and *philia*.

Later as an adult Jacob re-emerges and is reborn again in the arms of Michaela, whose compassionate witness to his retelling of a history of loss knits him together in the womb of her love:

Michaela's hands above her head; I stroke the fragile place on the back of her smooth upper arms. She is sobbing. She has heard everything – her heart an ear, her skin an ear. Michaela is crying for Bella.

The light and heat of her tears enter my bones.
The joy of being recognized and the stabbing loss: recognized for the first time . . .
Each night heals gaps between us until we are joined by the scar of dreams. My desolation exhales in the breathing dark.

(p. 182)

The sharing of their past becomes a knitting together of histories in their newly spun relationship:

Michaela offers her ancestors to me. I'm shocked at my hunger for her memories. Love feeds on the protein of detail, sucks fact to the marrow.

(p. 179)

Listening to her brings a sense of absolution: 'I cross over the boundary of skin into Michaela's memories, into her childhood' (p. 185). Her love, her vitality, her compassion and her warmth bring Jacob back from the land of the dead. This is another vital form of exogamous initiation: just as there is the theme of the angel who descends from the heavens in order to enjoy human (and hence mortal) love, Jacob has to ascend from the shades of death into being fully alive.

Jacob then vicariously enters the landscapes of Michaela's childhood:

> I enter the landscape of her adolescence, which I receive with a bodily tenderness as Michaela relaxes and imperceptibly opens towards it . . . I knew then I would show her the land of my past as she was showing me hers. We would enter the Aegean in a white ship, the belly of a cloud. Though she will be the foreigner, *agapē* at an unfamiliar landscape, her body will take to it like a vow.
>
> (p. 186)

It is in such sharing of memories that Jacob and Michaela are reconceived, as a new entity, as a fully conjoined couple. Jacob finally enters the present:

> Finally, Michaela takes me to one of the meccas of her childhood, a birch forest growing out of white sand.
> This is where I become irrevocably unmoored. The river floods. I slip free the knot and float, suspended in the present.
>
> (p. 188)

Two bodies interpenetrate, sharing two past lives, within a landscape imprinted with the images, sounds, smells, and mythic meanings of this past. In embracing our mortal coil, we embrace the sacrament of this present, alive, flesh-and-blood moment:

> What does the body make us believe? That we're never ourselves until we contain two souls. For years corporeality made me believe in death. Now, inside Michaela yet watching her, death for the first time makes me believe in the body.
>
> (p. 189)

In the mythic narratives generated by their respective inherited histories, the past of both forms a duet, each line of the melody intertwining and interweaving but still distinctly itself. The whole becomes polyphony. Jacob and Michaela's love is an act of standing in awe in the face of each other and their lives, an awe that bears traces of a sense of the holy, rapturous and terrifying.

The soul that stands in awe experiences a sense of root or radical wonder, an astonishment before the depths and heights that seem to be opening up within. It stands wordless on the edge of time, the brink of death. It has its own brilliant sparks of the divine.

(Hirsch, 1999, p. 257)

This is the attitude of wonder in which Jacob and Michaela live their love. Such transformation moves them towards the conception of new life, a child symbolic of their love

I pray that soon my wife will feel new breath inside her own. I press my head against Michaela's side and whisper a story to her flat belly.

Child I long for: if we conceive you, if you are born . . . Light the lamp, cut a long wick. One day when you've almost forgotten, I pray you'll let us return. That through an open window, even in the middle of a city, the sea air of our marriage will find you. I pray that one day in a room lit only by night snow, you will suddenly know how miraculous is your parents' love for each other. My son, my daughter: May you never be deaf to love.

(p. 195)

Chapter 16

Laetitia, liveliness and love

> Most men ebb and flow in wretchedness between the fear of death and
> the hardships of life; they are unwilling to live, and yet they do not know
> how to die.
>
> (Seneca, *Epistulae Morales*, I. 17)

Seminal to therapeutic work with couples and individuals is finding ways to
enhance the courage, to cross the abyss from apathy into a more alive state
of becoming. Partners sometimes collude with each other to shut down on a
possible moment of shared liveliness. There is a tension between loving and
living fully in the knowledge of mortality – ours and our beloved's – and
only half-living because we are too scared of the fullness of our life and
death. Unconsciously triggering discord in the face of the possibility of
relational harmony is sometimes due to fear of what such unity brings with
it. We fear the vulnerability and exposure entailed by intimacy. The
mutability of such moments also gives rise to fear of their loss.

A poignant article in the *Sydney Morning Herald* of 13 January 2001 by
Martin Armiger described a spell in hospital. He observed that the critical
factor for each man in Ward 21 was how much he invested or did not invest
in life:

> In the corner of Ward 21 at St Vincent's Hospital in Darlinghurst,
> there is a long thin man who never gets out of bed. Neither does he
> speak if he can help it, nor feed himself . . . His legs are as thin as pins,
> fleshless, the scant muscles and sinews exposed like an anatomy
> drawing. His skin is like paper that has been left in a drawer too long.
> He holds his arms up, elbows turned outwards, as if he may be attacked
> at any moment by unknown enemies . . . Two nights later I wake in the
> dark and hear a small mewling sound . . . I have never heard the
> slightest murmur from him before . . . The thought occurs to me that he
> might be dying, that after practically willing himself into the grave,

now, on the very edge, he wants to come back. He may be, in his quiet way, calling out. I tell myself that I am being fanciful, close my eyes and fall back into sleep.

(Armiger, 2001, p. 2)

In the morning he is dead . . .

Then some Italians come, and inject life into the place: the ward is transformed from 'a place of contiguous, disjunctive, private sufferings to a place of shared and public life'. The same challenges, such as being made to walk to the toilet, so passively resisted by the first man, are greeted with enthusiasm. Giovanni wants to go home, but can't leave until he proves he can walk without a frame. On the day of his test Giovanni:

puffs himself up like a weight lifter. The nurse lays out a tape on the floor. He is supposed to walk without deviation the length of the tape and back in less than 40 seconds. He grips his walking sticks . . . hurls himself up the line, puffing hard, rounds the turn, staggering slightly now, but, with a skip and a hop, makes the finish line with a second to spare. We all shout 'Bravo!' whistle and cheer . . . Giovanni looks blank-faced, stunned perhaps, at the enormity of his achievement, then does a victory lap, shaking hands with the old men in their beds, the physios and trainers; the whole ward celebrating, for a moment, our Olympian, our Virgil.

(p. 3)

This article sharply portrays the difference between having one foot in the grave as opposed to being in love with life, and what physiological effect such torpidity or liveliness has.

Depression as a defence against joy

Can some forms of depression be a defence against joy? By joy I mean *joie de vivre* a capacity to rejoice in the happiness of others and emotional aliveness. Such a form of enjoyment is an active achievement requiring intellectual, emotional and physical muscle. We can defend against sadness, grief, emptiness, depression and the 'tears of things'. But might depression sometimes be a defence against the energetic work involved in enjoyment?

There are of course many issues to consider – such as how to recognize and understand the process by which joy might become manic, unmitigated, excessive, or pushed down into depression. A further question is how to differentiate joy from sentimentality, which sometimes hides a repressed sadism. Joy must always be considered in the context of other affects, for example its relationship with the pleasure principle, desire and power, love and hate.

There are complex developmental reasons leading to why a given individual has more or less 'stacked on the side of life'. Winnicott shows how we are all marked by dead or numb spots, if not by a pervasive deadness, that, at the deepest levels, bear witness to a lapse of existence that once seemed endless. These may derive from an emotionally dead or preoccupied mother (the nameless dread that Bion speaks of when maternal containment has failed) or from a too-long absence, which will seem like an *evil eternity* – the $x+y+z$ minutes (Winnicott, 1971, p. 114) when the mother did not return, thus engendering in the baby a primordial break in life's continuity. The infant's ability to experience and symbolize life-enhancing connectedness with its supporting milieu is lost. Primitive defences of a form of half-aliveness are organized to defend against a repetition of 'unthinkable anxiety', of a process of fissuring the links between self and other, and between self and self. An original aliveness is blanked out in the face of this ghastly horror. If the return from such nothingness into aliveness and vitality is greeted with the same absent presence, the child may mould itself around the need for self-obliteration.

Weininger (1996) explores the topic of what is entailed for a life to be predominantly constructive rather than destructive of self and relationships, and what it takes for psychoanalysis to tip the balance on the side of life. He describes the pain of unlived, mislived or half-lived lives, of patients who feel dead, stall life and undo whatever they try to build. He shows the deadly consequences when we, ourselves afraid of liveliness, recoil from each other's growth in aliveness, how we 'choke on and swallow ourselves, drop into a deadness worse than death, initiate destructive actions that deaden ourselves more . . . To what extent can we turn things around?' (Eigen, 1996, p. xv).

Love of life entails ontological courage, and hard and brutally honest work on ourselves, dissolving destructive repetitious relational patterns. We are trying, perpetually, to move out of psychically dead imprisonment into a shared, unsentimental freedom of being with each other. It is not that real, gloriously passionate and majestic love does not exist, so much that when it is presented to us, we often turn away out of timidity, faltering, hesitant, reluctant to rise to its occasion.

Joie de vivre

> To be alive is all.
>
> (Winnicott, 1963/1984a, p. 192)

In the Greek tradition joy does not exist as an untrammelled force in itself. It is always seen in a relational context to other emotions. Therefore it is a quality that is variably negative or positive. For example, for the Stoics, joy must be understood in terms of the absence of fear or anxiety and is dependent upon, a reasoned view of nature. For the Epicurians, joy has to do with the lessening of pain. For the Sceptics, joy is so transient and mixed with alternative emotions that it must never be relied upon as an absolute.

In all three traditions true joy is to be achieved together with peace of mind and the absence of harmfully passionate over-emotionality, particularly fear, aggression, obsessive desire and frustration. Absolute joy can be dangerous and destructive if it is aggressive. Abandoned joy was encapsulated (contained) in Bacchanalian festivals (later the Carnivale). Untrammelled joy may swing into its opposite (*enantiodromia*) and lead to disappointment, depression, regret, remorse, the 'come down' after exuberant joy.[1]

In the Renaissance, the Greek idea that joy needed to be mediated by other emotions was further explored. Passion was seen as a passive emotion, joy as active, something actively created rather than merely experienced. The problem concerned how to express an individual joy without harming another, or becoming excessive. The solution was to have joy mediated by understanding, responsibility and reason. True joy also goes hand in hand with equanimity.

In the seventeenth century[2] joy was subdivided into various categories: a basic libido, *cupiditas* (sheer lust), *gaudium* (ongoing enjoyment), *hilaritas* (cheerfulness) and *laetitia* which is a beatitude. Joy as beatitude can only be achieved where there is mental acquiescence, the peace of mind such as described in 'the peace of God which passeth all understanding'.

Joy is related to happiness, and for Aristotle happiness is linked to intelligence, wisdom, generosity, self-control, courage and sociability. I would add, to being able to love deeply and altruistically.

Transformations in love

We are all always living with a dim intimation of an ultimately unknowable and therefore unspeakable 'no-thing' which is beyond our limits and knowledge and yet to which we belong, and which continuously informs us although we turn a blind eye to it. Bion called this 'O', which he defines as ultimate reality, godhead, absolute truth, the infinite or the thing-in-itself. Grotstein associates it with Lacan's (1966/1977) register of the Real: 'The Real is Kant's "thing-in-itself", Bion's Absolute Truth, Ultimate reality, an experience beyond imaging, imagining, and symbolising' (Grotstein, 2000, p. 273).

1 See Nussbaum, 1994.
2 See Lloyd, 1996.

Although O is ultimately unknowable, it is inferred through its transformations. Such transformations are dynamic and disruptive and bring
about catastrophic change, as in an irruption of O, a disturbing fact, which
overturns the status quo. Our life task is its realization: 'The most, and the
least that the individual person can do is to be it' (Bion, 1970, p. 141).
Transformations in O require 'disciplined abandonment of memory, desire,
understanding, sense impressions' and ego itself (Grotstein, 1997b). O is
apprehended through a *via negativa*: 'O is a dark spot that must be illumi-
nated by blindness' (Bion, 1970, p. 88).

Intuition, the 'seventh servant' (Bion, 1970), Spinoza's 'knowledge of the
third kind', is a moment of seeing, knowing that and understanding how we
are part of God or Nature. We can enjoy moments of illumination when
we discern our place in the scheme of things, the connections, the inter-
relations, a primordial experience of eternity, or of the timeless.

Such moments of inherent excellence where we have a brush with O,
behold and sense the magnitude of O, are accompanied by the 'tears of
things' and by a profound recognition of and remorse for our failures to
live up to our truths, our falling short of the mark. At such moments we
mourn our lost opportunities and the hurts we have inflicted. At-one-ment
with O and atonement are linked.

We may feel so intimidated by such majesty that we avoid, through
numerous disguised subterfuges, rising to the occasion of ourselves, now,
here, this minute. Resistance is resistance to O: 'Resistance operates because
it is feared that the reality of the object is immanent' (Bion, 1965, p. 82).

> When in the presence of the Other, I say, 'Here I am!' this 'Here I am!'
> is the place through which the Infinite enters into language, but without
> giving itself to be seen.
>
> (Levinas, 1982/1985, p. 106)

'Here I am! Here I am!' Only when we answer the call of the lover who is
our beloved are we fully individuated, according to the Jewish philosopher
Rosenzweig, who likens the call of the lover to God calling Abraham
(Moyn, 2005, p. 148). God calls Abraham twice, and it is only the second
time, when he answers 'Here I am' to God, that Abraham achieves 'genuine
selfhood'. 'I become an "I" only thanks to the Thou of the divine, who calls
and therefore individuates my self' (p. 148). Such I–Thou dialogue depends
upon acknowledgement of alterity. Rosenzweig writes: 'Only when the I
acknowledges the Thou as something external to itself . . . that is, only
when it makes the transition from monologue to authentic dialogue, only
then does it become that I' (Rosenzweig, as cited in Moyn, 2005, p. 148).
Love allows one to be true to the gap between God and human, while
nonetheless bridging the distance between them.

The epiphany of the beloved's face is a 'rupture of the *I–Thou*' relation, an *illeity* signifying both 'holiness' and 'separation' (Levinas, 1961/1969, p. 256) and also a poignant responsiveness to the fragility of humanity:

> Love aims at the Other; it aims at him in his frailty . . . To love is to fear for another, to come to the assistance of his frailty. In this frailty as in the dawn arises the Loved, who is the Beloved . . . The epiphany of the Beloved is but one with her *regime* of tenderness. The *way* of the tender consists in an extreme fragility, vulnerability. It manifests itself at the limit of being and non-being, as a soft warmth where being dissipates into radiance.
>
> (Levinas, 1961/1969, p. 256)

Grotstein (2000) states that neurosis is the 'postponement of the fateful consequences of rendezvous with O' (including O of oneself and O of the other), whereas psychosis is the 'abnegating disavowal and discrediting of it altogether'. Standing defenceless before the Real make us 'shudder and shrink away from the dread of the Real (O)', yet 'the power to encompass and countenance it qualifies one as having undergone a transformation in O, which corresponds to a numinous, spiritual experience' (Grotstein, 2000, p. 273), a transformation in love.

Here I unite Spinoza's concept of conatus, the endeavour to persist in one's being, a movement towards intuitive knowledge, true individuation, Bion's transformations in O and truth as *alétheia*. 'The ego, in seeking to disguise, repress, or alter the unconscious, becomes disingenuous and dissembles the truth' (Grotstein, 1997b). Yet truth remains behind all that disguises it. Stripping away the layers of conceptualization we reveal O, even if it is also beyond comprehension.

In the mystical space of non-duality, seeing and being seen, we feel brushed by eternity, *ruach Elohim*, in the vastness of space, seeing all phenomena as interdependent, feeling in loving harmony with the world. This is out-flowing, not in-turned.

Laetitia

T. S. Eliot declared that human beings cannot bear very much reality (Eliot, 1935/1959). As Bion said, 'Resistance is only manifest when the threat is contact with what is believed to be real' (1965, p. 147). Human beings cannot bear very much pain but perhaps even more they cannot bear very much joy. I use the Latin term *laetitia* to describe both the joyful, ecstatic, vertiginously blissful state found in moments of inherent excellence where we experience the fundamental non-duality of subject and object, self and world, such as in an states where there is communion with the other, and also a more continuous state of being in the love which passeth all understanding.

> With you, the world remains fluid. Words are ethereal. The sensible remains sweet and carnal: living, pulsating. It is light like the birds, the flowers, the angels. It is felicity. Fragile, too, in its incomplete incarnation.
>
> (Irigaray, 1994/2000, p. 11)

What I am writing of here shares some of the qualities of *jouissance* as described by Barthes, Lacan,[3] Kristeva, Eigen and others. However, my sense of *laetitia* goes beyond their use of *jouissance*. It is closer to the sense of bliss described in states of union, states of mystical non-duality in Tantric Buddhism. However, I also add to the equation a sense of the particular: this person I am with, with all their uniqueness, mortality, difference, is who I am finding myself in communion with, in this moment. To join that deeply and intimately with another goes beyond desire, pleasure, beyond limitations. It is not for the faint-hearted, it destroys the self as we knew it, opens us out, explodes structures of fixity. As Clark defines it, 'jouissance is the experience wherein fixity of state melts, where identity vaporises, where impossibilities of definition open up infinite possibilities' (Clark, 2000, p. 12).

Such rejoicing is the perfect antidote to envy, which cannot bear the existence of another's goods, powers or beauty. To rejoice in another's richness is to enjoy them non-possessively, beyond desire.

In intimate relations we play with how much *laetitia* we can stand, for how long we can sustain it before trepidation, forces of apathy call forth a break, a shutting down on *laetitia*. This play between *laetitia* and creating limitations or shutting down is a second-by-second choice. Emily Dickinson

---

3 I use the term *laetitia* to differentiate my concept from the Lacanian use of the term *jouissance*. *Jouissance* originally means enjoyment. Diderot wrote a definition of *jouissance* as idiopathic, bound up with romantic love as meaning enjoyment, which he defines as 'to enjoy' as 'to know, to experience, to feel the advantages of possession' through enjoyment of the beloved. He asks, is there 'anything that can make us happier than the possession and enjoyment of a being who thinks and feels as you do, who has the same ideas, who experiences the same sensations, the same ecstasies, who brings her affectionate and sensitive arms towards yours, who embraces you, whose caresses will be followed with the existence of a new being who will resemble one of you' (Diderot, 1751/1967, p. 96).

Over time Lacan (Evans, 1996) developed his idea of *jouissance* and uses the term variously: there are at least three Lacanian meanings for *jouissance* – phallic *jouissance*, *jouissance* of the Other, and sexual *jouissance*. Lacan saw *jouissance* as phallic, and not relational, unconcerned with the subjectivity of the other. *Jouissance* is always linked to the pleasure principle and therefore to pain: as in the enjoyment of the pain of pleasure and the enjoyment of the pleasure of pain. In 1970 Lacan posited a feminine *jouissance* as a 'supplementary *jouissance*' (S20, 58) which is beyond the Phallus, a *jouissance* of the Other.

unflinchingly embraced the pith and marrow of things: 'Dare you see a soul *at the White Heat?*' she asks. She wrote, 'I find ecstasy in living', and could not understand why such bliss and fullness of life had to be carefully portioned out in bits by most people.

> Why Bliss so scantily disburse –
> Why Paradise defer –
> Why floods be served to Us – in Bowls –
> I speculate no more –
>
> (Dickinson, as cited in Hirsch, 1999, p. 89)

Such a state beyond categories combining the bliss and clarity of enlightenment is well-attested in Buddhism:

> A person in a peak-experience of, say, pure aesthetic perception and enjoyment feels himself at his best and fullest. He feels more perceptive and contented than at other times, but the feeling he experiences defies categorisation.
>
> (Guenther, 1976, p. 37)

Possessive desire is a defence, a prohibition against going beyond a certain limit in *jouissance*. We use desire to tyrannically attempt to control the plenitude of a moment, to catch it, distil it, define it, close down on it:

> As fast as heart opens, imaginary ego rushes in with fictitious claims and self-serving scripts. The ego incessantly bends the *jouissance* of the Other to its prevailing catalogue of desires. Indeed, a servile tyrannical ego may be expert at attuning itself to the desire of the Other, in order to capture *jouissance*.
>
> (Eigen, 1998, p. 148)

Against this, we find that to not control but to surrender to its greater satisfaction is to taste something which, once tasted, makes the fairy-floss substitute reveal itself for the poor shadow that it is: 'Once tasting the beauty and depth of such an opening, it is difficult to return to tyranny without regrets . . .' (Eigen, 1998, p. 148).

Psychotherapy is about creating or finding ways to understand and melt the old restrictive patterns of defence against life and relationship, and so to increase the capacity for *laetitia*, for life, for becoming. True intimate relations necessitate a sacrifice of control in the service of *laetitia*, realizing that 'I am not the imaginary hero of my omnipotent ego dreams, nor is the other what I imagined. We are much worse and better than anything we thought we were or wanted' (Eigen, 1998, p. 150). As a patient, Jackie, said:

I suddenly realized the opposite of love is not hate, but control. And I so need to control my partner Josh, because it feels so unsafe when I don't. That was why I so freaked out when I had my first child. I suddenly realized I wasn't boss of the universe. It was so scary, yet I also felt such an overwhelming sense of relief, in fact celebration.

Laetitia involves the capacity to feel more: including to bear more suffering as well as more joy. As Ogden points out, the goal of analysis is to 'upset (unsettle, decentre, disturb, perturb) the . . . given of the patient's conscious beliefs and narratives by which he creates illusions of permanence, certainty and fixity of the experience of self and of the people who occupy his internal and external worlds' (Ogden, 1997, p. 12).

No two moments of *laetitia* are the same, each is a new revelation requiring us to rise to the occasion of ourselves in this place in a new way: we are continually 'learning on the job', living frugally on the surprise of finding the plenitude of being:

> You and I as living gods, bearers of *jouissance* who serve the *jouissance* of the Other do not exist as something we can posit. What does not exist is the you I say you are, the me you want me to be. My version of you does not cover the territory. What you say about you does not either . . . It is precisely the you I don't know that makes the you I know bearable . . . What counts more than knowing is the *Ein Soph* of you, the unknowable, indefinable You. Always, the inexhaustible Mystery.
>
> (Eigen, 1998, p. 150)

In the Drunken Song in Zarathustra, Nietzsche speaks of joy in the sense that I have used the term *laetitia*:

> All Joy wants eternity of all things, wants honey, wants lees, wants drunken midnight, wants tombs, wants tomb-tears comfort, wants gilded evening glow.
>
> *What* does joy not want? It is thirstier, more cordial, hungrier, more terrible, more secret than all woe; it wants *itself*, it bites into *itself*, the ring's will strives in it; it wants love, it wants hatred, it is over rich, gives, throws away, begs that one might take it, thanks the taker, it would like to be hatred, so rich is joy that it thirsts for woe, for hell, for hatred, for disgrace, for the cripple, for *world* – this world, oh, you know it!
>
> All joy wants eternity, wants deep, deep eternity.
>
> (Nietzsche, 1883/1966, p. 436)

Chapter 17

Alétheia: becoming in love

This book has encompassed a terrain concerning the quest for authenticity in love, from the *pathos* of distorted perceptions and misconstructions to the shocking revelation of the truth through iconoclasms of alterior love, unfolding into the infinitely expanding horizons of becoming in love. Love has been presented as consisting of a palette of aspects of love and inter-dependently conditioned by alterity, intersubjectivity and exogamy. To say love is intersubjective is to say that the two lovers are interdependent, mutually influencing each other, neither completely conjoined, nor com-pletely independent. Exogamous love is the desire to cross the intersubjective space, yet difference and opacity continually reassert the space between us and thus keep each of us forever unreached and unreachable. If our subjectivity is forever in flux, each encounter is a new manifestation of the limitless being and ever-becoming *eudaimonia* of each other.

In becoming in love we transcend our egocentric limitations into an ecstasy of co-inherence in which we also retain a separation-in-union. It is at-one-ment. It is also atonement because a natural aspect of at-one-ment is sorrow and remorse for all our failings, our faults, our lies, our cover-ups, our almost wilful misunderstandings. Through atonement we find the deepest reconciliation with each other possible: we heal our disseveration.

Our enigmatic nature is always revealing itself as if for the first time, a shock and a delight. When desire does not unconsciously seek to destroy, incorporate, possess or cannibalize the other, we may find ourselves liberated into a joyful appreciation and gratitude for simply being who we are, making us more fully human and open to the needs of others, to the agonies and sorrows of life.

Our love life has a personal and a social history: the pinnacles of love to which we aspire are obscured and compromised by political, cultural as well as psychological obstacles. Primary love, which originates from our first caregivers, moves out from the family of origin and into the world, just as love predicated on narcissism transforms into love based on a valuing of the alterity of the other. Yet our ability to move from original love, and various narcissistic modalities, into mature love based on an appreciation of our beloved's subjectivity, is beset with developmental impediments, unresolved complexes belonging to the endogamous spheres of our past.

One vision hovering over this work was that of the Buddhist Four Noble Truths which encompass the actuality of dissatisfaction, its causes, the truth of the cessation of suffering and the truth of a path to cessation. There is the truth of the suffering of interpersonal destructiveness and relational discontent. There is the truth of the many causes of dissatisfaction and disappointment including obscuration, misperceptions and deluded views. We become immured in the mire of endogamous interlocking and intra-locking scenes that are superimposed upon our relationships, imprisoning us in an ever more confusing realm of distortions, enmity, misunderstanding and alienation. There is the possibility of another way of being – an ultimately ecstatic ontophany of becoming in love. There is a path of cessation of relational destructiveness, dissatisfaction and delusion through realizing and integrating insight into the nature of reality which has been there all along, beneath the phantasmagoria. When we arrive, there is a sense of being where we were always meant to be.

Enlightenment is simply the name for a change in perspective (Guenther, 1976, p. 66) in which we see more clearly, unimpeded by the layers of projections based on our manifold erroneous views. True enlightenment based on non-grasping and insight into the interdependence of all phenomena has as its quality limitless love, compassion, enjoyment and appreciation of the value of all human beings:

> The supreme source is the total state of one's self, the authentic condition that totally pervades everything, beyond any border; centre and direction, without any duality . . .
>
> (Norbu, 1986, p. 53)

In this book I have described my concept of the exogamous quest as an endeavour to take delight in the freedom, epiphany and alterity of the beloved and to ever deepen and authenticate our becoming O in love. This quest does not proceed in a straight line and often 'goes off the rails'. Yet when we untangle our confused emotional contortions there can be a sense of being with each other where we always were meant to be, and on another level always have been, a sense of grace. From the perspective of 'being here' our inherent clear awareness is primordial and timeless, it does not evolve or develop with experience. There is nothing to achieve, for we are already that who we are, yet we work to achieve that nothingness. Like the clouds covering the sky, to use a famous Buddhist metaphor for enlightenment, the sky is always as it always was and is and will be, the sky. Or in the words of the Sufi poet:

Thou art a shadow and in love with the sun: the sun comes, the shadow is naughted speedily.

(Rûmi)

Love's work is a process of ever deepening our clarity, understanding, compassion and courage: it is a stripping away of all that is not authentic, it is a *via negativa*, it is *alétheia*.

In all love and other interpersonal relations, in all couplings, there is a sense of something beyond, a third mysterious and elusive presence, a spirit to open our eyes to move us. This third presence can be seen as our intuition, our inkling, our seventh servant, although caught in webs of deceit and delusion. Such opening out to this reality entails a personal and a mutual effort, an honesty and a faith of nerve which is emotionally hard, but is also our greatest erotic possibility. It is through the exogamous conatus that *eros* becomes an ethical opus.

Although the focus has been very much the couple, about personal and interpersonal ethics, there are also wider cultural and political implications of this theory of exogamous love. Through such becoming in love we deepen our compassion and understanding of others, our ability to apprehend and celebrate alterity, to be lovers of all others.

The contrast is between imagination, curiosity and negotiation on the one hand, and on the other hand, intolerance leading to metaphorical or actual war instead of mediation and understanding. The question to ask is whether psychotherapy and a philosophy of love have something therapeutic to offer concerning the impact of the personal worlds of our relationships with each other on world concerns. I see couples every day whose relational failures leave them in a kind of Sartrian 'hell is other people'. Their desperate alienation and destructiveness spill out into their immediate environment, and flow outwards to have nefarious repercussions upon their children unto the next generation. This influence is two-way: there is a great deal of disillusionment and despair rippling inwards demanding attention to questions such as whether we can live our lives more harmoniously, whether we can sit down together and find solutions, alleviate the sense of panic which incites us to unreflective, unconsidered action. Therapy reminds us that slow, painstaking, incremental work still is the only thing that has a long-term benefit. And its results are achievements forever needing to be won again and again, in this new moment, now. This last points to the ethical attendants of love: generosity, compassion and the embodied, active expressions of love's virtues.

This book has been an exploration into a philosophy and psychology of embodied, passionate love relations. To embrace love fully is to confront the whole range of ultimate questions: eternity and mortality, self and other, identity and difference, limitation and increase, illusion and disillusionment, union and separateness, mind–body relations, pleasure and pain, procreation and destruction, the sublime and the mundane. Such love enters a state of exultation beyond lust and desire, which is simultaneously close to the 'tears of things', as well as a supreme, inordinate felicity.

The quest for true love weaves a meandering path, moving onwards, then, despite prohibitions to the contrary, we look back to old modes, encountering numerous psychological obstacles, repeating and recreating pathological aspects of early relationships. Yet the path of love is not always a regression, it can be a circumambulation of the real. The spiral moves upwards towards an end, to O, or backwards to the familiar and safe. Yet O is at our beginning as it is at our end. It is more about discovering and becoming who we always are. As Schelling put it, 'the end is like the beginning and the beginning like the end, a kind of eternity, since it is not a sequence of time but only one time' (Schelling, as cited in Dupré, 1975, p. 671). Rituals of initiation in love redefine 'return' to mean to turn again, in an ever new and ever deepening way.

To reach the unreachable infinitude of becoming we walk the path of love, through horror and splendour, agony and joy, through quotidian misconceptions into revelation, transfiguration and beatitude, becoming in O in *alétheia* in love, truth, being and love.

Bibliography

Allen, W. (Writer/Director) (1992). *Husbands and wives* [Motion picture]. United States: Columbia TriStar.

Andreas-Salomé, L. (1914). Zum typus weib [About women]. *Imago 3*, 1–4.

Andreas-Salomé, L. (1951). *Lebensrückblick, grundriss einigher lebenserinnerungen* [Looking back at one's life, a life retrospective: an outline of a handful of life's memories] (E. Pfeiffer, ed.). Zurich: Max Niemans Verlag & Wiesbaden.

Arendt, H. (1996). *Love and Saint Augustine* (J. Scott and J. Stark, eds). Chicago: Chicago University Press.

Aristotle (2004). *The Nicomachean ethics* (J. Thomson, trans.). London: Penguin.

Armiger, M. (2001, January 13). Waiting for life and death. *Sydney Morning Herald, Spectrum*, pp. 2–3.

Armstrong, J. (2002). *Conditions of love: The philosophy of intimacy*. London: Penguin.

Augustine (1961). *Confessions* (R. S. Pine-Coffin, trans.). London: Penguin (original work written 400).

Balázs, B. (1960). *A Kékszakállu herceg vára.* [Duke Bluebeard's castle]. Budapest, Hungary: Magyar Helikon.

Balint, M. (1952). *Primary love and psychoanalytic technique*. London: Maresfield.

Balint, M. (1959). *Thrills and regressions*. London: Maresfield (reprinted by Karnac, 1987).

Balint, M. (1968). *The basic fault*. London: Basic Books.

Barnes, J. (2004). *The lemon tree*. London: Picador.

Baron-Cohen, S. (1995). *Mindblindedness*. London: MIT Press.

Bartók, B. (1907). *Two portraits*, op. 37, movement I. Budapest, Hungary: Károly Rozsnyai.

Bartók, B. (1925). *Bluebeard's castle*. Vienna: Universal Edition.

Bayley, J. (1998). *Iris: A memoir of Iris Murdoch*. London: Duckworth.

Benjamin, J. (1988). *The bonds of love*. New York: Pantheon.

Benjamin, J. (1995). *Like subjects, love objects*. New Haven, CT: Yale University Press.

Benjamin, J. (1998). *Shadow of the other: Intersubjectivity and gender in psychoanalysis*. London: Routledge.

Benvenuto, B. and Kennedy, R. (1986). *The work of Jacques Lacan: An introduction*. London: Free Association Books.

Bergmann, M. (1980). On the intrapsychic function of falling in love. *Psychoanalytic Quarterly 49*, 56–77.

Bernasconi, R. and Critchley, S. (eds) (1991). *Re-reading Levinas*. Bloomington: Indiana University Press.

Bernstock, J. (1991). *Under the spell of Orpheus*. Edwardsville: Southern Illinois University Press.

Bick, E. (1968). The experience of the skin in early object relations. *International Journal of Psychoanalysis 49*, 484–486.

Bick, E. (1986). Further considerations on the functioning of skin in early object relations: findings from infant observation integrated into child and adult analysis. *British Journal of Psychotherapy II*, 292-299.

Bion, W. (1961). *Experiences in groups*. London: Tavistock.

Bion, W. (1963). *Elements of psychoanalysis*. London: Heinemann.

Bion, W. (1965). *Transformations*. London: Karnac.

Bion, W. (1967). *Second thoughts*. London: Heinemann.

Bion, W. (1970). *Attention and interpretation*. London: Tavistock.

Bion, W. (1977). *Two papers: The grid and the caesura* (J. Salomâo, ed.). Rio de Janiero: Imago Editora.

Bion, W. (1983). *Learning from experience*. Northvale, NJ: Jason Aronson (original publication 1962).

Bion, W. (1991). *A memoir of the future*. London: Karnac.

Bion, W. (1992). *Cogitations*. London: Karnac.

Blake, W. (2004). *The complete poems* (A. Ostriker, ed.). Oxford: Oxford University Press.

Blanchot, M. (1993). *The infinite conversation* (S. Hanson, trans.). Minneapolis: University of Minnesota Press (original work 1969).

Bollas, C. (1987). *The shadow of the object*. New York: Columbia University Press.

Borges, J. (1999). *Selected non-fictions* (Eliot Weinberger, ed.). New York: Viking.

Bowlby, J. (1969–1980). *Attachment and loss*. London: Hogarth.

Bowlby, J. (1979). *The making and breaking of affectional bonds*. London: Tavistock.

Bowlby, J. (1988). *A secure base: Clinical applications of attachment theory*. London: Routledge.

Bowra, M. (1961). *Medieval love-songs*. London: Athlone Press.

Brandchaft, B. (1994). To free the spirit from its cell. In R. Stolorow and G. Atwood (eds), *The intersubjective perspective* (pp. 57–76). Northvale, NJ: Jason Aronson.

Britton, R. (1989). The missing link: parental sexuality in the Oedipus complex. In J. Steiner (ed.), *The oedipus complex today* (pp. 83–101). London: Karnac.

Britton, R. (1992). The oedipus situation and the depressive position. In R. Anderson (ed.), *Clinical lectures on Klein and Bion* (pp. 34–45). London: Routledge.

Britton, R. (1998). *Belief and imagination*. London: Routledge.

Britton, R. (2004). Narcissistic disorders in clinical practice. *Journal of Analytical Psychology 49*(4), 477–490.

Brookner, A. (1983). *Look at me*. London: Penguin.

Brookner, A. (1987). *A friend from England*. London: Cape.

Brown, L. (ed.) (1993). *New shorter Oxford English dictionary*. Oxford: Clarendon Press.

Buber, M. (1987). *I and thou* (R. Gregor-Smith, trans.). Edinburgh: T & T Clark (original work published 1923).

Buber, M. (2002). *Between man and man* (R. Gregor-Smith, trans.). London: Routledge (original work published 1947).

Bullock, A. and Trombley, S. (eds) (1977). *The new Fontana dictionary of modern thought*. London: HarperCollins.

Carson, A. (1986). *Eros: The bittersweet*. Princeton, NJ: Princeton University Press.

Cavarero, A. (1995). *In spite of Plato* (S. Anderline-D'Onofrio and A. O'Healy, trans.). Cambridge: Polity Press (original work published 1990).

Chatalian, G. (1974). A review of R. H. Robinson: The Buddhist religion: A historical introduction. *Journal of Indian Philosophy 2*(3–4), 355–372.

Clark, G. (1987). Animation through the analytical relationship: the embodiment of self in the transference and counter-transference. *Harvest Journal for Jungian Studies 33*, 104–114.

Clark, G. (2000). Mind–body intimacies and pains. Unpublished manuscript.

Clark, G. (2006). A Spinozan lens onto the confusions of borderline relations. *Journal of Analytical Psychology 51*(5), 735–741.

Clulow, C. (1993). *Rethinking marriage*. London: Karnac.

Cocteau, C. (Director) (1960). *Orphée* [Motion picture]. Paris: Les Editions Cinegraphiques.

Cocteau, J. (1972). *Three screenplays* (C. Martin-Sperry, trans.). New York: Grossman.

Coleridge, S. (1999). *The rhyme of the ancient mariner* (P. Fry, ed.). Boston: Bedford (original work published 1798).

Collin, F. (1994). Philosophical differences. In F. Thébaud (ed.), *A history of women: Toward a cultural identity in the twentieth century* (pp. 261–297). Cambridge, MA: Belknap Press.

Colman, W. (1993). Marriage as a psychological container. In S. Ruszczynski (ed.), *Psychotherapy with couples* (pp. 70–99). London: Karnac.

Colman, W. (1996). Aspects of anima and animus in oedipal development. *Journal of Analytical Psychology 41*(1), 37–57.

Compte-Sponville, A. (2001). *A small treatise on the great virtues* (C. Temerson, trans.). New York: Metropolitan Books (original work published 1996).

Corbin, H. (1972).*Theophanies and mirrors: Idols or icons?* Dallas, TX: Spring.

Critchley, S. (2002). 'Introduction'. In S. Critchley and R. Bernasconi (eds), *The Cambridge companion to Levinas* (pp. 1–33). Cambridge: Cambridge University Press.

Critchley, S. and Bernasconi, R. (eds) (2002). *The Cambridge companion to Levinas*. Cambridge: Cambridge University Press.

Davidman, J. (1951). The longest way round. In D. Wesley Soper (ed.), *These found the way: Thirteen converts to Protestant Christianity*. Philadelphia: Westminster Press.

Demény, J. (ed.) (1971). *Béla Bartók letters*. London: Faber and Faber.

de Rougemont, D. (1983). *Love in the western world* (rev. edn). (M. Belgion, trans.). Princeton, NJ: Princeton University Press (original work published 1940).

Derrida, J. (1999). *Adieu to Emmanuel Levinas* (P. Brault and M. Naas, trans.). Stanford, CA: Stanford University Press (original work published 1997).

Dickinson, E. (1960). *The complete poems of Emily Dickinson* (T. H. Johnson, ed.). Boston: Little, Brown, and Company.

Diderot, D. (1967). 'Jouissance', *The encyclopedia* (S. Gendzier, trans.). New York: Harper and Row (original work published from 1751).

Donne, J. (1933). *The poems of John Donne* (H. Grierson, ed.). Oxford: Oxford University Press (original work published 1751).

Dorati, A. (1983). *Notes of seven decades.* Detroit, MI: Wayne University Press.

Dorsett, L. (1983). *And God came in.* New York: Macmillan.

Dupré, A. (1975). Alienation and redemption through time and memory: an essay on religious time consciousness. *Journal of the American Academy of Religion 43*(4), 671–679.

Eigen, M. (1996). Forward. In O. Weininger, *Being and not being* (pp. xiii–xv). London: Karnac.

Eigen, M. (1998). *The psychoanalytic mystic.* London: Free Association Books.

Eliade, M. (1958). *Rites and symbols of initiation.* New York: Harper.

Eliot, T. S. (1959). Burnt Norton. In T.S. Eliot, *Four quartets* (pp. 189–196). London: Faber (original work published 1935).

Ellenberger, H. F. (1970). *The discovery of the unconscious.* New York: Basic Books.

Ellmann, R. (1987). *Oscar Wilde.* London: Penguin.

Epicurus (1993). *The essential Epicurus* (E. O'Connor, trans.). New York: Prometheus.

Evans, D. (1996). *An introductory dictionary of Lacanian psychoanalysis.* London: Routledge.

Fairbairn, W. R. D. (1943). The war neuroses – their nature and significance. In *Psychoanalytic studies of the personality* (pp. 256–287). London: Routledge & Kegan Paul.

Fairbairn, W. R. D. (1952a). *Psychoanalytic studies of the personality.* London: Routledge & Kegan Paul.

Fairbairn, W. R. D. (1952b) Endopsychic structure considered in terms of object-relationships. In D. Scharff and E. Fairbairn-Birtles (eds), *Psychoanalytic studies of the personality* (pp. 82–132). London: Routledge & Kegan Paul (original work published 1944).

Fairbairn, W. R. D. (1994). Observations on the nature of hysterical states. In B. E. Fairbairn and D. E. Scharff (eds), *From instinct to self: Selected papers of W. R. D. Fairbairn.* Northvale, NJ: Jason Aronson (original work published 1954).

Federn, P. (1953). *Ego psychology and the psychoses.* New York: Basic Books.

Fisher, J. (1999). *The uninvited guest: Emerging from narcissism towards marriage.* London: Karnac.

Fonagy, P. and Target, M. (1996). Playing with reality: I. Theory of mind and the normal development of psychic reality. *International Journal of Psycho-Analysis 77*, 217–233.

Fordham, M. (1957). *New developments in analytical psychology.* London: Routledge.

Fordham. M. (1976). *The self and autism.* London: Heinemann.

Fraiberg, S., Adelson, E. and Shappiro, V. (1975). Ghosts in the nursery: a psycho-analytic approach to the problem of impaired infant–mother relationships. *Journal of the American Academy of Child Psychiatry 14*, 387–422.

Freedman, R. (1996). *Life of a poet: Rainer Maria Rilke*. Evanston, IL: Northwestern University Press.

Freud, S. (1945). *The interpretation of dreams* (A. A. Brill, trans.). London: George Allen & Unwin (original work published 1900).

Freud. S. (1955). Group psychology and the analysis of the ego. In J. Strachey (ed. and trans.), *The standard edition of the complete psychological works of Sigmund Freud* (Vol. 18, pp. 67–145). London: Penguin (original work published 1921).

Freud, S. (1961). Civilisation and its discontents. In J. Strachey (ed. and trans.), *The standard edition of the complete psychological works of Sigmund Freud* (Vol. 21, pp. 59–149). London: Hogarth Press (original work published 1930).

Freud, S. (1977a). Three essays on sexuality and other works. In J. Strachey (ed. and trans.) and A. Richards (ed.), *Penguin Freud library* (Vol. 7, pp. 33–171). London: Penguin (original work published 1905).

Freud, S. (1977b). Family romances. In J. Strachey (ed. and trans.) and A. Richards (ed.), *Penguin Freud library* (Vol. 7, pp. 217–227). London: Penguin (original work published 1909).

Freud, S. (1977c). On the universal tendency to debasement in the sphere of love. In J. Strachey (ed. and trans.) and A. Richards (ed.), *Penguin Freud library* (Vol. 7, pp. 243–261). London: Penguin (original work published 1912).

Freud, S. (1984a). Instincts and their vicissitudes. In J. Strachey (ed. and trans.) and A. Richards (ed.), *Penguin Freud library* (Vol. 11, pp. 105–107). London: Penguin (original work published 1915).

Freud, S. (1984b). The unconscious. In J. Strachey (ed. and trans.) and A. Richards (ed.), *Penguin Freud library* (Vol. 11, pp. 159–223). London: Penguin (original work published 1915).

Freud, S. (1984c). Narcissism: an introduction. In J. Strachey (ed. and trans.) and A. Richards (ed.), *Penguin Freud library* (Vol. 11, pp. 59–99). London: Penguin (original work published 1914).

Freud, S. (1984d). Mourning and melancholia. In J. Strachey (ed. and trans.) and A. Richards (ed.), *Penguin Freud library* (Vol. 11, pp. 245–269). London: Penguin (original work published 1917).

Freud, S. (1985). Creative writers and day-dreaming. In J. Strachey (ed. and trans.) and A. Dickson (ed.), *Penguin Freud library* (Vol. 14, pp. 129–143). London: Penguin (original work published 1908).

Freud, S. (2001). Two case histories. In J. Strachey (ed. and trans.), *The standard edition of the complete psychological works of Sigmund Freud* (Vol. 10, pp. 3–149). London: Hogarth Press (original work published 1909).

Freud, S. and Breuer, J. (2004). *Studies in hysteria* (N. Luckhurst, trans.). London: Penguin (original work published 1895).

Frie, R. (1997). *Subjectivity and intersubjectivity in modern philosophy and psycho-analysis: A study of Sartre, Binswanger, Lacan, and Habermas*. Lanham, MD: Rowman & Littlefield.

Fullerton, P. (1996). Attachment and loss in the marital relationship. Unpublished manuscript.

Fullerton, P. (2001). Defensive marital choice: no difference, killing off the challenge. In *A world of difference: The dynamics of working psychoanalytically with couples* (pp. 4–12). Society for Psychoanalytic Marital Psychotherapy International Conference, Keble College, Oxford.

Gay, P. (1986). *The bourgeois experience: Victoria to Freud: Vol. 2: The tender passion.* New York: W.W. Norton.

Gilbert, M. (1989). *On social facts.* Princeton, NJ: Princeton University Press.

Gill, C. (1999). Introduction. In C. Gill (ed. and trans.), *Plato: The symposium* (pp. x–xlvi). London: Penguin.

Gordon, R. (1993). *Bridges: Metaphor for psychic processes.* London: Karnac.

Green, A. (1975). The analyst, symbolization, and absence in the analytic setting (On changes in analytic practice and analytic experience) – In memory of D.W. Winnicott. *International Journal of Psycho-Analysis 56*, 1–22.

Green, A. (2000). *The chains of Eros: the sexual in psychoanalysis* (L. Thurston, trans.). London: Rebus Press (original work published 1997).

Grotstein, J. (1985). *Splitting and projective identification.* Northvale, NJ: Jason Aronson.

Grotstein, J. (1994). Notes on Fairbairn's metapsychology. In J. Grotstein and D. Rinsley (eds), *Fairbairn and the origins of object relations* (pp. 112–151). London: Free Association Books.

Grotstein, J. (1997a). 'Internal objects' or 'chimerical monsters': the demonic 'third forms' of the internal world. *Journal of Analytical Psychology 42*(1), 47–81.

Grotstein, J. (1997b). Bion's 'transformation in O' and the concept of the 'transcendent position'. Retrieved February 2005 from http://www.sicap.it/~merciai/bion/papers/grots.htm

Grotstein, J. (2000). *Who is the dreamer who dreams the dream?: A study of psychic presences.* Hillsdale, NJ: Analytic Press.

Grotstein, J. and Rinsley, D. (eds) (1994). *Fairbairn and the origins of object relations.* London: Free Association Books.

Grotstein, J. (2005). Projective *trans*identification: An extension of the concept of projective identification. *International Journal of Psychoanalysis 86*, 1051–1069.

Guenther, H. (1976). *The tantric view of life.* Boston: Shambhala.

Hamilton, W. (1951). Introduction. *The symposium* (pp. 12–29). London: Penguin.

Hardy, T. (1986). *A pair of blue eyes.* London: Penguin (original work published 1878).

Hegel, G. (1977). *Phenomenology of spirit* (A. V. Miller, trans.). Oxford: Oxford University Press (original work published 1807).

Heidegger, M. (1962). *Being and time* (J. Macquarrie and E. Robinson, trans.). Oxford: Blackwell (original work published 1927).

Hillman, J. (1989). *A blue fire: The essential James Hillman* (T. Moore, ed.). London: Routledge.

Hirsch, E. (1999). *How to read a poem.* New York: Harvest.

Hobson, R. (1974). Loneliness. *Journal of Analytical Psychology 19*(1), 71–90.

Hobson, R. (1985). *Forms of feeling.* London: Tavistock.

Holmes, R. (1996). *Attachment, intimacy, autonomy.* Northvale, NJ: Jason Aronson.

Holmes, R. (1998). *Coleridge: Darker reflections.* London: HarperCollins.

Hopkins, G. M. (1985). *Poems and prose of Gerard Manley Hopkins.* London: Penguin.

Hughes, J. (1994). Fairbairn's revision of libido theory: the case of Harry Guntrip. In J. Grotstein and Rinsley D. (eds), *Fairbairn and the origins of object relations* (pp. 250–275). London: Free Association Books.

Huxley, A. (1965). *Point, counter point*. New York: Perennial (original work published 1928).

Impala, P. (2001). Poems. Unpublished.

Irigaray, L. (1985). *This sex which is not one* (C. Porter and C. Burke, trans.). New York: Cornell University Press (original work published 1977).

Irigaray, L. (1991). Questions to Emmanuel Levinas: on the divinity of love. In R. Bernasconi and S. Critchley (eds), *Re-reading Levinas* (pp. 109–119). Bloomington: Indiana University Press.

Irigaray, L. (2000). *To be two* (M. Rhodes and M. Cocito-Monoc, trans.). London: Athlone Press (original work published 1994).

James, W. (1981). *The principles of psychology*. Cambridge, MA: Harvard University Press (original work published 1890).

Jones, E. (1953–1957). *Life and work of Sigmund Freud* (Vols. 1–3). New York: Basic Books.

József, U. (n.d.). Sleeve notes for Béla Bartók's *Bluebeard's castle*. Qualiton, Hungary, LPX 1001.

Jung, C. G. (1966a). *Two essays on analytical psychology: The collected works of C. G. Jung* (Vol. 7, R. F. C. Hull, trans.). London: Routledge (original work published 1935).

Jung, C. G. (1966b). Psychology of the transference. In R. F. C. Hull (trans.), *The collected works of C. G. Jung* (Vol. 16, pp. 163–327). London: Routledge & Kegan Paul (original work published 1946).

Jung, C. G. (1966c). The therapeutic value of abreaction. In R. F. C. Hull (trans.), *The collected works of C. G. Jung* (Vol. 16, pp. 163–327). London: Routledge & Kegan Paul (original work published 1928).

Jung, C. G. (1967). *Memories, dreams and reflections*. London: Fontana.

Jung, C. G. (1969). The structure and dynamics of the psyche. In R. F. C. Hull (trans.), *The collected works of C. G. Jung* (Vol. 8). London: Routledge & Kegan Paul (original work published 1954).

Jung, C. G. (1977). Mysterium coniunctionis: an inquiry into the separation and synthesis of psychic opposites in alchemy. In R. F. C. Hull (trans), *The collected works of C. G. Jung* (Vol. 14). London: Routledge & Kegan Paul (original work published 1955).

Jung, C. G. (1988). *Nietzsche's 'Zarathustra'* (Vols 1–2, J. Jarrett, ed.). Princeton, NJ: Princeton University Press.

Jung, C. G. (1991). Marriage as a psychological relationship. In R. F. C. Hull (trans.), *The collected works of C. G. Jung* (Vol. 17, pp. 187–205). London: Routledge (original work published 1931).

Jung, E. (1957). *Animus and anima*. Dallas, TX: Spring Publications.

Kalsched, D. (1996). *Inner world of trauma*. London: Routledge.

Kaufmann, W. (ed. and trans.) (1966). *The portable Nietzsche*. London: Chatto & Windus.

Kaufmann, W. (1992). *Discovering the mind: Vol 2. Nietzsche, Heidegger and Buber*. New Brunswick, Canada: Transaction.

Keats, J. (1952). *Letters* (M. Forman, ed.). London: Oxford University Press.

Kern, S. (1992). *The culture of love: Victorians to Moderns*. Cambridge, MA: Harvard University Press.

Kernberg, O. (1975). *Borderline conditions and pathological narcissism*. New York: Jason Aronson.

Kernberg, O. (1995). *Love relations*. New Haven, CT: Yale Haven Press.

Kiberd, D. (2003). At full speed: inside the mind of W. B. Yeats – and outside. *Times Literary Supplement*, September 26, pp. 3–5.

Klein, M. (1935). A contribution to the psychogenesis of manic-depressive states. *International Journal of Psycho-Analysis 16*, 145–174.

Klein, M. (1955). On identification. In M. Klein, P. Heimann, S. Isaacs and J. Riviere (eds), *New directions in psycho-analysis: The significance of infant conflict in the pattern of adult behaviour* (pp. 309–345). London: Hogarth Press.

Klein, M. (1988). Love, guilt and reparation. In M. Klein and J. Riviere, *Love, guilt and reparation and other works* (pp. 57–119). London: Norton (original work published 1937).

Klein, M. (1992a). Notes on some schizoid mechanisms. In M. Klein, *Envy and gratitude and other works (1946–1963)* (pp. 1–24). London: Karnac (original work published 1946).

Klein, M. (1992b). The origins of transference. In M. Klein, *Envy and gratitude and other works (1946–1963)* (pp. 48–56). London: Karnac (original work published 1952).

Knox, J. (2003). Trauma and defences: their roots in relationship. An overview. *Journal of Analytical Psychology 48*(2), 201–207.

Kohut, H. (1984). *How does analysis cure?* Chicago: University of Chicago Press.

Kristeva, J. (1982). *Powers of horror: An essay on abjection* (L. Roudiez, trans.). New York: Columbia University Press (original work published 1980).

Kristeva, J. (1987). *Tales of love* (L. Roudiez, trans.). New York: Columbia University Press (original work published 1983).

Kristeva, J. (1991). *Strangers to ourselves* (L. Roudiez, trans.). New York: Harvester (original work published 1988).

Lacan, J. (1977). *Écrits* (A. Sheridan, trans.). New York: Norton (original work published 1966).

Laplanche, J. (1999). *Essays on otherness*. London: Routledge.

Lawrence, D. H. (1994). *Complete poems* (D. Herbert Lawrence, ed.). Hertfordshire: Wordsworth Editions.

Ledermann, R. (1986). Pathological sexuality and paucity of symbolisation in narcissistic disorder. *Journal of Analytical Psychology 31*(1), 23–45.

Lessing, D. (1995). *Under my skin*. London: Flamingo.

Lessing, D. (1996). *Love, again*. London: Flamingo.

Levinas, E. (1969). *Totality and infinity* (A. Lingis, trans.). Pittsburgh, PA: Duquesne University Press (original work published 1961).

Levinas, E. (1985). *Ethics and infinity* (R. Cohen, trans.). Pittsburgh, PA: Duquesne University Press (original work published 1982).

Levinas, E. (1990). *Nine Talmudic readings* (A. Aronowicz, trans.). Bloomington: Indiana University Press (original work published 1968).

Levinas, E. (1996a). Is ontology fundamental? In A. Peperzak, S. Critchley and R. Bernasconi (eds), *Basic philosophical writings* (pp. 1–11). Bloomington: Indiana University Press (original work published 1951).

Levinas, E. (1996b). Meaning and sense. In A. Peperzak, S. Critchley and R.

Bernasconi (eds), *Basic philosophical writings* (pp. 33–65). Bloomington: Indiana University Press (original work published 1964).

Levinas, E. and Kearney, R. (1986). Dialogue with Emmanuel Levinas. In R. Cohen (ed.), *Face to face with Emmanuel Levinas*. Albany, NY: State University of New York Press.

Lewis, C. S. (1955). *Surprised by joy*. London: Harvest.

Lewis, C. S. (1960). *The four loves*. London: Fontana.

Lewis, C. S. (1961). *A grief observed*. London: Faber and Faber.

Lewis, W. Hamilton (1982). *Brothers and friends: The diaries of Major Warren Hamilton Lewis* (C. Kilby and M. Lamp Mead, eds). San Francisco: Harper & Row.

Lingis, A. (1981). Translator's introduction. In E. Levinas, *Otherwise than being* (pp. xvii–xlvii). Pittsburgh, PA: Duquesne University Press.

Lloyd, G. (1994). *Part of nature*. Ithaca, NY: Cornell University Press.

Lloyd, G. (1996). *Spinoza and the Ethics*. London: Routledge.

Lucretius (1982). *De rerum natura* (W. H. D. Rouse, trans.). Cambridge, MA: Harvard University Press (original work written 60 BC).

Lyons, A. (1993). Husbands and wives: the mysterious choice. In S. Ruszczynski (ed.), *Psychotherapy with couples* (pp. 44–55). London: Karnac.

Lyons, A. and Mattinson, J. (1993). Individuation in marriage. In S. Ruszczynski (ed.), *Psychotherapy with couples* (pp. 104–126). London: Karnac.

Mahler, M. (1971). A study of the separation-individuation process – and its possible application to borderline phenomena in the psychoanalytic situation. *Psychoanalytic Study of the Child 26*, 403–424.

Mahler, M., Pine, F. and Bergmann, A. (1975). *The psychological birth of the human infant*. New York: Basic Books.

Main, M. and Solomon, J. (1986). Discovery of a new, insecure-disorganized/disoriented attachment pattern. In T. B. Brazelton and M. Yogman (eds), *Affective development in infancy* (pp. 95–124). Norwood, NJ: Albex.

Mann, T. (1928). *The magic mountain* (H. Lowe-Porter, trans.). London: Secker & Warburg (original work published 1924).

Mason, A. (1994). A psychoanalyst looks at a hypnotist: a study of *folie à deux*. *Psychoanalytic Quarterly 63*, 641–679.

Mattinson, J. and Sinclair, I. (1979). *Mate and stalemate*. Oxford: Blackwell.

Meares, R. (2000). *Intimacy and alienation*. London: Routledge.

Meares, R. (2005a). *The metaphor of play* (2nd edn). London: Routledge.

Meares, R. (2005b). Analogical structure of the narrative of self. In R. Meares and P. Nolan (eds), *The self in conversation IV* (pp. 124–138). Sydney: ANZAP.

Mellers, W. (1987). *The masks of Orpheus*. Manchester: Manchester University Press.

Meltzer, D. (1967). *The psychoanalytic process*. London: Clunie Press.

Meltzer, D. (1975). Adhesive identification. *Contemporary Psychoanalysis 11*, 289–310.

Meltzer, D. (1992). *The claustrum*. London: Clunie Press.

Meltzer, D. (1994). A contribution to the metapsychology of cyclothymic states. In A. Hahn (ed.), *Sincerity and other works: Collected papers of Donald Meltzer* (pp. 90–122). London: Karnac (original work published 1963).

Michaels, A. (1996). *Fugitive pieces*. London: Bloomsbury.

Mighall, R. (2000). Introduction. *The picture of Dorian Gray* (pp. ix–xxxv). London: Penguin.

Miller, M. (1951). Nature in the Faerie Queen, *English Literary History 18*, 191–200.

Milner, M. (1934). *A life of one's own.* London: Virago.

Milner, M. (1987). *The suppressed madness of sane men.* London: Routledge.

Mitchell, S. (2002). *Can love last: The fate of romance over time.* New York: Norton.

Moreux, S. (1953). *Béla Bartók.* London: Harvill Press.

Moyn, S. (2005). *Origins of the other: Emmanuel Levinas between revelation and ethics.* Ithaca, NY: Cornell University Press.

Nietzsche, F. (1966). *The portable Nietzsche* (W. Kaufmann, ed. and trans.). New York: Viking Press.

Norbu, N. (1986). *The crystal and the way of light* (J. Shane, ed.). London: Penguin.

Nozick, R. (1989). *The examined life: Philosophical meditations.* New York: Simon & Schuster.

Nussbaum, M. (1986). *The fragility of goodness.* Cambridge: Cambridge University Press.

Nussbaum, M. (1994). *Therapy of desire.* Princeton, NJ: Princeton University Press.

Nussbaum, M. (2001a). *The fragility of goodness.* Cambridge: Cambridge University Press.

Nussbaum, M. (2001b). *Upheavals of thought: The intelligence of emotions.* Cambridge: Cambridge University Press.

Ogden, T. (1989). *The primitive edge of experience.* London: Karnac.

Ogden, T. (1992). *Projective identification and psychotherapeutic technique.* London: Karnac.

Ogden, T. (1994). *Subjects of analysis.* Northvale, NJ: Jason Aronson.

Ogden, T. (1997). *Reverie and interpretation: Sensing something human.* Northvale, NJ: Jason Aronson.

Ovid (1955). *The metamorphoses. Book III* (M. Innes, trans.). Harmondsworth: Penguin.

Peperzak, A. (1996). Preface. In A. Peperzac (ed. and trans.), *Emmanuel Levinas: Basic philosophical writings* (pp. vii–xvii). Bloomington: Indiana University Press.

Perrault, C. (1989). *Cinderella and other tales from Perrault.* London: Methuen Children's Books.

Perry, W. (ed.) (1971). *A treasury of traditional wisdom.* Bedford: Perennial Books.

Phillips, A. (1988). *Winnicott.* London: Fontana.

Phillips, A. (2000). *Promises, promises: Essays on literature and psychoanalysis.* London: Faber and Faber.

Pickering, J. (1996). Béla Bartók and the quest for the beloved: a study of Bluebeard's Castle. *Temenos: Australian Jungian and Cultural Review 3*, 20–29.

Pickering, J. (2001). Exogamy: the relational self. *Australasian Journal of Psychotherapy 20*, 117–141.

Pickering, J. C. (2002). Moving metaphors of self. In R. Meares (ed.), *The self in conversation* (pp. 123–143). Sydney: ANZAP.

Pincus, L. (1962). *The marital relationship as a focus for casework.* London: Tavistock.

Plato (1951). *The symposium* (W. Hamilton, trans.). London: Penguin.

Plato (1989). *The symposium* (A. Nehamas and P. Woodruff, trans.). Indianapolis, IN: Hackett.

Plato (1999). *The symposium* (C. Gill, trans.). London: Penguin.

Poincaré, H. (1952). *Science and method*. New York: Dover.

Post, G., Underwood, L., Schloss, J. and Hurlbut, W. (2001). *Altruism and altruistic love*. New York: Oxford University Press.

Rhode, E. (1994). *Psychotic metaphysics*. London: Karnac.

Rickman, J. (ed.) (1957). *A general selection from the works of Sigmund Freud*. New York: Anchor.

Rilke, R. M. (1981). *An unofficial Rilke* (M. Hamburger, ed. and trans.). London: Anvil Poetry.

Rilke, R. M. (1992). *Duino elegies* (D. Oswald, trans.). Zurich: Daimon Verlag (original work published 1923).

Rose, G. (1997). *Love's work*. London: Vintage.

Rosenfeld, H. (1964). On the psychopathology of narcissism: a clinical approach. *International Journal of Psycho-Analysis 45*, 332–337.

Rosenfeld, H. A. (1987). *Impasse and interpretation*. London: Tavistock.

Rosenzweig, F. (1935). Epigraph: Bücher über Hegel. *Kleinere Schriften*. Berlin: Schocken.

Ruszczynski, S. (ed.) (1993). *Psychotherapy with couples*. London: Karnac.

Samuels, A. (1989). *The plural psyche*. London: Routledge.

Samuels, A. (1993). *The political psyche*. London: Routledge.

Samuels, A. (2001). *Politics on the couch*. London: Profile Books.

Sartre, J. P. (1958). *Being and nothingness* (H. Barnes, trans.). London: Methuen (original work published 1943).

Sartre, J. P. (1967). *No exit: Four contemporary French plays* (S. Gilbert, trans.). New York: Random House (original work written 1944).

Schacter, D. (1996). *Searching for memory: The brain, the mind and the past*. New York: Basic Books.

Scheler, M. (1954). *The nature of sympathy*. London: Routledge & Kegan Paul.

Schwartz, J. (1999). *Cassandra's daughter*. London: Penguin.

Schwartz-Salant, N. (1982). *Narcissism and character transformation*. Toronto: Inner City Books.

Scruton, R. (1986). *Sexual desire: A moral philosophy of the erotic*. New York: Free Press.

Scurr, R. (2002). Review of Anita Brookner's 'The next big thing'. *The Times Literary Supplement*, June 21, p. 24.

Searle, J. R. (1990). Collective intentions and actions. In P. R. Cohen, M. E. Pollack and J. L. Morgan (eds), *Intentions in communication* (pp. 401–415). Cambridge, MA: MIT Press.

Seligman, E. (1982). The half-alive ones. *Journal of Analytical Psychology 27*(1), 1–20.

Sibley, B. (1985). *Shadowlands*. London: Hodder & Stoughton.

Singer, I. (1966). *The nature of love: Plato to Luther*. New York: Random.

Smith, S. (2003). *Spinoza's book of life: Freedom and redemption in the Ethics*. New Haven, CT: Yale University Press.

Spielrein, S. (1994). Destruction as a cause of coming into being. *Journal of Analytical Psychology 39*(2), 155–187.

Spinoza, B. (1994). *A Spinoza reader: The Ethics and other works* (E. Curley, ed. and trans.). Cambridge: Cambridge University Press (original publication 1677).

Steiner, G. (1978). *Heidegger*. London: Fontana.

Stendhal (Marie Henri Beyle) (1957). *Love* (G. and S. Sale, trans.). London: Penguin (original work published 1822).

Stern, D. (1985). *The interpersonal world of the infant*. New York: Basic Books.

Stewart, M. (2006). *The courtier and the heretic: Leibniz, Spinoza, and the fate of God*. New York: W. W. Norton & Company.

Symington, N. (1983). The analyst's act of freedom as agent of therapeutic change. *International Review of Psycho-Analysis 7*, 27–40.

Symington, N. (1985). Phantasy effects that which it represents. *International Journal of Psycho-Analysis 66*, 43–47.

Symington, N. (1986). *The analytic experience*. London: Free Association Books.

Symington, N. (1993). *Narcissism: A new theory*. London: Karnac.

Symington, N. and Symington, J. (1996). *The clinical thinking of Wilfred Bion*. London: Routledge.

Taylor, C. (1989). *Sources of the self*. Cambridge: Cambridge University Press.

Tuomela, R. (1995). *The importance of us: A philosophical study of basic social notions*. Stanford, CA: Stanford University Press.

Tustin, F. (1972). *Autism and childhood psychosis*. London: Hogarth.

Veress, S. (1949). Bluebeard's castle. *Tempo 13*, 32–36.

Virgil (1964). *The eclogues and georgics of Virgil* (C. Day Lewis, trans.). New York: Anchor Books.

Wajnryb, R. (2001). *The silence: How tragedy shapes talk*. Sydney: Allen & Unwin.

Weininger, O. (1996). *Being and not being*. London: Karnac.

Wild, J. (1969). Introduction. In E. Levinas, *Totality and infinity* (pp. 11–21). Pittsburgh, PA: Duquesne University Press.

Wilde, O. (2000). *The picture of Dorian Gray* (R. Mighall, ed.). London: Penguin (original work published 1891).

Wilson, A. N. (1990). *C. S. Lewis: A biography*. London: Flamingo.

Winnicott, C. (1989). D.W.W.: a reflection. In D. Winnicott, *Psychoanalytic explorations* (pp. 1–21). London: Karnac.

Winnicott, D. (1944). *Getting to know your baby*. London: Heinemann.

Winnicott, D. (1971). *Playing and reality*. London: Penguin.

Winnicott, D. (1984a). Communicating and not communicating leading to a study of certain opposites. In D. Winnicott, *The maturational processes and the facilitating environment* (pp. 37–55). London: Karnac (original work published 1963).

Winnicott, D. (1984b). The development of the capacity for concern. In D. Winnicott, *The maturational processes and the facilitating environment* (pp. 73–82). London: Karnac (original work published 1963).

Winnicott, D. (1988). *Human nature*. London: Free Associaton Books.

Winnicott, D. (1992a) The manic defence. In D. Winnicott, *Through paediatrics to psycho-analysis* (pp. 129–145). New York: Brunner/Mazel (original paper published 1935).

Winnicott, D. (1992b). Mind and its relations to the psyche-soma. In *Through paediatrics to psycho-analysis* (pp. 243–245). London: Tavistock (original work published 1949).

Wispé, L. (1987). History of the concept of empathy. In N. Eisenberg and J. Strayer (eds), *Empathy and its development* (pp. 17–37). Cambridge: Cambridge University Press.

Wordsworth, W. (1961). Recollections of early childhood. In A. Quiller-Crouch (ed.), *Oxford book of English verse: 1250–1918*. Oxford: Oxford University Press.

Wyschogrod, E. (2000). *Emmanuel Levinas: The problem of ethical metaphysics*. New York: Fordham University Press.

Wyschogrod, E. (2003). Autochthony and welcome: discourses of exile in Levinas and Derrida. *Journal of Philosophy and Scripture 1*(1), 36–42.

Yovel, Y. (ed.) (1999). *Desire and affect: Spinoza as psychologist*. New York: Little Room Press.

Index

Abraham x
Absolute Idealists 42, 56
adhesive identification 23, 106, 224
agapē 18, 25–6, 211, 236; *see also caritas*
aggression 31, 48, 88, 115, 123, 156, 157, 241
albatross 3, 4, 10, 15
Alcibiades 101, 217–18
Alétheia (unconcealment: Greek metaphor for truth) xii, 6, 12, 93, 94, 104, 147, 208, 226, 243, 247, 249; exogamy 66; negative capability 44; revelation of reality 226; selected facts 98; *see also* truth
aliveness 9, 28, 239, 240
Allen, Woody 112
alpha function 87, 92–3, 180
alterity 6, 8n6, 12, 13, 27, 40–52, 61, 63, 117, 135, 154, 248; altruistic love 27; appreciation of 12, 115, 227, 247, 249; cultural difference 72; defences against 100, 107, 151-2, 206; depressive position 114; developmental capacity for 47–9, 71, 78, 223; exogamous love 66, 151, 211; historical contributions 42–4; I-Thou dialogue 242; intolerance of 73, 151–2, 153; mother's personhood 71; negative capability 44; opacity 44–5, 58; paradox of 12, 13; *xenia* 29; *see also* Other
altruism 6, 26, 27, 97; altruistic love 5n1, 19, 25, 30, 41, 56, 97, 211; depressive position 114; exogamous love 211
ambivalence 19, 36, 49, 109, 115, 116, 214, 222n4; defences against 222n4; depressive position 114, 115; exogamous love 211, 215; melancholia 154–5
analytic object 90n4
analytic relationship 63–4, 192
analytic third 90, 91, 180
anātman 13, 205; *see also* non-self
ancestry 234–6; *see also* intergenerational matters
Andreas-Salomé, Lou 128–30, 195–6
anger 105n1, 109, 155

anima xi, 31, 71, 103
anxiety 87, 88, 101, 105n1, 112, 143, 150, 155, 179, 221, 240
archetype x, 71
Arendt, Hannah 26
Aristophanes 20, 21, 34, 125
Aristotle 25, 117, 241
Armiger, Martin 238–9
Armstrong, John 220
arrow metaphor for truth 6; *see also* truth
attachment ix, 23, 84, 120–2, 128; conflicts between attachment styles 122, 126, 127; 'secure base' 85–6, 120, 128; separation trauma 134n3
attachment styles 85, 121, 122, 126, 127, 128; dismissing/avoidant 121; insecure-ambivalent 121, 122, 123, 126; insecure-avoidant 121, 122, 123, 126; preoccupied/ambivalent 121n1; secure 121; unresolved/disorganized 121n1
Augustine 10, 26, 48

Balint, Michael 51, 124, 127, 156, 192
Barnes, J. 152
Bartók, Bela 16, 183–90
Bayley, John 212–13
beauty 161, 162, 179, 185, 186, 189, 214, 244; platonic 32, 33, 217
Being (Being in love) 5, 8, 11, 12, 13, 17, 22, 23, 27, 41, 42, 44, 46, 47, 54, 56, 57, 66, 67, 72, 74, 124, 154, 179, 181, 188, 208, 218, 219, 220, 243, 246, 247, 248, 250; *see also* becoming
becoming, 21, 55, 56, 191, 208, 238, 245; becoming in love, (becoming in O) 7, 8, 12, 13, 14, 15, 16, 30, 62, 65, 66, 67, 83, 183, 211, 225, 227, 229, 247, 248, 249, 250
Benjamin, J. 49, 50, 62, 77, 221
Berkeley, George 8, 219, 221
beta elements 59, 86, 87–8, 92, 147
Bick, Esther 86, 106

Bion, Wilfred ix, 92–4, 104, 243; beta elements 59, 86, 87–8, 92, 147; catastrophic change 182, 195, 227, 229, 242; container-contained 87, 89, 183; 'K' 16, 215, 222; 'minus K' 222–3; 'minus love' 31; myth 14n14, 93; nameless dread 240; narcissism 153; no-thing 13; 'O' ix, 6–7, 11, 12, 13, 30, 32, 44, 64, 66, 67, 181, 221–2, 225, 227, 228, 241, 242, 243, 248; paranoid-schizoid/depressive positions 115; projections 117; projective identification 87, 105, 109, 123; relational view of self 53; reverie 87, 88; 'selected fact' 93n14, 94, 98, 100n3, 147, 149, 175; transformations 7, 88, 222, 227, 228, 242, 243; unknowable nature of ultimate truth 44, 181, 221, 222, 241, 242, 243; without memory, desire or understanding 44–5, 58, 114, 222, 224, 225, 226, 234n4, 242
Blake, William 31
Blanchot, M. 52
Blue Murder 197, 199
Bluebeard's Castle (Bartók) 16, 183–90, 192–3, 197–8
body 58–60, 230; *see also* embodiment and mind–body relations
Bollas, Christopher 105–6, 170
Borges, J. 54
Bowlby, John ix, 85–6, 120–1, 156
Bräten, Stein ix
breast 48; part-object relating 111
Breton, André 180
Breuer, Joseph 140
Britton, R. 74, 78, 89, 114, 157, 159; triangular space 74, 89
Brookner, Anita 165, 167–75
Buber, Martin 19, 56, 57
Buddha 84
Buddhism 5, 9, 13, 19, 27, 45, 206, 214; David/Sibylla story 201, 205; egocentrism 27; enlightenment 214, 248; Four Immeasurables 19; Four Noble Truths 34, 248; joy 9n9; mirror metaphor 160, 180-1; non-attachment 45–6; non-self (anātman) 13, 55, 181; primordial nature 181; stream metaphor 55; Vajrayāna 244, 245
Butler, Judith 61

care 6, 9, 19, 44, 48, 56, 84, 154, 202, 211
caritas 26; *see also agapē*
Carson, A. 22
Cartesian dualism 55, 56
cast as Other 26n6, 72
change 8, 32, 41, 62, 93, 100, 129, 144, 145, 148, 150, 175, 183, 195, 202, 206
Christianity 26, 58, 62, 214
Clark, G. 60n7, 71, 244

clinging 121, 122–3, 125, 126, 127, 130
closeness 48, 109, 117, 121, 122, 123, 124, 125, 127–8, 157, 212, 223, 224
closeness-distance 30, 40, 122, 123, 126-8, 187, 212n1
Cocteau, Jean 196
Coleridge, Samuel Taylor 4, 10n12, 15, 43
Colman, Warren 71n4, 86, 88
compassion 5, 6, 18n2, 19, 42, 211, 214, 236, 248, 249
Compte-Sponville, A. 34, 212
conatus 66, 67, 78, 85, 220, 227, 229, 243, 249
conjoint selected fact 94, 147, 149, 178, 180
consciousness 42, 55, 74, 133, 135, 144, 187; *see also* stream of consciousness; self-consciousness
containment 15, 85–90, 93, 95, 114, 120, 127, 129, 135, 143, 226; 'borrowed' 87, 92, 145, 150; narcissistic patients 180; therapeutic space 143; *see also* self-containment
conversational model 56n5; *see also* Hobson and Meares
countertransference x, 15, 85, 91, 144, 205
couple relationships 84–5, 86, 90, 223–4
couple therapy 11, 84–5, 88, 143, 238, 249; *alétheia* 104; Bion's grid 92–4; conjoint selected fact 94, 147; developmental and defensive object-choices 98–102; incremental change 150; interlocking traumatic scene 149–50; intersubjective third 90, 91; narcissism 167, 175–8, 180; splitting and projection 109–11; thin-skinned patients 158–9
'covenant' concept 97
cross-cultural marriage 72
cross-dressing 175–8
cupidity 26

Dante Alighieri 33, 96
Darwin x
Davidman, Joy 16, 227–33
de Rougemont, D. 72
death 35–6, 37, 154, 194, 219, 236, 238; Davidman/Lewis relationship 231–2; of (false) self 21, 35, 62, 66, 194, 236; fear of, 87, 88, 95, 238
death instinct 31n8; *see also thanatos*
defences 12, 31, 98, 116, 240; ambiguity 222n4; avoidance 16, 21n3, 30, 33, 36, 40, 128, 153, 155, 166, 179, 195, 203, 212, 218, 229, 242; David/Sibylla story 203, 205; depression as defence against joy 239–40; fantasies as 141, 150; idealization 214; impediments to intimacy 208; narcissistic 174, 175, 179; paranoid-schizoid position 112; predictions 225; shared 100–1
depression 175, 239–40

depressive position 66–7, 72, 78, 113–15; exogamy 215; failure of transition 195; narcissism 153, 179, 180
Derrida, Jacques 40
desire 5, 18, 19, 20, 22, 34, 35, 52, 64, 84, 98, 109, 113, 115, 141, 162, 166, 172, 173, 218, 226, 230, 239, 241, 244, 245, 247, 248, 249, 250; acquisitive 34, 57; being without 45–6; egocentrism 27; Irigaray 26n6; Lacan 35, 244; oedipal 69; possessive 245; sexual 33, 111; see also eros
destruction/destructiveness 31, 48, 84, 195; Spielrein's theory of destruction as a cause of coming into being 31
destructive patterns of relating 8, 10, 16, 66, 70, 78, 84, 88, 94, 114, 145, 149, 150, 157, 188, 195, 221, 223, 240
dialogue 30, 57, 60, 72, 73, 166, 208, 242
Dickinson, Emily 244–5
Diderot, Denis 244n3
difference 6, 20, 23, 27, 39, 41, 42, 44, 50, 61, 63, 72, 73, 78, 100, 109, 115, 121, 125, 160, 179; see also Otherness; alterity
Dionysus xii, 194, 218
disavowal 222n4
discovery 5, 36, 216–17; of each other beneath misconceptions 36, 63, 211, 223; of selected fact 94; see also alétheia, revelation
disillusionment 165, 166, 212, 215–16, 249
distance 123, 127–8; see also closeness-distance
domesticity and the erotic 28, 29, 69, 83, 113, 125, 231, 232
Donne, John 151
double-identity theory 60
dreams/dreaming ix, 93, 201
dualism 13, 41, 55, 56, 58, 195, 196, 206
Duke Bluebeard's Castle (Bartók) 16, 183–90, 192–3, 197–8

Echo see narcissus/narcissism
echolalia 163, 165, 173, 174
ecstasy 22, 63, 214, 245, 247
ego 13, 22, 23, 57, 77, 109, 123, 132, 152, 155, 214, 242, 243; body-ego 59; dissolution of 31, 34, 35; idealization 214; lost object 155; narcissism 152–3; repression 132n1; transcendence of 52, 247; see also self
ego ideal xi, 155
egocentricity 9, 20, 27, 52, 84, 114, 215, 228, 245, 247; see also self-centredness
Eigen, Michael 225, 240, 244, 245, 246
einfühlung 19, 42; see also empathy
Eliot, T. S. 12, 243
embodiment 58–60, 61, 192, 218, 249
emotions 19, 20, 31, 221; ambivalence 115–16; co-created emotional

environment 104, 111, 115; depressive position 114–15; detached from original context 133; joy mediated by 241; K 222; layering 116; negative capability 92; oscillations 109, 114, 154, 216; polarizing 128; psychosomatic cause and effect 59; shared unconscious emotional material 60; splitting 98, 109–11; transformation of emotional material 88; translocated (displaced) emotional material 100, 105, 109; trauma 144
empathy 6, 9, 18n2, 74; alterity 41–2; depressive position 114; heteropathic 42; idiopathic 43; mind-mindedness 86; mirroring 154, 179; narcissistic patients 180; projective identification 109; Romantics 42–3; secure relationships 86; vicarious introspection 109; see also einfühlung
emptiness 205; inner/psychological emptiness 56, 153, 154, 156, 169, 179, 239; see also śūnyatā
endogamy (psychological) 8, 10, 66, 67–8, 69, 70, 71, 84, 102, 130, 225, 248; endogamous transferences and projections 35, 66; endogamous partner choice 10, 15, 66; ideological and fear of difference 73; Oedipus as myth of 73; tensions between exogamy and 29, 66; see also exogamy
enlightenment 7, 8, 9n9, 35, 214, 245, 248
enmeshment 90, 121, 122, 125, 127, 182
envy x, 84; 'minus K' 222–3; narcissism 156, 157, 170, 171–2, 173; rejoicing as antidote to 244
Epicurus 14, 25, 32
epiphany and love 8, 41, 191, 243, 248
epistemology 56; and alterity 42
epistemophilic impulse 220–1, 222
equanimity 19, 124, 241
erastes 162
Erikson x
eromenos 162
Eros (god of love) 6, 18, 19, 22, 218
eros (love) x, 18, 22, 28, 164, 211, 229, 249; friendship 25; interpretations of 19; Levinas 23, 50; as relational force of connection 28, 34, 35; Socrates 34, 217–18; storge conflict with 29; see also love
erotic love 29, 32–3; see also love-making; sexual love
'erotics of the socks' 28, 231
eternity 31–2, 227, 242, 243, 246, 249, 250
eudaimonia 9, 247
Eurydice 155, 191, 193–6, 202, 203, 205, 207–8
exogamy 7–8, 13, 65–79, 211–26, 247, 249; anima 71; detachment from family 69–71;

dissolution of identity 31; Grotstein xi, xii; obstacles to 78; recognition of ancestry 234; thresholds of love 182
expectations 46–7, 182; as impediment to love 5, 11, 46-7, 117, 150, 208

face-to-face encounter 6, 12, 30, 50–1, 58, 153, 191, 236, 243; Levinas 50, 51, 58; narcissistic defence against 153
Fairbairn, W. R. D.: disappointment leading to intrapsychic orientation 133n3; idealization 213; internalization 49, 54; moral defence 213; relational view of self 53, 156; 'Siamese twinship' 125; splitting 123n2
fantasies 12, 192; as defences 141, 150; Freud 69; negative 46–7; shared unconscious 107, 134, 140; see also phantasies
Farrer, Austin 233
father 75–7, 78, 131–2, 142–3, 200
feminism 61
fetishism 111
Fisher, J. 89, 153, 179
folie à deux 106, 109
Fordham, Michael 70n3, 133n3, 156
forgiveness 211
Fraiberg, S. 144
Freud, Sigmund x, 13, 34, 196, 221; autoeroticism 97; detachment from family 65, 66; developmental trajectory of love 77; disavowal 222n4; domestic/erotic love dichotomy 29; ego 77; 'erotic revolution' xii; exogamous rites of passage 66, 77; fathers 77; gender 61; goal of psychoanalysis 13; homosexuality 160n2; idealization 213, 214; incorporation of the other 31; mourning and melancholia 36, 154-5; narcissism 154; oedipal defeat as gift of liberation 65; Oedipus complex 73; parents 70n3; regressive (endogamous) motivations for love 34, 96; repression 132n1; second sight 96; sexual curiosity 220; trauma 140; two currents of love 69
A friend from England (Brookner) 165
friendship 18, 24–5, 29, 30, 40, 74, 78, 172, 189, 229, 232; see also philia
Fugitive pieces (Michaels) 149, 221, 234–7

Gay, P. 67
gaze 51, 152; annihilatory 129, 187, 188
gender 61, 75, 117, 188
Gilbert, M. 64n8
God 5, 228, 241, 242; agapē 26; Godhead and O 225; hospitality 30; ladders of love 33
Goethe, Johann Wolfgang von 43
grandiosity 152, 153, 156, 163, 174, 175
gratitude 31, 32, 42, 116, 169, 211, 247
Greeks, Ancient 18–19, 162

Green, A. 78, 90n4
Gresham, Joy see Davidman, Joy
grief 37, 179; related to narcissism, melancholia 154, 179
Grotstein, James S. ix–xii, 12n13, 62, 123, 140, 141n10; 'background presence' 70n3; chimerical monsters 140; 'covenant' concept 97; 'O' 241, 242, 243; pathological relationships 123n2; projective identification 105n1, 109; projective transidentification 107, 144n11; the Real 241; subjectivity 7, 62, 64n8; 'subjugating third' 144n11
Guenther, H. 27, 245
Guntrip, Harry 69–70

Hardy, Thomas 111–12
hate 27, 31, 77, 98, 114, 115–16, 155, 221, 246; ambivalence 109, 111, 114
Hegel, Georg Wilhelm Friedrich 163, 169
Heidegger, Martin xii, 56, 57
Heraclitus 98
Herder, Johann Gottfried von 42
heteropathic identification 106
Hinduism 19
Hirsch, E. 237
Hobson, Robert 49, 56
Holderlin, Hans 43
holding the relationship in mind 48, 219–20
Holmes, R. 10n12, 121
homosexuality 160n2, 162, 194
Hopkins, Gerald Manley 55
hospitality 10n12, 29–30
hostility 84, 98, 124
Huxley, A. 51

I-Thou relations 19, 57, 72–3, 208, 211, 242–3
iconoclasm of love 11, 233
Idealists 42, 48, 49, 56, 58, 221
idealization x, 112, 208, 213–15, 216; Davidman/Lewis relationship 227, 228, 233; selfobject needs 156
identification 106, 117; idiopathic versus heteropathic 106; maternal 113, 139, 160n2; narcissism 153, 155; see also projective identification
identity 31, 43, 55, 59; dissolution of 31, 61–2; double-identity theory 60; gender 61
idiopathic identification 106
illusion 226
images (as obscuring reality of other, false, distorted) 11, 12, 71, 90, 100, 103, 104, 109, 112, 119, 214-5, 233; see also mirror image; narcissism
imago 69, 75
improvisation 135, 150

incest 69
incompletion (sense of) 34–5
individuation 7, 13, 50, 77, 117, 206, 243;
    couple relationships 85, 102; Jung 54
infant development ix, x–xi; capacity for
    alterity 48; effects of separation trauma
    121-2, 134n3; Fairbairn 49, 123, 156;
    Fordham 133n3; Freud 77, 97; Klein
    67n1, 72, 98, 113, 114, 156; need for
    merger 125; object relations 123n2;
    oceanic bliss idea 34; pre-verbal memory
    systems 140-1, 153; Winnicott 48, 76, 115,
    140, 153, 156, 192, 212, 219
infant research 53–4, 141n10
insecure-avoidant attachment style see
    attachment
intergenerational matters 70, 100, 140
intergenerational trauma 100, 140, 141,
    142–3, 145–7, 148, 150
interlocking scenes 11, 16, 131-50, 160, 162,
    176, 180, 248
internal working models 121, 128
internalization 49, 54, 139–40
interpretation 59, 88, 93, 147, 158–9, 180
intersubjective instinct ix
intersubjective/analytic third 90–2, 143, 147,
    149; see also Ogden, Thomas
intersubjectivity 9–10, 13, 52, 62–3, 192, 247;
    Bluebeard's Castle 189; David/Sibylla
    story 204–5, 207; Idealism/Romanticism
    42; mother-infant relationship 49–50;
    narcissistic denial of 153; oedipal situation
    73, 74; projections 104; uterine life 154
intersubjective/relational space 10, 15, 23, 63,
    74, 116, 138, 182, 188, 192; relation to
    therapeutic space 84, 85, 86, 87, 90, 92,
    143, 144, 180, 192; see also marital space;
    transitional space; therapeutic space;
    triangular space
intimacy 12, 52, 117, 127–8, 233–4, 238;
    discovery 216; enmeshed-avoidant
    attachment 122; exogamous love 211; fear
    of 46, 238; impediments to 11, 67, 83, 208;
    improvisation 135, 150; remembrance 45;
    sexual 132; solitude 122, 127, 128, 211,
    212–13; thresholds of 45, 66, 182, 192,
    208, 227
introjection x, 49, 98, 139, 233; David/Sibylla
    story 205; extractive 105–6, 170; maternal
    object 54
intuition 13, 242, 249
Irigaray, Luce 26n6, 33–4, 43, 60, 61, 62–3,
    221, 244

Jacques, Francis 72–3
James, William 10, 55
joie de vivre 28, 88, 226, 239, 240–1
Jones, E. 96

jouissance 244, 245, 246
joy 9n9, 19, 63, 212, 239, 240–1, 246;
    enjoyment 27, 211, 239, 241, 244, 245, 248
József, Ujfalussy 188
Judaism 6n4
Jung, C. G. 14, 21, 113, 196; analytic
    relationship 63–4; anima 71; container-
    contained 89; domestic/erotic love
    dichotomy 29; double-identity theory 60;
    psyche and matter 59; relational view of
    self 54; traumatic complex 145
Jung, Emma 113
Jungian analysis 13

'K' 16, 215, 222
kairos 11, 164
Kalsched, D. 205
Kant, Immanuel 55, 221–2
Keats, John 16, 44
Kernberg, Otto 23, 35, 52, 169, 170
Klein, Melanie 67, 72, 96–7, 221;
    ambivalence 116; depressive position
    113–14, 195; narcissism 155–6; paranoid-
    schizoid position 111; projective
    identification 105; unconscious phantasy
    98, 134n6
knowledge 33, 56, 218–19, 220–1, 222–3;
    false/stale 226; see also epistemology;
    epistemophilic instinct; K; negative
    capability
Knox, J. 134n3, 141n10
Kohut, Heinz 56n5, 156, 227
Kristeva, Julia 18, 43, 61, 72, 152

Lacan, Jacques 35, 241, 244n3
ladders of love 33, 77, 102
laetitia 227, 241, 243–6
language 6n5, 13, 60–1, 242; and
    autobiographical memory 135; embodied,
    60-1; inadequacies of 13, 18; gender 61;
    and trauma 135; and true dialogue 30; of
    uncertainty 94
Laplanche, J. 43, 140, 141
Lawrence, D. H. 28–9
Ledermann, R. 156
Lessing, Doris 223
Levinas, Emmanuel 20, 21–2, 28, 46, 56, 243;
    alterity 6n3, 44, 50; altruism 26; beyond
    ontology 44; eros 23, 50; face-to-face
    encounter 50–1; hospitality 30; the Infinite 242; other
    beyond comprehension 218–19; relational
    third 64; subjectivity 41; substitution 26
Lewis, C. S. 11, 16, 36, 58, 158, 227–33
liberation (from stuck psychic states) 63, 65,
    76
libido 27, 77, 111, 214
Lingis, A. 26

Lloyd, Genevieve 61
loneliness 23, 153, 186, 190, 223; David/
    Sibylla story 203, 205, 206; existential 55,
    56
Look at me (Brookner) 167–75
loss xi, 32, 36, 124; anxiety about 125; coming
    to terms with 211; melancholia 154–5;
    narcissism 154
love 5–9, 18–37, 247–50; alterity 6, 40, 42,
    50; ambivalence 115–16; *Bluebeard's
    Castle* 186, 187, 188; cupidity 26, 241;
    Davidman/Lewis relationship 227–33;
    dissolution of identity 61–2; domestic/
    erotic dichotomy 28–9; erotic 29, 32–3;
    existential alienation 56; exogamous
    65–79, 211–26, 247, 249; face-to-face
    encounter 50–1; at first sight 96; Freud
    77, 97; *Fugitive pieces* 234–7; Grotstein
    ix–xii; I-Thou dialogue 57, 242–3;
    iconoclasm of 11–12; increase in 212;
    interdependence with alterity, exogamy,
    intersubjectivity 13, 15; intersubjectivity
    9–10; Irigaray 43; liebstod (love and
    death) 35–6; Merleau-Ponty 56–7;
    mother-infant relationship 114; narcissism
    152, 166; negative capability 44;
    paradoxes of 12–13; pathologies 83–4;
    primary 156; psychological impediments
    to 16, 66, 78, 83, 84, 124, 154, 213;
    psycho-somatic interpenetration 60; quest
    for 65, 250; revelation of other person 52;
    romantics on 32, 43; therapy 13–14;
    thresholds of 182; transformations in
    241–3; and truth 5, 6, 11, 12, 14, 16;
    unconditional 19; *see also eros, agapē,
    philia, storge, xenia, nomos*
love-making 33–4; *see also* erotic love; sexual
    love

Mahler, Margaret 49–50, 76
malignant third 144, 145–6, 149, 150, 157,
    164, 180
manic-depression 225–6
Mann, Thomas 35
marital fit 97
marital/relational third *see* relational third;
    thirdness
marital/relational space 10, 97, 102, 134; *see
    also* intersubjective space
marriage 8, 85, 141–2, 200; containment 85,
    89; cross-cultural 72; Davidman/Lewis
    relationship 229–30; demands for
    proposal 137–8; exogamy 65–6;
    interlocking traumatic scene 140; solitude
    212; thresholds of love 182
masochism 24, 163, 165, 169, 174
master-slave metaphor (Hegel) 163–4, 169,
    173, 174

Meares, R. 55, 56n5, 132, 133, 135
melancholia 11, 36, 154–5, 191
Meltzer, D. 106, 223, 224
memory 149, 224–5, 226, 233–6;
    autobiographical 135; Bion 44–5, 222,
    224, 225, 226; relation to mourning and
    melancholia 155, 233; traumatic 132–3,
    135–6, 144, 145–6
merger 23, 50, 125; *see also* symbiosis
Merleau-Ponty, Maurice 56–7
Michaels, Anne 16, 149, 221, 234–7
Miller, Henry 196
Milner, Marion 181, 215
mind, theory of 42, 49, 74
mind-body relations 57, 58–60, 196, 230, 249
'minus K' 222–3
'minus L' (minus love) 31
mirroring 26, 48, 110, 153, 156, 158, 176, 177,
    207
mirror metaphor 160, 180-1
mirror: reflection motif in narcissism 151-81
misogyny 194, 203, 205
monadism (psychological) 21, 49–50, 55, 74,
    159, 180, 183, 186, 208
monologue (opposed to true dialogue) 57,
    152, 166, 208, 242
Moreux, Serge 188
Morgan, Christiana 195–6
mother 48, 49–50, 75; ability to see as person
    48, 70, 71, 114; baby's gaze at 51;
    container-contained 87; David/Sibylla
    story 206, 207; depressive position
    113–14; detachment from 69–70; fusion
    with 23, 71; 'good-enough' 69n2, 219;
    identification with 113, 139, 160n2;
    internalization of 139; introjection of
    maternal object 54; intrusive 124, 219,
    224; life-giving 155; nameless dread 240;
    non-verbal communication 153; oedipal
    desires 76; paranoid-schizoid position
    111; preoccupied 47, 240; projections 71;
    Rilke/Andreas-Salomé relationship 129,
    130; traumatic scenes 142
mourning 36, 124, 154-5, 175, 180, 232–3; *see
    also* Freud (mourning and melancholia)
Murdoch, Iris 212–13
Murray, Henry 196
myth 14–15, 16, 34, 93, 193–5; Bion on 14;
    Greek (Oedipus) 73-5; Orpheus and
    Eurydice 191-208; personal 14-15

Narcissus/narcissism 16, 151–64, 247; Balint
    156; Britton 159; and couple therapy 158-
    9, 167, 175-8, 180-1; of echo 151, 152,
    160-3, 165–81; endogamy 66; feminine
    128, 130; Fordham 156; Freud 154-5,
    160n2; homosexuality 160n2; idealization
    213; impediments to intimacy 208; infancy

77; Kleinian theories of 155-6; Lederman
156; myth of 152, 160, 164, 166, 172, 178;
narcissistic combinations 161-3;
narcissistic intralocking scene 157,
159–64, 165, 167, 171, 173; object-choice
97; *Picture of Dorian Gray* (Oscar Wilde)
164; Pausanius's version 178; role of Echo
165–81; sado-masochism 163–4;
Rosenfeld 157-8; schizoid personality 49;
selfobject 156–7; theories of original 154-
6; thick- and thin-skinned 157–8, 170
narratives of self 93n8, 135, 140, 234, 236
negative capability 16, 44, 92, 93n10, 94,
224–6; and discovery of conjoint selected
fact 180; exogamy 215; Keat's definition
of 16, 44; narcissistic patients 180
negative fantasy 46–7
Neisser, Karl 96
Nietzsche, Friedrich 53, 56, 128, 246
Nin, Anaïs 195–6
nomos 18
non-attachment 13, 45–6
non-duality 13, 23, 206, 211, 243, 244
non-self 13; *see also* anātman
Norbu, Chögyal Namkhai 248
Novalis 43
Nozick, R. 64n8
Nussbaum, Martha 14, 33, 162, 218

'O' 6–7, 11, 12, 19, 221–2, 225, 250;
emptiness 181; exogamy 65, 66; no-thing
13; numinous presence of 67;
transformations in 7, 8, 32, 227, 228,
241–3
object-choice/partner choice xi, 3, 10, 15, 66,
67–8, 69, 85, 96–7, 122, 129;
developmental and defensive 98–102,
108–9, 147, 152; endogamous 10, 67–8, 69;
exogamous 66, 97; homosexual 160n2;
narcissistic 153, 179
object relations 23, 84, 98, 104; anima/animus
71n4; awareness of 119; couple therapy
91, 98; endogamy 66; internalization 49,
139, 140; narcissistic 151, 154, 155–6, 157,
170, 179; part-object relating 111–12, 115;
relational view of self 53
ocnophile 127
oedipal desires 69, 76
oedipal issues in narcissism 77
oedipal situation 66, 71n4, 73–4, 77, 78–9;
and thirdness 77
Oedipus: complex resolution 78; fathers 75-7;
as myth of endogamy 73-5
Ogden, Thomas 9, 17, 43, 62, 90–1, 109,
144n11, 192, 195, 205, 246
omnipotence 49, 98, 153, 233
ontological relation: Levinas on 44
ontology 44

Orpheus 155, 187, 191, 192–6, 202, 203, 207
orphic complex 193, 205, 208
Other xi, 12, 20, 40; exogamy 7; face-to-face
encounter with the 50–1; idiopathic
identification 106; incorporation of the 31;
jouissance 244n3, 245, 246; knowledge of
the 218–19, 220–1; Levinas 22; narcissism
151–2; *see also* alterity; difference

pain 244n3; defences against 116, 159, 175,
215, 226, 230; loss, 33, 36, 154, 157, 230;
not knowing 222, 223; psychic 33, 37, 65,
69, 84, 88, 111, 154, 206, 212, 240; related
to pleasure principle and *jouissance*
244n3; *see also* rejection; suffering
paranoid-schizoid position 66–7, 72, 111–13,
114; failure of transition to depressive
position 195; narcissism 153, 179, 180;
oscillation between depressive position
and 115, 153
parents 75, 77–8; 'extra-verbal' messages 140;
influence on partner choice 67–8, 96–7,
102; oedipal situation 73–4, 78; *see also*
father; mother
part-object relating 111–12, 115
partner choice *see* object-choice
pathos 14, 16, 19n2, 50, 83-4
Peperzak, A. 41
personality traits 99, 117
phantasies: grandiose 152; incest 69; intrusive
223–4; memory systems 134n6; mother–
infant relationship 114; projective
identification 105n1; shared unconscious
97–8, 107, 134, 138, 140; *see also* fantasies
phantom presences 140, 144, 150
phenomenology 57
philia 18, 24, 25, 235; *see also* friendship
philobat 127
The Piano (film) 198, 206
Plato 18, 19, 20, 21, 32, 34, 58, 102, 160, 217,
221
pleasure principle 77, 239, 244n3
Poincaré, H. 94, 147
Post, G. 27
privacy 124, 188, 220, 223–4; *see also* space;
solitude
projection 71, 83, 90, 104, 112, 117–19; beta
elements 87; containment 88; David/
Sibylla story 205; destructiveness 84;
exaggerations 113; idealization 214;
imaginal realm 192; impediments to true
love 5, 11, 66, 83, 84, 90, 98, 208; intrusive
223; maternal 103; mutual 106–7; shared
unconscious phantasies 98
projective identification 104, 112, 123; beta
elements 86; Bion's reformulation 87, 185;
controversies concerning 185n1; Klein's
original formulation 105; mutual 92, 97,

104, 105, 106–7, 117, 138; narcissistic
    object relations 156; positive use of 109
psychoanalysis 13, 73; gender 61;
    intersubjectivity 62; mind-body dualism
    58; narcissism 154; relational view of self
    53–4; *see also* therapy
psychosis (abnegation of O) 243

quest concept 8

reality 6–7, 11–12, 192, 243; exogamous love
    211; foursquare 11, 42, 49, 71, 72, 111,
    114, 167, 211, 212, 214, 226; knowledge of
    221; of other 8, 11, 12, 13, 33, 40, 49, 52,
    58, 62, 151, 211, 242; psychic 117, 201,
    205, 206, 221, 222; revelation of 226;
    ultimate/absolute 5, 6-7, 11-12, 42, 67,
    181, 228, 241, 248; unknowable nature of
    40, 44, 62, 66, 181, 221, 222, 243, 246; *see
    also* 'O'
reciprocity 26, 27, 30, 223; reflective capacity
    87, 89–90, 92, 135, 135n8, 145, 149, 150
reflective consciousness 132, 133
rejection (fear of) 45, 102, 115, 116, 125, 137
rejoicing (as virtue) 19, 32, 215, 244
relational configurations 120–30, 191, 204
relational theory: relational school of
    psychoanalysis 7, 13, 53, 54, 56, 83, 84,
    90; *see also* self (relational view of)
relational third/marital third 23, 61, 63–4, 85,
    86, 89, 90-2, 127, 147, 159, 178, 211, 227,
    228; *see also* intersubjective third; marital
    third
relational view of self 13, 21, 53–4, 57–8, 84,
    102, 121, 141n10, 154, 156
reparation 48, 114, 116
repetition compulsion 98, 100, 147, 226, 234
repression 109, 132n1, 162, 163, 196, 239
Rilke, Rainer Maria 128–30, 182, 196, 212
rites of passage 21, 66
romantic stages 215–16
Romantics 34, 42–3
Rose, Gillian 25, 63, 68, 128, 230
Rosenfeld, H. 157
Rosenzweig, Franz 28, 31, 40, 186–7, 208,
    242
Ruszczynski, S. 72n5

sadism 155, 156, 205, 239
sado-masochism 163–4, 165, 174
Samuels, A. 75n7, 76n9, 76n10
Santayana, George 213
Sartre, Jean-Paul 188, 196
Scheler, Max 33n9, 106
Schelling, Friedrich Wilhelm Joseph von 250
schizoid states 13, 30, 33, 45, 49, 59, 128, 218
Schopenhauer, Arthur 31, 56, 84
Schwartz, J. 76

Scruton, Roger 27
Scurr, R. 165
SeaChange 3
Searle, J. R. 64n8
sehnsucht 34, 43
'selected fact' 94, 98, 149; Bion 100n3;
    conjoint 147, 178, 180; *see also* Bion;
    Poincaré; self
self 7, 22, 26; altruism 27; body-mind self
    59–60; divided 196; intersubjectivity 9–10,
    74; isolated 186–7; narcissism 153, 156;
    non-relational view of 154; relational view
    of 53–4, 57–8, 84, 154, 156; 'selving' 55;
    subject-centred 208; transparent 221; *see
    also* ego
self-centredness 12, 13, 26, 27, 35, 52, 57, 58,
    114; *see also* egocentricity
self-consciousness 42
self-containment 87, 109, 122, 127, 224;
    Andreas-Salomé 128, 129; narcissism 153;
    uterine life 154
self-deception 109
self-destruction 193
self-image (narcissism) 109, 151, 161, 162,
    169, 173
self psychology 56n5
self-reflection 74, 154; *see also* reflective
    capacity
self-surrender 23–4
selfobject 156–7, 159, 180, 227
Seneca 238
sensuality 28, 65, 69
separation 36, 50, 75, 78, 121, 126; anxiety
    about 125; defence against pain of 157;
    denial of 153; holding in mind 220;
    dismissing reaction to 134n3, 179; *see also*
    individuation
sexual desire 33
sexual difference 72
sexual love 23, 129; *see also* erotic love; love-
    making
sexual satisfaction 116
Shakespeare, William ix–x
shame 110, 132, 137–8
shared unconscious phantasy/phantasies 97-8,
    107, 134, 138, 140; *see also* Klein;
    unconscious fantasy
Singer, Irving 18n1, 213
Socrates 33, 34, 53, 217, 218
solipsism 27, 49, 55–6, 154, 186, 189, 208
solitude 40, 117, 121, 122, 124, 168, 169, 183,
    211, 212–13
soul 21, 58, 164, 169, 188, 195, 208, 237
soul-mates 20, 183, 188–9, 207
Spielrein, Sabina 31, 113, 195–6
Spinoza, Benedict de 8, 27, 67, 242, 243
splitting 98, 109–11, 112, 123n2
Steiner, G. 8

Stendhal (Marie Henri Beyle) 213
Stern, Daniel ix, x, 54n2
storge 18, 29, 235
stories 14–15, 16; see also narratives of self;
    myth
strange 43, 44, 71, 72, 230; see also uncanny
stranger 10, 18, 29, 30, 40, 41, 43, 53, 72, 101,
    125, 229, 235; see also xenia
stream of consciousness 10, 45, 55, 135; see
    also consciousness; James, William
subjectivity 7, 13, 21, 23, 35, 42, 247, 248; co-
    created 62; conjoint subjectivity of couple
    22, 64n8, 90 (see also relational third);
    development of 73; intersubjective third
    90; Levinas 41, 44; oedipal situation 73
    (and development of subjectivity) 74, 79;
    of other 109, 151, 248; see also
    intersubjectivity
'subjugating third' 144n11
substitution: doctrine of 230; Levinas 26
suffering 14; cessation of 243; created by
    desire 27, 32, 34, 84; and pathos 83; see
    also pain
śūnyatā 13, 181, 205, 206
symbiotic union 23, 34, 49, 97, 125, 154, 180;
    see also merger
symbol/symbolic 3, 10, 13, 33, 35, 75, 78, 101,
    115, 133, 139, 147, 178, 182, 223, 233, 240,
    241
Symington, Neville 46, 93, 106, 140, 155,
    156n1, 175, 222
sympathy 18, 19n2, 49, 177

telos 21; teleological x, 8, 21, 34, 63, 65, 67,
    84, 85, 90, 178, 207, 211, 227, 234
temenos 84, 85
tenderness 69, 109, 116, 243
thanatos 31n8, 164
therapeutic space 87, 91, 92, 143
therapy 13–14, 84, 245, 249; see also couple
    therapy; psychoanalysis
thirdness 73–4, 75, 85, 90, 249; analytic third
    90, 91, 180; exogamous love 211;
    intersubjective third 90–2, 143, 147, 149;
    malevolent/malignant third 144, 145–6,
    149, 150, 157, 164, 180; relational third/
    marital third 23, 61, 63–4; see also
    analytic/intersubjective third; relational/
    marital third
thresholds of love 8, 12, 16, 52, 66, 130, 182,
    189, 191, 192, 195, 227, 229
transcendence 23, 35, 42, 44, 221
transference x, 85, 91, 227; marital/relational
    15, 85, 91, 109, 144; see also
    countertransference
transformations in love 7, 8, 16, 83, 195, 208,
    229, 233, 237, 243
trauma: children of survivors of 148;

conscription 135–6, 142; impediments to
    intimacy 208; intergenerational 100, 140,
    141, 142–3, 145–7, 148, 150; interlocking
    traumatic scene 136–40, 148, 149–50, 162,
    176, 180; intralocking traumatic scene
    133–6, 144, 147, 159–64; Jung's traumatic
    complex 145; memory systems 132–3,
    135–6, 144; narcissistic patients 180
Trevarthen, Colwyn ix
triangular space 74, 89, 160, 169; see also
    Britton
trust 86, 88, 135, 211, 220
truth 5–6, 7, 9, 12, 13, 14, 33, 100, 164, 217,
    226, 234, 235, 250; arrow metaphor 12,
    22; Buddhist Four Noble Truths 34, 248;
    'O' 241, 243; see also alétheia
Tuomela, R. 64n8
Tustin, F. 165
typecasting 113

Ulrich of Lichtenstein 24
ultimate reality 6–7, 241; see also 'O'
uncanny 41, 43, 44, 72, 140
underworld 193, 194, 195, 204, 207
unknown/unknowability of other, of O/
    ultimate reality 40, 44, 56, 62, 63, 66, 180,
    181, 215, 221, 222, 223, 241, 242, 243, 246
uterine life 154

Virgil 193, 195
vitality see aliveness
voyeurism 206

Wajnryb, R. 148
Walpole. Horace 212n1
Weininger, O. 240
wholeness 19, 20, 21; as individuation 34,
    206, 215
Wild, J. 30, 58
Wilde, Oscar 160, 164
Winnicott, Clare 213
Winnicott, Donald: aliveness 9, 240; capacity
    to be alone 212; dead spots 240;
    environmental mother 70n3; esse est
    percipi 219; fathers 75–6; going on being
    9, 45, 128, 140; 'good-enough' mother
    69n2; mother-infant relationship 48, 78,
    191–2; mother's gaze 153; privacy 223;
    relational view of self 54, 156; self located
    in body 60; transitional space 48, 86;
    unpredictability 213
Wolff, Toni 113, 195–6
Wyschogrod, E. 30, 50

xenia 18, 29–30, 235
xenophobia 43, 72

Young, Edward 53